D0986654

the AMAZING SPIDER-MAN

THE COMPLETE CLONE SAGA EPIC

SPIDER-MAN: THE COMPLETE CLONE SAGA EPIC BOOK 2. Contains material originally published in magazine form as AMAZING SPIDER-MAN #395-399, SPECTACULAR SPIDER-MAN #218-221, SPIDER-MAN #54-56, SPIDER-MAN UNLIMITED #8, WEB OF SPIDER-MAN #120-122 and SPIDER-MAN: FUNERAL FOR AN OCTOPUS #1-3. Second edition. First printing 2017. ISBN# 978-1-302-90366-4. Published by MARVEL WORLDWIDE, INC., a subsidiary of MARVEL ENTERTAINMENT, LLC. OFFICE OF PUBLICATION: 135 West 50th Street, New York, NY 10020. Copyright © 2017 MARVEL No similarity between any of the names, characters, persons, and/or institutions in this magazine with those of any living or dead person or institution is intended, and any such similarity which may exist is purely coincidental. **Printed in the U.S.A.** ALAN FINE, President, Marvel Entertainment; DAN BUCKLEY, President, TV, Publishing & Brand Management; JOE QUESADA, Chief Creative Officer; TOM BREVOORT, SVP of Publishing; DAVID BOGART, SVP of Business Affairs & Operations, Publishing & Partnership; C.B. CEBULSKI, VP of Brand Management & Development, Asia; DAVID GABRIEL, SVP of Sales & Marketing, Publishing; JEFF YOUNGQUIST, VP of Production & Special Projects; DAN CARR, Executive Director of Publishing Technology; ALEX MORALES, Director of Publishing Operations; SUSAN CRESPI, Production Manager; STAN LEE, Chairman Emeritus. For information regarding advertising in Marvel Comics or on Marvel.com, please contact Vit DeBellis, Integrated Sales Manager, at vdebellis@marvel.com. For Marvel subscription inquiries, please call 888-511-5480. **Manufactured between 12/2/2016 and 1/9/2017 by LSC COMMUNICATIONS INC., SALEM, VA, USA.**

the AMAZING SPIDER-MAN

THE COMPLETE CLONE SAGA EPIC BOOK 2

WRITERS
Tom Brevoort, Tom DeFalco, J.M. DeMatteis, Todd DeZago, Mike Kanterovich, Terry Kavanagh, Tom Lyle & Howard Mackie

PENCILERS
Mark Bagley, Sal Buscema, Steven Butler, Phil Gosier, Stewart Johnson, Ron Lim, Tom Lyle, Mike Manley & Tod Smith

INKERS
Sal Buscema, Harry Candelario, Sam De La Rosa, Randy Emberlin, Scott Hanna, Don Hudson, Larry Mahlstedt, Al Milgrom, Tom Palmer, Joe Rubinstein & Bill Sienkiewicz

COLORISTS
John Kalisz, Bob Sharen, Kevin Tinsley & Chia-Chi Wang

LETTERERS
Sue Crespi, Steve Dutro, Loretta Krol, Bill Oakley, Jeff Powell, Clem Robins, Joe Rosen, Dave Sharpe and Richard Starkings & Comicraft

EDITORS
Mark Bernardo, Bob Budiansky, Eric Fein, Danny Fingeroth & Mark Powers

Front Cover Artist: Steven Butler
Front Cover Colorist: Chris Sotomayor

Collection Editor: Mark D. Beazley
Associate Managing Editor: Kateri Woody
Senior Editor, Special Projects: Jennifer Grünwald
VP Production & Special Projects: Jeff Youngquist
SVP Print, Sales & Marketing: David Gabriel
Research: Jeph York
Production: ColorTek & M. Hands
Book Designer: Arlene So

Editor In Chief: Axel Alonso
Chief Creative Officer: Joe Quesada
Publisher: Dan Buckley
Executive Producer: Alan Fine

MARVEL COMICS
THE AMAZING SPIDER-MAN
© 1994 MARVEL ENT. GROUP, INC.
$1.50 US
$2.05 CAN/UK £1.25
395
NOV
02457
APPROVED BY THE COMICS CODE AUTHORITY
BACK FROM THE EDGE PART 1 OF 4
BAGLEY & MAHLSTEDT
THE PUMA
RETURNS--
MORE VICIOUS AND
BRUTAL THAN EVER!

...IT'S ALL HERE?
EVERY CENT.
THANK YOU, MANNY--
--YOU NEVER LET ME DOWN.
WOULDN'T THINK OF IT, MISTER WHITE.
OF COURSE YOU WOULDN'T.
YOU JUST KEEP WORKING YOUR TERRITORY AS WELL AS YOU'VE BEEN--AND YOUR CUT OF THE BUSINESS IS GOING TO GROW AND GROW.
SOUNDS GOOD T'ME, MISTER WHITE.
YOU HAVE MY NUMBER IN PRINCETON?
uh-huh.
I WANT YOU TO CALL ME ON THURSDAY AFTER THE SHIPMENT COMES IN FROM--
GRROWWRR
WHAT THE %$#*!! WAS THAT?
CLIFFORD WHITE, THIRTY-ONE YEARS OLD, DEVOTED HUSBAND, FATHER, AND DRUGLORD-- RACES FOR THE DOOR...
...HE CAN'T SAY WHY.
LOUD NOISES ARE, AFTER ALL, COMMON-PLACE IN MANHATTAN--EVEN AT THREE A.M.
CARS BACKFIRE, TRUCKS RUMBLE, DRUNKS BELLOW, WOMEN SCREAM.
BUT THIS SOUND FREEZES WHITE'S BLOOD. SCARES HIM-- TO THE BOTTOM OF HIS SOUL.
GRRRRR

AND WITH GOOD REASON.
RROWWURRRR
...B-BOYS...
BOYS--
I... ah... NEED A LITTLE HELP HERE.
MANNY--?
OH, MY GOD--!

KRAK!
DON'T LET IT KILL ME!
PLEASE--
--DON'T LET IT KILL ME!
PUMA--
--NO!
RELIEF FLOODS HIM--BUT THE SENSATION IS SHORT-LIVED...
...BECAUSE THIS WOMAN'S EYES PIN WHITE TO THE WALL AS SURELY AS THE CAT'S CLAWS; BORE INTO THE DEPTHS OF HIS SOUL. PIERCE HIS COMFORTABLE LIES...
...HIS ALL-TOO ILLUSORY SELF-IMAGE.
WAVES OF NAKED EMOTION WASH OVER HIM. PAIN AND DESPERATION. HEARTBREAK AND FEAR. ALL FUNNELED THROUGH THIS WOMAN...
...POURED, LIKE BOILING OIL, INTO EVERY CORNER OF HIS PSYCHE.
AND HE KNOWS--AS HE SCREAMS HIS THROAT RAW--THAT WHAT HE'S FEELING IS THE PAIN HE'S CAUSED...
...THE SUFFERING AND ANGUISH OF EVERY ADDICTED WRETCH WHOSE LIFE HE'S HELPED DESTROY.
AND HE WISHES, WITH ALL HIS HEART...

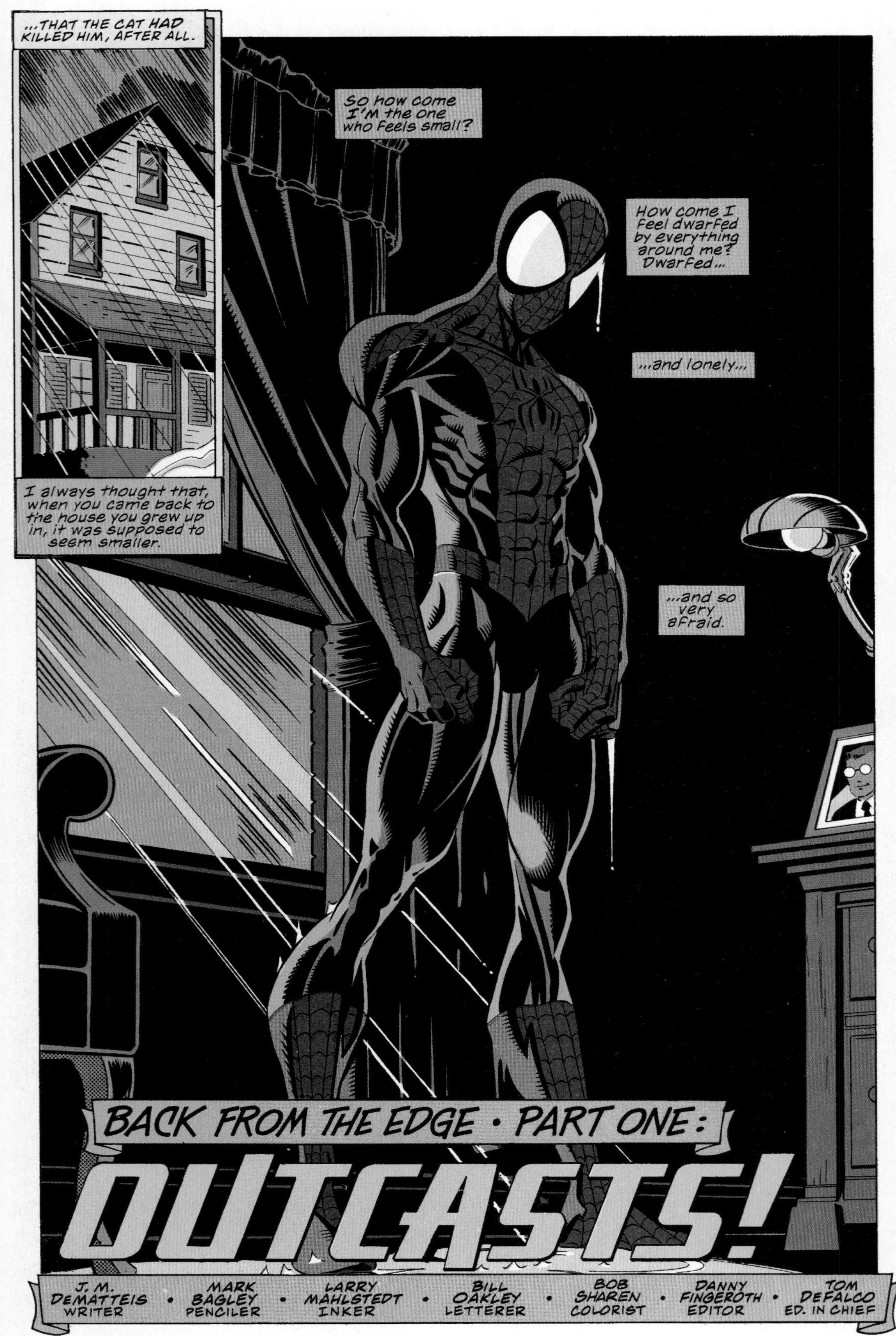
...THAT THE CAT HAD KILLED HIM, AFTER ALL.
I always thought that, when you came back to the house you grew up in, it was supposed to seem smaller.
So how come I'M the one who feels small?
How come I feel dwarfed by everything around me? Dwarfed...
...and lonely...
...and so very afraid.
BACK FROM THE EDGE • PART ONE:
OUTCASTS!
J. M. DEMATTEIS WRITER • MARK BAGLEY PENCILER • LARRY MAHLSTEDT INKER • BILL OAKLEY LETTERER • BOB SHAREN COLORIST • DANNY FINGEROTH EDITOR • TOM DEFALCO ED. IN CHIEF

Why am I here, anyway? What do I think I'm going to find crawling through the shadows of AUNT MAY'S house?
Certainly not her. She's a few blocks from here, in Forest Hills Hospital ... dying. And this house is empty of everything...
...except the ghosts of the past.
MY past.
NO--this ISN'T my past. It's HIS. PETER PARKER'S.
And as far as I'm concerned, Parker is dead. Dead and buried.
I'm just the mask now. Just-- the SPIDER.
Or am I?
The truth of the matter is... after my ordeal at Ravencroft...*
...I don't know WHO I am: a mask or a face. A Spider...
*IN LAST MONTH'S "POWER AND RESPONSIBILITY" CROSSOVER.-- DANNY

...or a man.
Maybe THAT'S why I'm here.
I can't deal with Parker's life, Parker's world as it is today. But here... I can at least remember his yesterdays.
As hard as it was for me, growing up without parents-- there were a lot of wonderful times in this house with Aunt May and Uncle Ben.
I was loved here. Protected.

I WAS HAPPY.

IDIOT!
No point in trying to hold on to ghosts-- they'll only slip through your fingers.
The past is dead.
As dead as Uncle Ben.
And Aunt May...?
No. I can't... I WON'T... even think about that!
Let PARKER worry himself sick. Let Parker weep. Let him MOURN.
I'm the mask. I'm the SPIDER.
I don't know if that's what I want...
...but it's what I NEED.
HOME.

IT'S NOT A WORD MARY JANE WATSON-PARKER WAS EVER VERY COMFORTABLE WITH.
FOR SOME PEOPLE, THE PLACE THEY GREW UP IN HOLDS WARM MEMORIES: MOMENTS TO BE HIDDEN IN THE SECRET CORNERS OF THE HEART AND TREASURED, PROTECTED, THROUGHOUT THE YEARS.
BUT MARY JANE RAN AWAY FROM HOME, FAMILY, AND MEMORIES COLD AS ICE A LONG TIME AGO.
SO WHY, SHE WONDERS, STANDING -- FAR TOO LONG -- OUTSIDE THE DOOR OF HER SISTER'S HOUSE, HAVE I COME BACK TO PITTSBURGH?
WHY NOT TURN AND RUN; GET ON THE NEXT PLANE TO NEW YORK AND--
BUT IT'S TOO LATE. HER HAND HAS KNOCKED, ALMOST WITHOUT HER REALIZING IT. AND THE DOOR HAS BEEN OPENED...
...ON THE PAST.
MARY JANE--?
I WAS... IN THE NEIGHBORHOOD AND I THOUGHT--
THAT IS... I, UM... AH...
Y'THINK MAYBE I CAN COME IN?

WELCOME HOME.
HOME TO THESE TWO IS THE NIGHT.
BOTH WERE ONCE HUMAN. BOTH HAD FAMILIES, JOBS, LIVES OF RICHNESS AND COMPLEXITY.
NOW, NOCTURNE AND PUMA MOVE THROUGH SHADOWS, OVER ROOFTOPS, LIVE IN ABANDONED BUILDINGS AND COLLAPSED TUNNELS.
BUT AT LEAST THEY HAVE EACH OTHER... MOVING TOGETHER IN A GRACEFUL DANCE; THE BEAST ALWAYS AT THE READY, WAITING TO RESPOND TO HIS MISTRESS'S EVERY COMMAND.
THE MISTRESS ALWAYS THERE WITH A SOFT LOOK OR COMFORTING TOUCH, TO EASE THE MONSTER'S PAIN.
BUT TONIGHT THEIR FOCUS ISN'T ON EACH OTHER -- BUT ON A TORMENTED SOUL WHOSE PSYCHIC CRY HAS BEEN CALLING TO NOCTURNE FOR WEEKS NOW.
A CRY THAT HAS, AT LONG LAST...

...GROWN TOO LOUD TO IGNORE.
IT'S--
--TIME!
SPEECH COMES HARD FOR NOCTURNE--AND THE HUGE EFFORT RARELY SEEMS JUSTIFIED.
HER COMMON MODE OF COMMUNICATION IS FAR EASIER... AND FAR MORE DIRECT.
FOR NOCTURNE CAN CHANNEL EMOTION--THE RAW CLAY OF THE PSYCHE--"SPEAKING" IN A LANGUAGE MORE ELOQUENT THAN WORDS.
AND WHAT SHE CHANNELS, SHE RECEIVES: CATCHING JOY AND SUFFERING, ANGER AND ELATION, AS EASILY AS WE WOULD CATCH THE SCENT OF SUMMER GRASS.
IN THE WEEKS AFTER SHE WAS TRANSFORMED FROM POLICE DETECTIVE ANGELA CAIRN INTO THIS LEATHER-WINGED NIGHT-CREATURE, THE PSYCHIC WINDS BLEW HARD...
...NEARLY OVER-WHELMING HER.
BUT, WITH TIME, WITH PRACTICE, SHE HAS BEEN ABLE TO MASTER THIS NEW WAY OF HEAR-ING. OF BEING.
SO SHE LISTENS--AND SAILS ABOVE THE RAIN-WASHED MANHATTAN STREETS... THEN ACROSS THE WATER INTO QUEENS.

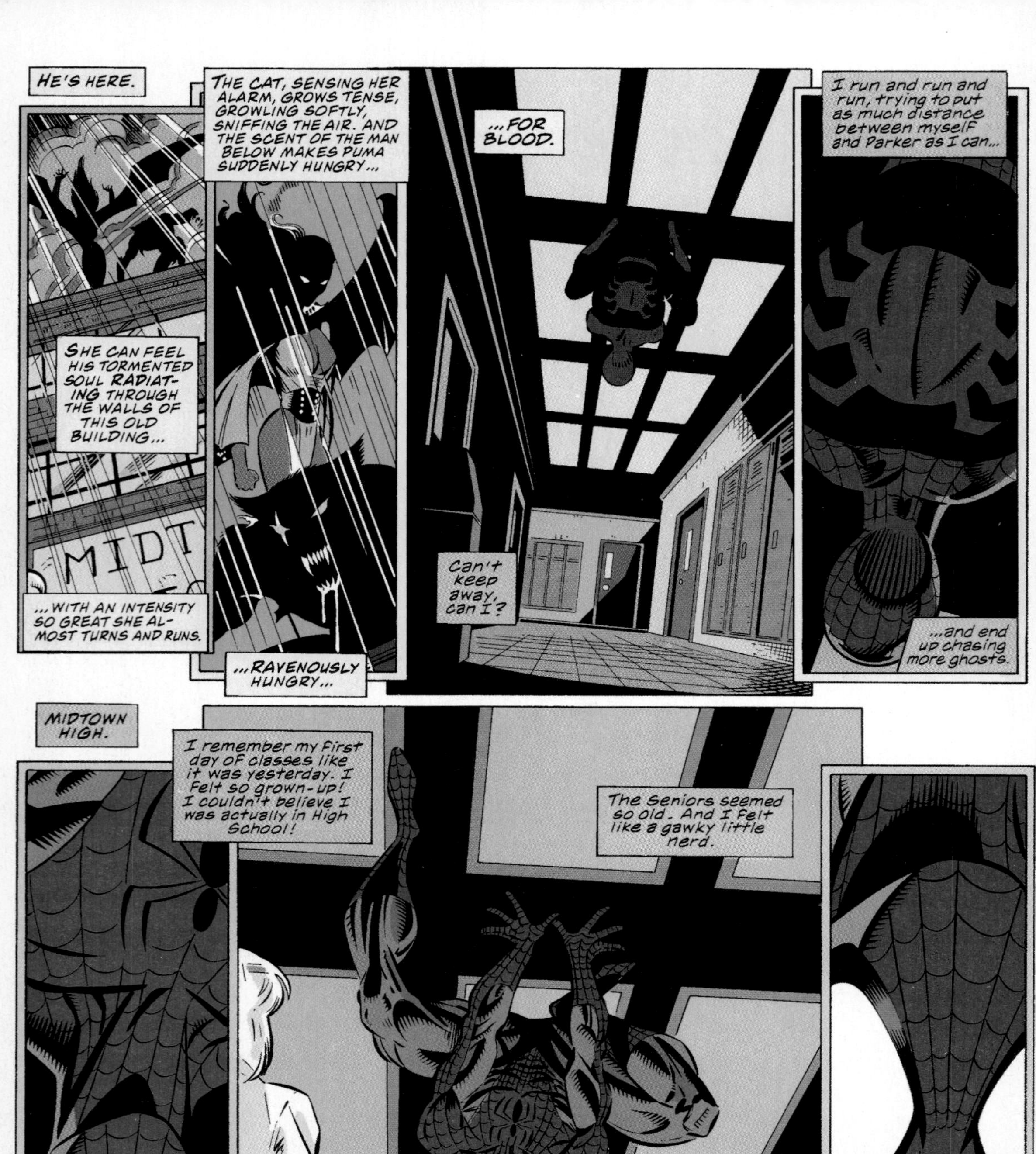
HE'S HERE.
SHE CAN FEEL HIS TORMENTED SOUL RADIATING THROUGH THE WALLS OF THIS OLD BUILDING...
MIDT
...WITH AN INTENSITY SO GREAT SHE ALMOST TURNS AND RUNS.
THE CAT, SENSING HER ALARM, GROWS TENSE, GROWLING SOFTLY, SNIFFING THE AIR. AND THE SCENT OF THE MAN BELOW MAKES PUMA SUDDENLY HUNGRY...
...RAVENOUSLY HUNGRY...
...FOR BLOOD.
Can't keep away, can I?
I run and run and run, trying to put as much distance between myself and Parker as I can...
...and end up chasing more ghosts.
MIDTOWN HIGH.
I remember my first day of classes like it was yesterday. I felt so grown-up! I couldn't believe I was actually in High School!
The Seniors seemed so old. And I felt like a gawky little nerd.
I think I was here for two months before another kid even TALKED to me.

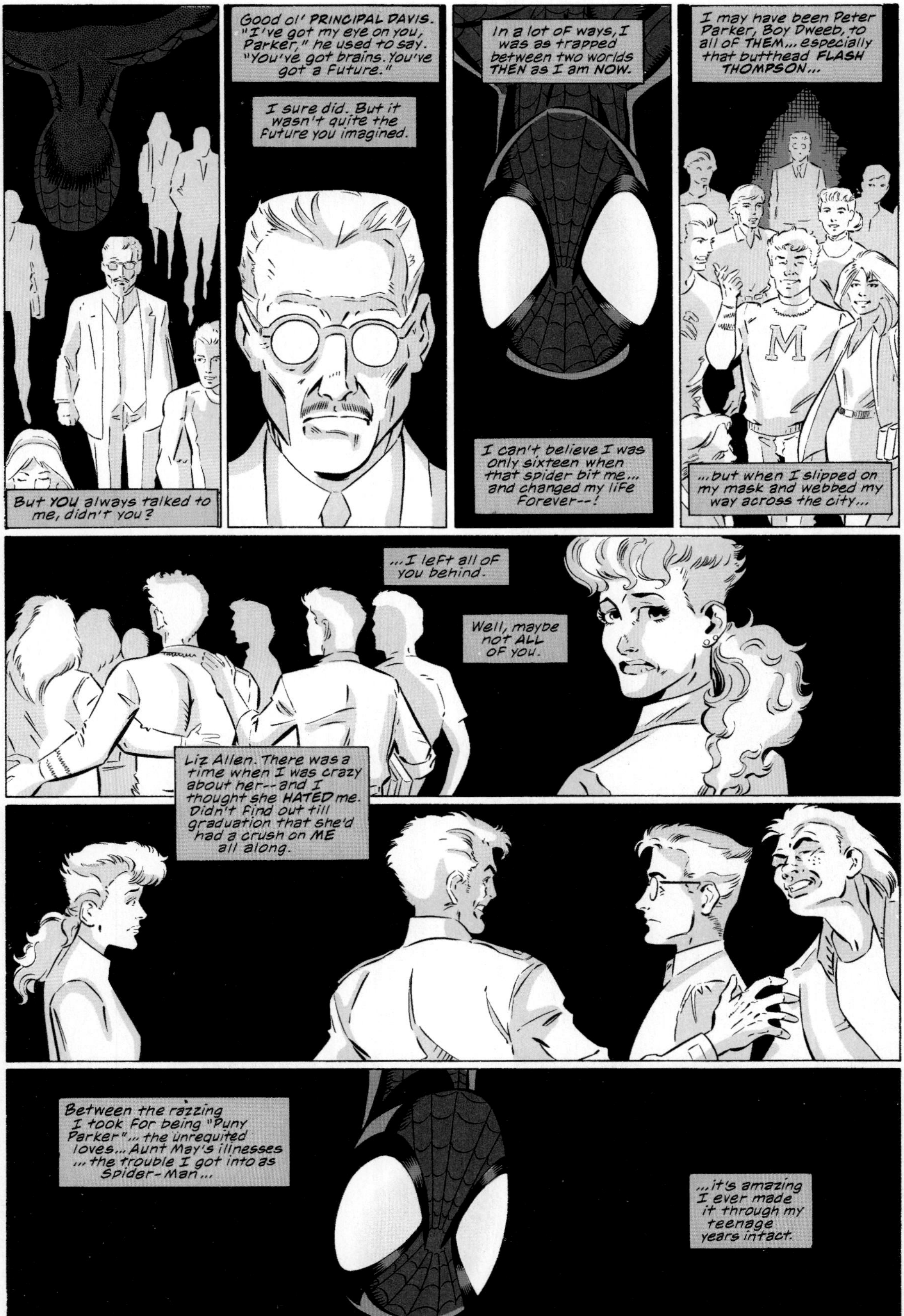

But YOU always talked to me, didn't you?

Good ol' PRINCIPAL DAVIS. "I've got my eye on you, Parker," he used to say. "You've got brains. You've got a future."
I sure did. But it wasn't quite the future you imagined.

In a lot of ways, I was as trapped between two worlds THEN as I am NOW.
I can't believe I was only sixteen when that spider bit me... and changed my life forever--!

I may have been Peter Parker, Boy Dweeb, to all of THEM... especially that butthead FLASH THOMPSON...
...but when I slipped on my mask and webbed my way across the city...

...I left all of you behind.

Well, maybe not ALL of you.

Liz Allen. There was a time when I was crazy about her--and I thought she HATED me. Didn't find out till graduation that she'd had a crush on ME all along.

Between the razzing I took for being "Puny Parker"... the unrequited loves... Aunt May's illnesses ... the trouble I got into as Spider-Man...

...it's amazing I ever made it through my teenage years intact.

But I'll say THIS for you, kid : for all your problems, all your adolescent angst, you really STRUGGLED to make a life for yourself...
...to have friends, take care of your family, get your career at THE BUGLE in gear.
Being Peter Parker MEANT something to you, didn't it? Even when you put on the mask, you didn't become something OTHER... some carefully-constructed Spider-Thing.
You were just Peter... doing your best to get by.
What would you do, kid, if you knew what I know now? If you could look into the future and see how it would all turn out?
Despite all your struggles, it didn't work. You're still the nerd walking in the back of the hall, all alone. Still on the outside.

Only thing is--it's a lot COLDER out here than you could ever--
GRROWWRRR

--IMAGINE--?!
Why the devil did I COME here?!

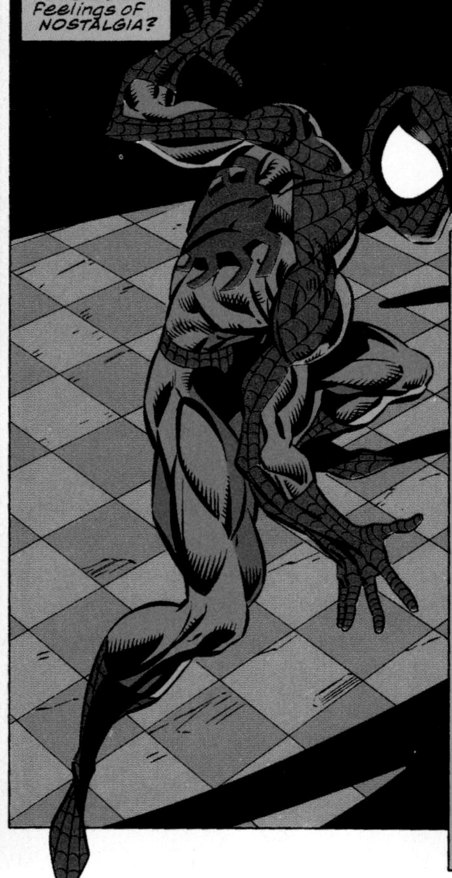
To give in to some stupid, useless feelings of NOSTALGIA?
To let my guard down and become VULNERABLE?

Haven't I learned by now that the second I DO that...

...THE DEVILS COME SWARMING OUT OF THE SHADOWS?!
PUMA!
Another one I watched die: brought down in a hail of bullets.*
ROWWRR
* IN SPECTACULAR SPIDER-MAN #193. --DANNY
SH
And yet here he is, back from the grave --like ALL his miserable kind.
THE GOOD ONES... THE DECENT ONES... THEY STAY DEAD--
--BUT THE ANIMALS LIKE YOU--
KEEP
COMING

BACK!
KROOOOM!
IT WILL TAKE MORE THAN THIS RAIN OF BLOWS TO STOP THE CAT.

HE HUNKERS THERE, SNARLING, EYES BURNING WITH HATE. THE VERY SIGHT OF THIS SPIDER-THING IS DISTURBING TO HIM --REMINDING PUMA OF A LIFE HE'D RATHER FORGET, REPRESS, DENY.

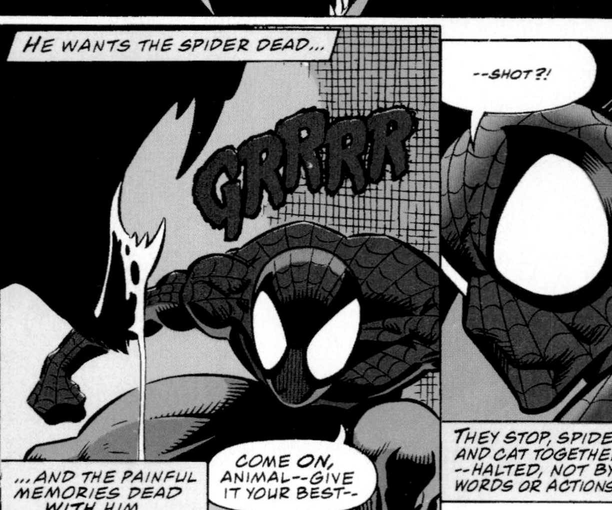

HE WANTS THE SPIDER DEAD...
GRRRR
...AND THE PAINFUL MEMORIES DEAD WITH HIM.
COME ON, ANIMAL--GIVE IT YOUR BEST--
--SHOT?!
THEY STOP, SPIDER AND CAT TOGETHER --HALTED, NOT BY WORDS OR ACTIONS...

...BUT BY A POWERFUL PRESENCE--!

ANGELA CAIRN--?

NOT... CAIRN.

NOCTURNE.

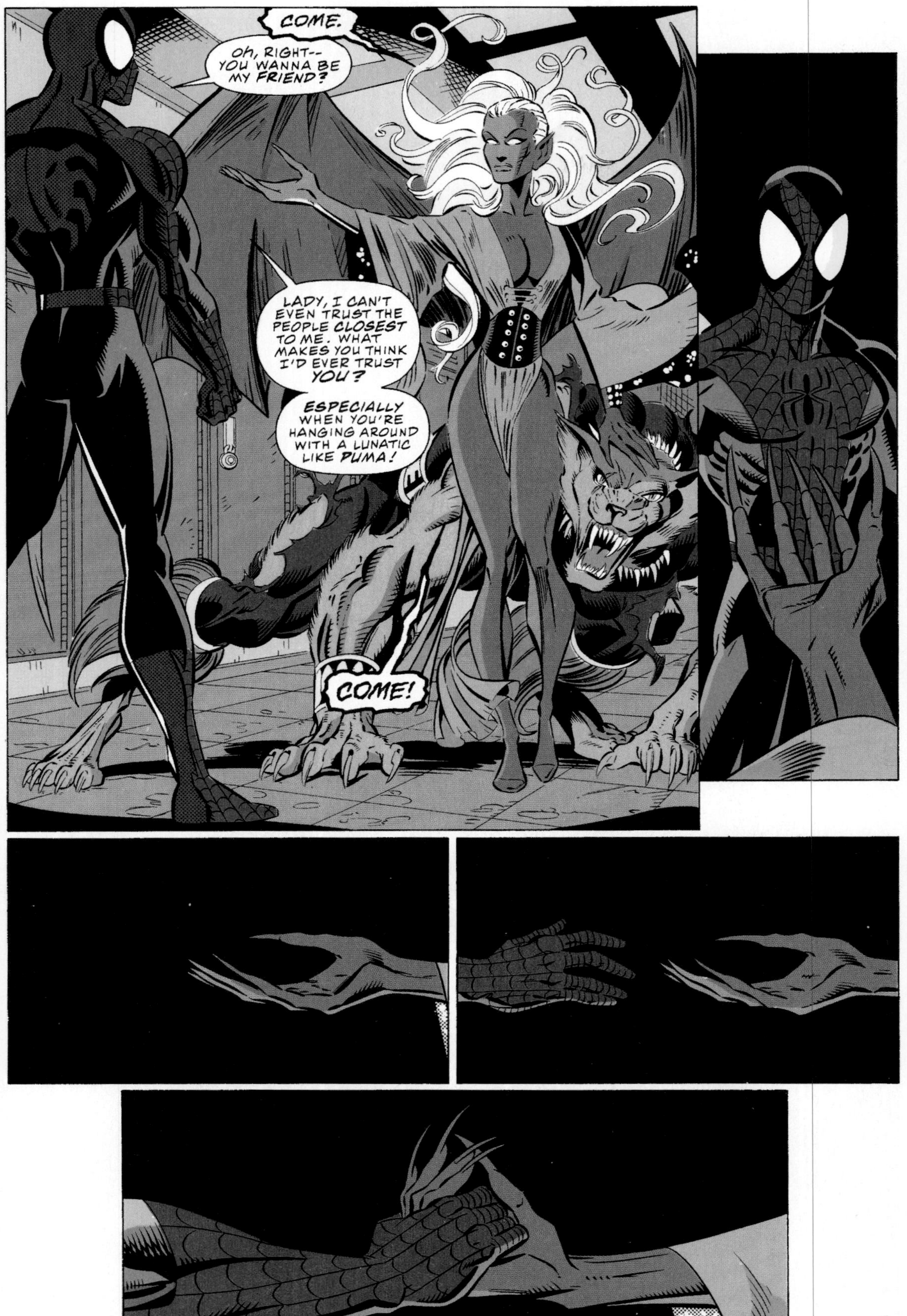
COME.
Oh, RIGHT--
YOU WANNA BE MY FRIEND?
LADY, I CAN'T EVEN TRUST THE PEOPLE CLOSEST TO ME. WHAT MAKES YOU THINK I'D EVER TRUST YOU?
ESPECIALLY WHEN YOU'RE HANGING AROUND WITH A LUNATIC LIKE PUMA!
COME!

I HAVE BEEN ...LISTENING TO YOUR PAIN, SPIDER-MAN.
SOMETHING HAS BROKEN... YOUR SPIRIT.
POISONED IT.
YOU HELPED ME... WHEN ZEMO'S MACHINE... MUTATED ME.* NOW I--
--WANT TO HELP YOU.
MY PAIN IS MY BUSINESS. I DON'T WANT YOUR HELP--OR ANYBODY ELSE'S.
THE ONLY REASON I CAME UP HERE TO INWOOD PARK WITH YOU--IS TO WARN YOU ABOUT PUMA.
*SPECTACULAR SPIDER-MAN ANNUAL #13.-- Danny
DON'T YOU REALIZE THAT THOMAS FIREHEART'S A MURDERER?
IF I HADN'T STOPPED HIM A FEW MONTHS BACK, HE WOULD HAVE ASSASSINATED SENATOR MAGUIRE!
ISN'T IT OBVIOUS... THAT FIREHEART... IS AS DEAD AS ANGELA CAIRN? AS DEAD... AS THE MAN... BEHIND YOUR MASK?
YOU DIDN'T COME... TO WARN ME. YOU CAME... BECAUSE YOU ARE LOST... AND FRIGHTENED... AND SO VERY TIRED...
...OF BEING ALONE.
SPARE ME THE PSYCHOBABBLE! YOU DON'T KNOW ME! YOU DON'T KNOW THE FIRST THING ABOUT ME!
THE EFFORT TO SPEAK... IS EXHAUSTING ME. I HAVE HAD ENOUGH OF WORDS.
ROWRR
THEY BREED DECEIT... AND SUSPICION.
FEAR--
--AND LIES!
HER HAND IS HOT... EVEN THROUGH HIS MASK.
HE'S BURNING.
NOT A BURNING OF FLESH, BUT OF MIND. NOCTURNE'S CONSCIOUSNESS RADIATES INTO HIM...

...AND THE PAST --HER PAST-- COMES ALIVE!
HE SEES THROUGH HER EYES; FEELS THROUGH HER HEART. AND WHAT HE FEELS MOST OF ALL -- IS LONELINESS.
A PART OF ANGELA CAIRN MAY HAVE REJOICED AT HER TRANSFORMATION INTO THIS NIGHT-SONG... THIS NOCTURNE... BUT SHE WASN'T PREPARED FOR THE PROFOUND ALONENESS THAT ATE AT HER.
SHE TOOK SOME COMFORT IN HER ROLE AS PROTECTOR OF LOST SOULS LIKE HERSELF: OUTCASTS AND UNTOUCHABLES; THE SHUNNED, THE ABUSED, THE REJECTED.
BUT HER LONELINESS REMAINED.
THAT'S WHY, WHEN SHE FOUND THE CAT SLEEPING THERE IN THE ALLEY, SHE REJOICED. FOR SHE KNEW, INTUITIVELY...
...THAT SHE'D FOUND A KINDRED SPIRIT. A COMPANION.
HE'D BEEN SHOT RECENTLY... BADLY WOUNDED. THERE WAS INFECTION... FEVER... BUT SOMEHOW HIS BODY HAD SURVIVED.

As she reached out--taking Thomas Fireheart's pain into herself and accelerating his healing--she saw that the man he'd once been was buried, deep in the Puma's consciousness, and no effort on her part could draw him out.

But the cat was grateful for her help; and, with a stubborn loyalty and a stubborn pride, he *followed* her that night...

...and every night thereafter.

Wow. Y'think you could *warn* me the next time you do that?

Look, I understand how it must have *been* for you--

--but you can't just ignore Fireheart's crimes! His past--

--is as irrelevant as mine... or yours. What we've done ...who we've *been*... doesn't matter.

We are... who we are--

--now--

NOCTURNE --ARE YOU ALL RIGHT?
THE STRAIN... OF THE... JOINING--
I'D BETTER GET YOU OVER TO--

GROWWR
EASY, PUMA! I WAS JUST TRYING TO HELP HER--
ROOWWRR

PUMA--STOP!
HE...ah... DOESN'T SEEM TO BE LISTENING...!

NO, NOT LISTENING: REMEMBERING. AN ANIMAL'S MEMORIES, DIM AND OBSCURE...
...OF THE MAN HE USED TO BE.
THOMAS FIREHEART WAS THE FINAL PRODUCT OF A CENTURIES-LONG BREEDING EXPERIMENT. TRAINED SINCE CHILDHOOD TO CARRY THE MOUNTAIN LION MEDICINE. TO BE THE PROTECTOR OF HIS TRIBE.
(THE SPIDER!)
SAVIOR OF HIS PEOPLE.
(THE SPIDER!)
BUT THE PUMA MEDICINE SEDUCED HIM, CONSUMED HIM. HE SURRENDERED CONTROL OF HIMSELF TO THE CAT--AND DISGRACED HIS PEOPLE...DEFILED HIS SOUL.
(ALWAYS THERE-- TO WITNESS OUR SHAME!)
FELL, LIKE LUCIFER...
(KILL HIM--AND WE KILL OUR SHAME-- KILL OUR PAST!)
...INTO A HELL OF HIS OWN MAKING.
(WE CAN BE FREE!)

Bremen Public Library

Puma's lost it...
AROWWRRR
...not that I'm surprised.
I should've taken him down the first chance I had.
But no, I had to listen to PARKER again. Had to let my guard down... start thinking Nocturne was right.
That what Fireheart needed was compassion. That maybe, together, we could all find a little friendship.
SHRAKT!
A little peace.
But see where trust gets you?
See where HOPE gets you?

Nocturne was right about ONE thing:
Peter Parker doesn't exist any more. He's as dead as Thomas Fireheart.
There's just the Puma and the Spider...
...AND ONLY ONE OF US IS COMING OUT OF THIS ALIVE!
TO BE CONTINUED-- IN THE PAGES OF SPECTACULAR SPIDER-MAN #218!
AND NEXT MONTH IN AMAZING-- "DEADMEN!"--GUEST-STARRING DAREDEVIL!
(IF YOU THOUGHT THE RETURN OF THE CLONE WAS SOMETHING... WAIT'LL YOU SEE WHAT HAPPENS TO SPIDEY NEXT!)

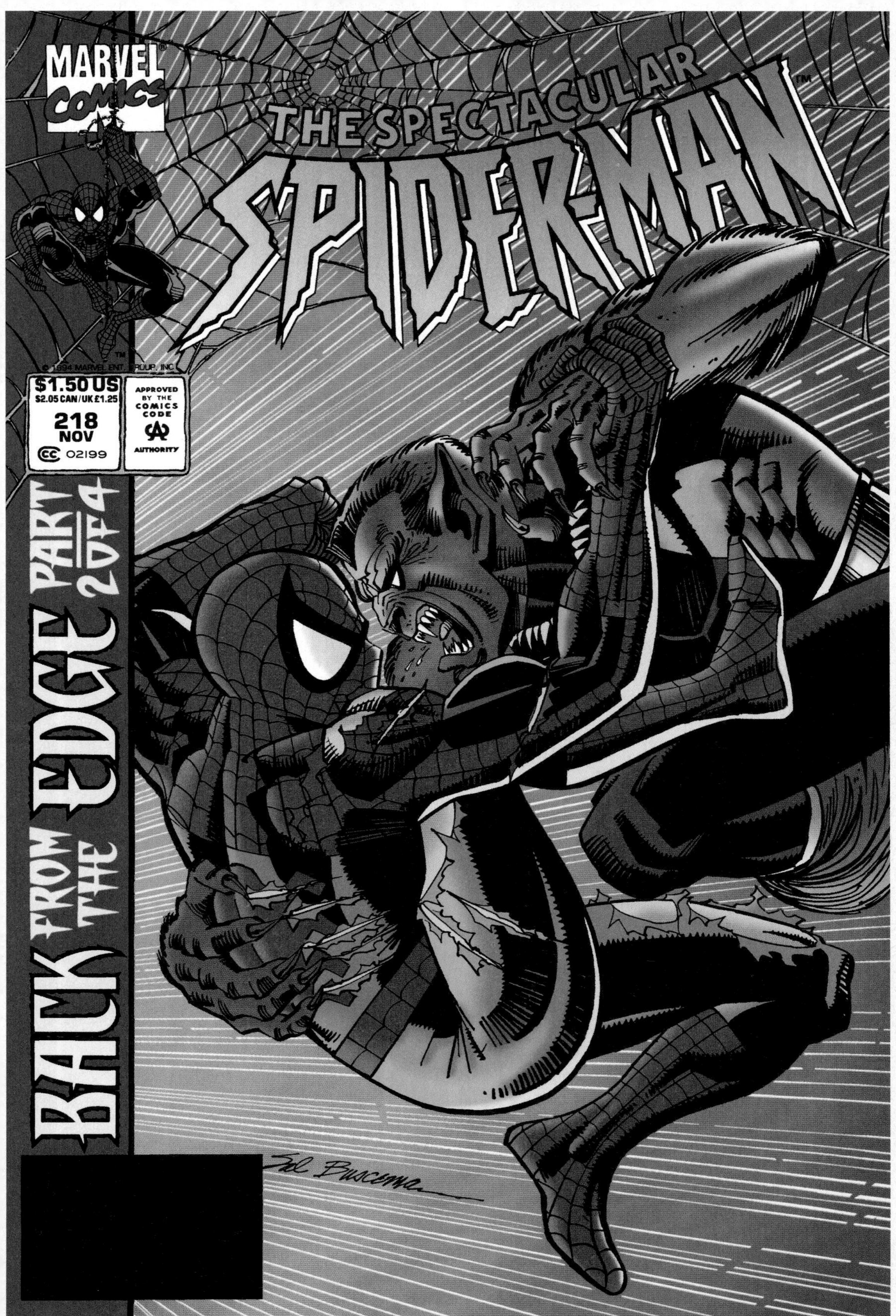

MARVEL COMICS
THE SPECTACULAR SPIDER-MAN
© 1994 MARVEL ENT. GROUP, INC.
$1.50 US
$2.05 CAN/UK £1.25
218
NOV
CC 02199
APPROVED BY THE COMICS CODE AUTHORITY
BACK FROM THE EDGE PART 2 OF 4
Sal Buscema

BITTEN BY A RADIOACTIVE SPIDER, STUDENT PETER PARKER GAINED THE PROPORTIONATE STRENGTH AND AGILITY OF AN ARACHNID! ARMED WITH HIS WONDROUS WEB-SHOOTERS, THE RELUCTANT SUPER HERO STRUGGLES WITH SINISTER SUPER-VILLAINS, MAKING ENDS MEET, AND MAINTAINING SOME SEMBLANCE OF A NORMAL LIFE!

STAN LEE PRESENTS: **THE SPECTACULAR SPIDER-MAN**

BACK FROM THE EDGE--PART 2
WHEN MONSTERS ROAM!
Somewhere, buried deep within this SNARLING, SLAVERING beast lies the broken, battered humanity of a man named THOMAS FIREHEART...
...the result of generations of selective breeding designed to produce a powerful SHAMAN for his tribe--possessing the spirit of both MAN... and MOUNTAIN LION.
Recently, though, the BALANCE was upset. The human SPIRIT was beaten... abandoned... rejected.
Now there is only THE PUMA!

PLOT TOM DeFALCO · ART SAL BUSCEMA · SCRIPT TODD DEZAGO · LETTERS CLEM ROBINS · COLORS JOHN KALISZ · EDITOR MARK POWERS · GROUP EDITOR DANNY FINGEROTH

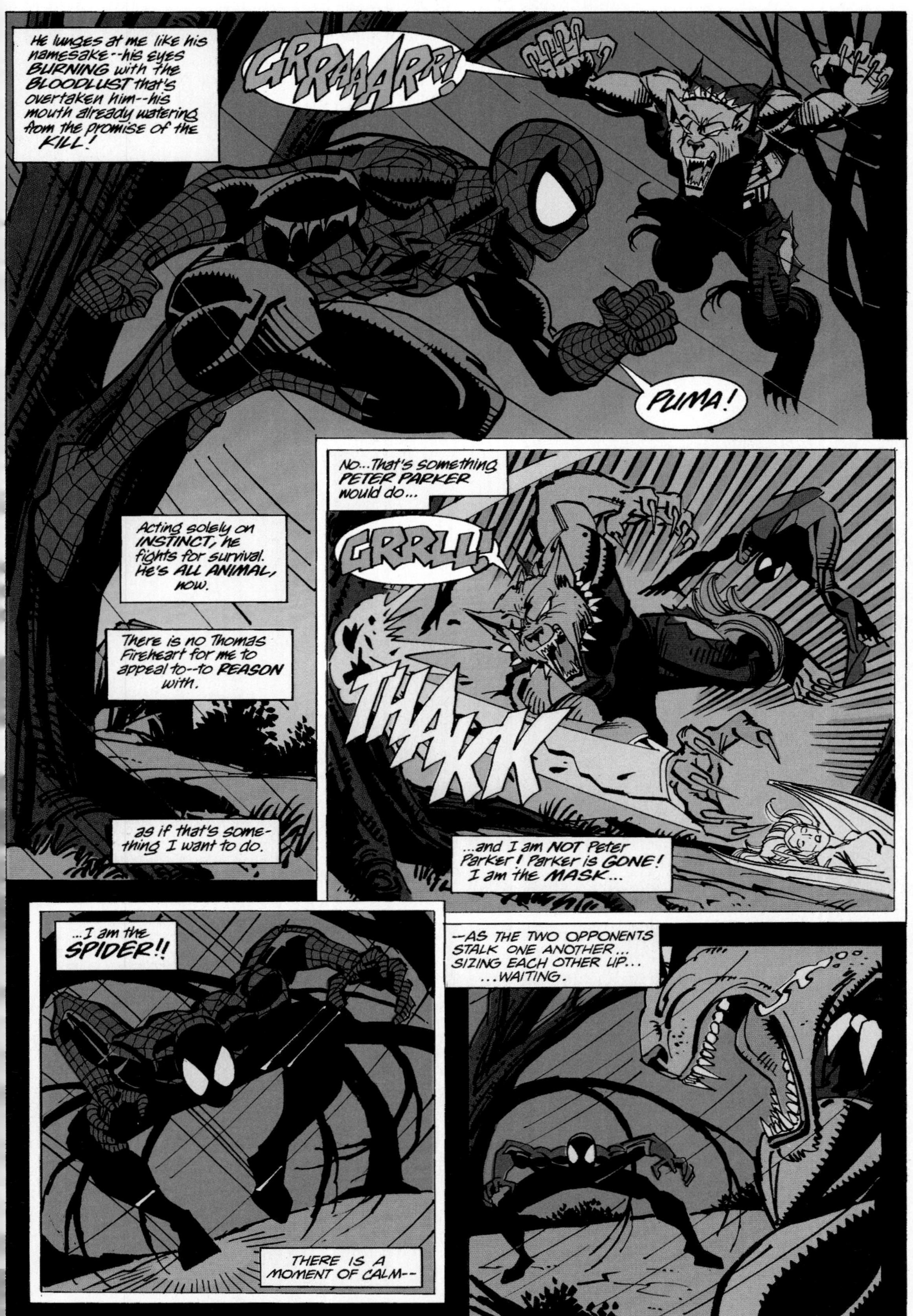
He lunges at me like his namesake--his eyes BURNING with the BLOODLUST that's overtaken him--his mouth already watering from the promise of the KILL!
GRRAAARR!
PUMA!
Acting solely on INSTINCT, he fights for survival. He's ALL ANIMAL, now.
There is no Thomas Fireheart for me to appeal to--to REASON with.
as if that's something I want to do.
No...That's something PETER PARKER would do...
GRRLL!
THAKK
...and I am NOT Peter Parker! Parker is GONE! I am the MASK...
...I am the SPIDER!!
THERE IS A MOMENT OF CALM--
--AS THE TWO OPPONENTS STALK ONE ANOTHER... SIZING EACH OTHER UP... ...WAITING.

...TO SPRING!

THEY BATTLE AS ANIMALS--LIGHTNING-QUICK REFLEXES EVADING DEADLY CLAWS--PRIMAL INSTINCTS GUIDING LEAPS AND LUNGES--

SSNRLL!

--THE PUMA WANTING THE SPIDER DEAD--HOPING TO EXTINGUISH THE PAIN AND ANGER THAT THE MEMORY OF HIM BRINGS.

THE SPIDER...

...GIVING UP ANOTHER CHUNK OF HIS HUMANITY WITH EVERY BLOW--BECOMING MORE BRUTAL--

MORE VICIOUS--
OOOOOHHHH.

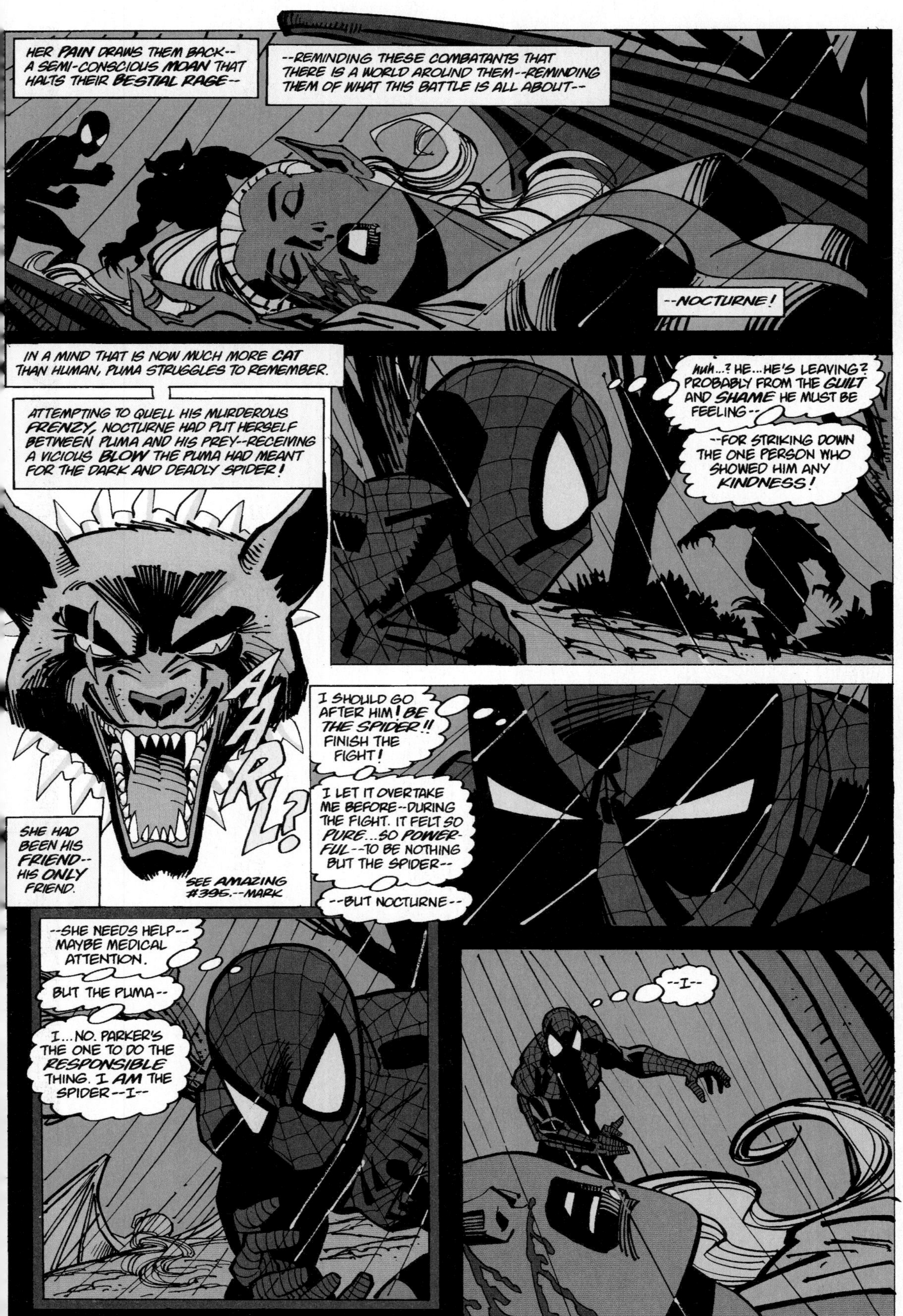
HER PAIN DRAWS THEM BACK-- A SEMI-CONSCIOUS MOAN THAT HALTS THEIR BESTIAL RAGE--
--REMINDING THESE COMBATANTS THAT THERE IS A WORLD AROUND THEM--REMINDING THEM OF WHAT THIS BATTLE IS ALL ABOUT--
--NOCTURNE!
IN A MIND THAT IS NOW MUCH MORE CAT THAN HUMAN, PUMA STRUGGLES TO REMEMBER.
ATTEMPTING TO QUELL HIS MURDEROUS FRENZY, NOCTURNE HAD PUT HERSELF BETWEEN PUMA AND HIS PREY--RECEIVING A VICIOUS BLOW THE PUMA HAD MEANT FOR THE DARK AND DEADLY SPIDER!
huh...? HE...HE'S LEAVING? PROBABLY FROM THE GUILT AND SHAME HE MUST BE FEELING--
--FOR STRIKING DOWN THE ONE PERSON WHO SHOWED HIM ANY KINDNESS!
AARRL?!
SHE HAD BEEN HIS FRIEND-- HIS ONLY FRIEND.
SEE AMAZING #395.--MARK
I SHOULD GO AFTER HIM! BE THE SPIDER!! FINISH THE FIGHT!
I LET IT OVERTAKE ME BEFORE--DURING THE FIGHT. IT FELT SO PURE...SO POWERFUL--TO BE NOTHING BUT THE SPIDER--
--BUT NOCTURNE--
--SHE NEEDS HELP-- MAYBE MEDICAL ATTENTION.
BUT THE PUMA--
I...NO. PARKER'S THE ONE TO DO THE RESPONSIBLE THING. I AM THE SPIDER--I--
--I--

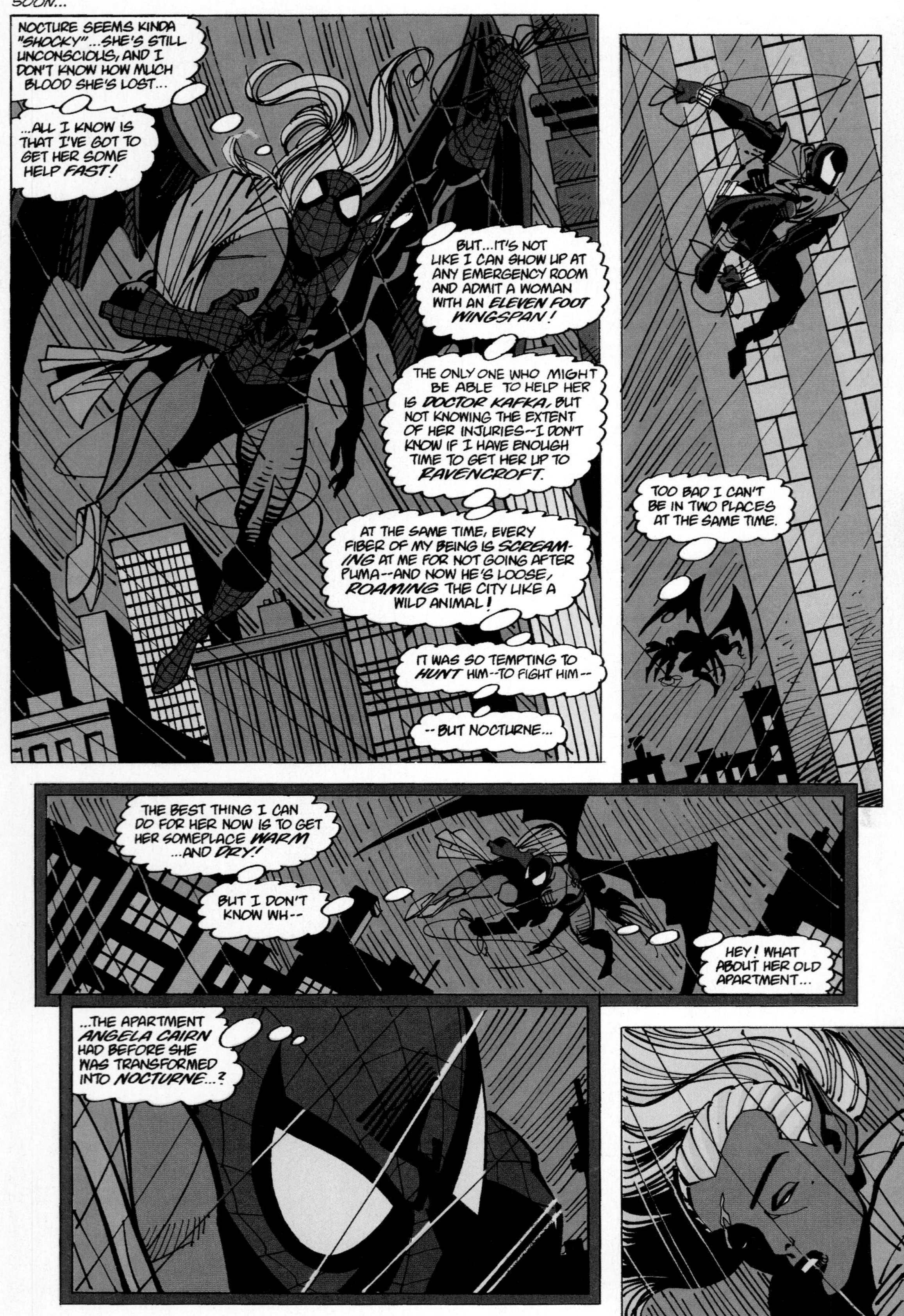
SOON...
NOCTURE SEEMS KINDA "SHOCKY"...SHE'S STILL UNCONSCIOUS, AND I DON'T KNOW HOW MUCH BLOOD SHE'S LOST...
...ALL I KNOW IS THAT I'VE GOT TO GET HER SOME HELP FAST!
BUT...IT'S NOT LIKE I CAN SHOW UP AT ANY EMERGENCY ROOM AND ADMIT A WOMAN WITH AN ELEVEN FOOT WINGSPAN!
THE ONLY ONE WHO MIGHT BE ABLE TO HELP HER IS DOCTOR KAFKA, BUT NOT KNOWING THE EXTENT OF HER INJURIES--I DON'T KNOW IF I HAVE ENOUGH TIME TO GET HER UP TO RAVENCROFT.
AT THE SAME TIME, EVERY FIBER OF MY BEING IS SCREAMING AT ME FOR NOT GOING AFTER PUMA--AND NOW HE'S LOOSE, ROAMING THE CITY LIKE A WILD ANIMAL!
IT WAS SO TEMPTING TO HUNT HIM--TO FIGHT HIM--
--BUT NOCTURNE...
TOO BAD I CAN'T BE IN TWO PLACES AT THE SAME TIME.
THE BEST THING I CAN DO FOR HER NOW IS TO GET HER SOMEPLACE WARM ...AND DRY!
BUT I DON'T KNOW WH--
HEY! WHAT ABOUT HER OLD APARTMENT...
...THE APARTMENT ANGELA CAIRN HAD BEFORE SHE WAS TRANSFORMED INTO NOCTURNE...?

EASY, CHIPPIE, EASY...
YA GOT NO REASON T'BE SCARED--
--WE JUST A BUNCHA GUYS CAUGHT OUT INNA RAIN--NOT BAD GUYS, JUS' COLD AN' HUNGRY.
WE WAS KINDA HOPIN' YA MIGHT "LEND" US A LITTLE O' DAT FOOD--
YEAH, AN' A LITTLE WARMTH--
SHUT UP, DUFF--
WHY, GISH HERE IS SO HUNGRY, HIS STOMACH'S BEEN GROWLIN' F'DAYS...
...AIN'T DAT RIGHT, GISH?
GROWWRR
HEH HEH YEAH, MY STOMACH'S BEEN GROWLIN'...
WHAT THE--?
GISH...? WUZZAT YER STOMACH...?
RRRAARRR
OH, MAN!!
WHAT THE @#&% IZZAT?
SNNNRRL

SKROOOAR
THUD
AAAAH!
CRASH

THEY SCURRY LIKE RATS OFF A SINKING SHIP--THEIR TERROR SEEMING TO FEED PUMA'S ANIMALISTIC FURY...

SNRR.. RAAR!

THE FEAR MADDENS HIM--

--ENRAGES HIM--

--YET SOMEWHERE BEHIND THE RED MIST OF HIS RAGE, THE SMALL PART OF HIM THAT IS STILL THOMAS FIREHEART REMEMBERS--

--THAT HE IS ALREADY RESPONSIBLE FOR INJURING ONE INNOCENT WOMAN TONIGHT.

Angela--NOCTURNE--said that she had been DRAWN to me--that she had SENSED my pain--

--that she knew I had given in to the SPIDER--and abandoned my life as PETER PARKER.

Just as FIREHEART gave in to the Puma--just as ANGELA CAIRN ceased to exist when she became Nocturne.

And I wonder--did I subconsciously bring her here to prove her WRONG...?
...to prove MYSELF wrong...?
I'm surprised that there are lights on in Angela's apartment...

...the place SHOULD be deserted.

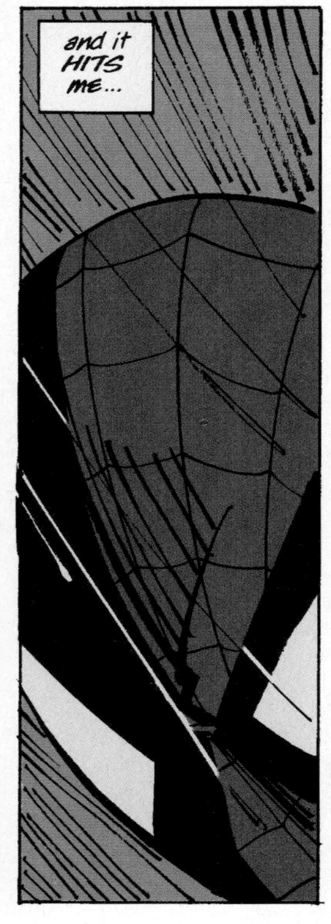

and it HITS me...

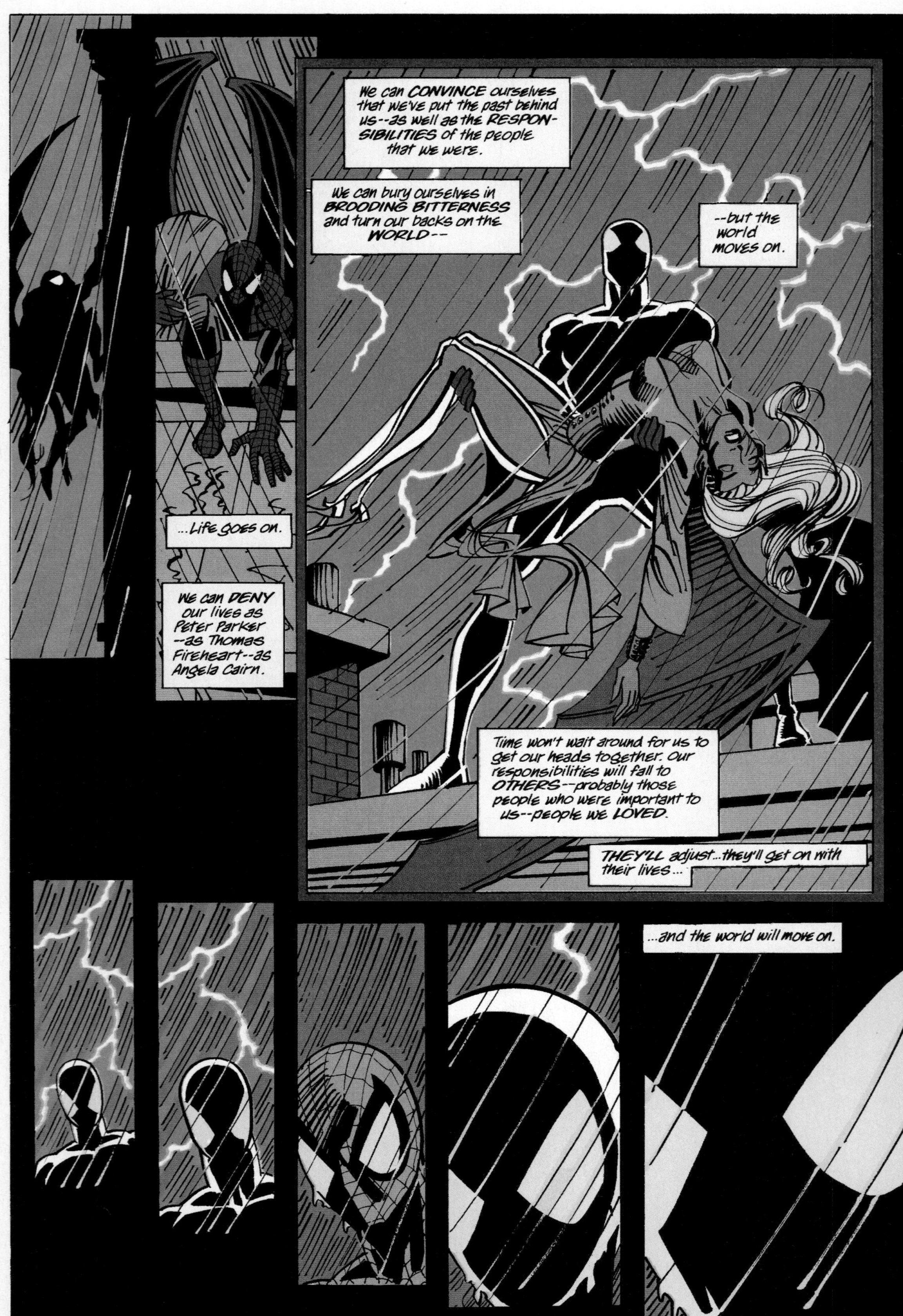
...Life goes on.
WE can DENY our lives as Peter Parker --as Thomas Fireheart--as Angela Cairn.
We can CONVINCE ourselves that we've put the past behind us--as well as the RESPONSIBILITIES of the people that we were.
We can bury ourselves in BROODING BITTERNESS and turn our backs on the WORLD--
--but the world moves on.
Time won't wait around for us to get our heads together. Our responsibilities will fall to OTHERS--probably those people who were important to us--people we LOVED.
THEY'LL adjust...they'll get on with their lives...
...and the world will move on.

I OWE YOU SO MUCH, MAY--

--FOR THE OH SO MANY TIMES WHEN YOU WERE *THERE* FOR ME. FOR BEING SUCH A *KIND* AND *COMPASSIONATE FRIEND*--
--FOR BEING LIKE THE *SISTER* I NEVER HAD...!

I'VE ALWAYS ADMIRED YOUR *STRENGTH,* MAY. YOU'VE ALWAYS BEEN STRONG FOR ME...
...AND YOU'VE ALWAYS BEEN STRONG FOR *PETER*.

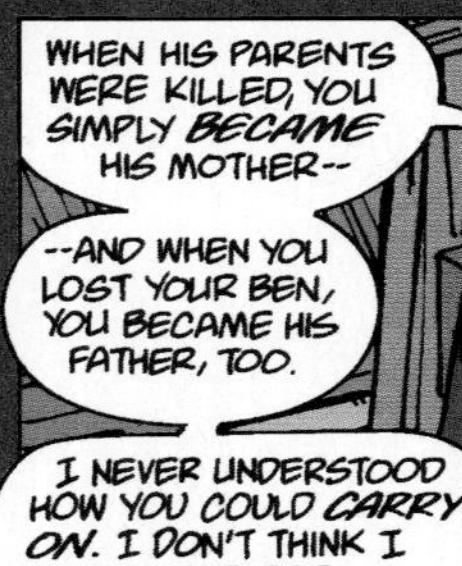
WHEN HIS PARENTS WERE KILLED, YOU SIMPLY *BECAME* HIS MOTHER--
--AND WHEN YOU LOST YOUR BEN, YOU BECAME HIS FATHER, TOO.
I NEVER UNDERSTOOD HOW YOU COULD *CARRY ON*. I DON'T THINK I COULD HAVE BEEN AS *BRAVE* AS YOU.

YOU DON'T HAVE TO BE STRONG ANYMORE, MAY.
YOU'VE DONE YOUR PART-- YOU'VE LIVED A GOOD LIFE AND RAISED A FINE YOUNG MAN--
--BUT YOU DON'T NEED TO FIGHT ANYMORE.

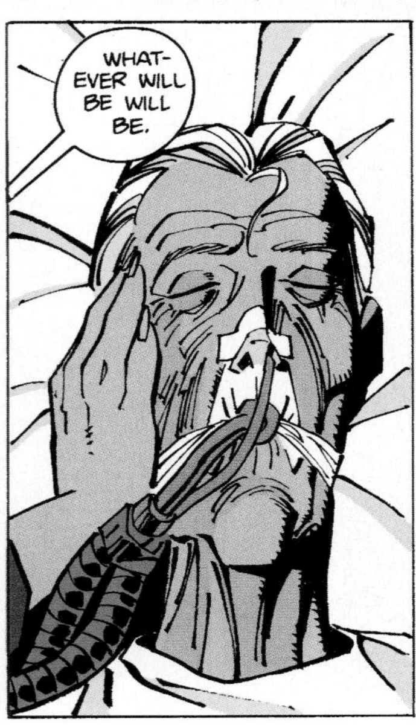
WHAT-EVER WILL BE WILL BE.

OOOOH...!
REST, ANGELA-- DON'T TRY TO TALK. I KNOW HOW HARD IT IS FOR YOU...
...NOT ANGELA ...I ...AM...
...PUMA?!
PUMA...?!?
YOU MUST BE DELIRIOUS, LADY! HOW CAN YOU BE SO WORRIED ABOUT HIM, AFTER WHAT HE DID TO YOU...?
HE PRACTICALLY RIPPED YOUR FACE OFF!
She answers, not with words, but with that power of hers. She reaches out with her EMOTIONS--

--and fills my head and my heart with her feelings for him. Her CONCERN --her CARE.
There is an understanding between them--a BOND. He needs us, and she knows where we'll find him--

--so that maybe we can HELP him to find himself.
Doesn't he at least deserve a SECOND CHANCE...?

Yeah... don't we all...?

PITTSBURGH...
...WHERE PETER'S WIFE MARY JANE PURSUES A QUEST ALL HER OWN...
I GUESS I WAS HOPING THAT YOU'D GIVE ME A SECOND CHANCE, GAYLE...

...THAT YOU AND DAD AND I COULD PUT OUR DIFFERENCES ASIDE LONG ENOUGH FOR US TO--MAYBE--BE A FAMILY AGAIN...

ALTHOUGH WE'VE ONLY TALKED ON HOLIDAYS AND BIRTHDAYS--I'VE NEVER TOLD YOU, GAYLE, HOW SORRY I AM--HOW MUCH I HATE MYSELF--
--FOR WHAT I DID TO YOU.
AND I AM SO SORRY...

I LOOK BACK AND I CAN'T BELIEVE HOW SELFISH I WAS--TO JUST ABANDON YOU WHEN YOU NEEDED ME THE MOST. I--
YOU DID WHAT YOU HAD TO DO, MARY JANE... YOU NEEDED TO DO WHAT WAS RIGHT FOR YOU. I WAS ANGRY WHEN YOU LEFT--BUT IT WASN'T LONG BEFORE I REALIZED THAT YOU WERE RIGHT.
IT WAS SELFISH OF ME TO ASSUME THAT YOU WOULD WANT TO STAY AND HELP ME.

AFTER TIMMY LEFT, AND MOM DIED, I WAS LEFT ALONE WITH TWO KIDS--BUT NONE OF THAT WAS YOUR RESPONSIBILITY--YOU HAD A LIFE OF YOUR OWN!
AND MAYBE I RESENTED YOU FOR THAT...

...BUT I NEEDED TO LEARN TO STAND ON MY OWN TWO FEET--I GUESS WE BOTH DID--AND WE DIDN'T TURN OUT SO BAD...!
AND SOMEHOW I ALWAYS KNEW THAT WE WOULD BE CLOSE AGAIN...LIKE MOM ALWAYS USED TO SAY --THINGS HAVE A WAY OF TURNING OUT RIGHT--
--"AS RIGHT AS RAIN!"

I MISS HER...
I THINK OF ALL THE THINGS I WISH I'D TOLD HER...
...AND... WELL...

...IF ANYTHING EVER HAPPENED TO YOU, OR DAD; I'D SPEND THE REST OF MY LIFE REGRETTING THAT I HAD NEVER TOLD YOU THAT I WAS SORRY...
...AND THAT I LOVE YOU BOTH.

Nocturne seems almost DRAWN to Puma--as if somehow, through their bond--their SYMBIOSIS, she can SENSE--
Huh...?
MY spider-sense is buzzing like--
DAREDEVIL!
Not Matt Murdock ...the NEW Daredevil! The one that showed up shortly after Murdock was KILLED.*
*MATT MURDOCK'S APPARENT DEATH WAS CHRONICLED IN DAREDEVIL #325.--MARK
What's HIS deal, I wonder?
Well,...Good Luck, pal! Those are HUGE shoes you're trying to fill...!
Matt Murdock...THERE'S a guy who just lost control--letting Daredevil's activities take priority in his life--putting Murdock in jeopardy--
--a mistake he paid for with his LIFE.

Sometime later we arrive at our destination --
--the dockside warehouse in which Angela was originally TRANSFORMED into Nocturne!*
SO WHAT'S THE STORY, ANGELA? WHY WOULD PUMA COME HERE?
IS THIS WHERE YOU'VE BEEN HOLING UP SINCE--
* IN SPECTACULAR SPIDER-MAN ANNUAL #13. --MARK
SPIDER-SENSE!! Like a four-alarm fire--
RRRAAARR!!
--as Puma--Fireheart--comes out of NOWHERE!!

SSNNRRLL!
No... I'm wrong! Fireheart's gone! The Puma's even more BESTIAL --more FERAL--than before! Every time I turn around it seems he's becoming more CAT-LIKE!!
And Nocturne's having less and less of an effect on him.
GRRRR--
-RRAAARR!!
--like it's MY FAULT!
The look in his eyes--like he's been BETRAYED --like she's turned AGAINST him--
And as I TENSE for the attack--
--DODGE the raking claws--
--as I'm drawn INTO the fight--
--the SPIDER is drawn OUT!

THAAT
THE BATTLE IS BRUTAL--
FSSSHH
--SAVAGE--
KASHH!
--VICIOUS--AS THE SPIDER DEFENDS HIMSELF AGAINST THE FURY OF HIS ATTACKER!
IN A DESPERATE ATTEMPT TO STOP THIS BATTLE, SHE ASSAULTS PUMA WITH A BARRAGE OF EMOTION-- REACHING OUT WITH AN INTENSE CALM--
--SEEKING TO RE-ESTABLISH HER BOND WITH HIS BURIED HUMAN SPIRIT! ONLY TO FIND--
--THAT THAT IS A WASTED EFFORT...!

MEANWHILE...

--PROBLEM IS THAT BOTH YOU AND DAD WERE ALWAYS SO STUBBORN. AND IF EVEN MENTIONED THE WORD "COMPROMISE"--YOU'D BOTH LOOK AT ME LIKE I WAS FROM MARS!
WELL--HOPEFULLY WE'VE ALL GROWN SOME. I JUST WANT DAD TO SEE--
MOMMY--
--I HAD A BAD DREAM. I DREAMED THAT YOU AND DADDY WERE GONE... AN' I WAS ALL--
--ALL ALONE!

OH, HONEY--!
KEVIN--! IT'S ALL RIGHT!

IT WAS ONLY A DREAM--AND THEY'RE NOT REAL.
YOUR MOMMY IS RIGHT HERE, AND SHE WOULD NEVER LEAVE YOU!
IT'S OKAY, MUFFIN-- EVERYTHING IS OKAY--

--EVERYTHING IS "RIGHT AS RAIN."

THIS IS A FIGHT OF SURVIVAL--
--A BATTLE TO THE DEATH.
KNOWING THIS, NOCTURNE RESOLVES HERSELF TO A COURSE OF ACTION--
--AWAITS AN OPENING--
--AND LEAPS--
--THROWING HER BODY BETWEEN THE TWO COMBATANTS--!
AND THOUGH THE STRAIN ON HER EMPATHIC ABILITIES IS NEAR UNBEARABLE, SHE CREATES BETWEEN THEM--BECOMES, ACTUALLY--AN EMOTIONAL CONDUIT--
--BUFFETING...BOMBARDING BOTH OF THESE MEN WITH THE ANGUISH, GUILT, AND PAIN OF THE OTHER. LETTING THEM EXPERIENCE FIRSTHAND--
--WHAT IT IS TO BE THE SPIDER...

...AND WHAT IT IS
TO BE THE PUMA.
WRAPPED WITHIN ONE ANOTHER,
THEY ARE BOUND BY EMOTION.
AND THOUGH IT TAKES ONLY A
MOMENT--

--IT IS AN EXPERIENCE NEITHER OF THEM WILL SOON FORGET!
FOR THE SPIDER, IT IS A MOMENT OF ENLIGHTENMENT--
--OF UNDERSTANDING.
FOR THE OTHER--
--IT HAS A FAR MORE SOBERING EFFECT...
...AS SLOWLY, SUBCONSCIOUSLY, FIGHTING BACK THE BEAST--
--THE MAN ONCE KNOWN AS THOMAS FIREHEART--
--RECLAIMS HIMSELF!
Fireheart! No matter what he's been through--I can't let him just walk away!
He may be a victim of his own power, but he has to PAY for his crimes...!
Nocturne protests with a hand on my arm. Her power ENVELOPES me in a wave of CALM--
--like before.

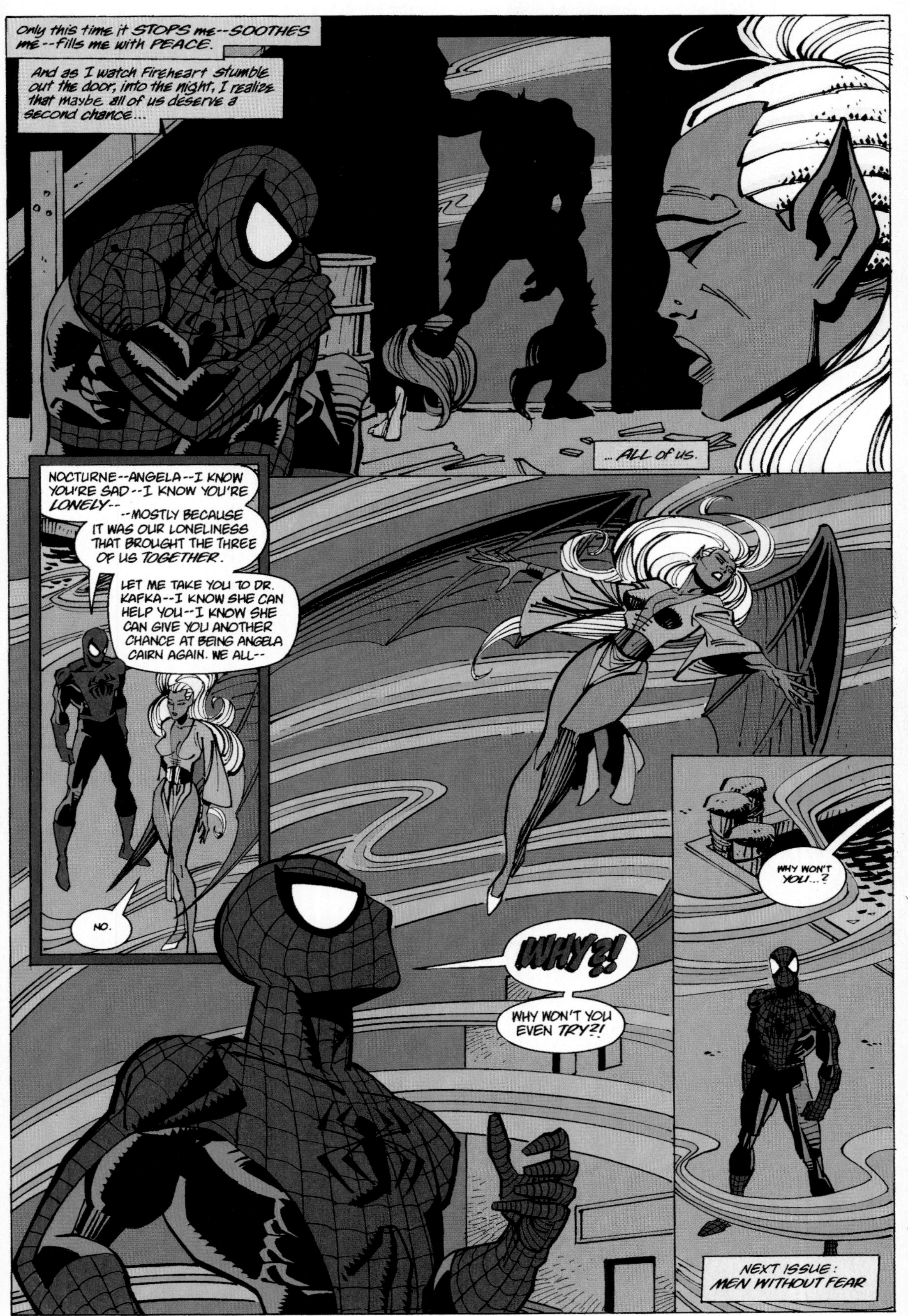
Only this time it STOPS me--SOOTHES me--fills me with PEACE.
And as I watch Fireheart stumble out the door, into the night, I realize that maybe all of us deserve a second chance...
...ALL of us.
NOCTURNE--ANGELA--I KNOW YOU'RE SAD--I KNOW YOU'RE LONELY--
--MOSTLY BECAUSE IT WAS OUR LONELINESS THAT BROUGHT THE THREE OF US TOGETHER.
LET ME TAKE YOU TO DR. KAFKA--I KNOW SHE CAN HELP YOU--I KNOW SHE CAN GIVE YOU ANOTHER CHANCE AT BEING ANGELA CAIRN AGAIN. WE ALL--
NO.
WHY?!
WHY WON'T YOU EVEN TRY?!
WHY WON'T YOU...?
NEXT ISSUE: MEN WITHOUT FEAR

MARVEL COMICS
THE AMAZING SPIDER-MAN
© 1994 MARVEL ENT. GROUP, INC.
$1.50 US
$2.05 CAN/UK £1.25
396
DEC
02457
APPROVED BY THE COMICS CODE AUTHORITY
SIDE-BY-SIDE WITH DAREDEVIL
BACK FROM THE EDGE PART 3 OF 4
...AND THE MOST SHOCKING ENDING OF ALL!

BITTEN BY A RADIOACTIVE SPIDER, STUDENT **PETER PARKER** GAINED THE PROPORTIONATE STRENGTH AND AGILITY OF AN ARACHNID! ARMED WITH HIS WONDROUS WEB-SHOOTERS, THE RELUCTANT SUPER HERO STRUGGLES WITH SINISTER SUPER-VILLAINS, MAKING ENDS MEET, AND MAINTAINING SOME SEMBLANCE OF A NORMAL LIFE!

Stan Lee PRESENTS: THE AMAZING SPIDER-MAN®

PLEASE, WILSON-- DON'T INSULT ME.
AAAAA!
ROK!
YOU THINK I'D LET A PIECE OF GARBAGE LIKE YOU SHOOT ME IN THE BACK?
IF YOU DON'T WANT THE OTHER HAND BROKEN, I SUGGEST YOU ANSWER MY QUESTION.
WHERE'S LELAND OWLSLEY?
I DUNNO, MAN! I DUNNO!
ALL I HEAR'S WHAT'S ON THE STREET!
THEY SAY HE'S OUT-- AN' HE'S GOT SOMETHIN' BREWIN'--
--SOMETHIN' BIG!
GIVE ME THE DETAILS.
I SWEAR THAT'S ALL I KNOW! I SWEAR T' GOD!
KRONK!

IF YOU DON'T STOP TAKING THE LORD'S NAME IN VAIN, WILSON--
SPAKK!
--YOU'LL NEVER GET TO HEAVEN.
YOU CAN COME DOWN NOW.
YOU'VE BEEN FOLLOWING ME... MIRRORING MY EVERY MOVE--
--FOR THREE NIGHTS NOW.
AND NO ONE CAN DO THAT WITHOUT ME NOTICING.

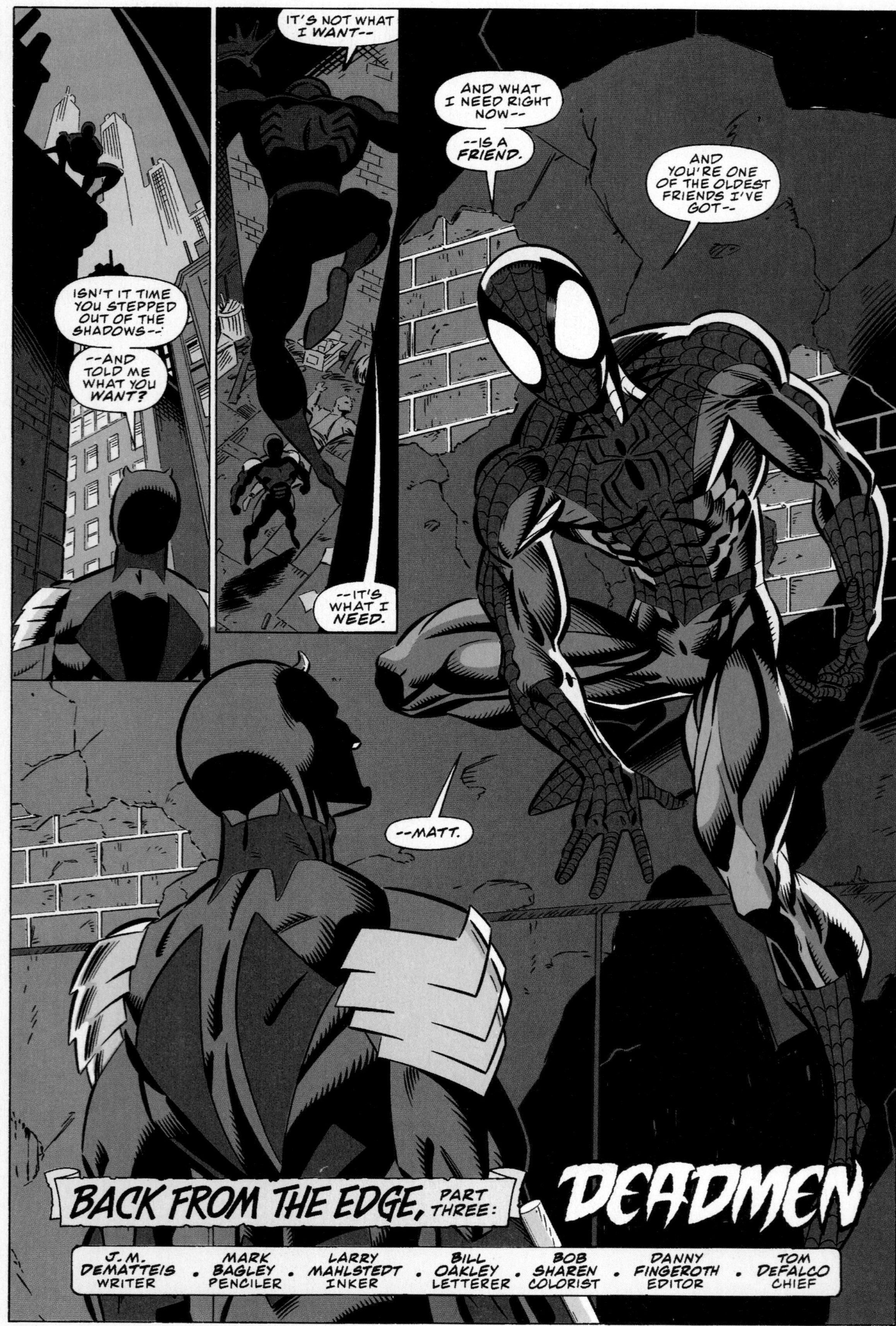
ISN'T IT TIME YOU STEPPED OUT OF THE SHADOWS--
--AND TOLD ME WHAT YOU WANT?
IT'S NOT WHAT I WANT--
--IT'S WHAT I NEED.
AND WHAT I NEED RIGHT NOW--
--IS A FRIEND.
AND YOU'RE ONE OF THE OLDEST FRIENDS I'VE GOT--
--MATT.
BACK FROM THE EDGE, PART THREE: DEADMEN
J.M. DEMATTEIS WRITER
MARK BAGLEY PENCILER
LARRY MAHLSTEDT INKER
BILL OAKLEY LETTERER
BOB SHAREN COLORIST
DANNY FINGEROTH EDITOR
TOM DEFALCO CHIEF

YOU'VE GOT THE WRONG MAN. THE DARE-DEVIL YOU KNOW IS BURIED SIX FEET IN THE GROUND.
LET HIM REST IN PEACE.
MATT, PLEASE --DON'T WALK AWAY FROM ME!
MATT MURDOCK IS DEAD.
RING BELL
SO AM I.
MICE.

Brainless, frightened little mice, scurrying around. Waiting for me to swoop down and effortlessly devour them. But the question is...
...do I want to?
Questions? Doubts?
Once I would have simply scooped the mice up, chewed them to pieces, and spit them out... without a second thought.
But I'm not the man I once was, am I? I've discovered I have a conscience. I know shame...
...and guilt.
But of course, acknowledgement of such feelings doesn't mean that they're in any way useful. Or desirable.
I lived without them for many years; perhaps I should discard them again. Perhaps I will...
...once I answer another-- far more provocative --question:
Who am I?
I was born Leland Owlsley. Yet the world calls me the Owl.
What, I wonder, shall I call myself?

I WAS ONCE LIKE ALL OF YOU DOWN THERE; BLAND AND WITLESS. CAREFUL TO OBSERVE SOCIETY'S RULES AND BOUNDARIES.
I HAD A THRIVING BUSINESS. A LOVING FAMILY. I PERFORMED ACTS OF CHARITY AND GOODNESS.
BUT LELAND OWLSLEY'S SOUL--WAS DEAD.
WHEN I FINALLY STEPPED OVER THE EDGE... SPREAD THE OWL'S WINGS AND FLEW INTO THE NIGHT...
...I TASTED A FREEDOM, A DIZZYING EUPHORIA, THAT RAISED UP MY DECOMPOSING SOUL--AND, AT LONG LAST, GAVE ME LIFE!
TO BREAK THE BONDS OF LAW AND MORALITY... TO STEAL, TO LIE, TO TERRORIZE AND MURDER... THESE THINGS BECAME MY REASONS FOR EXISTENCE.
BUT SOMEWHERE IN THE OWL'S HEART, OWLSLEY'S VOICE WAS HEARD--CRYING FOR REDEMPTION...FOR HUMANITY.
AND I LISTENED: SURRENDERING MY WINGS AND GIVING MYSELF UP TO THE VERY WORLD I'D FOUGHT SO HARD TO ESCAPE FROM.
BUT I COULDN'T BEAR THE PSYCHIATRISTS, PROBING MY EVERY IMPULSE... THE JUDGES AND PROSECUTORS SCREECHING FOR MY HEAD. ABOVE ALL... I COULDN'T BEAR THE PRISON WALLS CONFINING ME...
...REDUCING OWLSLEY AND THE OWL BOTH...
ah--HERE YOU ARE!
...TO SOMETHING EVEN SMALLER THAN A MOUSE.

YOU'RE LATE FOR OUR MEETING, OWLSLEY.
DON'T CALL ME THAT.
A TRIFLE TOUCHY TONIGHT, eh?
OH, WELL... COME ALONG NOW, BROTHER--WE HAVE QUITE A BIT TO TALK ABOUT.

IS THIS WHY I ESCAPED? DID I LEAVE A TRAIL OF BLOOD AND BROKEN BONES BEHIND ME SO THAT I COULD RETURN TO A WORLD POPULATED BY HIS KIND?
I'M NOT YOUR BROTHER, VULTURE--

--AND I NEVER WILL BE.
SO YOU SAY, MY FRIEND.
SO YOU SAY.

I keep reading the first paragraph of this article over and over...
...but it just won't penetrate. I might as well be reading Latin.
You're doing good, Mary Jane: can't sleep. Can't read.
Every nerve-ending in your body is tingling. Stomach's turning over.
Well, what did I expect coming back to Pittsburgh? Being here in my sister Gayle's house... I can almost smell the past. And it's not exactly a sweet scent.
When Peter and I would go over to May's for dinner-he'd spend hours sometimes just rooting around through his old things...

...telling me stories about his childhood... how wonderful it was growing up there.
I come home and I'm ready for the intensive care ward.

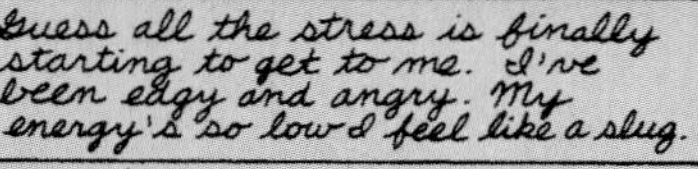
Guess all the stress is finally starting to get to me. I've been edgy and angry. My energy's so low I feel like a slug.
And knowing that I'm going to confront my father tomorrow sure isn't helping things.

Gayle's done her best, God bless her, to make me feel comfortable. Part of the family.
But the truth of the matter is; being part of this family...

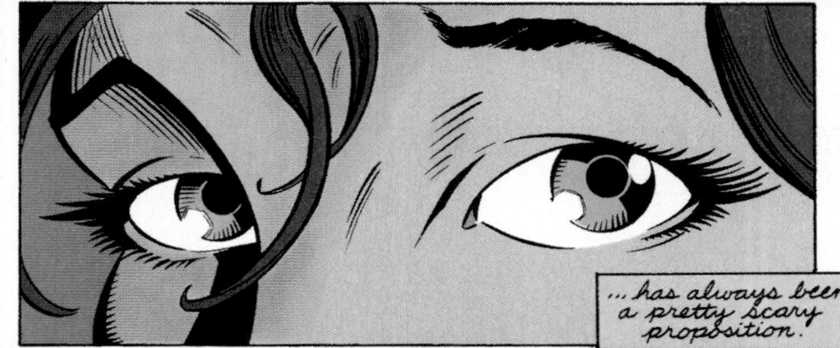
...has always been a pretty scary proposition.

OKAY, NOW I'LL BE THE PRINCESS AND YOU BE MY LADY-IN-WAITING.
WHY CAN'T I BE THE PRINCESS?
'CAUSE I SAID SO.
OH. OKAY.

HEY--
--HOW THE DEVIL AM I SUPPOSED TO GET ANY WRITING DONE WITH YOU KIDS MAKING SO MUCH NOISE OUT HERE?!

BUT, DADDY... WE WERE PLAYING QUIET... JUST LIKE YOU TOLD US.

DON'T TALK BACK TO ME, YOU LYING LITTLE $#*%!!
I-I'M SORRY, DADDY.

I'M SORRY.

PENNY FOR YOUR THOUGHTS, SIS.

I DOUBT IF THEY'RE WORTH THAT MUCH.

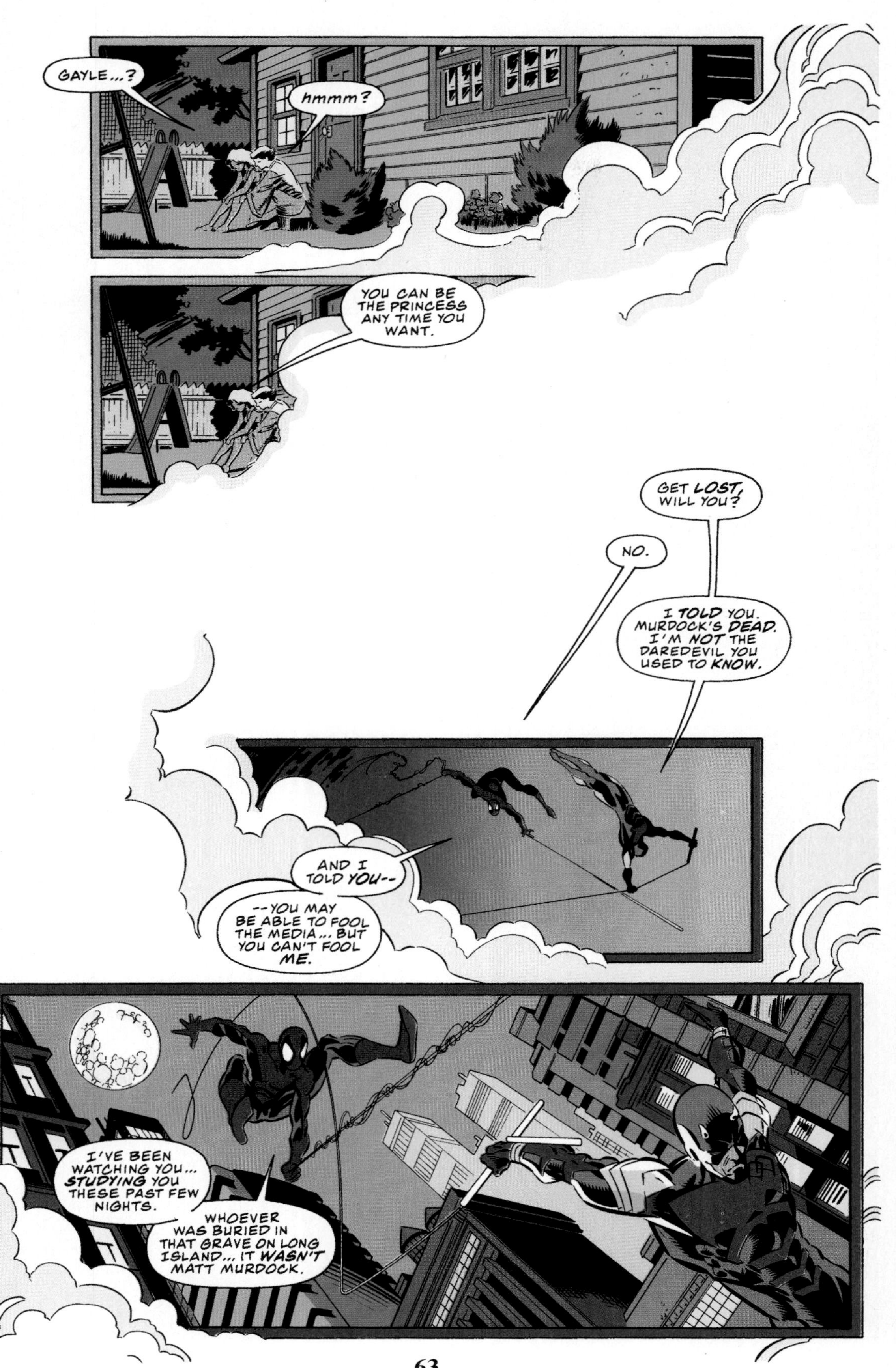
GAYLE...?
hmmm?
YOU CAN BE THE PRINCESS ANY TIME YOU WANT.
GET LOST, WILL YOU?
NO.
I TOLD YOU. MURDOCK'S DEAD. I'M NOT THE DAREDEVIL YOU USED TO KNOW.
AND I TOLD YOU--
--YOU MAY BE ABLE TO FOOL THE MEDIA... BUT YOU CAN'T FOOL ME.
I'VE BEEN WATCHING YOU... STUDYING YOU THESE PAST FEW NIGHTS.
WHOEVER WAS BURIED IN THAT GRAVE ON LONG ISLAND... IT WASN'T MATT MURDOCK.

WE MAY NOT HAVE BEEN BEST FRIENDS-- BUT YOU'RE THE CLOSEST THING TO A KINDRED SPIRIT I'VE EVER KNOWN!
YOU AND I SHARED OUR SECRETS... WE SHARED OUR STRUGGLES. NOT JUST AS DAREDEVIL AND SPIDER-MAN--
--BUT AS MATT MURDOCK AND PETER PARKER.
SMART MOVE, THERE--GIVING AWAY YOUR SECRET TO A TOTAL STRANGER!
IF THIS IS THE WAY YOU OPERATE, PAL-- I'M AMAZED MURDOCK EVER GAVE YOU THE TIME OF DAY.
LISTEN TO ME, BLAST IT!
I'M IN TROUBLE HERE! MY WHOLE LIFE'S BEEN RIPPED APART--
--AND I DON'T KNOW WHERE ELSE TO TURN!
GET THIS THROUGH YOUR THICK HEAD: I'M NOT MURDOCK--
--AND EVEN IF I WAS--
--THERE'S NOTHING I CAN DO TO HELP YOU!

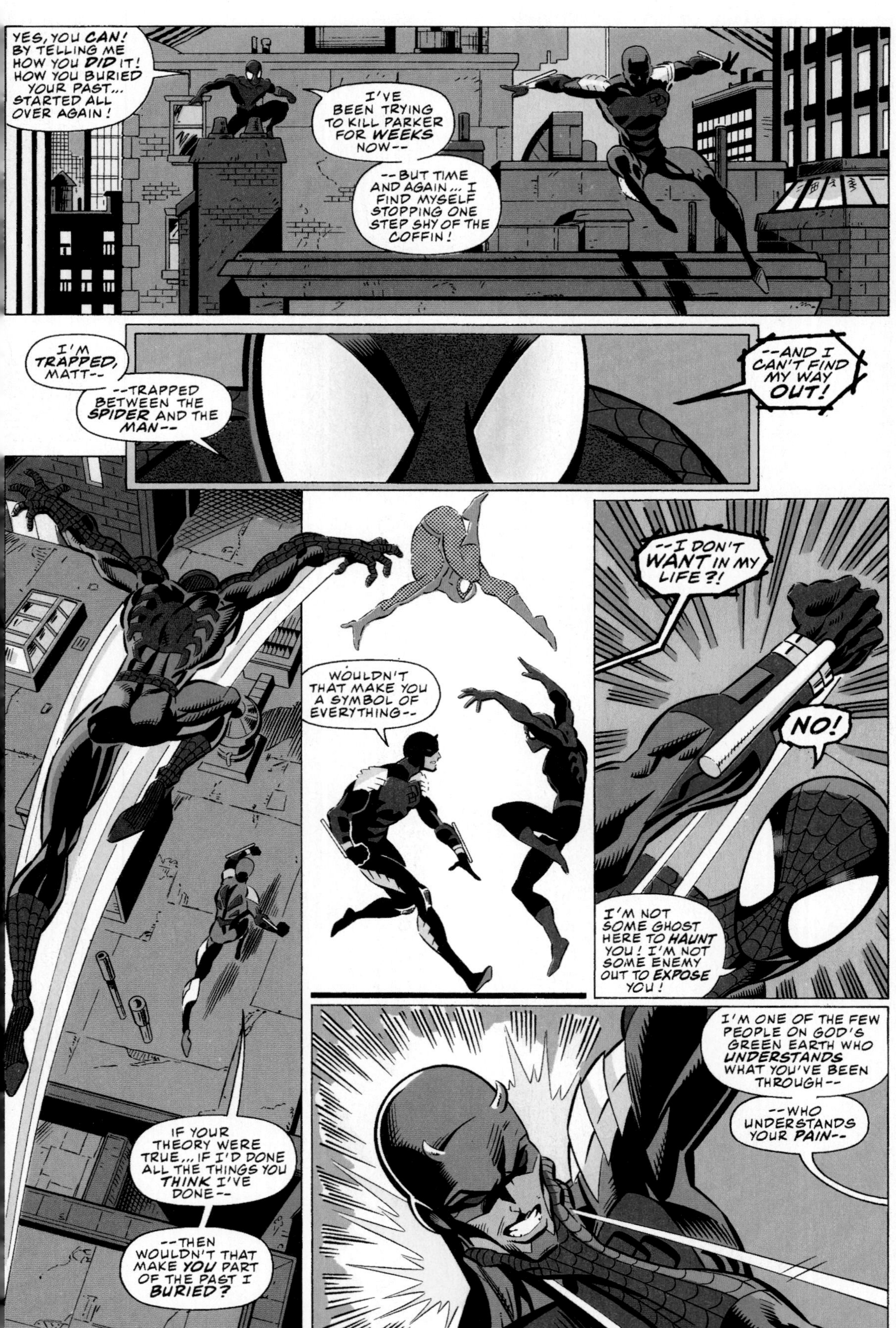
YES, YOU CAN! BY TELLING ME HOW YOU DID IT! HOW YOU BURIED YOUR PAST... STARTED ALL OVER AGAIN!
I'VE BEEN TRYING TO KILL PARKER FOR WEEKS NOW--
--BUT TIME AND AGAIN... I FIND MYSELF STOPPING ONE STEP SHY OF THE COFFIN!
I'M TRAPPED, MATT--
--TRAPPED BETWEEN THE SPIDER AND THE MAN--
--AND I CAN'T FIND MY WAY OUT!
IF YOUR THEORY WERE TRUE... IF I'D DONE ALL THE THINGS YOU THINK I'VE DONE--
--THEN WOULDN'T THAT MAKE YOU PART OF THE PAST I BURIED?
WOULDN'T THAT MAKE YOU A SYMBOL OF EVERYTHING--
--I DON'T WANT IN MY LIFE?!
NO!
I'M NOT SOME GHOST HERE TO HAUNT YOU! I'M NOT SOME ENEMY OUT TO EXPOSE YOU!
I'M ONE OF THE FEW PEOPLE ON GOD'S GREEN EARTH WHO UNDERSTANDS WHAT YOU'VE BEEN THROUGH--
--WHO UNDERSTANDS YOUR PAIN--

--AND WHO NEEDS YOU TO UNDERSTAND MINE!
REMOVE THE HAND.
I--I'M SORRY. I DIDN'T MEAN TO--
LOOK, I WON'T BOTHER YOU ANY MORE, OKAY? IT'S JUST THAT--
STOP APOLOGIZING AND LET'S GO.
GO? GO WHERE?
TO PAY OUR RESPECTS TO THE DEAD.

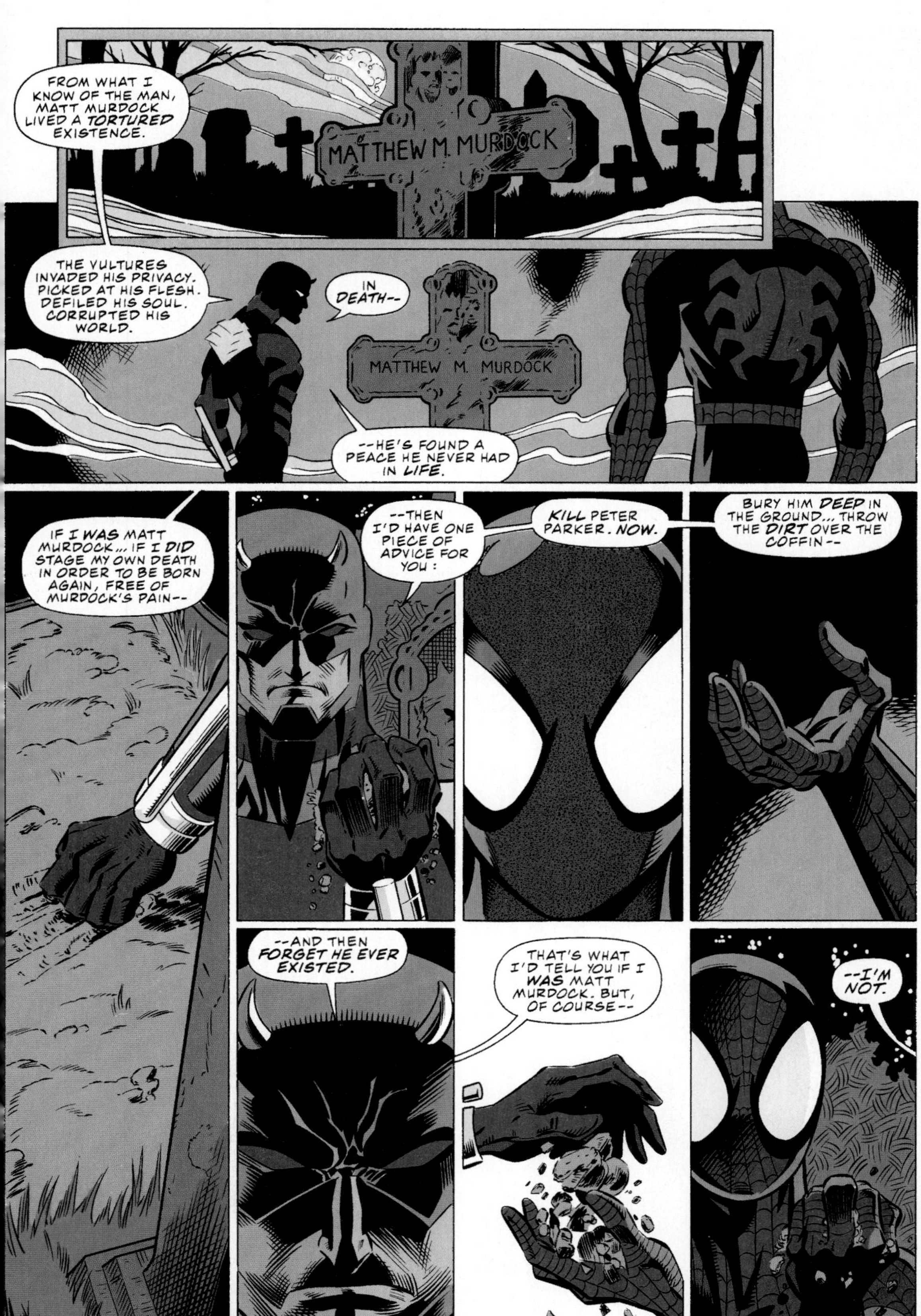

MATTHEW M. MURDOCK
FROM WHAT I KNOW OF THE MAN, MATT MURDOCK LIVED A TORTURED EXISTENCE.
THE VULTURES INVADED HIS PRIVACY. PICKED AT HIS FLESH. DEFILED HIS SOUL. CORRUPTED HIS WORLD.
IN DEATH--
MATTHEW M. MURDOCK
--HE'S FOUND A PEACE HE NEVER HAD IN LIFE.
IF I WAS MATT MURDOCK... IF I DID STAGE MY OWN DEATH IN ORDER TO BE BORN AGAIN, FREE OF MURDOCK'S PAIN--
--THEN I'D HAVE ONE PIECE OF ADVICE FOR YOU:
KILL PETER PARKER. NOW.
BURY HIM DEEP IN THE GROUND... THROW THE DIRT OVER THE COFFIN--
--AND THEN FORGET HE EVER EXISTED.
THAT'S WHAT I'D TELL YOU IF I WAS MATT MURDOCK. BUT, OF COURSE--
--I'M NOT.

NOW WHAT DO YOU WANT?

I DUNNO. COUPLE O' LONELY GUYS LIKE US--
--I FIGURED MAYBE WE COULD GO SPLIT A PIZZA ...GRAB A COUPLE OF BEERS ...SEE A MOVIE--

--HUNT FOR THE OWL?

WHAT AM I DOING HERE... IN THIS DEGENERATE WRECK OF A MANSION IN BROOKLYN?
WHAT AM I DOING HERE... IN THE COMPANY OF THIS DEGENERATE WRECK OF A MAN?

I SOUGHT HIM OUT AS SOON AS I RETURNED TO NEW YORK.
BUT WHY?

BECAUSE I HEARD THE TALE OF THE CHAMELEON'S SIMULACRA; HOW ADRIAN TOOMES SIPHONED THEIR LIFE-FORCE AND RENEWED HIS OWN?
HOW HE KILLED THE WEAK, CANCER-RIDDLED OLD MAN HE'D BEEN--AND WAS REBORN AS THE NEW VULTURE?

DID I HOPE THAT, BY JOINING FORCES WITH HIM, STUDYING HIM, I COULD FATHOM A WAY TO BE RID OF OWLSLEY--AND EMBRACE THE OWL ONCE AGAIN?
OF COURSE, THERE'S ANOTHER OPTION I HAVEN'T CONSIDERED.

PERHAPS IT'S NOT OWLSLEY--BUT THE OWL I'M TRYING TO KILL. OR PERHAPS...
...IT'S BOTH?
...ARE YOU LISTENING TO ME, OWLSLEY?
I TOLD YOU NOT TO CALL ME THAT.
SLIP OF THE TONGUE.
BELIEVE ME, MORE THAN ANYONE, I UNDERSTAND YOUR DESIRE TO BE RID OF YOUR... FORMER SELF. WHEN I SLOUGHED OFF MY OLD SKIN, I VOWED THAT I'D BLOT OUT ALL THOUGHT... ALL MEMORY... OF THE DODDERING WEAKLING I WAS.
IN FACT--THAT'S WHY WE'RE HERE!
IN THIS SYRINGE IS A CERTAIN FORMULA... A CHEMICAL VIRUS... WHICH I OBTAINED AT NO SMALL RISK FROM AN ARMY RESEARCH LABORATORY.
IT'S THE KEY, MY FRIEND, TO BURYING OWLSLEY AND TOOMES--
--ONCE AND FOR ALL.

YOU'RE A PHILOSOPHICAL MAN. SO TELL ME : WHAT IS THE KEY TO IDENTITY?
IS IT OUR OWN KNOWLEDGE OF OURSELVES... OR OTHER PEOPLE'S KNOWLEDGE OF US?
IF I SAY THAT I AM NO LONGER ADRIAN TOOMES... THAT I AM THE NEW VULTURE NOW AND FOREVER, DOES THAT MAKE IT SO?
OR DOES THE MEMORY OF TOOMES IN OTHER PEOPLE'S MINDS MEAN THAT HE STILL EXISTS?
NOW WHERE DID I PUT THAT--?
ah... HERE HE IS!
P-PLEASE ...DON'T HURT ME!
I SNATCHED THIS SPECIMEN OFF THE STREETS OF LOWER MANHATTAN THIS MORNING. SCAVENGING FOOD OUT OF A GARBAGE CAN.
HE'S IN THE ROOM WITH US. HE SEES US. HE RECOGNIZES US AS THE VULTURE AND THE OWL.
BUT IF HE CEASES TO EXIST--
--DON'T WE?
DO YOU SEE WHAT I'M GETTING AT? ONCE I DIE IN HIS MIND--
--I'M LEFT FREE TO TOTALLY REINVENT MYSELF, IN WHATEVER IMAGE I CHOOSE!
VULTURE --STOP THIS!

THIS MAN HAS DONE YOU NO HARM! GIVE HIM THE ANTIDOTE... NOW!
DIDN'T YOU HEAR WHAT I SAID? HE WAS EATING BREAKFAST OUT OF A TRASH CAN! HIS LIFE DOESN'T MATTER!

IT MATTERS TO ME!

THE ANTIDOTE!
NOW!
SHIKK

AS YOU WISH...
...BROTHER.

OH, DEAR. I JUST REMEMBERED.

THE ARMY SCIENTISTS HADN'T GOTTEN THAT FAR IN THEIR RESEARCH.

THERE IS NO ANTIDOTE.
SNAKKT!

HIS NECK!
YOU SNAPPED HIS NECK!
WHY?!
WOULD YOU RATHER HE SUFFERED... THE WAY OUR VICTIMS ARE GOING TO SUFFER? WOULD YOU RATHER HE ENDURE DAYS OF TORTURE-- AND THEN A SLOW AGONIZING DEATH?
"OUR VICTIMS" ?!?
WHAT ARE YOU TALKING ABOUT?
MY BIRDS WILL CARRY THIS VIRUS OUT INTO THE CITY! ONE BY ONE, EVERY-ONE WHO EVER KNEW ADRIAN TOOMES AND LELAND OWLSLEY-- WILL DIE!
AND THEIR DEATHS WILL MAKE US FREE.
OH, PLEASE-- DON'T LOOK SO SHOCKED! ISN'T THIS WHY YOU CAME TO ME? ISN'T THIS WHAT YOU WANT-- MORE THAN ANYTHING ON EARTH?
NO!!
I'LL HAVE NO PART OF YOUR INSANE PLAN! I'LL HAVE NO PART OF YOU!
YOU CAN RUN FROM ME, BROTHER-- BUT YOU CAN'T HIDE.
AND DO YOU KNOW WHY?
WE'RE TWO OF A KIND!

WHY DID I RUN? BECAUSE I WAS REPULSED BY WHAT HE'S PLANNING?
OR BECAUSE -- I WAS SO SORELY TEMPTED?
ARE ALL MY SELF-DOUBTS... ALL MY BURNING QUESTIONS ...JUST SMOKE-SCREENS-- MASKING THE TRUTH THAT THE VULTURE SEES SO PLAINLY?
"TWO OF A KIND."
IF WE ARE... IF THAT MAN IS A MIRROR OF MY OWN HEART... IF MY DESTINY IS TO BE A SOULLESS SCAVENGER, SWOOPING DOWN OUT OF THE SKIES... THEN HEAVEN HELP ME.
AND HEAVEN HELP THE WORLD.
AND SO I MUST RETURN TO THE ORIGINAL QUESTION. PERHAPS... THE ONLY QUESTION:
WHO AM I?
OWL!

THE MAN WHO WORE THIS COSTUME BEFORE ME OFFERED YOU A SECOND CHANCE. HE OFFERED YOU HOPE.
AND YOU SPIT IN HIS FACE.
YOU DISGRACED HIS MEMORY.
TIME TO PAY UP, OWL. TIME TO GIVE THE DEVIL HIS DUE.
HOW DARE YOU PASS JUDGEMENT ON ME!
SHIKK
YOU DON'T KNOW ME! YOU CAN'T HOPE TO KNOW ME!
I WARN YOU... I WARN YOU BOTH: LEAVE. NOW. OR LEARN WHO I TRULY AM--
--TO YOUR EVERLASTING REGRET!
WISE UP, OWL--
--MAYBE YOU COULD HOLD YOUR OWN AGAINST ONE OF US... BUT NOT TWO! WHY NOT MAKE IT EASY ON YOURSELF AND--
CAWWW!
Shriiik!
SPIDER-MAN! ARE YOU--?

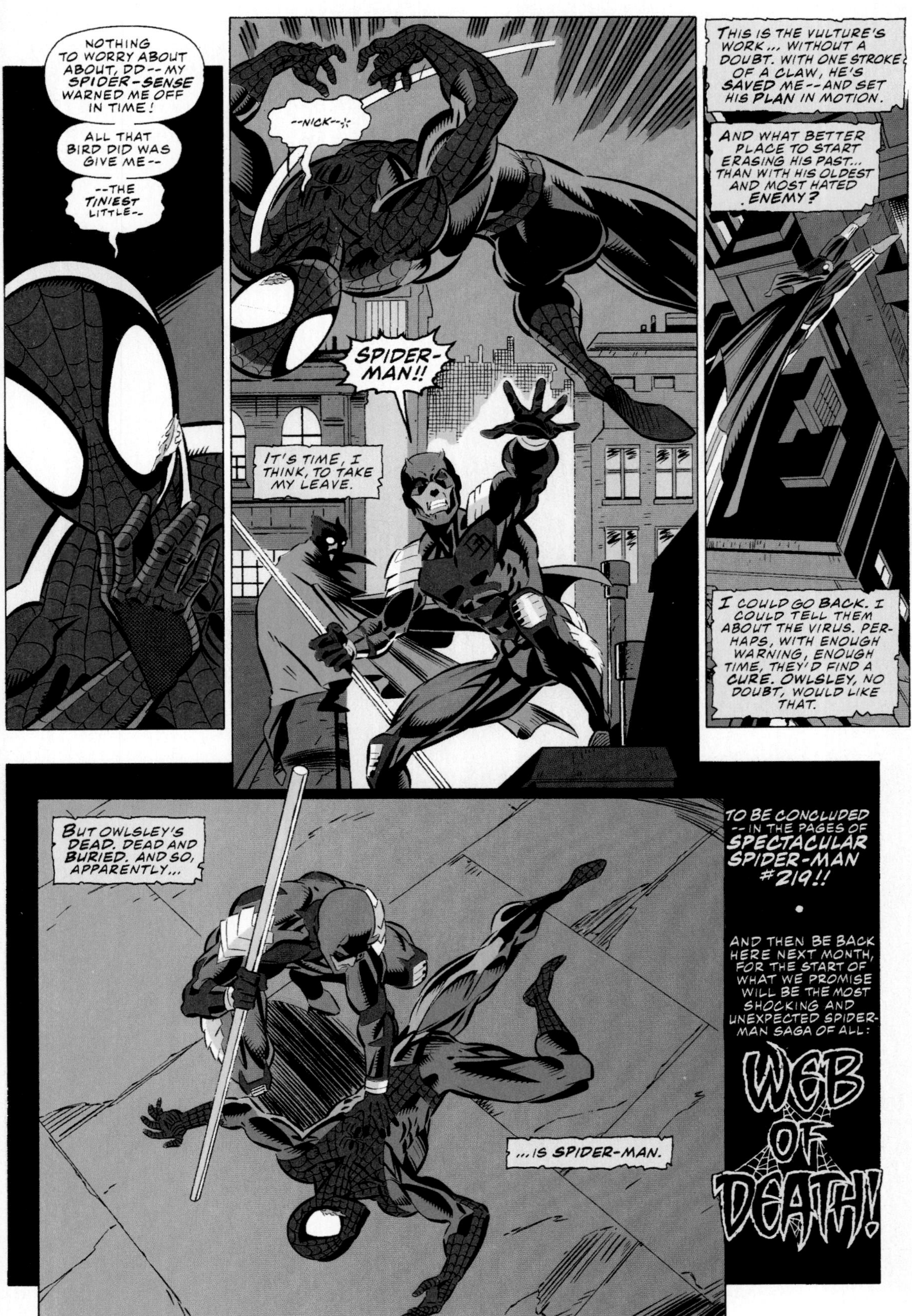
NOTHING TO WORRY ABOUT, DD-- MY SPIDER-SENSE WARNED ME OFF IN TIME!
ALL THAT BIRD DID WAS GIVE ME--
--THE TINIEST LITTLE--
--NICK--
SPIDER-MAN!!
IT'S TIME, I THINK, TO TAKE MY LEAVE.
THIS IS THE VULTURE'S WORK... WITHOUT A DOUBT. WITH ONE STROKE OF A CLAW, HE'S SAVED ME--AND SET HIS PLAN IN MOTION.
AND WHAT BETTER PLACE TO START ERASING HIS PAST... THAN WITH HIS OLDEST AND MOST HATED ENEMY?
I COULD GO BACK. I COULD TELL THEM ABOUT THE VIRUS. PERHAPS, WITH ENOUGH WARNING, ENOUGH TIME, THEY'D FIND A CURE. OWLSLEY, NO DOUBT, WOULD LIKE THAT.
BUT OWLSLEY'S DEAD. DEAD AND BURIED. AND SO, APPARENTLY...
...IS SPIDER-MAN.
TO BE CONCLUDED --IN THE PAGES OF SPECTACULAR SPIDER-MAN #219!!
AND THEN BE BACK HERE NEXT MONTH, FOR THE START OF WHAT WE PROMISE WILL BE THE MOST SHOCKING AND UNEXPECTED SPIDER-MAN SAGA OF ALL:
WEB OF DEATH!

MARVEL COMICS

THE SPECTACULAR SPIDER-MAN IS DYING!

$1.50 US
$2.05 CAN/UK £1.25
219
DEC
02199

APPROVED BY THE COMICS CODE AUTHORITY

GUEST-STARRING DAREDEVIL!

BACK FROM THE EDGE PART FOUR

IS IT TOO *LATE* TO *SAVE* THE LIFE HE'S FOUGHT TO RECLAIM?

Sal Buscema

Michel Lê '94

BITTEN BY A RADIOACTIVE SPIDER, STUDENT PETER PARKER GAINED THE PROPORTIONATE STRENGTH AND AGILITY OF AN ARACHNID! ARMED WITH HIS WONDROUS WEB-SHOOTERS, THE RELUCTANT SUPER HERO STRUGGLES WITH SINISTER SUPER-VILLAINS, MAKING ENDS MEET, AND MAINTAINING SOME SEMBLANCE OF A NORMAL LIFE!

STAN LEE PRESENTS: THE SPECTACULAR SPIDER-MAN

SPIDER-MAN...?
SPIDER-MAN!
COME ON, PETER...
HIS HEART'S POUNDING LIKE A JACKHAMMER --THUNDERING IN MY EARS--
--AND IT DOESN'T TAKE A BLIND MAN TO SEE THAT HIS RESPIRATION IS WAY UP...!
WHATEVER POISON WAS ON THE CLAWS OF THE OWL'S VULTURE WENT STRAIGHT INTO SPIDEY'S SYSTEM WHEN THE BIRD RAKED HIS FACE!*
HE SHOULD BE IN A HOSPITAL, BUT DO I DA--
...DEVIL...?
DAREDEVIL...! I'VE GOT TO--
*AS DETAILED IN AMAZING SPIDER-MAN #396 ("BACK FROM THE EDGE," PART 3). --MARK
EASY, PETER, YOU SHOULD--
NO.
LOOK.
THE OWL--!
MY RADAR-SENSE IS PICKING HIM UP, TOO--
--WAITING TO SEE THE RESULTS OF HIS WORK.
WELL, IF HE CAN BE THAT BOLD--

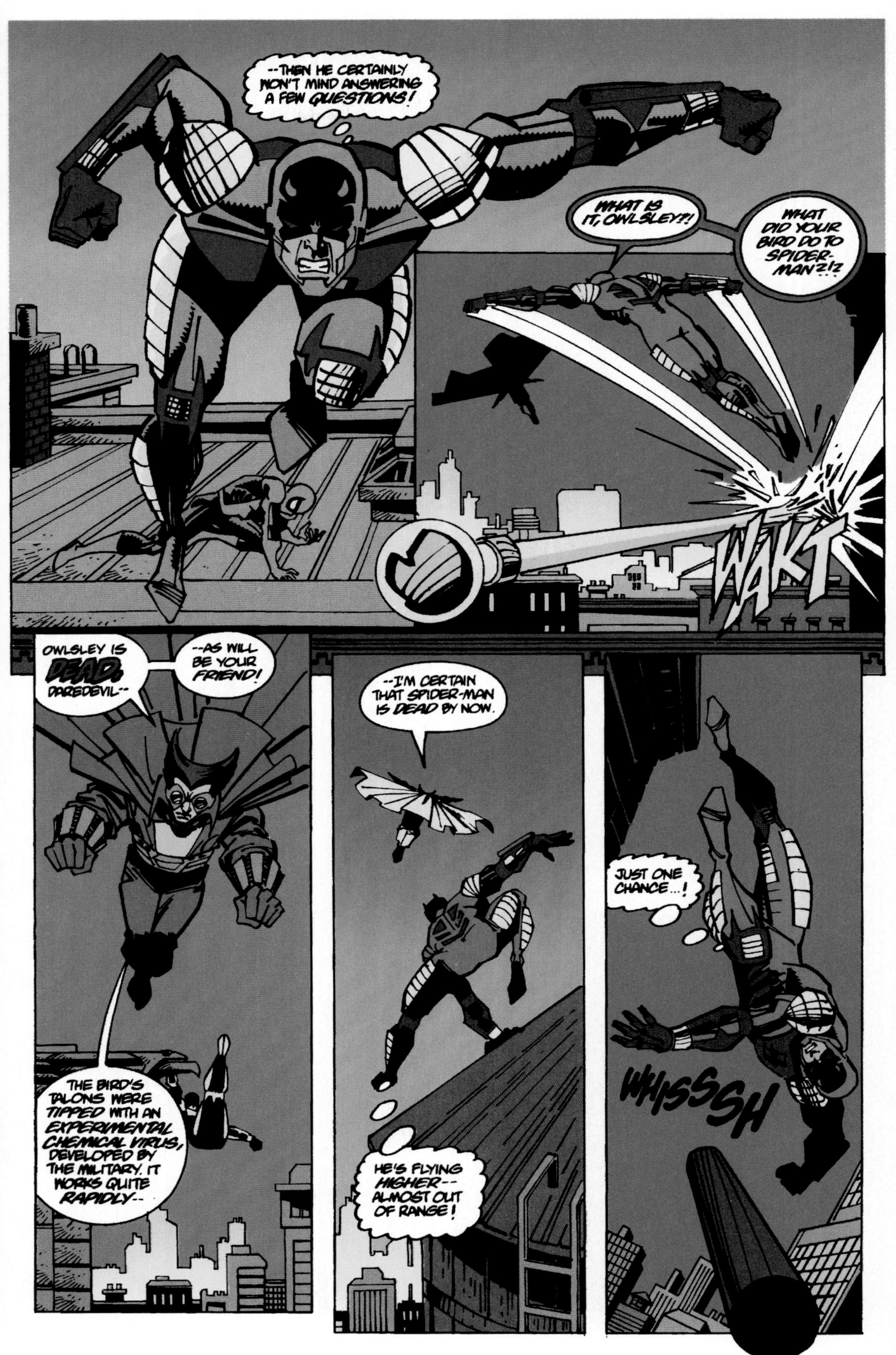
--THEN HE CERTAINLY WON'T MIND ANSWERING A FEW QUESTIONS!
WHAT IS IT, OWLSLEY?!
WHAT DID YOUR BIRD DO TO SPIDER-MAN?!?
WAKT
OWLSLEY IS DEAD, DAREDEVIL--
--AS WILL BE YOUR FRIEND!
THE BIRD'S TALONS WERE TIPPED WITH AN EXPERIMENTAL CHEMICAL VIRUS, DEVELOPED BY THE MILITARY. IT WORKS QUITE RAPIDLY--
--I'M CERTAIN THAT SPIDER-MAN IS DEAD BY NOW.
HE'S FLYING HIGHER-- ALMOST OUT OF RANGE!
JUST ONE CHANCE...!
WHISSSH

VULTURE?!
NOT TO WORRY, "BROTHER"--
--I'VE EVERY-THING WELL IN HAND! I SEE MY CARRIER "PIGEON" DID ITS JOB ON SPIDER-MAN--
THAPP
--LET'S SEE IF WE CAN'T MAKE IT TWO-FOR-TWO!
THE VULTURE--
--AND MY RADAR IS PICKING UP TWO MORE BIRDS--PROBABLY CARRYING THE SAME DRUG THEY USED ON SPIDER-MAN...!
WOOOSH
THIS MIGHT BE TRICKY! BY CLIMBING SO HIGH, I'VE LEFT MYSELF EXPOSED --I'LL HAVE TO--

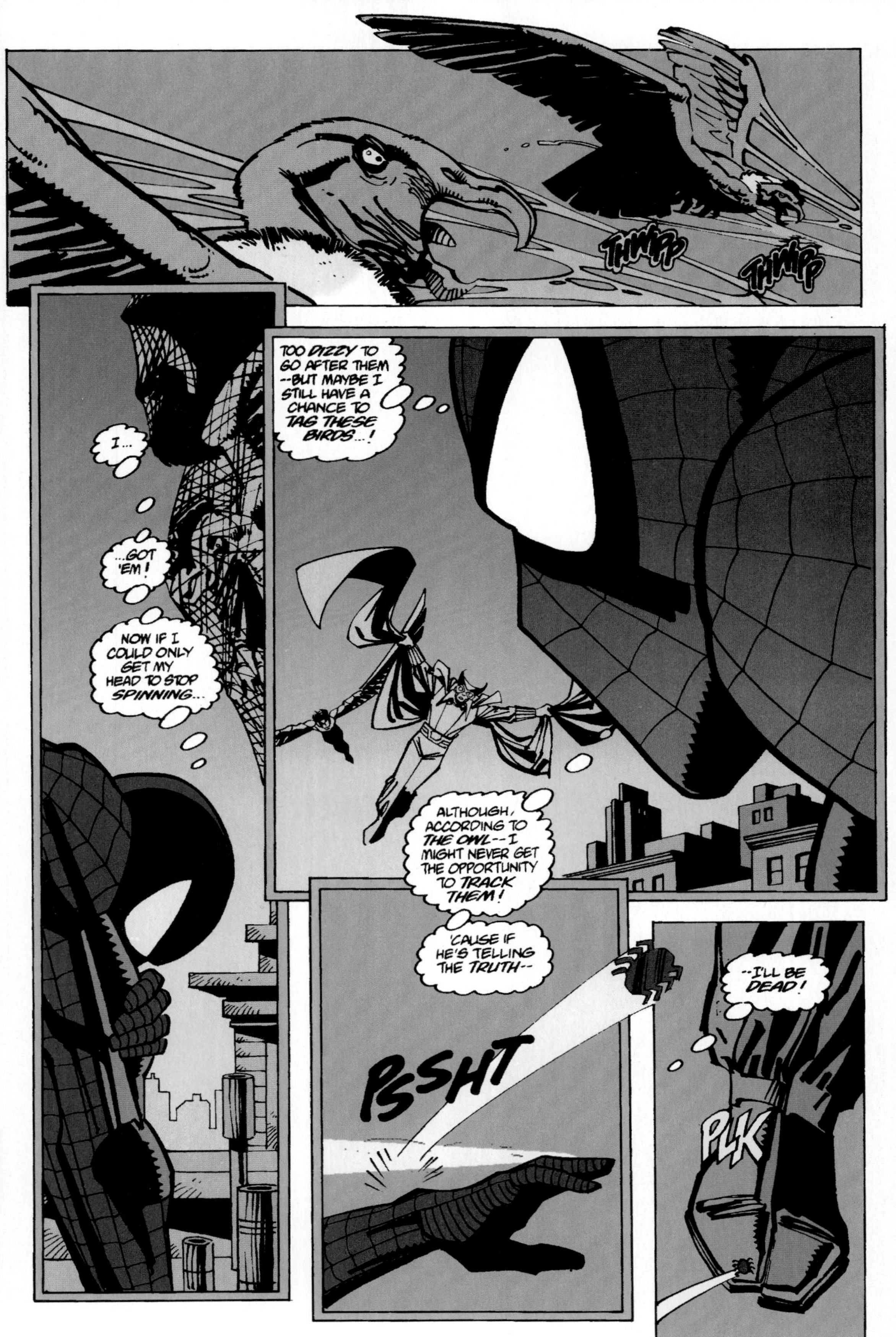
THWIPP
THWIPP
I...
...GOT 'EM!
NOW IF I COULD ONLY GET MY HEAD TO STOP SPINNING...
TOO DIZZY TO GO AFTER THEM --BUT MAYBE I STILL HAVE A CHANCE TO TAG THESE BIRDS...!
ALTHOUGH, ACCORDING TO THE OWL-- I MIGHT NEVER GET THE OPPORTUNITY TO TRACK THEM!
'CAUSE IF HE'S TELLING THE TRUTH--
PSSHT
--I'LL BE DEAD!
PLK

God, I'm so nervous, I hope he's not here...!
No I don't--I came all this way to do this ...so--

--so why am I so afraid...?!
My husband swings around in between buildings, for Pete's sake--
--so why can't I find the courage to simply knock on a motel room door...?

KNOCK KNOCK
7
There, I did it...
Could have been harder...

HI, DADDY...!

I'M GLAD YOU CAME, JANIE...

SO I RETURN TO ROOST --UNABLE TO ANSWER THE QUESTIONS WHICH PLAGUE ME. I FIND MYSELF DRAWN TO THIS DESOLATE MANOR.
GIVING IN TO TEMPTATION AND DARK DESPAIR...
IT'S ABOUT TIME YOU CAME BACK, OWLSLEY...!
...I FIND MYSELF IN LEAGUE WITH A MADMAN!!
I'VE TOLD YOU NOT TO CALL ME THAT. OWLSLEY'S DEAD!
SO YOU'VE SAID. AND YET WHEN I OFFER YOU A PLAN THAT WOULD TRULY BURY YOUR FORMER SELF FOREVER... YOUR REACTION WAS ONE OF HORROR AND REVULSION!
BUT I KNOW YOU BETTER THAN YOU KNOW YOURSELF, BROTHER! I KNEW THAT YOU'D SEE THE GENIUS OF SUCH A SCHEME--THAT YOU'D RETURN TO EMBRACE MY PLAN!
AND SO, IN HONOR OF MY FAITH IN YOU...
...I'VE BEGUN TO ERASE YOUR PAST FIRST.
YOU WHAT?!

PAUL GREYSON. A FORMER BUSINESS ASSOCIATE OF YOURS...?
I INFECTED HIM WITH THE VIRUS YESTERDAY...DURING HIS POWER-LUNCH. HE'LL DIE AT MIDNIGHT ...UNLESS...!
YOU SEE, I WASN'T COMPLETELY HONEST WITH YOU EARLIER WHEN I SAID THERE WAS NO ANTIDOTE...
...IT'S RIGHT HERE!
BUT SINCE YOU HAVE SOME TREPIDATION ABOUT THIS WHOLE THING, I'LL LET YOU DECIDE--
--WHETHER GREYSON RECEIVES IT OR NOT!
THIS IS INSANITY!!
THREATENED BY MY HESITATION, THE VULTURE HAS FORCED MY HAND, CHALLENGING ME TO ANSWER THE QUESTION THAT HAS RECENTLY BEEN MY BANE!
WHO AM I?!
THE OWL...OR OWLSLEY...?
CERTAINLY GREYSON'S LIFE MEANS NOTHING TO ME...YET TO LET HIM SIMPLY DIE LIKE THIS WOULD BE TO ACCEPT THE VULTURE'S MADNESS--!
SO DO I NOW RACE TO PASS THE VULTURE'S TEST...
...OR MY OWN...? TO PROVE ONCE AND FOR ALL WHETHER WE TRULY ARE TWO OF A KIND...?

MEANWHILE, AT THE PARKER RESIDENCE...

WE'RE RUNNING OUT OF TIME.

ALTHOUGH I'VE BEEN ABLE TO *ISOLATE* THE CHEMICAL THAT WAS COATING THE BIRD'S CLAWS--

--UNTIL I GET IT UNDER THE MICROSCOPE, I WON'T BE ABLE TO TELL IF IT'S THE *EXPERIMENTAL VIRUS* THE OWL *CLAIMS* IT IS...

...OR HOW *FAST* IT'S SPREADING!

BRINGING ME TO YOUR HOME, TAKING OFF YOUR MASK--

--YOU'RE AWFULLY *CAVALIER* WITH YOUR SECRET IDENTITY, AREN'T YOU?

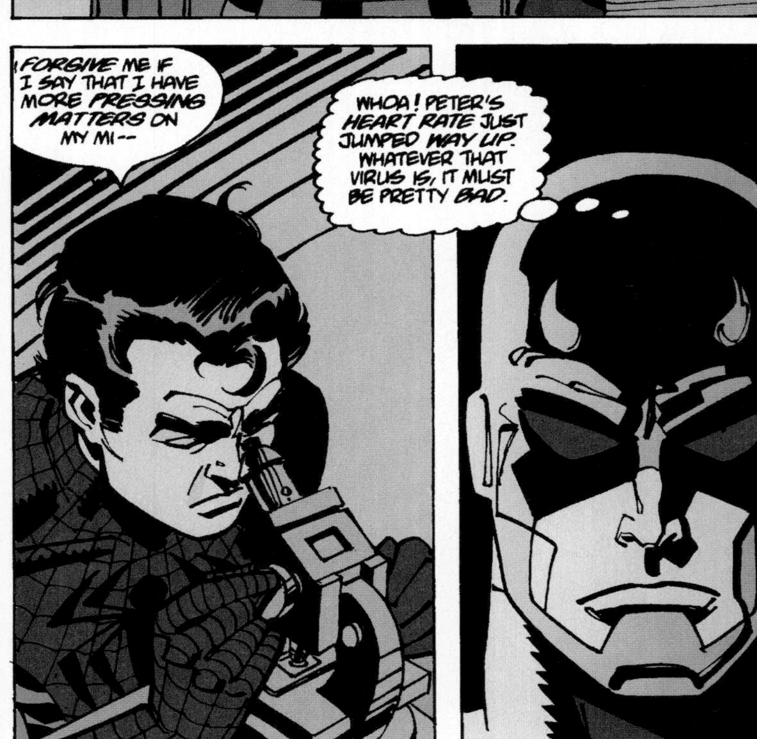

FORGIVE ME IF I SAY THAT I HAVE MORE PRESSING MATTERS ON MY MI--
WHOA! PETER'S HEART RATE JUST JUMPED WAY UP. WHATEVER THAT VIRUS IS, IT MUST BE PRETTY BAD.

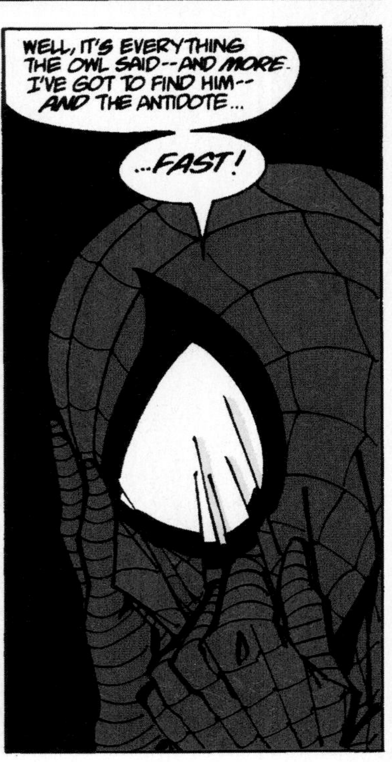

WELL, IT'S EVERYTHING THE OWL SAID--AND MORE. I'VE GOT TO FIND HIM--AND THE ANTIDOTE...
...FAST!

GREYSON.
HOW MANY TIMES IN THE CORPORATE ARENA DID WE WAGE WAR AGAINST ONE ANOTHER ...?
--PLAYING AT OUR INVISIBLE GAMES OF BOARDROOM POLITICS... CONFRONTING EACH OTHER ON BATTLEFIELDS OF CONTROLLING STOCK AND PROFIT MARGINS--
--AMASSING OUR TROOPS OF LAW FIRMS AND ACCOUNTANTS AS WE PREPARED TO JOIN IN MORTAL COMBAT?
FOR YOU I HELD AN ADMIRATION ONE MIGHT RESERVE FOR A WORTHY ADVERSARY...
...AND YET, WAS THERE EVER A MOMENT IN OUR TURBULENT ASSOCIATION THAT MY ADMIRATION TURNED TO HATRED...?
WAS THERE EVER A MOMENT I WISHED YOU DEAD...?
NO.
I HAVE COME HERE TO MAKE A DECISION...
COULD YOU POSSIBLY IMAGINE THE PIVOTAL ROLE YOU NOW PLAY IN MY LIFE...?
I HOLD YOUR LIFE HERE IN MY HAND--
--YOUR SALVATION.
BY MY INACTION--
--THE DECISION IS MADE.

PITTSBURGH.

...SO, I SEE YOU'RE STILL WRITING...?

NOTHING MUCH REALLY. SOME *FREELANCE* WORK FOR A LITTLE WEEKLY NEWS-PAPER—COVERING THE HIGH SCHOOL SPORTS, LOCAL EVENTS--AN OCCASIONAL HUMAN INTEREST PIECE...

IT ISN'T *FAULKNER,* BUT IT PAYS THE RENT.

AND WHAT EVER HAPPENED TO THE "*GREAT AMERICAN NOVEL*"...?

IT'S NOT IN ME ANYMORE, JANIE--I WENT DRY *YEARS* AGO--MAYBE EVEN BEFORE...
...

...
...I, *uh*...SEE YOU STILL HAVE THIS OLD *SMITH-CORONA*--
I REMEMBER THIS FROM WHEN I WAS LITTLE --OF COURSE IT LOOKED A LOT *BIGGER* TO *KID EYES*. THIS IS WHERE YOU DID YOUR WORK, AND GAYLE AND I WEREN'T TO GO ANYWHERE *NEAR*--

WHAT ARE YOU DOING WITH THIS?!
AFTER THE WAY YOU TREATED HER--THE WAY YOU DESERTED HER--HOW DARE YOU KEEP HER PICTURE AROUND?!
WHAT...?! DO YOU THINK I NEED YOU TO REMIND ME?! THAT'S WHAT THIS PICTURE IS FOR!
I LOVED YOUR MOTHER MORE THAN I EVER KNEW!
DO YOU THINK I'M PROUD OF THE WAY I TREATED HER?
YOU DON'T KNOW WHAT IT'S LIKE--TO KNOW THAT YOU HURT SOMEONE YOU LOVE--THAT YOU LET THEM DOWN--ABANDONED THEM--
--WISHING EVERY DAY THAT THERE WERE SOME WAY TO CHANGE THE PAST--
--HAVING NOTHING TO SHOW FOR YOURSELF BUT A LIFETIME OF REGRET...
JUST LIKE WHEN I--
WE...WE'RE TWO OF A KIND, DADDY...
I FEEL LIKE I DID THE SAME THING WHEN I RAN OUT ON GAYLE...I JUST LEFT...
SHE MEANT EVERYTHING TO ME AND I FORGOT WHAT WAS IMPORTANT --I FORGOT TO LET HER KNOW...
I DO KNOW HOW YOU FEEL, DADDY...

SOMEWHERE OVER BROOKLYN...
HOW'RE YOU DOING, SPIDER-MAN?
WE'RE RIGHT ON TRACK--I'M PICKING UP THE TRACER'S SIGNAL LOUD AND CLEAR.
IT SEEMS LIKE IF WE JUST KEEP HEADING SOUTHWEST, WE'LL--
I MEANT, HOW ARE YOU?!--NOT THE SIGNAL.
OH...WELL--I'M STILL A LITTLE DIZZY, BUT OTHER THAN THAT, I FEEL FINE.
LIAR.
HIS RESPIRATION IS STILL HIGH--AND I CAN PRACTICALLY FEEL THE HEAT OF HIS FEVER COMING THROUGH HIS COSTUME--HE'S BURNING UP--
--BUT HE WON'T STOP PUSHING HIMSELF --DRIVING HIMSELF UNTIL HE PINPOINTS--
"--OWL AND THE VULTURE!"
HOME THEN, BROTHER...?
I SEE THE ANTIDOTE IS STILL INTACT--SO YOU'VE FINALLY SEEN THE FOLLY IN DOING BATTLE WITH YOUR OWN DARK NATURE...?
HE IS RIGHT--
I AM HOME.

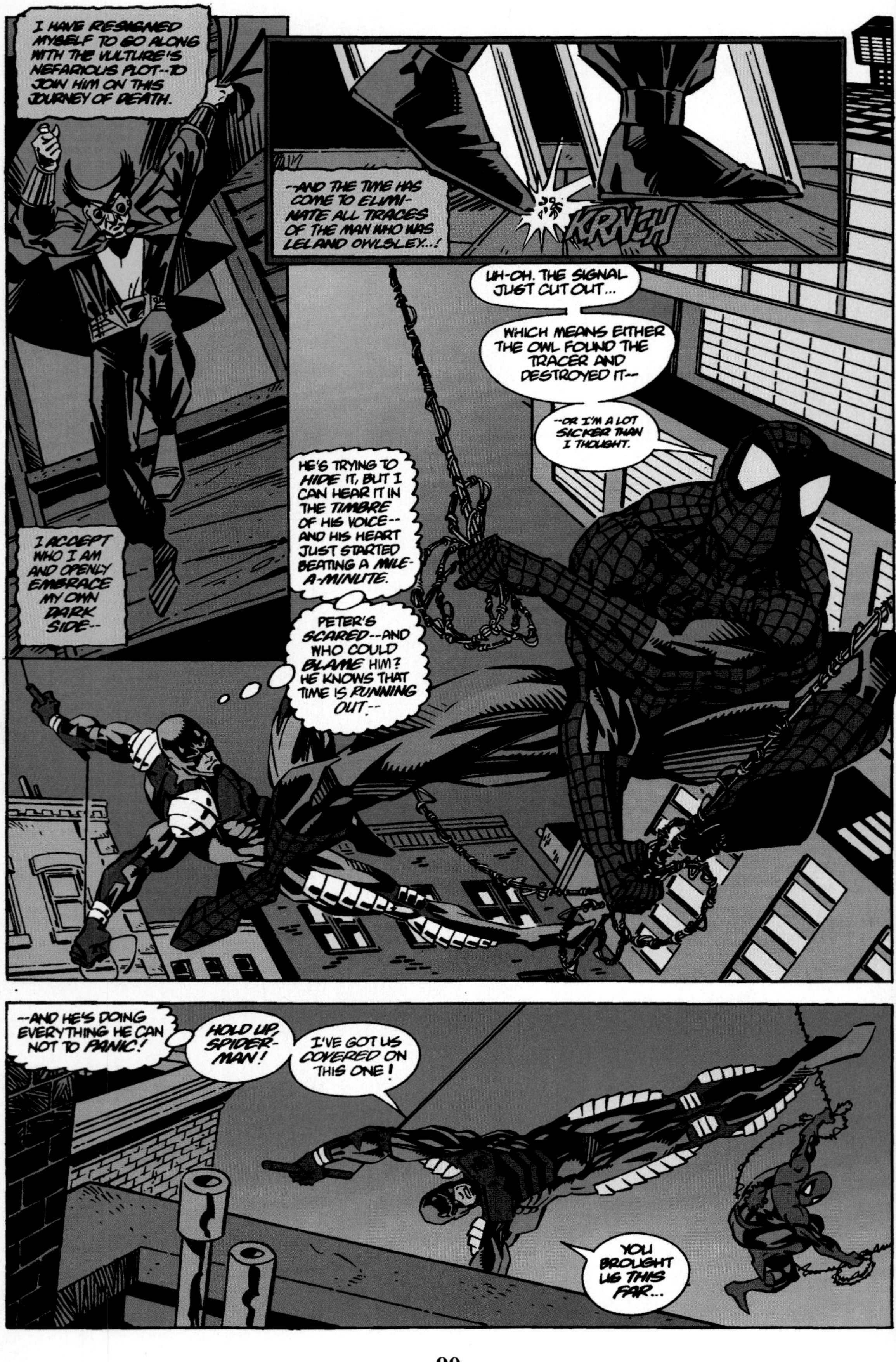

I HAVE RESIGNED MYSELF TO GO ALONG WITH THE VULTURE'S NEFARIOUS PLOT--TO JOIN HIM ON THIS JOURNEY OF DEATH.

--AND THE TIME HAS COME TO ELIMINATE ALL TRACES OF THE MAN WHO WAS LELAND OWLSLEY...!

KRNCH

UH-OH. THE SIGNAL JUST CUT OUT...

WHICH MEANS EITHER THE OWL FOUND THE TRACER AND DESTROYED IT--

--OR I'M A LOT SICKER THAN I THOUGHT.

I ACCEPT WHO I AM AND OPENLY EMBRACE MY OWN DARK SIDE--

HE'S TRYING TO HIDE IT, BUT I CAN HEAR IT IN THE TIMBRE OF HIS VOICE-- AND HIS HEART JUST STARTED BEATING A MILE-A-MINUTE.

PETER'S SCARED--AND WHO COULD BLAME HIM? HE KNOWS THAT TIME IS RUNNING OUT--

--AND HE'S DOING EVERYTHING HE CAN NOT TO PANIC!
HOLD UP, SPIDER-MAN!
I'VE GOT US COVERED ON THIS ONE!
YOU BROUGHT US THIS FAR...

"...LET'S SEE IF I CAN'T BRING US HOME."

IT IS A CENTERING--AND A REACHING--AS THE MAN CALLED DAREDEVIL OPENS HIMSELF TO THE ENVIRONMENT AROUND HIM...

AND THEN, HE BEGINS--

--SIFTING AND SORTING--FILTERING AND REFINING--

...AT ONCE, IT ASSAULTS HIM--OVERWHELMING HIM--BATTERING AT HIS HEIGHTENED SENSES IN A TIDAL WAVE OF SOUND AND ODOR.

HE ACCEPTS THEM WILLINGLY--NEVER BETRAYING THE PAIN OF THEIR SHARPNESS--THEIR HARSHNESS--ALL THE WHILE MAINTAINING HIS CALM.

--EXPLORING AND ELIMINATING EVERY SCENT AND SOUND AS HIS UNIQUE SENSES DRAW HIM NEARER AND NEARER TO HIS FINAL QUARRY.

REACHING--

--REACHING--

THERE IS NOTHING IN THE HUMAN EXPERIENCE THAT STIRS US AS DEEPLY AS WHEN WE REACH OUT--
WELL, I...I GUESS I'D BETTER GET GOING...

--SHARING WITH ANOTHER OUR FEELINGS AND EMOTIONS--
JANIE... IT...IT WAS SO GOOD OF YOU TO COME. I'M GLAD WE HAD THIS CHANCE TO TALK...

--LOOKING AT ONE ANOTHER WITH ONLY UNDERSTANDING AND CARING--
DAD ...I...

--REALIZING THAT IN COMMUNION--
OH, DADDY--

--IF ONLY BRIEFLY--
--LET'S MAKE THIS A BEGINNING--AND NOT ANOTHER ENDING!!
--TWO SOULS HAVE TOUCHED!

I'D LIKE THAT, JANIE...
I'D LIKE THAT A LOT!
THERE IS NOTHING LIKE OPENING YOUR HEART!

...AND TO BEST ACCELERATE OUR EFFORTS IN ERASING OUR RESPECTIVE PASTS, YOU'LL SUPPLY THE NAMES OF ANY OTHER ASSOCIATES WHO--
IF YOU TWO ARE THROUGH MAKING YOUR PARTY LIST--
--WE HAVE SOME QUESTIONS FOR WHICH WE'D LIKE TO BEAT THE ANSWERS OUT OF YOU!
SO--IT APPEARS THE SPIDER SURVIVES! MORE'S THE PITY--
--YET MAYBE ALL HE REQUIRES IS A HEALTHY SECOND DOSE!
SOON YOU'LL BOTH BE DEAD!
DEAD.
DEAD AND BURIED. I HAD THOUGHT LELAND OWLSLEY DEAD--THAT BY DESTROYING MY PAST, ONLY THE OWL WOULD REMAIN--
--THAT LELAND OWLSLEY WOULD BE GONE AND FORGOTTEN.

SHRAK
FOOL! ALL FIVE OF THOSE BIRDS CARRY THE VIRUS ON THEIR TALONS--AND IT'S OBVIOUS TO ME THAT SPIDER-MAN STILL SUFFERS FROM ITS DEVASTATING EFFECTS--!
HE'LL BE DEAD BEFORE HE HAS THE CHANCE TO STOP ALL OF THEM!
YOU TAKE CARE OF THE BIRDS WITH THE FEATHERS, SPIDEY --I'LL DEAL WITH THE ONE WITH THE RAZOR-TIPPED WINGS!
YET I AM THE OWL--AND I AM FORGOTTEN--
--LEFT OUT OF THE FIGHT--WAITING IN THE WINGS LIKE A WALLFLOWER --LOOKING FOR MY PLACE--
--WATCHING A MAN WHO VALIANTLY FIGHTS WITH THE STAGGERED MOVEMENTS OF A BODY RAVAGED BY SICKNESS--
--A WORTHY ADVERSARY--!
SHWOOSH
VULTURE'S RIGHT. PETER'S GETTING WORSE BY THE MINUTE--HIS TIME'S RUNNING OUT, SO WE'LL HAVE TO WRAP THIS UP QUICKLY...!
HAVE TO MAKE THIS WORK THE FIRST TIME--
--BECAUSE I MAY NOT GET A SECOND CHANCE!
I'D SAY YOUR AIM LEAVES A LOT TO BE DESIRED...!

OH, REALLY...
TOK
TOK
TOK
TOK
AHHHHH!
...I WOULDN'T SAY SO!
WAK
HOW'S THAT?!

THREE DOWN --TWO TO--
--GONE...?!

THWIPP
GREAT! I CAN BARELY STAND--MY HEAD IS SPINNING--BUT IF I DON'T GO AFTER THEM, THERE'S NO TELLING HOW FAR THAT VIRUS COULD SPREAD!

IF I CAN JUST--!

SNAGGED ONE--
--BUT THE OTHER ONE IS TOO FAR OUT OF RANGE! IT'S GOING TO GET AWA--

KAKT

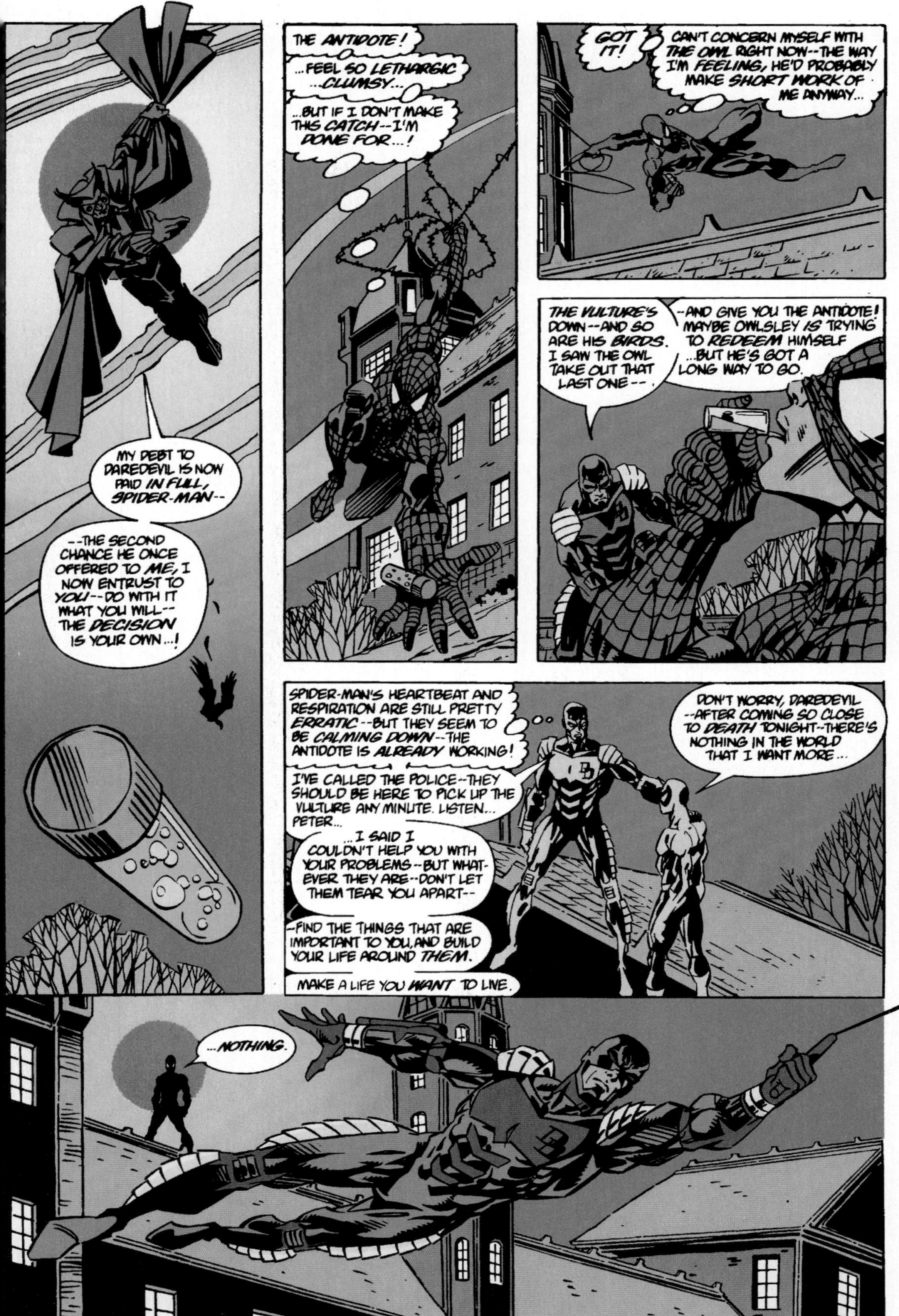
MY DEBT TO DAREDEVIL IS NOW PAID IN FULL, SPIDER-MAN--
--THE SECOND CHANCE HE ONCE OFFERED TO ME, I NOW ENTRUST TO YOU--DO WITH IT WHAT YOU WILL--THE DECISION IS YOUR OWN...!
THE ANTIDOTE!
...FEEL SO LETHARGIC ...CLUMSY...
...BUT IF I DON'T MAKE THIS CATCH--I'M DONE FOR...!
GOT IT!
CAN'T CONCERN MYSELF WITH THE OWL RIGHT NOW--THE WAY I'M FEELING, HE'D PROBABLY MAKE SHORT WORK OF ME ANYWAY...
THE VULTURE'S DOWN--AND SO ARE HIS BIRDS. I SAW THE OWL TAKE OUT THAT LAST ONE--.
--AND GIVE YOU THE ANTIDOTE! MAYBE OWLSLEY IS TRYING TO REDEEM HIMSELF ...BUT HE'S GOT A LONG WAY TO GO.
SPIDER-MAN'S HEARTBEAT AND RESPIRATION ARE STILL PRETTY ERRATIC--BUT THEY SEEM TO BE CALMING DOWN--THE ANTIDOTE IS ALREADY WORKING!
I'VE CALLED THE POLICE--THEY SHOULD BE HERE TO PICK UP THE VULTURE ANY MINUTE. LISTEN... PETER...
...I SAID I COULDN'T HELP YOU WITH YOUR PROBLEMS--BUT WHAT-EVER THEY ARE--DON'T LET THEM TEAR YOU APART--
--FIND THE THINGS THAT ARE IMPORTANT TO YOU, AND BUILD YOUR LIFE AROUND THEM.
MAKE A LIFE YOU WANT TO LIVE.
DON'T WORRY, DAREDEVIL --AFTER COMING SO CLOSE TO DEATH TONIGHT--THERE'S NOTHING IN THE WORLD THAT I WANT MORE...
...NOTHING.

"I WASN'T LYING TO DAREDEVIL--
"AFTER MONTHS OF TRYING TO RUN FROM MY PROB-LEMS--MY RESPONSI-BILITIES--MONTHS CONSIDERING GIVING UP MY LIFE AS PETER PARKER--
"--IT FINALLY TOOK MY DEATH TO MAKE ME SEE HOW MUCH THAT LIFE MEANS TO ME.

"I came to Pittsburgh hoping to find some answers--
"Answers to questions that I didn't even know I had. Looking to fill a space in my life that kept me from feeling complete somehow.
"I wanted to fix the things from my past that were keeping me from moving ahead--from going forward.
"It was hard...

"I'VE WATCHED SO MANY PEOPLE ON THE BRINK OF THE SAME DECISION--
"--THOMAS FIREHEART, ANGELA CAIRN--EVEN THE OWL WAS ON THE THRESHOLD OF DESTROYING HIS PAST--
"--ALL OF THEM BITTER AT HOW PAINFUL LIFE CAN BE.
"HOW FAR WILL THEY GO...?
"WILL IT TAKE THEIR DEATHS, AS WELL? LIKE IT DID FOR ME?

"...But I did it...!
"I made peace with my past--with my fathe and sister--its just a beginning, but I feel like part of the family again--
"--I don't think that I've been this happy--this confident--in a long, long time.

"NOT THE POSSIBILITY OF DEATH--BUT MY DEATH--
"--MY DEATH--
"--I CAN STILL FEEL THE VIRUS, SPREADING INSIDE ME, BURNING ME UP!
"I TESTED THE FEW DROPS LEFT. IT WAS TAP WATER.
" THE ANTIDOTE WAS A FAKE!"

"I'm ready to take on the world--and I can't wait to tell Peter--I've never felt so--
"Alive....!"
NEXT:
BIG NEWS!

MARVEL COMICS
WEB OF
SPIDER-MAN
FABULOUS
FLIP
BOOK
© 1994 MARVEL ENT. GROUP, INC.
$2.25 US
$3.05 CAN
120
JAN
02527
APPROVED BY THE COMICS CODE AUTHORITY
BEGINNING IN THIS ISSUE:
WEB OF LIFE 1 OF 4
THE SCARLET SPIDER...
THE MYSTERY MAN CALLED KAINE...
...AND THE GRIM HUNTER
...ON A COLLISION COURSE WITH DESTINY!
STEVEN -94-

BITTEN BY A RADIOACTIVE SPIDER, STUDENT **PETER PARKER** GAINED THE PROPORTIONATE STRENGTH AND AGILITY OF AN ARACHNID! ARMED WITH HIS WONDROUS WEB-SHOOTERS, THE RELUCTANT SUPER HERO STRUGGLES WITH SINISTER SUPER-VILLAINS, MAKING ENDS MEET, AND MAINTAINING SOME SEMBLANCE OF A NORMAL LIFE!

Stan Lee PRESENTS: **WEB OF SPIDER-MAN**™

AN ECHO IS ALL BEN REILLY EVER REALLY HEARS WHEN HE SPEAKS. A TRULY LATE-BLOOMING TWIN THAT NATURE NEVER INTENDED-- NEVER MADE ROOM FOR--
--THE CLONE OF PETER PARKER, THE AMAZING SPIDER-MAN.
CONCEIVED IN A LUST FOR REVENGE, AND BORN FULL-GROWN FROM THE MIND OF A MADMAN...
...TO FOREVER CHANGE THE LIFE OF THE ONE AND ONLY SPIDER-MAN.
BUT LIFE CHANGES PEOPLE INSTEAD.
HEROES AND VILLAINS ARE MADE, NOT BRED.
NCO SECURITY INC.
HEARD ABOUT YOUR JAILBREAK LAST NIGHT--
VRRRRM
--ALONG WITH THE TRAIL OF BODIES FROM THE STATE PEN TO THE EDGE OF THE CITY--
--AND SOMEONE'S GOT TO CLEAN UP THE MESS YOU MAKE!
POOM
DOES SPIDER-MAN KNOW YOU'RE RUNNING AROUND LOOSE TRYING TO OUTDO HIM, BUG BOY?
POOM

NOT THAT IT MATTERS TO ME. I LOVE CRUSHING DO-GOODERS.
NOT THIS TIME--

--CHALK-FACE.

I'VE GOT TO PUT SOME DISTANCE BETWEEN ME AND TOMBSTONE-- GIVE MYSELF A BREATHER.

KROOOM

RUNNING AWAY? THAT'S OKAY--

--I'LL FIND A NEW PLAYMATE--

--INSIDE THE ARMORED CAR!

UHNN...

EXACTLY WHAT I'VE BEEN TRYING TO AVOID ALL ALONG.

DRIVER JUST FOLLOWED STANDARD PROCEDURE-- DON'T STOP FOR ANYBODY OR ANYTHING DURING AN ATTEMPTED ROBBERY-- TO A FAULT. NOW HE'S UNCONSCIOUS...

...AND THIS ARMORED TRUCK'S COMPLETELY OUT OF CONTROL!

"RESTAURANT DEAD AHEAD IS PACKED WITH INNOCENT PEOPLE..."
312

...AND TOMBSTONE'S PULLED FREE ALREADY.
YOU CAN'T STOP ME...
...THIS PAYROLL HEIST WILL BANKROLL A WHOLE NEW START FOR ME--A NEW ORGANIZATION, NEW FAMILY! *
HAVE TO HIT THE BRAKES HERE--
*TOMBSTONE'S GOAL TO BE A CRIME BOSS WAS FOILED BACK IN SPECTACULAR SPIDER-MAN #'S 204-206. --ERIC
--WITHOUT HURTING THE SECURITY GUARDS INSIDE.
WEB-GAUNTLETS CAN ONLY ABSORB SOME OF THE IMPACT...
THWIP
...SO I'VE GOT TO SLOW THIS TANK'S MOMENTUM--
UHHF
--ONE S-STEP--
--AT A--
SKRRNNN
--TIME!
TOMBSTONE IS SPIDER-MAN'S OLD FOE--JUST ANOTHER IN A LONG LIST APPARENTLY--AND HE SHOULD BE SPIDER-MAN'S PROBLEM...

...BUT MY SPIDER-SENSE PICKED HIM UP FIRST.
I'LL SEE YOU BURIED UNDER THE ROCK YOU CRAWLED OUT FROM, PEST--!
NOT FROM THERE, CHUCKLES.
BIG TALK, COWARD.
AFRAID TO FACE ME LIKE A MAN...?
KRAK
URKK
WRONG QUESTION, TOMBSTONE!
TO THE WRONG MAN.
"I AM NOT A MAN."
WMP
IT BEGINS AGAIN-- THIS LITANY OF DENIAL--BUT...
HE WON--!
THE FREAK'S DOWN FOR THE COUNT!
THE SCARLET SPIDER SAVED US ALL!
HE'S A HERO--!
SOON, SPIDER.
VERY, VERY SOON.

THE KRAVINOFF ESTATE

SINCE THE TRAGIC DEATH OF ITS ORIGINAL OWNER--KNOWN TO THE WORLD AT LARGE AS *KRAVEN THE HUNTER*--THIS SPRAWLING MANSE HAS STOOD *EMPTY*. *

HOST TO NOTHING BUT *DUST* AND *ECHOES*.

*EXCEPT FOR A BRIEF PERIOD RECENTLY WHEN THE CHAMELEON OPERATED OUT OF THE ESTATE DURING THE "PURSUIT" STORYLINE.--ARCHIVIST ERIC

AN ECHO IS ALL *VLADIMIR KRAVINOFF* EVER REALLY HEARS WHEN HE SPEAKS. THE *CHILD* HIS INFAMOUS FATHER NEVER INTENDED--NEVER MADE ROOM FOR--

--THE *SON* OF THE *HUNTER*.

I'VE STUDIED EVERY DETAIL OF SPIDER-MAN'S METHODS--HIS MOVES, HIS HAUNTS, HIS WEAPONS--

--AND HIS LIMITS.

BUT I MEAN TO KNOW HIS VERY SOUL BEFORE THE HUNT IS THROUGH.

WE HAVE MORE IN COMMON NOW THAN YOU EVER DREAMED, FATHER ...
...THE SPIDER HAS SHAMED US BOTH.
YOU CHOSE TO ABANDON THE HUNT--TO SACRIFICE A LIFE OF HONOR AND RESPECT--
--HERE IN THIS HOUSE THAT WAS NEVER MY HOME.
BUT THE GRIM HUNTER WILL RISE ABOVE THE SINS OF THE FATHER.
AND THE KRAVINOFF NAME WILL BE CLEANSED...
...IN THE BLOOD OF SPIDER-MAN!
SHK
SHK
SHK

THE AIRCRAFT CARRIER INTREPID...
POOM
WHAT'S GOING ON UP THERE, SARGE?
WE'VE GOT A SURVIVING FACTION OF A.R.E.S.* TRYING TO RE-ESTABLISH THEMSELVES IN THE TERRORIST UNDERGROUND...
AMBL
*ASSASSINATION, REVOLUTION, EXTORTION AND SABOTAGE.--ERIC
"...WITH A VERY PUBLIC DISPLAY OF FORCE."
PHZZT
NH
FOUR DOWN...
PHZZT
...BARELY A DOZEN TO GO!
...WASTING YOUR TIME, KEN. THIS STORY IS GOING TO BE MINE!
KLK
KLK
WISHFUL THINKING, BETTY.
THE BYLINE'S MINE JUST LIKE THE INITIAL TIP WAS MINE--
FROM MY SOURCE, ELLIS. AND I GOT HERE LONG BEFORE YOU--
BY TAKING MY CAR FROM THE BUGLE GARAGE, BRANT...

"...ALL'S FAIR."
NAIL HIM GOOD!
COME ON, MEN, WORK LIKE A TEAM.
NEEDLE-TIPPED SPIDER-STINGERS STOPPED YOUR FEARLESS LEADER IN HIS TRACKS, CREW. BUT YOUR LASERS ARE STILL A MAJOR HEADACHE!
...THAT JUST NEEDS A FEW DOSES OF IMPACT WEBBING!
WHAT THE--?!
THWPH
THWPH
THWPH
SCARLET SPIDER'S SURROUNDED--
--LET'S FINISH HIM OFF!

NOOOO--!
PRETTY STUPID STRATEGY IN A *CIRCLE*, GANG...
...UNLESS YOU'RE REALLY COMMITTED TO A CAUSE.
NOT THE FIRST TIME I'VE HAD TO SAVE AN *IDIOT* FROM A *MORON*--

HOLD IT RIGHT THERE, SPIDER--!
HOW'D YOU KNOW ABOUT THE SITUATION HERE, HERO?
WERE YOU JUST PASSING BY...?! DID YOU HEAR THE NEWS BULLETINS...?!
WERE YOU OUT LOOKING FOR TROUBLE...?

GOT TO AVOID ANY UNNECESSARY PUBLICITY AND OFFICIAL QUESTIONS ABOUT MY IDENTITY THAT I CAN'T POSSIBLY ANSWER...

THWIP
...CAN'T EVEN UNDERSTAND MYSELF YET, FOR THAT MATTER.

EVEN AFTER ALL THIS TIME AWAY FROM THE SOURCE OF THE PROB--

BETTY BRANT... AGAIN.
STARING STRAIGHT AT ME. ALMOST AS IF SHE CAN SEE RIGHT THROUGH TO--
EMERGENCY
NO.

"THERE'S...SOMETHING IN HER EYES, ALL RIGHT."

BUT IT ISN'T RECOGNITION.
I'M NOT THE MAN SHE EVER KNEW...

"... THE REAL SPIDER-MAN NEVER SEEMS TO BE AROUND WHEN YOU NEED HIM ANYMORE.

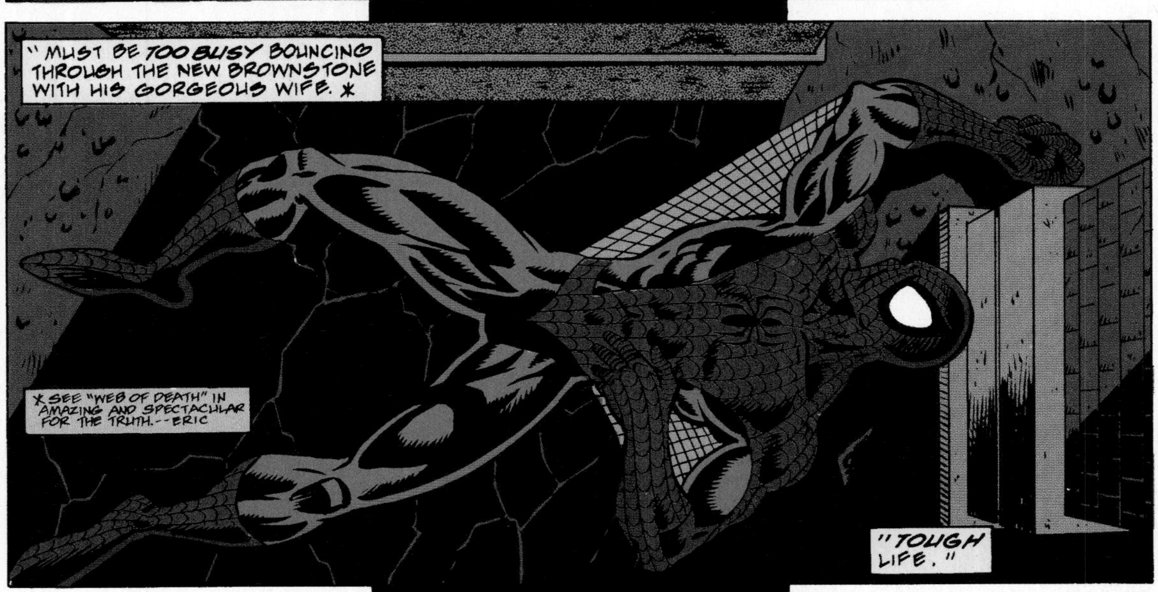

"MUST BE TOO BUSY BOUNCING THROUGH THE NEW BROWNSTONE WITH HIS GORGEOUS WIFE. *
* SEE "WEB OF DEATH" IN AMAZING AND SPECTACULAR FOR THE TRUTH.--ERIC
"TOUGH LIFE."

AS LONG AS MAY PARKER LIES NEAR DEATH IN A COMA--

--HER CONDITION THREATENING TO DETERIORATE AT THIS FOREST HILLS HOSPITAL--

--THE SPIDERS WILL NEVER BE FAR FROM EACH OTHER.
HIS NAME IS KAINE.
HE NO LONGER RECALLS IF IT'S A TITLE BORN, OR EARNED IN BLOOD. WHETHER HE CHRISTENED HIMSELF, OR WAS NAMED BY ANOTHER.
HE MAY HAVE KNOWN ONCE.
BUT NOT ANYMORE.
ALL HE KNOWS NOW, IS TRAGEDY...
...OF WHAT HAS BEEN...
...AND WHAT IS TO COME!

THE VISION ROLLS OVER HIM LIKE A THUNDEROUS WAVE. THIS IS CLEARER THAN THE FLASHES HE'S HAD BEFORE.
IT SMASHES THROUGH HIS DEFENSES.
HIS TERROR GROWS.
MARY JANE WATSON-PARKER RUNS FOR HER LIFE.
BUT IT'S A POINTLESS ACTION.
FOR, SOMETIME IN A NOT-DISTANT FUTURE, SHE IS DESTINED TO BE MURDERED.
BUT BY WHOM...
...IS NOT CLEAR.
THE VISION IS UNBEARABLE.
I MUST ACT--!

GREATER PITTSBURGH AIRPORT.
ALPHA
ALPHA

COME ON, GAYLE, SOMEONE'S GOT TO LET GO FIRST. THIS IS THE LAST FLIGHT BACK TO NEW YORK TONIGHT.
MARY JANE, CAN'T YOU STAY ANOTHER DAY? I ALREADY MISS YOU.
I'D LOVE TO, BUT I CAN'T. I HAVE TO GET BACK INTO MY LIFE-- BE THERE FOR PETER--
--AND AUNT MAY, WHEN SHE COMES OUT OF HER COMA.

I UNDERSTAND. JUST DON'T FORGET ABOUT ME.
AFTER ALL WE'VE BEEN THROUGH...?
YOU'LL ALWAYS BE A PART OF MY LIFE. WE'LL NEVER BE OUT OF TOUCH AGAIN.

THIS IS A NEW SIDE TO YOU, MARY JANE. I LIKE IT. YOU'RE POSITIVELY GLOWING.
THANKS, SIS. IT'S CALLED FAMILY.

BACK IN NEW YORK.
TOMBSTONE AND TERRORISTS IN THE SAME NIGHT. MIGHT AS WELL ADMIT IT...
...I NEEDED THAT.
AND THIS CITY'S BIG ENOUGH TO NEED ME BACK.
FOR THE FIRST TIME IN YEARS, I'M STARTING TO FEEL LIKE MY LIFE HAS A PURPOSE.
AND I WON'T PLAY GAMES WITH PETER PARKER'S LIFE.
BUT I CAN'T HELP FEELING GUILTY ABOUT THAT--CONSIDERING AUNT MAY'S CONDITION.
THWIP
I TRULY DESPISE THIS SCARLET SPIDER NAME THE BUGLE SADDLED ME WITH...
...BUT THE MASK HAS REAL POTENTIAL.
BY WEARING IT, IT OFFERS ME ANOTHER LIFE--ONE OF FREEDOM AND ENDLESS POSSIBILITIES--

"--AND SECOND CHANCES."
THE TRESPASSER'S PINNED BETWEEN THE MISSILE-LAUNCHER AND THE CONCES-SION STAND, SIR...
...THIS FLOATIN' MUSEUM'S SEEN MORE ACTION TONIGHT THAN IT DID IN THE WAR.
THE MEDIA CIRCUS PACKED IT IN HOURS AGO, BUT IT COULD BE ANOTHER CLOWN WORKING OVERTIME.
HOPE IT'S AN A.R.E.S. STRAGGLER THE LOCAL LAW MISSED...
...SO WE CAN SHOW 'IM HOW UNCLE SAM DEALS WITH--
BEST SHOW ME QUICKLY--
--'CAUSE, I'VE GOT YOU ALL LINED UP IN A ROW...

...LIKE LAMBS TO THE SLAUGHTER.

SHLK

AKK

GOOD MOVE, SOLDIER BOY.

POOT

SHLK

UHGG...

BUT NOT GOOD ENOUGH--

--TO STOP ME.

NEWS REPORTS WERE ACCURATE...
...I'M PICKING UP A SCENT...

SNF
SNF
...THE SPIDER HAS COME THIS WAY.

"...AND THE HUNT IS ON."
THIS REMINDS ME OF ALL THE REASONS PETER PARKER DONNED A MASK IN THE FIRST PLACE.
TO AVOID THE EXPECTATIONS AND JUDGMENTS OF THE WORLD AT LARGE...
...AND THE PEOPLE CLOSEST TO HIM.
TEK TEK TEK
I APPRECIATE THE SHOWY ENTRANCE, SPIDER...
...SO I'D CATCH YOUR REFLECTION IN THE SCREEN.
I'M TRYING TO QUIT SNEAKING, MS. BRANT...
...THAT'S WHY I'M HERE TONIGHT.
HOW'D YOU FIND ME?
DID YOU FOLLOW ME ALL THE WAY HOME FROM THE INTREPID, OR--
I'LL ANSWER WHATEVER QUESTIONS I CAN, MS. BRANT--
--BETTY--
--IF YOU CAN MAKE SOME TIME FOR ME.
FOR THE HOTTEST INTERVIEW OF THE YEAR...!?

BETTY'S GARDEN
THE NIGHT IS YOURS, RED.
WHERE DO WE BEGIN...?

FIRST THING I HAVE TO KNOW IS...

...WHAT DO YOU GET OUT OF THIS?
A CHANCE TO SET THE RECORD STRAIGHT--

--TO SOMEONE, SOMEWHERE--

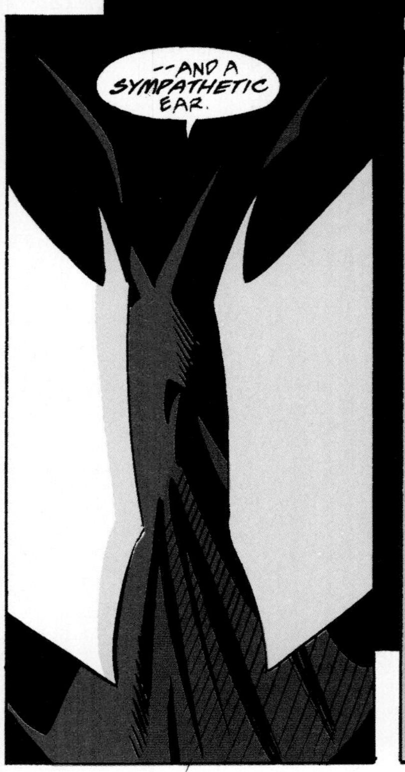
--AND A SYMPATHETIC EAR.

BAD CHOICE, SPIDER...

...I'M WORKING ON MY OBJECTIVITY.
I'VE LOST IT TOO OFTEN OVER THE YEARS, TOO EASILY--EVEN TOO RECENTLY WITH ARCHER BRYCE--*
* SEE WEB #'S 113-116. --ERIC.

"--TO REPEAT THE SAME MISTAKES."
THE SPIDER'S SCENT IS STRONG NOW.
THE THRILL OF THE HUNT IS--
--AN EXQUISITE PANG THAT SETS MY BLOOD TO BOILING.
EVERY FIBER OF MY BEING SCREAMS OUT IN ANTICIPATION--
--THE CLOSER I GET TO MY PREY.
WHO--?!
WHERE IS THE SPIDER?!

YOU JUST MISSED HIM, STRANGER--
--I THINK I SCARED HIM AWAY WITH MY HARDNOSED ATTITUDE!
BRAVE... LAST WORDS...
...IF THEY PROVE TO BE UNTRUE.
THE SPIDER'S TRAIL--

"--IS SURPRISINGLY SIMPLE TO FOLLOW."
DID I IMAGINE ALL THAT IN THE AIR BACK AT BETTY'S PLACE...? NOT EXACTLY FIREWORKS OR ANYTHING--
THWIP
--BUT MAYBE SOME SPARKS....!
I DON'T KNOW WHAT IT REALLY MEANS...

"...I ONLY KNOW IT'S GOOD TO BE ALIVE AGAIN."
I ALLOWED THE FEMALE TO SURVIVE-- IN CASE SHE'S NEEDED AS BAIT AGAIN--

--AND I'M FINALLY CLOSING IN ON THE SPIDER...!

"WEB OF LIFE" CONTINUES IN SPIDER-MAN #54, AND THEN SPINS BACK THROUGH HERE NEXT ISSUE--!
AND DON'T MISS SPIDER-MAN'S FIGHT FOR LIFE IN AMAZING AND SPEC--AND A VERY SPECIAL ANNOUNCEMENT IN SPEC #220--AS "WEB OF DEATH" TAKES OFF!

MARVEL COMICS
GIANT-SIZED FLIP BOOK
SPIDER-MAN®
WEB OF LIFE 2 OF 4
$2.75 US
$3.70 CAN
54
JAN
01372
APPROVED BY THE COMICS CODE AUTHORITY
IN THE SHADOW OF KAINE!
THE SCARLET SPIDER IN SOLO ACTION!
PLUS: THE GRIM HUNTER
TOM LYLE /94

THE DAILY BUGLE...
I'M GOING TO FIND HIM!
AND I'M GOING TO FIND HIM NOW!
AND THEN HE'LL PAY FOR WHAT HE'S DONE TO ME!
STAN LEE PRESENTS THE SCARLET SPIDER IN
WEB OF LIFE PART II
HOWARD MACKIE / TOM LYLE story & art SCOTT HANNA inks
SNARED
STARKINGS/COMICRAFT lettering KEVIN TINSLEY colors
DANNY FINGEROTH editor TOM DEFALCO editor in chief

KEN ELLIS...
...THAT'S THE GUY THAT SADDLED ME WITH THE "SCARLET SPIDER" NAME!
WHAT DID I EVER DO TO HIM?

PLACE IS EMPTY!
GIVES A WHOLE NEW MEANING TO THE PHRASE "GRAVEYARD SHIFT!"
NOT LIKE IN THE OLD DAYS. OR MAYBE IT'S JUST AN OFF NIGHT.
I REMEMBER JONAH HAD THIS PLACE HOPPING NIGHT AND DAY.

ROBBIE.
NED LEEDS.
BEN URICH.
THEY ALL PRACTICALLY LIVED HERE.

AND THEN THERE WAS PETER PARKER...
...TRYING TO HUSTLE UP SOME MONEY WITH FREELANCE PHOTOGRAPHS.

AND MOONING OVER JONAH'S SECRETARY... BETTY BRANT.
IT SEEMS LIKE YESTERDAY.
BETTY'S EYES...
...JONAH'S GRAVELLY VOICE.
PARKER!
WHAT ARE YOU DOING STANDING AROUND WHEN YOU COULD BE SNAPPING PHOTOS?!
ARE YOU LISTENING TO ME?

...WHAT ARE YOU DOING HERE?

THIS IS PRIVATE PROPERTY, BUDDY. I COULD HAVE YOU ARRESTED.
AND MOST PEOPLE KNOW THAT I'M NO FAN OF COSTUMED VIGILANTES.

YEAH... SORRY... I'M GOING.
WAIT. I HAVE SOMETHING I WANT TO SAY TO YOU.

I HEAR YOU'VE BEEN DOING LOTS OF GOOD THINGS SINCE YOU ARRIVED ON THE SCENE.
MY REPORTERS HAVE BEEN GIVING YOU SOME HEAD-LINES.
A REAL DO-GOODER, HUH?
THANKS, I--
WELL I'M NOT BUYING IT!

I DON'T TRUST ANY OF YOU MASKED "HEROES"!
MY PEOPLE ARE GOING TO KEEP AN EYE ON YOU.
IF YOU SLIP UP...WE'LL BE THERE TO REPORT THE FACTS.

FINE.
JUST ONE LAST THING, MISTER JAMESON...

YOUR PEOPLE HAVE BEEN WRITING ABOUT ME...
...CALLING ME THE SCARLET SPIDER DOESN'T MAKE ME TOO HAPPY.
I MIGHT HAVE MY LAWYERS CONTACT YOU ABOUT THAT.
JUST THOUGHT I'D WARN YOU!
WHY, OF ALL THE ARROGANT...
THAT FELT GREAT!
VISITING THE PAST... EVEN IF IT ISN'T REALLY MY PAST... FEELS GOOD. REAL GOOD.
LAST NIGHT SEEING BETTY...*
...TONIGHT CHEWING OUT JONAH...
...LIFE DOES HAVE ITS MOMENTS.
MAYBE I'VE GOT AN ANGEL LOOKING OVER MY SHOULDER, FOR A CHANGE.
AND THE MAN CALLING HIMSELF KAINE WATCHES...
...AND WAITS.
*WEB #120. -- Danny.

AT THAT MOMENT...
THIS PENTHOUSE APARTMENT ONCE BELONGED TO SERGEI KRAVINOFF, KNOWN AS KRAVEN THE HUNTER.
UPON HIS DEATH BY SUICIDE, IT -- AS ALL HIS WORLDLY POSSESSIONS -- WAS PASSED ON TO HIS ONLY CHILD...
...VLADIMIR, NOW CALLING HIMSELF THE GRIM HUNTER, A NAME TAKEN FROM A FABLE LEARNED AT HIS FATHER'S KNEE.
VLADIMIR IS A MAN WHO HAS INHERITED MANY OF HIS FATHER'S OBSESSIONS.
THE HUNT.
POWER.
AND BLOOD LUST FOR SPIDER-MAN.
YOUR ELIXIR HAS SERVED ME WELL, FATHER.

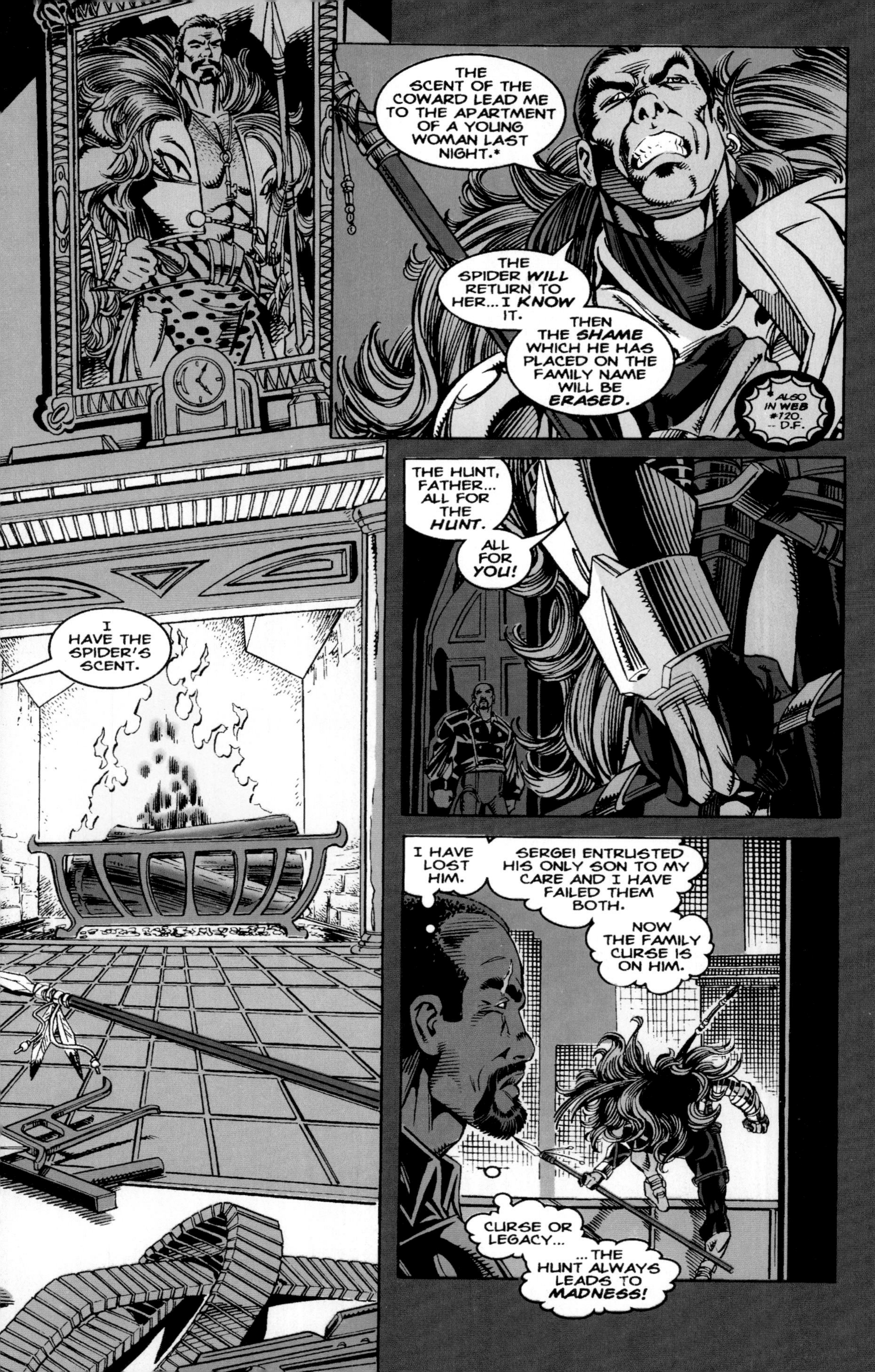
THE SCENT OF THE COWARD LEAD ME TO THE APARTMENT OF A YOUNG WOMAN LAST NIGHT.*
THE SPIDER WILL RETURN TO HER... I KNOW IT.
THEN THE SHAME WHICH HE HAS PLACED ON THE FAMILY NAME WILL BE ERASED.
* ALSO IN WEB #120. -- D.F.
I HAVE THE SPIDER'S SCENT.
THE HUNT, FATHER... ALL FOR THE HUNT.
ALL FOR YOU!
I HAVE LOST HIM.
SERGEI ENTRUSTED HIS ONLY SON TO MY CARE AND I HAVE FAILED THEM BOTH.
NOW THE FAMILY CURSE IS ON HIM.
CURSE OR LEGACY...
...THE HUNT ALWAYS LEADS TO MADNESS!

THE NEXT EVENING AT THE HOTEL WHICH BEN REILLY HAS BEEN CALLING HOME...
HEY, REILLY, WHERE'VE YOU BEEN KEEPING YOURSELF?
HOW'S THE STOMACH HOLDING UP?
IT WASN'T AS BAD AS IT LOOKED, BUT THANKS FOR YOUR HELP GETTING ME STITCHED UP.*
*WEB #119. -- Danny.
MAYBE WE CAN GET TOGETHER SOME TIME... WHEN YOU'RE FEELING UP TO IT?
MAYBE... THAT WOULD BE NICE.
A FEW MINUTES LATER...
LAST NIGHT BETTY BRANT AND NOW GABRIELLE...

YES!
THINGS ARE STARTING TO LOOK GOOD!

AND OUTSIDE...
...KAINE WATCHES.

AT THAT MOMENT...
PARK AVENUE MEDICAL CENTER
GEEZ! I HATE DOCTORS!
ROOM 5
SEEMED LIKE I SAT IN THAT WAITING ROOM FOR HOURS BEFORE GETTING IN TO SEE HIM...
...AND NOW HE'S GOT ME WAITING AGAIN!
DON'T KNOW WHY I EVEN CAME.
I'VE JUST BEEN FEELING A LITTLE RUN DOWN IS ALL.
MY STOMACH'S BEEN UPSET, BUT WITH ALL THAT'S GOING ON WITH AUNT MAY IN THE HOSPITAL AND PETER LOSING IT...
...I WOULDN'T BE SURPRISED IF I GAVE MYSELF AN ULCER.
WHAT IS TAKING HIM?
AHEM! MRS. PARKER...
...COULD YOU COME INTO MY OFFICE?
WE NEED TO TALK.

LATER, IN A SECTION OF THE CITY EVEN THE POLICE AVOID...
...KAINE WALKS.
NOW PETER PARKER AND BEN REILLY SLEEP.
LET THEM.
I WALK THE NIGHT... TAKE TO THE SHADOWS... SEEKING COMFORT WHICH ELUDES ME.
TRAP DOOR LIVE.
THIS IS MY DESTINY.
I SEEK COMFORT... ACCEPTANCE...
SNAP
...AND FIND ONLY PAIN!

PAIN.

IT HAS BEEN MY CONSTANT COMPANION THROUGHOUT THE YEARS.

THE PAIN OF ISOLATION.
THE PAIN OF REJECTION.

MY PAIN.

A PAIN WHICH I FREELY TRANSFER TO OTHERS.

THIS IS MY DESTINY.
DEATH IS THEIRS.

SOMEWHERE IN THE CITY, SPIDER-MAN LIES ON A ROOFTOP WRAPPED IN A FEVERISH SLEEP.
POISONED BY THE VULTURE, DEATH LOOMS LARGE IN HIS DREAMS.
ELSEWHERE, BEN REILLY SLEEPS PEACEFULLY FOR THE FIRST TIME IN YEARS...
...AS DREAMS OF A LIFE THAT COULD BE DANCE THROUGH HIS HEAD.
AND KAINE...
HE NEITHER SLEEPS NOR DREAMS.
HE STANDS ALONE WRAPPED IN THE SHADOWS OF THE NIGHT.
APART EVEN AS THE DREAMS OF PETER PARKER AND BEN REILLY ARE HEADED ON A COLLISON COURSE.
DREAMS SHARED AS IF WITH ONE MIND...

FRAGMENTED DREAMS.
DREAMS FILLED WITH STAINLESS STEEL...BRIGHT LIGHTS... ANTISEPTIC SMELLS...
DREAMS OF A BIRTH.
A LABORATORY.
AND THEN AN EMPTINESS... A DARKNESS WHICH SEEMS TO HIDE THE ANSWERS TO SO MANY QUESTIONS.
THE DREAMS THUNDER THROUGH THE SLEEP OF BOTH MEN WITH SUCH SPEED AND INTENSITY THAT LITTLE IS UNDERSTOOD.
ENOUGH ONLY TO LABEL THE DREAMS NIGHTMARES.
AT THAT MOMENT...
...KAINE DOUBLES OVER AS SEARING AGONY CUTS THROUGH HIS BRAIN.
THE SOURCE OF THE PAIN IS UNKNOWN TO HIM.
IT IS DIFFERENT THAN THE PAIN THAT ACCOMPANIES HIS PRECOGNITIVE FLASHES.
KAINE WAITS FOR THE PAIN TO SUBSIDE... AND TO UNDERSTAND IT...
KAINE CAN DO NOTHING MORE THAN WAIT.
NO.
OMIGOD! IT'S STARTING!

SOMEWHERE IN THE BERKSHIRE MOUNTAINS OF MASSACHUSETTS...
SEWARD TRAINER IS A SCIENTIST...A MAN OF VISION.
HE HAS DEVOTED HIS LIFE TO THE PURSUIT OF KNOWLEDGE...
...AND THE PRACTICAL APPLICATION OF THAT WHICH HE FINDS.
BREEP
THE OUTSIDE LINE?
NO ONE HAS THAT NUMBER, BUT...
BEN? IS THAT YOU, BOY? WHERE'VE YOU BEEN? WHERE ARE YOU?
I CAME BACK TO NEW YORK.
I'M WORRIED, SEWARD...FEELING WEIRD...DISTURBING DREAMS...
COULD DEGENERATION HAVE STARTED ALREADY?
BEN..! WHY COULDN'T YOU HAVE STAYED AROUND LONG ENOUGH TO FINSH THE TESTING?
STAY WHERE YOU ARE! I'M COMING TO NEW YORK!

A SHORT TIME LATER...

I NEED TO CLEAR MY HEAD.

I NEED SOMEONE TO TALK TO.

I NEED...

...BETTY!

"THERE SHE IS.STILL SO BEAUTIFUL.

"SHE'S A SYMBOL OF A *PAST* THAT CAN NEVER BE MINE.

"BUT A FUTURE--?"

EXCUSE ME!
HI... I WAS JUST THINKING ABOUT YOU.

I WAS WONDERING IF YOU'D LIKE TO FINISH WHERE WE LEFT OFF LAST NIGHT?
MAYBE YOU WANT A LITTLE MORE INFO FOR YOUR STORY.

I'M OFF THE STORY. IT BELONGS TO KEN ELLIS NOW.

Oh... SORRY... DIDN'T MEAN TO BOTHER YOU...
I'LL GO.
NO. WAIT.

I TOOK MYSELF OFF THE STORY. IT'S TIME EVERYTHING WASN'T JUST *WORK* FOR ME.
I NEED A LIFE, TOO.

I KNOW I SHOULD BE AFRAID OF YOU, BUT...
...THERE'S SOMETHING ABOUT YOU...I CAN'T DESCRIBE IT...
...IT'S AS THOUGH I'VE KNOWN YOU FOR A VERY LONG TIME.
FRA KOOM
A SUDDEN BURST OF INSTINCT FLASHES THROUGH THE SCARLET SPIDER'S HEAD...
...SOMETHING HE HAS COME TO KNOW AS HIS SPIDER-SENSE.
IT WARNS HIM OF DANGER THE INSTANT BEFORE IT STRIKES...
...AND HE CARRIES HIMSELF AND BETTY TO SAFETY!
WHO ARE YOU?
YOU KNOW WHO I AM, SPIDER!
AND YOU KNOW WHY I AM HERE!

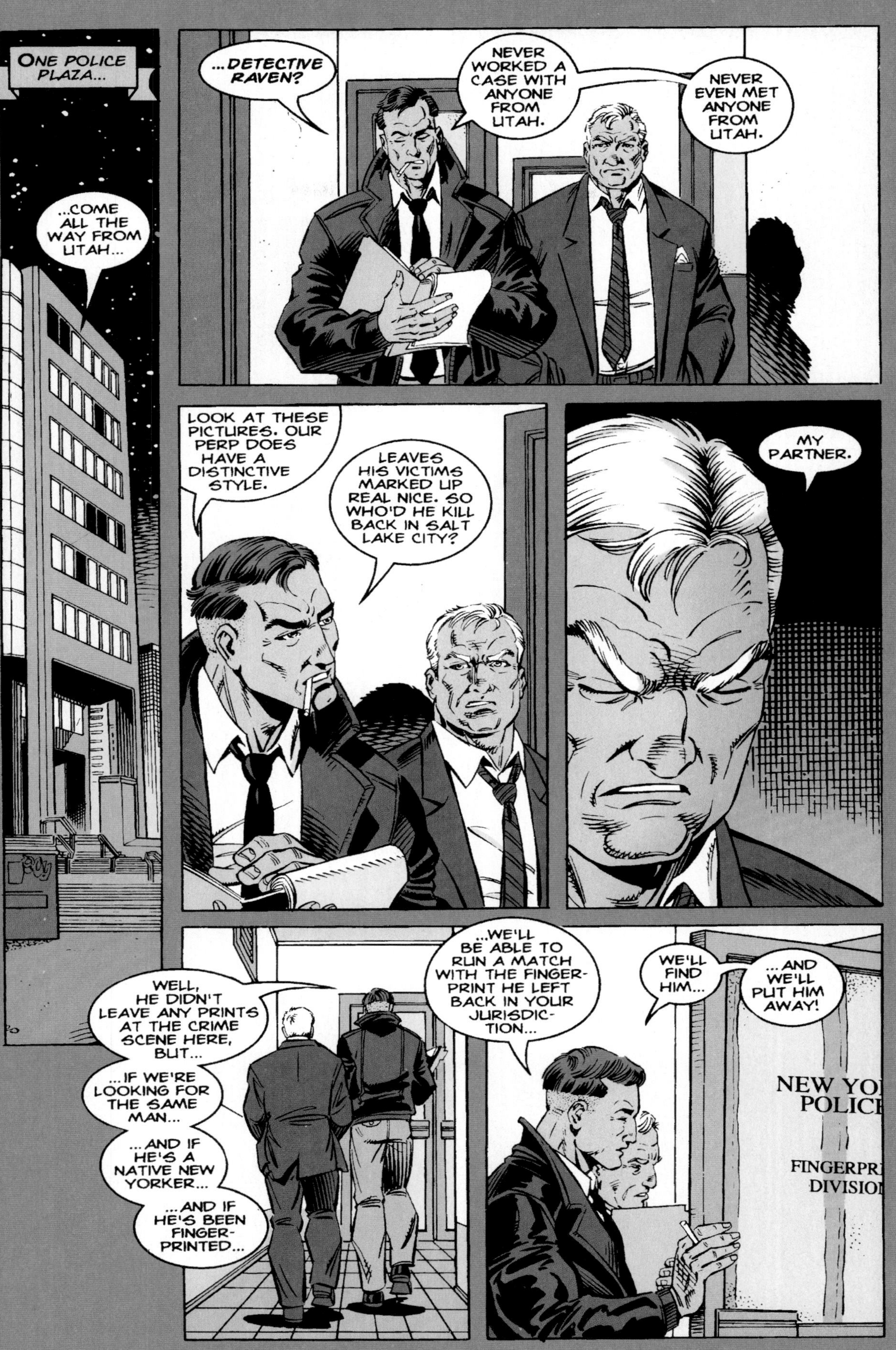
ONE POLICE PLAZA...
...COME ALL THE WAY FROM UTAH...
...DETECTIVE RAVEN?
NEVER WORKED A CASE WITH ANYONE FROM UTAH.
NEVER EVEN MET ANYONE FROM UTAH.
LOOK AT THESE PICTURES. OUR PERP DOES HAVE A DISTINCTIVE STYLE.
LEAVES HIS VICTIMS MARKED UP REAL NICE. SO WHO'D HE KILL BACK IN SALT LAKE CITY?
MY PARTNER.
WELL, HE DIDN'T LEAVE ANY PRINTS AT THE CRIME SCENE HERE, BUT...
...IF WE'RE LOOKING FOR THE SAME MAN...
...AND IF HE'S A NATIVE NEW YORKER...
...AND IF HE'S BEEN FINGER-PRINTED...
...WE'LL BE ABLE TO RUN A MATCH WITH THE FINGER-PRINT HE LEFT BACK IN YOUR JURISDIC-TION...
WE'LL FIND HIM...
...AND WE'LL PUT HIM AWAY!
NEW YO
POLICE
FINGERPR
DIVISIO

YOU'VE GOT THE WRONG MAN, MISTER.
NOW, BETTY, I'D LIKE YOU TO GO INSIDE SO I CAN TALK TO THIS GENTLEMAN CALMLY.
I'M NOT GOING ANYWHERE! THIS IS MY BACK-YARD AND HE'S TRES--
BETTY, NOW! PLEASE.
THE WOMAN IS IN NO DANGER. IT IS YOU I SEEK.
DID YOU HOPE THAT IN CHANGING YOUR COSTUME I WOULD LOSE YOUR TRAIL?
DID YOU THINK THAT MY FATHER DID NOT TEACH ME BETTER?
A MAN CANNOT CHANGE HIS SCENT AS EASILY AS HIS CLOTHES.
I HAVE NO IDEA WHAT YOU'RE TALKING ABOUT!

IT MATTERS NOT, COWARD! THIS HUNT CONCLUDES NOW!
HAVE IT YOUR WAY!
YOUR PROJECTILES ARE NEW... NO? BUT QUITE USELESS AGAINST MY BODY ARMOR!

AND AS YOU SEE, I HAVE PROJECTILES OF MY OWN.
YEAH, I SEE THEM. BUT THE THING ABOUT PROJECTILES...

...IS YOU CAN'T HIT WHAT YOU CAN'T CATCH!

HE'S FOLLOWING. GOOD.
NEED TO LEAD HIM AWAY FROM HERE.

I KNOW HE SAID BETTY'D BE SAFE --
-- BUT SOMEHOW HE DOESN'T SEEM LIKE THE TRUSTWORTHY TYPE.

WHERE ARE YOU, COWARD?
HIDING WILL SERVE NO PURPOSE.
I WILL TRACK YOU DOWN TO THE ENDS OF THE EARTH IN ORDER TO AVENGE MY FATHER'S DEATH.
STILL DON'T KNOW WHAT YOU'RE TALKING ABOUT AND --
-- I HAD NO INTENTION OF HIDING!
JUST LOOKING TO GAIN THE UPPER HAND.
YOUR ACTIONS CONFIRM YOU AS THE COWARD YOU ARE... AND ALWAYS HAVE BEEN!
AND YOU GAIN NOTHING!
STILL YOU UNDERESTIMATE MY SPEED... MY AGILITY...
...YOU EXPECT MY FATHER, BUT I AM STRONGER, FASTER THAN KRAVEN!
KRAVEN? YOU'RE KRAVEN'S SON?!

DO NOT TAUNT ME!
YOU KNOW WHO I AM!
YOU KNOW THAT YOU WERE RESPONSIBLE FOR THE STAIN ON MY FAMILY NAME!
IT WAS YOU, SPIDER, WHO DROVE MY FATHER TO MADNESS... TO TAKE HIS OWN LIFE!
NO! IT WASN'T ME!
LIAR!
HIS JOURNAL TELLS THE TALE --
-- MY FATHER'S WORDS HAVE CONDEMNED YOU FROM BEYOND THE GRAVE!
ONLY YOUR DEATH WILL APPEASE HIS RESTLESS SPIRIT!
YOU REALLY ARE INSANE, AREN'T YOU?
SHOOP

THEY SAID SUCH A THING ABOUT MY FATHER... AND ABOUT HIS MOTHER BEFORE HIM.
THOSE WERE LIES.
MY FATHER WAS DRIVEN TO HIS DEATH BY YOU...
FOOL! SEE HOW EASILY I EVADE YOUR ATTACK!
BUT... EVEN AS I WATCH YOU MOVE...
...NO... IT CANNOT BE.
YOU ARE NOT HIM.
THE SCENT IS THE SAME... THAT IS CURIOUS, BUT OF NO CONSEQUENCE TO ME.
THE FIGHTING STYLE IS SLIGHTLY DIFFERENT. I KNOW THE MAN I FOUGHT... AND YOU ARE NOT HIM.
I MUST FIND SPIDER-MAN.
I CAN'T LET HIM ESCAPE!
HE ENDANGERED BETTY, AND...
BETTY! I'VE GOT TO MAKE SURE SHE'S OKAY!

YOU ALL RIGHT?
I CALLED THE POLICE --
-- I WAS WORRIED ABOUT YOU. I STILL CAN'T SHAKE THE FEELING THAT YOU ARE FAMILIAR -- THAT WE'VE KNOWN EACH OTHER BEFORE.
NO.
I'M NOT THE PERSON YOU THINK I AM.
HE WOULD HAVE HANDLED THIS BETTER.
I NEVER SHOULD HAVE FOOLED MYSELF INTO THINKING I COULD HAVE A REAL LIFE.
IT WON'T HAPPEN AGAIN.
I'M SORRY TOO.
SORRY...
...I'VE GOT TO HUNT DOWN THAT MANIAC.
READ WEB #121 FOR PART THREE OF "WEB OF LIFE"
THEN BE BACK NEXT ISSUE FOR THE LIFE-SHATTERING CONCLUSION, AS DEATH COMES CALLING FOR ONE OF OUR CAST!

MARVEL COMICS
WEB OF SPIDER-MAN®
$1.50 US
$2.05 CAN
121
FEB
APPROVED BY THE COMICS CODE AUTHORITY
WEB OF LIFE 3 OF 4
KAINE vs. THE SCARLET SPIDER
Phil '94 + R.E.

BITTEN BY A RADIOACTIVE SPIDER, STUDENT PETER PARKER GAINED THE PROPORTIONATE STRENGTH AND AGILITY OF AN ARACHNID! ARMED WITH HIS WONDROUS WEB-SHOOTERS, THE RELUCTANT SUPER HERO STRUGGLES WITH SINISTER SUPER-VILLAINS, MAKING ENDS MEET, AND MAINTAINING SOME SEMBLANCE OF A NORMAL LIFE! AND NOW HE'S GOT HIS RETURNED CLONE TO CONTEND WITH!

Stan Lee PRESENTS: WEB OF SPIDER-MAN™

C'MON, SWEETHEART-- JUMP FOR IT! THAAAT'S IT!
OH, YA ALMOST GOT IT THAT TIME!
GIMME MY CLOCK BACK!
YEAH, DUTCH--MAYBE YA SHOULD HURRY UP AN' GIVE IT TO HER!
JUS' POP A CAP IN HER AN' LET'S GET OUTTA HERE!
HER NAME IS ANNIE--
--SHE HAD A LIFE ONCE. SHE HAD FRIENDS AND A FAMILY... A HOUSE... A HOME--
--THESE THINGS FILLED HER LIFE, AND SHE HAD BEEN HAPPY--
--BUT THAT WAS LONG AGO.
NOW THAT LIFE IS TOO PAINFUL TO REMEMBER. HER EXISTENCE THESE DAYS IS ONLY IN SURVIVING ONE DAY TO THE NEXT... FINDING FOOD... STAYING WARM.
WEB OF LIFE
PART THREE
THE HUNTING
TODD DEZAGO GUEST WRITER
PHIL GOSIER GUEST BREAKDOWNS
DeLa ROSA & EMBERLIN FINISHES
STEVE DUTRO LETTERS
KEVIN TINSLEY COLORS
ERIC FEIN EDITS
DANNY FINGEROTH GROUP EDITS
BOB BUDIANSKY CHIEF EDITS

COME ON... COME ON...
IT DON'T BELONG TO YOU! IT'S NOT YOUR PROPERTY! GIMME MY CLOCK!
THE RAGGED TRAPPINGS OF HER NEW LIFE BARELY FILL A BATTERED SHOPPING CART...

THIS CLOCK'S A PIECE A' JUNK, YA OLD HAG! IT'S TRASHED! IT DON'T EVEN WORK!

THEN WHY WOULD YOU WANT IT?

HEH HEH-- HEY, ROSS-- HOW 'BOUT THIS?
HERE'S A CHICK FOR YA!

LAURA!

YOU LEAVE MY BABY GIRL ALONE!
YOU PUT HER BACK!
YOU PUT MY LAURA BACK RIGHT THIS MINUTE!

WAK
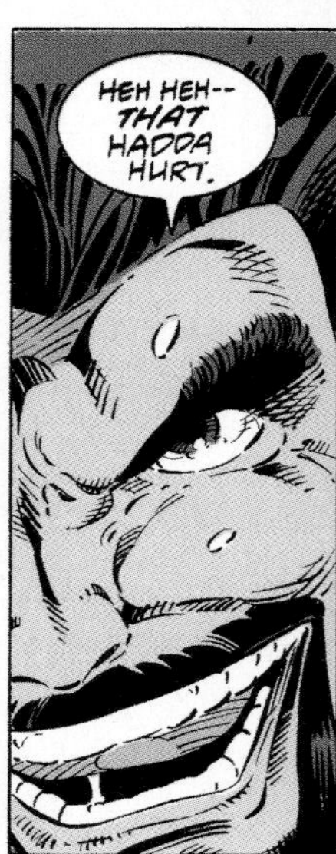
HEH HEH-- THAT HADDA HURT.

SO WILL YOU!
HUH?

WHAK
CHOK

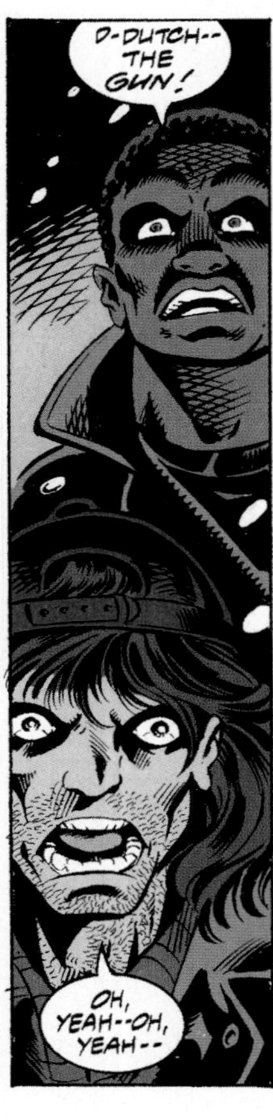
D-DUTCH-- THE GUN!
OH, YEAH--OH, YEAH--

TH-THAT'S ENOUGH, FREAK! WE WERE J-JUS' GONNA POP SOME SCABS IN THE PARK-- BUT I DON'T MIND PUTTIN' SOME HOLES IN YOU, TOO! DON'T--
HIS NAME IS KAINE...

--CULKK--!
...AND HE MOVES WITH A BRUTAL GRACE--VICIOUSLY DISPATCHING THE PUNKS AS IF ON A WHIM--MOMENTARILY DISTRACTED FROM AN AGENDA NO MAN CAN FATHOM...!
NOT ME, MAN! I'M NOT DIGGIN' ON THIS...I'M JUS' ALONG FOR THE RIDE!
KRAK
WE WUZ ONLY PLAYIN' WITH HER, MAN--WE WUZ PLAYIN'!
I DON'T CARE.
KRAKT
THA-THANK...
...THANK--
KRNCH

MANHATTAN AT TWILIGHT--AS THE STREETS AND SIDEWALKS OF THE CITY ARE DUSTED WITH THE FIRST SNOW OF THE SEASON--
--MOST PEOPLE WALK HUNCHED OVER, BRACING THEMSELVES AGAINST THE BITTER WINDS THAT HOWL THROUGH THESE CANYONS--
--NEVER GLANCING UPWARD, WHERE, THROUGH THE FALLING SNOW, THEY MIGHT CATCH A GLIMPSE OF--
--THE SCARLET SPIDER!
NO PARKING
PLEASE, LET ME GET THERE AHEAD OF HIM!
I'M ONLY ASSUMING THAT IT WOULD TAKE THE GRIM HUNTER SOME TIME TO PICK UP PETER'S SCENT--TO TRACK HIM BACK TO HIS APARTMENT--
--AND WHEN THE HUNTER GETS THERE...I WANT TO BE THE ONE WAITING THERE TO MEET HIM!
THE GRIM HUNTER TRACKED ME--TO BETTY BRANT'S PLACE--BELIEVING I WAS PETER--WANTING TO KILL SPIDER-MAN--*
--BUT THE SCENT WAS WRONG, HE SAID...
...WHICH MAKES SENSE...EVEN THOUGH I'M PETER'S CLONE, OUR SCENTS WOULDN'T BE EXACTLY THE SAME--OUR PHEROMONE OUTPUT MUST BE DIFFERENT.
*IT HAPPENED IN SPIDER-MAN #54--WEB OF LIFE PART 2. --ERIC

BUT THE HUNTER GOT AWAY FROM ME--!

I JUST *HOPE* THAT IN THE TIME IT TOOK FOR ME TO STOP OFF AT HOME AND STOCK UP ON *WEB-FLUID* AND *STINGERS*--

--THAT THE HUNTER DIDN'T GET THE *ADVANTAGE* AND LOCATE PETER BEFORE I CAN GET OVER THERE!

ALL THIS TIME I'VE BEEN WORRYING THAT MY PRESENCE MIGHT *COMPROMISE* PETER'S LIFE... AND NOW I JUST MIGHT BE ABLE TO *SAVE IT!*

uhm... I'M REALLY IN *NO RUSH*...

...WE REALLY DON'T NEED TO BE GOING *SO FAST*...

THIS...? PAL, THIS IS *NOTHIN'!* I BEEN DRIVIN' A HACK NOW FER 22 YEARS. I *KNOW* HOW T'DRIVE IN THE SNOW...

...THE *TRICK* IS NEVER T'HIT THE--

SAFE
CAUTIOUS
COURTEOUS

LOOK OUT!

HOLY CRUD!

THE BRAKES WON'T CATCH! I GOT NO CONTROL!
WE'RE SKIDDING!
WHA--? SPIDER-SENSE--WHOA, LOOKS LIKE I'M AT THE RIGHT PLACE AT THE RIGHT TIME!
A WELL-PLACED WEBLINE SHOULD DO THE TRICK.
THWIPP
SHLPSPROING
W-WE STOPPED? HOW COULD WE HAVE POSSIBLY STOPPED...?!
I THOUGHT WE WAS DEAD FER SURE.
IT'S LIKE A MIRACLE!
34th ST.

THE KRAVINOFF ESTATE.
AS I LOOK DOWN ON VLADIMIR KRAVINOFF, I AM AFRAID THAT IN HIS IMPASSIONED BID TO CONTINUE HIS FATHERS LEGACY--
--TO CARRY ON WITH HONOR AND TRADITION THE KRAVINOFF NAME...
...HE HAS ALSO INHERITED THE THE MADNESS THAT BROUGHT KRAVEN TO HIS DEATH.
HE FOLLOWS SO CLOSELY NOW IN HIS FATHER'S FOOTSTEPS THAT HE CANNOT SEE THAT HE, TOO, HAS FALLEN VICTIM TO SUCH INSANE OBSESSION!
HE IS DRIVEN NOW BY ONE PURE AND BURNING TRUTH--THAT HE WILL HAVE COMPENSATION FOR HIS FATHER'S DEATH--
--DESPITE THE FACT THAT KRAVEN TOOK HIS OWN LIFE--
--THAT HE WILL HAVE HIS REVENGE--
--THAT THE GRIM HUNTER WILL DESTROY SPIDER-MAN!

AND THE ROLE I AM INTENDED TO PLAY IN THIS MAD DRAMA?
I CAN ONLY BE AN OBSERVER--WATCHING IN FRUSTRATION AS HE PLUMMETS EVEN FASTER--
--SO LOST IS HE TO MY WORDS.
VLADIMIR...
...THE SON OF MY CLOSEST FRIEND. AND AS YOU GREW TO MANHOOD, YOUR FATHER ALLOWED ME TO SHARE IN HIS PRIDE.
--SPIRALING DEEPER AND DEEPER INTO THIS ABYSS OF SELF-DESTRUCTION!
HOW EASY IT WAS FOR ME TO SEE IN YOU THE SON I NEVER HAD. HOW EASY, WHEN HE DIED, WAS IT FOR ME TO TAKE ON HIS MANTLE AS YOUR FRIEND, TEACHER, AND CONFIDANTE.
MY APPEALS TO HIS SENSIBILITIES FALL ON DEAF EARS--SO CONSUMED IS HE WITH THIS OVER-POWERING DESIRE--
AND HOW DIFFICULT IT IS FOR ME NOW, TO WATCH YOU CHOOSE THIS COURSE--TO LOSE YOU TO THIS OBSESSION, AS WELL!

MY MIND SEARCHES FOR THE WORDS -- ALL THE WHILE KNOWING THAT THE WORDS WOULD HAVE NO MEANING --
--AND IT'S ALL I CAN DO TO STIFLE THE URGE TO SCREAM AT YOU, BEG OF YOU, PLEAD WITH YOU NOT TO CONTINUE ON THIS PATH! DENY THIS DEMENTED LEGACY--!
-- I WISH THERE WAS SOME WAY I COULD REACH YOU, SAVE YOU FROM THIS INSANITY.
BUT THERE IS NOT.
YOUR RESOLVE IS MUCH TOO STRONG. YOUR RATIONALE BASED ON MADNESS.
AND SO I WILL KEEP MY COUNSEL --
--RESIGNING MYSELF TO THE FACT THAT YOU WILL NOT BE TURNED FROM THIS COURSE. I WILL BE YOUR EYES WHILE YOU ARE BLINDED BY THIS ILLNESS --
-- I WILL BE THERE TO AID YOU, SHOULD MATTERS DICTATE--
--TO PROTECT YOU IF I CAN-- IF ONLY FROM YOURSELF...
THE HUNT IS ON, GREGOR! THE SCENT OF MY PREY IS AROUND ME! AND SO IS THE SMELL OF DEATH!
I TAKE IT THE HELICOPTER IS SUPPLIED WITH THE ITEMS WE DISCUSSED?
JUST AS YOU REQUESTED, VLADIMIR--
--JUST AS YOU WISH.

THE 28TH PRECINCT, MIDTOWN MANHATTAN--

--AS VISITING DETECTIVE JACOB RAVEN AND NEW YORK DETECTIVE CONNOR TREVANE WORK LATE INTO THE DECEMBER NIGHT.

THIS LOOKS LIKE THE WORK OF THE SAME MAN.

...BECAUSE I DON'T KNOW WHY ANYONE WOULD WANT TO COPY A SIGNATURE SLAYING LIKE THIS!

WHEN I FIRST GOT THIS CASE TWO YEARS AGO, BACK IN SALT LAKE CITY, I FIGURED IT WAS GOING TO BE EASY! HE'D REVEAL HIMSELF.

YOU DON'T DO WHAT HE DID AND THEN GO HOME AND GET A GOOD NIGHT'S SLEEP--!

THAT'S WHERE I MADE MY MISTAKE-- I WAS THE ONE WHO COULDN'T GET ANY SLEEP! I'VE BEEN ACHING OVER THIS ONE FOR A LONG TIME.
THIS KILLER IS COLD--HIS SOUL IS DEAD--

--HE BEATS HIS VICTIMS TO DEATH WITH HIS BARE HANDS-- THEN HE LEAVES THAT--
--THAT MARK!
ANYBODY WHO'D DISFIGURE HIS VICTIMS THAT WAY HAS GOT TO BE DEMENTED! AND NOW WE GOT A MATCH ON HIS PRINTS--!

BUT THAT'S WHERE IT GETS FISHY, JACOB. THIS GUY MAY BE TWISTED... BUT HE'S SMART!
SO WHY'D HE ALL OF A SUDDEN GET STUPID ENOUGH TO LEAVE A PRINT AT A CRIME SCENE...?
A LOTTA THESE GUYS HE PUT DOWN WERE MOB--THEY WERE TRAINED. THEY WERE GOOD, AND HE WALKED THROUGH 'EM LIKE THEY WERE NOTHIN'!
YOU DON'T ELUDE THE COPS THIS LONG BY BEIN' CARELESS... THE PRINT ISN'T PERFECT--
NO. BUT IT'S ENOUGH.
ENOUGH TO CONVINCE ME HE'S HERE IN NEW YORK.
AND I THINK IT'S TIME WE PAID A VISIT TO THE MAN WITH THE MATCHING FINGER-PRINTS.

THE BROWNSTONE APARTMENT OF PETER AND MARY JANE PARKER.
SO FAR, SO GOOD. IT LOOKS LIKE I BEAT THE GRIM HUNTER HERE...
...NOW IT'S JUST A MATTER OF STAYING OUT OF SIGHT WHILE I STAKE THE PLACE OUT.
OF COURSE, THE WAY THIS STORM IS BUILDING I'M GOING TO BE A VERY INCONSPICUOUS SNOW-MAN IN NO TIME.
I FEEL LIKE I'M PLAYING AT BEING SOME KIND OF GUARDIAN ANGEL HERE. AS MUCH AS I DON'T WANT TO INTRUDE INTO PETER'S LIFE--
--I FEEL THAT I SOMEHOW OWE IT TO HIM TO LOOK OUT FOR HIM-- I KNOW THE HUNTER IS STALKING HIM--
--BUT I CAN'T JUST LEAVE HIM OUT IN THE COLD! AND ALTHOUGH THIS CHIMNEY IS ACTING AS A GREAT WINDBREAK, IT'S ALSO BLOCKING MY VIEW!
THAT CALLS FOR A CHANGE OF VENUE!

--AND HOPEFULLY A BETTER PERSPECTIVE!
SO THIS WOULD BE REILLY'S DESTINATION...?! BUT WHAT BRINGS HIM HERE?
IS IT SOME BURNING VOYEURISTIC DESIRE THAT DRAWS HIM TO PARKER? TO OBSERVE A LIFE THAT HAS COMPLETENESS? TO DWELL ON THE "MIGHT-HAVE-BEEN"?
IN ANY CASE, AS HE WATCHES PARKER, I WILL BE WATCHING HIM!
AND I WON'T ALLOW ANYTHING TO GET IN MY WAY!
CHOOM
JUST AS I WON'T ALLOW REILLY TO INTERFERE WITH MY PLANS FOR PETER AND MARY JANE PARKER.

THERE, THAT'S BETTER. NOW IT'S TIME TO JUST SIT AND PLAY THE SPIDER-- WATCHING MY "WEB" AND WAITING FOR MY "PREY"--
--HUNTING THE HUNTER!

C'MON, HUNTER-- "STEP INTO MY PARLOR..."
I'M WAITING!
KRNCH

WHA...?

THAKK

KRTHWAM

unnh SOMEONE--CREPT UP ON ME--SPIDER-SENSE DIDN'T GO OFF!
GOTTA GET MY HEAD TOGETHER-- FOR A SECOND THERE THE GUY LOOKED LIKE--

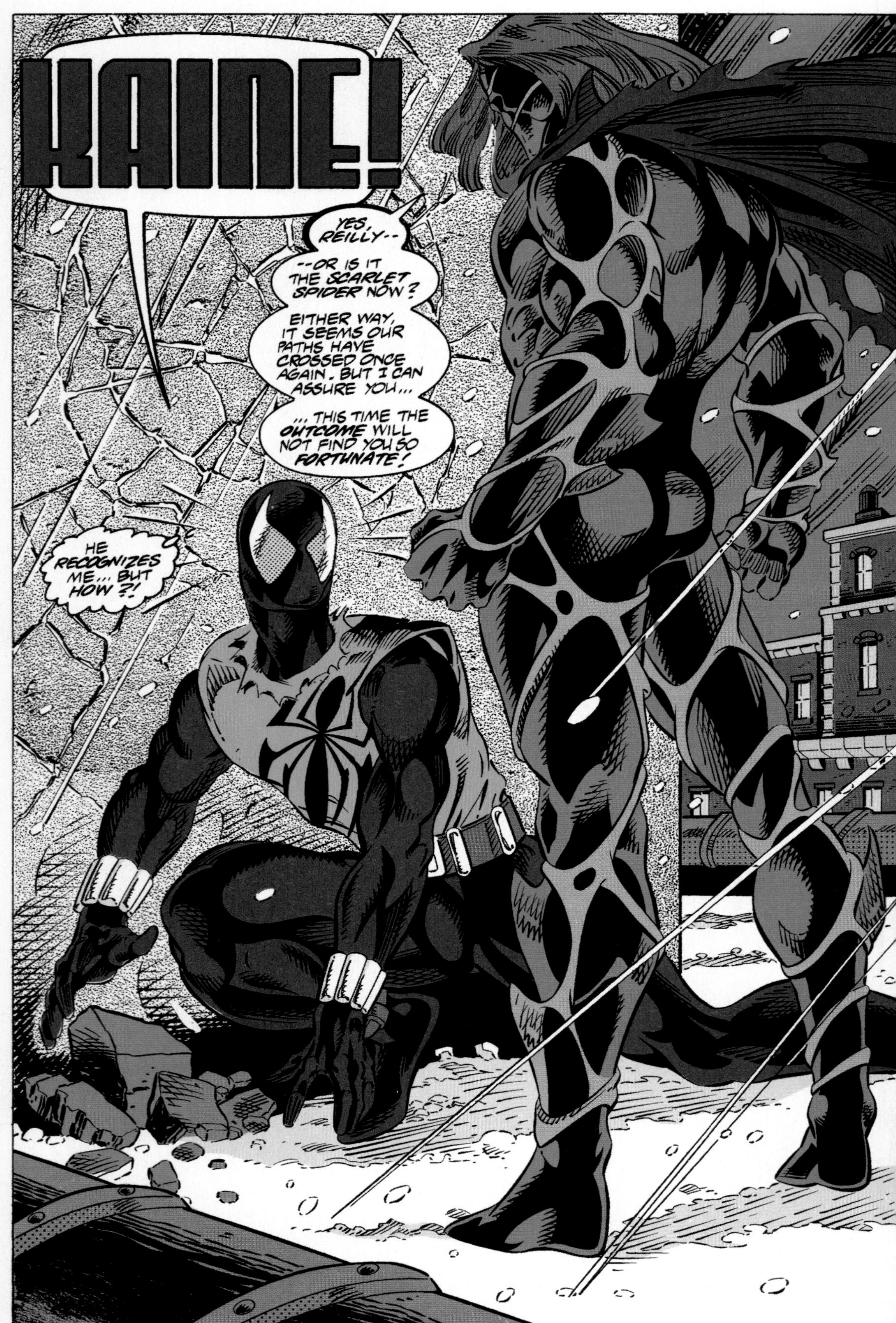
KAINE!
YES, REILLY--
--OR IS IT THE SCARLET SPIDER NOW?
EITHER WAY, IT SEEMS OUR PATHS HAVE CROSSED ONCE AGAIN. BUT I CAN ASSURE YOU...
...THIS TIME THE OUTCOME WILL NOT FIND YOU SO FORTUNATE!
HE RECOGNIZES ME... BUT HOW?!

CAN'T WORRY ABOUT THAT NOW-- I HAVE TO PUT KAINE DOWN FAST! GOTTA KEEP HIM OFF-BALANCE--
THAK
BRAM
--CAN'T LET HIM GET THE ADVANTAGE--
--KEEP HIM ON THE DEFENSIVE--
RURNT
--AND WAIT FOR AN OPENING!
THP
THP
THERE.
HOW DO YOU LIKE THOSE STINGERS, KAI--
--OH GREAT!

IF AT FIRST YOU DON'T SUCCEED--
THWUP
THWUP
--SWITCH TO IMPACT WEBBING!

ThWph
ThWph

SO NOW THAT I HAVE YOUR UNDIVIDED ATTENTION, MAYBE YOU WON'T MIND ANSWERING A FEW QUESTIONS, LIKE--
--WHAT BRINGS YOU TO NEW YORK?

KRA
CHNK

TOMK

IRONICALLY ENOUGH, REILLY--
--YOU DO.
unnh

AND I'VE ARRIVED JUST IN TIME TO ATTEND YOUR FUNERAL.
MMF.
HUH?
OH, NO. I ALMOST FORGOT--THE GRIM HUNTER!
URK--
HAVE TO GET AWAY FROM KAINE-- STOP THE HUNTER FROM--
CHKK-KK
HE'S STRANGLING ME--TRYING TO CRUSH MY WINDPIPE-- AND HE COULD DO IT, TOO!
I'M STARTING TO BLACK OUT! GOT TO--
SMAPP

UNNH...
TUNK
C'MON, BEN-- SHAKE IT OFF! YOU'VE GOT WORK TO DO--
--YOU'VE GOTTA STOP THE HUNTER!
YEAH, RIGHT--AS SOON AS I TAKE CARE OF--
THOOM

MEANWHILE, ON THE ADJACENT ROOFTOP--
I HAVE FOUND HIM, FATHER--! I HAVE TRACKED MY ENEMY TO HIS LAIR--
--MY PREY TO HIS DEN!
HIS FOUL SCENT BURNS AT MY NOSTRILS, BUT SO, TOO, DOES THE SMELL OF DEATH!
EVERY FIBER OF MY BEING, EACH ONE OF MY ENHANCED SENSES, TELLS ME THAT THE KILL IS NEAR...!
I STAND AT THE PRECIPICE OF MY DESTINY. ONCE I ELIMINATE HIS MEAGER SECURITY DEVICES, I SHALL SLAY THE SPIDER-MAN--
--AND CLEANSE FOREVER THE STAIN HE HAS PLACED ON OUR FAMILY NAME!
YOU WILL BE AVENGED, FATHER--
--AND I WILL HAVE FULFILLED THE LEGACY YOU HAD LEFT TO ME-- THE LEGACY OF KRAVEN!
ALL MY LIFE, ALL MY TRAINING-- EVERY HUNT, AND EVERY KILL--HAVE PREPARED ME FOR THIS MOMENT!
HOW FITTING THAT THE SPIDER SHOULD DIE IN HIS OWN--
--EH...?

YOU INTERFERE WITH DESTINY HERE, STRANGER! IN COMING HERE, YOU HAVE MADE A FATAL ERROR--
--BUT I GUARANTEE, IT IS A MISTAKE THAT WILL BE YOUR LAST!
SO WE SHALL SEE...
UNH. GOTTA STOP... THEM... GOT... ...STOP THEM BOTH! IF I DON'T...
...PETER'S DEAD...
CHUFF
"WEB OF LIFE" CONCLUDES--WITH A SHOCKING DEATH--IN SPIDER-MAN #55! THEN, NEXT MONTH, BE HERE FOR PART 1 OF THE "SMOKE AND MIRRORS" CROSSOVER--FEATURING THE RETURN OF THE CLONE'S CREATOR: THE JACKAL!

MARVEL COMICS
$1.95 US
$2.65 CAN/UK £1.25
55
FEB
01321
APPROVED BY THE COMICS CODE AUTHORITY
SPIDER-MAN
WEB OF LIFE
4 of 4
KAINE...
SCARLET SPIDER...
GRIM HUNTER...
...ONE WILL
DIE!

SNOW FALLS ON NEW YORK CITY.
SOMEWHERE ON A ROOFTOP LIES THE MAN THE NEWSPAPERS HAVE LABELED THE SCARLET SPIDER.
HE CAN THINK OF HIMSELF ONLY AS BEN REILLY.
HE'D LIKE TO THINK OF HIMSELF SIMPLY AS A MAN WITH EXTRAORDINARY POWERS AND A GREAT SENSE OF RESPONSIBILITY.
A SENSE OF RESPONSIBILITY WHICH PUSHED HIM TO TRY TO STOP THE GRIM HUNTER FROM GETTING TO AND KILLING PETER PARKER.
STAN LEE PRESENTS THE SCARLET SPIDER IN
END HUNT
WEB OF LIFE PART IV
HOWARD MACKIE WRITER
MIKE MANLEY GUEST PENCILER
JOE RUBINSTEIN GUEST INKER
STARKINGS/ COMICRAFT LETTERING
KEVIN TINSLEY COLORS
DANNY FINGEROTH EDITOR
BOB BUDIANSKY EDITOR IN CHIEF
NOW, HIS BRUISED AND BLOODIED FACE CRUSHED AGAINST THE SNOWY ROOFTOP, BEN IS NOT FEELING TOO POWERFUL OR RESPONSIBLE.
HE IS FEELING ONLY PAIN, FEAR, AND A SENSE OF FAILURE.
ALL INFLICTED AT THE HANDS OF THE MAN CALLING HIMSELF KAINE.*
AND THE PAIN SERVES AS A REMINDER THAT BEN IS NOTHING MORE THAN A CLONE OF PE PARKER.
THROUGH HIS PAIN, HE CURSES HIMSELF AS A POOR EXCUSE FOR A MAN...
...AND FOR A HERO.
*SEE WEB OF SPIDER-MAN #127. --DANNY

KAINE.
HE'S HERE. FOLLOWING ME AGAIN.
STRONGER... MORE SAVAGE THAN I REMEMBERED.
TORE INTO ME... THROUGH ME... LIKE I WAS NOTHING.
AGAIN. WHY DOES HE DO THIS TO ME?
WHY DOESN'T HE JUST KILL ME?
STOPPED ME FROM GETTING INTO PARKER'S APARTMENT... FROM STOPPING THE GRIM HUNTER.
NOW HE'S GOING FOR PARKER, TOO.
WHY?
HE AND THE GRIM HUNTER BOTH ARE AFTER SPIDER-MAN.
CAN'T LET THEM DO THIS!
GOT TO STOP KAINE AND THIS GRIM HUNTER BOTH.
THWIP
GOT TO TRY.

GOT TO PUSH THROUGH THE PAIN.
THROUGH THE FEAR.
STAY FOCUSED ON AUNT MAY.
DO IT... SAVE PARKER'S LIFE... FOR HER.
EVERYTHING FOR HER.
THWIPP

ON A NEARBY ROOFTOP...
KAINE AND THE GRIM HUNTER CIRCLE EACH OTHER IN A DANCE OF CERTAIN DEATH.
NEITHER HAS EVER LAID EYES ON THE OTHER BEFORE, AND YET...
...EACH IS READY TO KILL THE OTHER.
I DO NOT KNOW WHO YOU ARE, OR WHY YOU DARE STAND IN THE WAY OF MY REACHING THE SPIDER, BUT...
...YOUR INTERFERENCE WILL BRING YOU ONLY DEATH!

THIS HUNTER IS POWERFUL...
COULD HE BE THE ONE I SEEK?
HE STALKS SPIDER-MAN... WOULD KILL HIM.
...FAST...
...DEADLY.
CAUSED ME TO ACT PREMATURELY.
CAUSED ME TO LASH OUT AT REILLY.
I MUST PUT AN END TO THIS ONE.
HE CANNOT BE ALLOWED TO INTERFERE WITH ALL THAT I HAVE STRIVEN TO ACCOMPLISH.
HE MUST DIE.
AS MUST THEY ALL.
HE HAS FORCED MY HAND.

AT THAT MOMENT...
NO SIGN OF EITHER OF THE BAD GUYS OUT HERE.
I'VE GOT TO KNOW.
GOT TO MAKE SURE THAT PETER AND HIS WIFE ARE SAFE.
DARK INSIDE.
QUIET.
EMPTY.
SO THIS IS WHERE HE LIVES.
WHERE HE HAS A LIFE.
A HOME...
...A FAMILY.
THINGS I COULD NEVER DARE HOPE FOR...
...NEVER DARE DREAM.

BUT I DO DREAM.
DREAM OF THE WAY THINGS COULD HAVE BEEN.
TORTUROUS DREAMS WHICH ONLY SERVE TO REMIND ME OF...
...HOW EMPTY MY LIFE IS.
THIS IS CRAZY!
WHY DO I DO THIS TO MYSELF?
GOT TO GET OUT OF HERE! FIND KAINE AND THE GRIM HUNTER!
STOP DREAMING.

ELSEWHERE...
THERE WAS A TIME THAT NOT A SINGLE SPECK OF DUST WAS ALLOWED TO EXIST IN THIS STATE-OF-THE-ART LABORATORY.
BUT THAT WAS LONG AGO.
A MAN ENTERS THE LABORATORY AND IMMEDIATELY FEELS AS THOUGH HE IS RETURNING TO A LONG-LOST HOME.
A HOME HE LEFT RELUCTANTLY, BUT HASTILY.
CALL R.G.K. FOR LAB EQUIPMENT
SO LONG AGO.
AND WITH THE FLIP OF A LIGHT SWITCH...
...SEWARD TRAINER, ONE OF THE WORLD'S LEADING GENETICISTS, IS HOME.
OKAY, BEN, YOU GOT ME TO COME BACK*.
ALL I HAVE TO DO IS FIND YOU...
...BEFORE IT'S TOO LATE.
*LAST ISSUE. -- Danny.

MEANWHILE, THE STORM AND THE BATTLE BETWEEN KAINE AND THE GRIM HUNTER RAGE ON.
NEITHER MAN SEEMS TO BE AFFECTED BY THE BITTER COLD, THE DRIVING WINDS OR THE BLINDING SNOW.
BOTH ARE TOO DRIVEN BY A BLOOD RAGE TO NOTICE THE ELEMENTS.
GOT TO REST -- CATCH MY BREATH.
BETWEEN MY BATTLE WITH THE GRIM HUNTER AND THE BEATING I TOOK FROM KAINE, I'VE GOT TO ASK MYSELF...
...WHAT MAKES ME THINK I CAN TAKE THE TWO OF THEM ON TOGETHER?

IT WOULD BE A LOT EASIER... SMARTER EVEN... TO JUST LET THE TWO OF THEM TEAR EACH OTHER APART... GO IN AND PICK UP THE PIECES AFTERWARD.
BUT, I JUST CAN'T DO IT.
THWIPP
HERE... LIFE IS JUST STARTING TO GO MY WAY...
NO --
LOSING IT...DIZZY...
...CAN'T...
...HANG...
...AND I'M THROWING MYSELF IN BETWEEN TWO GUYS WHO WILL PROBABLY KILL ME.
WHUMP
I HAVE HIM!
HE IS ON THE DEFENSIVE NOW.
HE DIES.

NO.
THEY'RE GOING TO KILL EACH OTHER.
GOT TO STOP THEM. GOT TO...
YOU ARE A WILD ONE...
...AND UNEXPECTED.
UNDER OTHER CIRCUMSTANCES, I WOULD WELCOME HUNTING YOU, BUT TONIGHT...
...SPIDER-MAN IS MY PREY!
KRA
KOOM
WE WILL FINISH THIS ANOTHER DAY.
TOO WEAK TO STOP KAINE.
GOT TO GET A MICRODOT TRACER ON HIM BEFORE HE GETS AWAY.
GOT HIM!
THINK I'LL COLLAPSE NOW...

A SHORT AND PAINFUL TIME LATER...
STARTING TO FEEL A LITTLE BETTER.
CAN'T AFFORD TO REST FOR TOO LONG. STILL GOT TO NAIL KAINE.
YEAH, LIKE THAT'S GOING TO BE EASY.
HAVE JUST ENOUGH TIME TO LOAD UP ON SOME WEB CARTRIDGES AND MAYBE THAW OUT MY TOES A LITTLE BIT.
NICE COSTUME, YOUNG MAN, BUT ISN'T IT JUST A LITTLE COLD TO BE PARADING AROUND IN YOUR UNDER-WEAR?
WHO THE--?
THAT IS YOU UNDER THERE... ISN'T IT, BEN?
SEWARD? YOU CAME?

OF COURSE I DID. DID YOU THINK I'D PASS UP THE CHANCE OF FINISHING UP OUR LITTLE TESTING?
THANK YOU.
IT'S GOOD TO SEE A FAMILIAR... A FRIENDLY... FACE.
YOU LOOK TERRIBLE, KID.
I'M FINE, SEWARD.
BANGED UP, BRUISED, AND NOT SURE I CAN CUT IT AS A SUPER HERO, BUT FINE.
GLAD TO HEAR IT, YOUNG FELLA. NOW LET'S GET YOU PACKED UP AND OUT OF THIS RAT HOLE. THERE'S PLENTY OF ROOM AT MY LAB FOR YOU.
HE'S HERE, SEWARD.
KAINE. I'VE ALREADY HAD A RUN-IN WITH HIM. I'VE GOT TO GO BACK AFTER HIM TONIGHT.
HE'S GOING TO KILL AGAIN. I'VE GOT TO STOP HIM.
NOT AGAIN. NOT HIM!

ELSEWHERE...
I WON'T LET HIM ESCAPE.
THE GRIM HUNTER COULD BE THE ONE.
THE ONE I HAVE SEEN IN MY...
...VISIONS!
AGAIN... A PRECOGNITIVE GLIMPSE INTO THE FUTURE.
LIVE
THE PAIN IS OVERWHELMING!
MARY JANE!
SPIDER-MAN'S WIFE!
SHE IS TO BE MURDERED!

IT'S GOING TO HAPPEN SOON.
SHE WILL DIE...
...AND HE WILL SUFFER!
I HAVE NO CHOICE.
MY ROLE IS CAST.
I MUST FIND HER...
...NOW!

CENTRAL PARK...
THE GRIM HUNTER MOVES THROUGH THE DRIVING SNOW WITH THE STEALTH OF A JUNGLE CAT.
EVERY ONE OF HIS ENHANCED SENSES IS FOCUSED ON THE TRACKING OF HIS PREY: SPIDER-MAN.
AND THEN...
WHAT'S THIS?
KAINE... HIS SCENT IS IN THE AIR.
HE HAS THE AUDACITY TO STALK ME?
VERY WELL.
GREGOR! THIS IS VLAD. COME TO ME... NOW.
I WILL NOT BE HUNTED, KAINE.
SINCE YOU SEEK AN ENDING...
...LET IT HAPPEN TONIGHT!

A SHORT TIME LATER...
THE TRAIL ENDS HERE.
IT'S AS THOUGH THE GRIM HUNTER HAS DISAPPEARED FROM THE FACE OF THE --
WHY DO YOU SEEK YOUR DEATH, MAN?
WHO ARE YOU THAT SEEKS ME... SEEKS YOUR DEMISE? UNTIL TONIGHT I HAD NO QUARREL WITH YOU.
IT WAS THE SPIDER I HUNTED.
BUT NOW...!

AND NOW, BECAUSE OF YOUR PURSUIT OF THE SPIDER...
...YOU WILL DIE!
ALL THINGS CONCERNING SPIDER-MAN CONCERN ME!
HIS LIFE IS MINE!
GENTLEMEN! I'D LOVE TO SAY IT'S BEEN TOO LONG...
...BUT THAT WOULD BE FIBBING!
NOW, KAINE OLD BUDDY, WHY DON'T YOU WRESTLE WITH MY IMPACT WEBBING FOR A WHILE?
I INVENTED IT WITH YOUR UGLY FACE IN MIND!

YOU HAVEN'T LEARNED ANYTHING ABOUT ME IN ALL THESE YEARS...HAVE YOU?
HOW MANY TIMES DO I HAVE TO BEAT YOU DOWN?
A FEW MORE, I GUESS!
AND EVERY TIME YOU DO, I'LL JUST COME BACK AND TRY A LITTLE HARDER.
UNLESS YOU KILL ME, THAT IS.

KILLING YOU WOULD MAKE THINGS TOO EASY FOR YOU. I WANT YOU TO SUFFER.
THIP THIP THIP
LUCKY ME. GUESS YOU'RE ABOUT THE BEST FRIEND I HAVE, THEN.
NOW, HOW ARE THOSE STINGERS FEELING?
I INVENTED THEM WITH YOU IN MIND AS WELL. YOU SHOULD BE EXPERIENCING SOME MUSCULAR PARALYSIS JUST ABOUT...
...NOW!!
LOOKS LIKE THEY WORKED.
KRAK
GREAT! NOW I'VE GOT TO SAVE KAINE FROM DROWNING!
THIS JUST ISN'T MY DAY!
SEVERAL MINUTES LATER...
TERRIFIC! CAN'T FIND KAINE, AND NOW THE GRIM HUNTER IS GONE!
I'VE GOT TO DRY OFF AND TRY TO WARN PARKER ABOUT THIS.
I'M SURE HE'LL BE MORE THAN HAPPY TO SEE ME!

THE OTHER SIDE OF THE PARK...
YOU ARE GOOD, KAINE.
BUT NOT GOOD ENOUGH.
DEFEATED BY THE SCARLET SPIDER, YOU ESCAPED.
NOW YOU ARE LIKE A WOUNDED GREAT BEAST.
ONE THAT MUST BE DISPOSED OF.
YOU CANNOT HIDE... CANNOT RUN... FROM ME!
IT WOULD HAVE BEEN BETTER FOR YOU TO HAVE LET ME ESCAPE.
PERHAPS.

BUT IT SEEMS WE SEEK THE SAME PREY, KAINE.
ONLY ONE OF US CAN BE ALLOWED TO COLLECT THE TROPHY.
THE SPIDER WILL BE MINE. I SWEAR THIS IN MY FATHER'S NAME.
IT'S NOT GOING TO HAPPEN.
AS GREGOR, AIDE AND MENTOR TO THE GRIM HUNTER, ARRIVES ON THE SCENE...
...HE WITNESSES THE TWO PREDATORS CIRCLING EACH OTHER.
EACH TAKING IN THE OTHER'S EVERY MOVEMENT UNTIL...
...THE ATTACK SPILLS INTO THE SHADOWS OF THE NIGHT AND...
...THE BATTLE IS OVER IN AN INSTANT.
SNAP
ALL IS SILENT EXCEPT FOR THE DRIVING WIND.

FIRST KAINE STAGGERS FROM THE SHADOWS... WOUNDED.
THEN GREGOR WATCHES AS VLADIMIR -- THE GRIM HUNTER -- STEPS FROM THE SHADOWS.
IN HIS HEART, GREGOR KNOWS THE OUTCOME OF THE BATTLE.
HIS GREATEST FEAR HAS BEEN REALIZED.
GREGOR... I HAVE FAILED...
...FAILED MY FATHER... FAILED YOU...
...FORGIVE ME...
HE HAS BEEN MARKED.
HE DIES.
AS SHALL MANY OTHERS.
3
AS KAINE DISAPPEARS INTO THE STORM, GREGOR HOLDS THE LIFELESS BODY OF WHAT IS THE CLOSEST TO A SON HE HAS EVER KNOWN.
AND EVEN AS HIS GRIEF OVERWHELMS HIM...
...A PLAN OF VENGEANCE BEGINS TO FORM.
WEB OF LIFE ENDS HERE, BUT DO NOT MISS THE STUNNING DEATH IN NEX WEEK'S SPECTACULAR SPIDER-MAN – AND THEN THE SMOKE & MIRRORS CROSSOVER WHICH BEGIN IN WEB #122 AND CONTINUES THRU AMAZIN AND THIS MAG – IT'S CLONE MADNESS AT ITS ULTIMATE!

MARVEL COMICS
THE AMAZING SPIDER-MAN
FABULOUS FLIP BOOK
© 1994 MARVEL ENT. GROUP, INC.
$2.25 US
$3.05 CAN
397
JAN
02457
APPROVED BY THE COMICS CODE AUTHORITY
WEB OF DEATH 1 OF 4
THE LAST SPIDEY/DOC OCK SAGA OF ALL TIME BEGINS HERE!
BAGLEY & MAHLSTEDT
BUT FIRST A DYING SPIDEY'S GOT TO GET PAST STUNNER!

I AM KAINE-- AND I KNOW YOU, SPIDER-MAN...
...BETTER THAN YOU KNOW YOURSELF.
THE SECRETS OF YOUR PAST, THE TRAGEDIES OF YOUR FUTURE; THE DEPTH OF YOUR LONELINESS, THE INTENSITY OF YOUR PAIN.
BUT YOU, MY FRIEND, CAN NEVER KNOW ME. AND THAT'S EXACTLY HOW I WANT IT.
FROM THE DAY I FIRST DREW BREATH, I STOOD ALONE. SEPARATE. WITHOUT LOVE. WITHOUT FAMILY. WITHOUT HOPE.

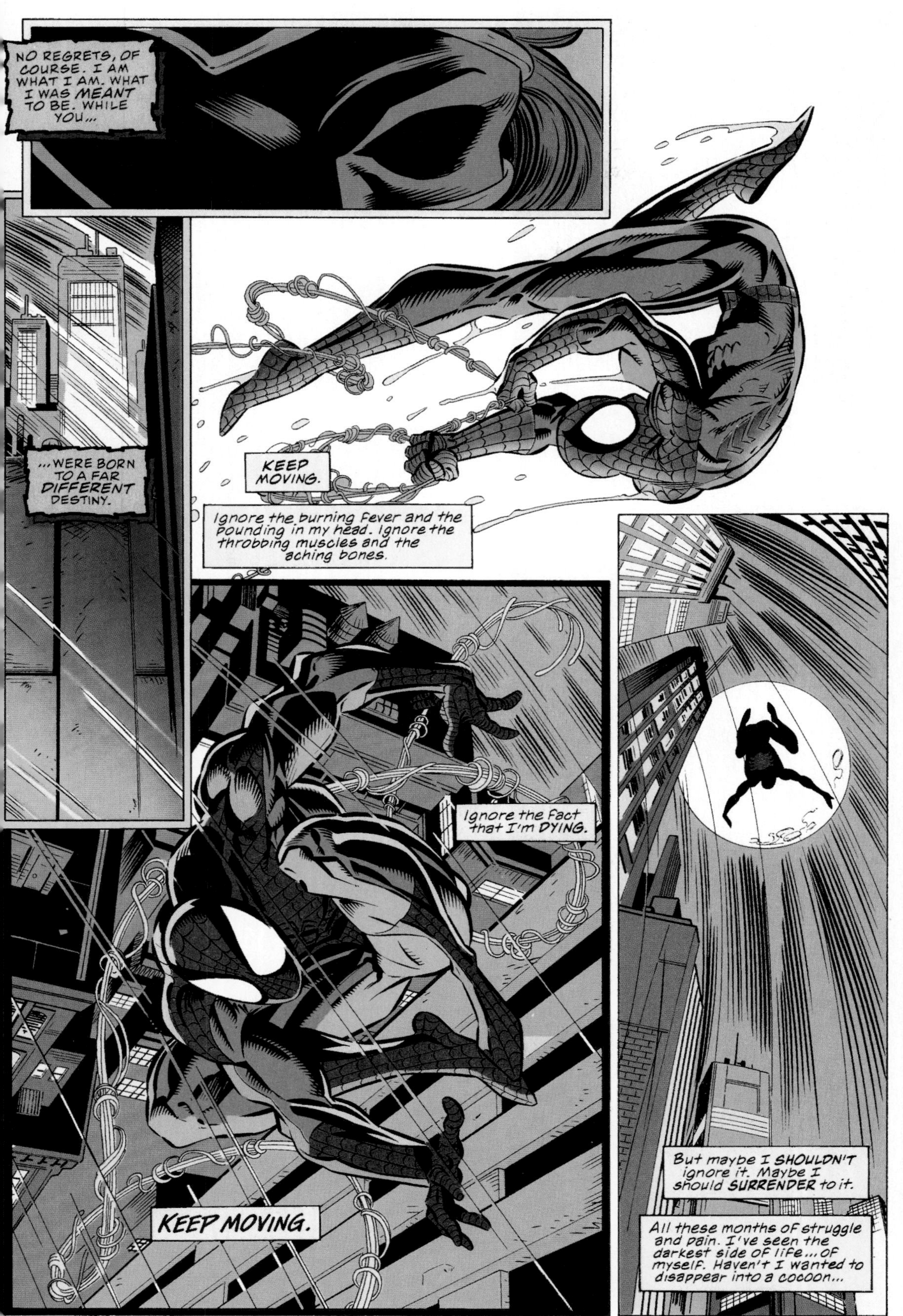
NO REGRETS, OF COURSE. I AM WHAT I AM. WHAT I WAS MEANT TO BE. WHILE YOU...
...WERE BORN TO A FAR DIFFERENT DESTINY.
KEEP MOVING.
Ignore the burning fever and the pounding in my head. Ignore the throbbing muscles and the aching bones.
Ignore the fact that I'm DYING.
KEEP MOVING.
But maybe I SHOULDN'T ignore it. Maybe I should SURRENDER to it.
All these months of struggle and pain. I've seen the darkest side of life... of myself. Haven't I wanted to disappear into a cocoon...

...give up the world and just...
THWIP!
...FADE AWAY?
What WAS that? Like a door... opening in my mind.
Like a fragment of feeling... a broken piece of memory...
...that I never knew I HAD!
Must be the fever. Can't gather up my thoughts. Can't concentrate.
Can't even shoot my webbing straight.

At the rate I'm going, I'll end up killing MYSELF...
...before this CHEMICAL VIRUS the Vulture infected me with...
...even gets a chance to...
do
the
job...
ALL THESE YEARS.

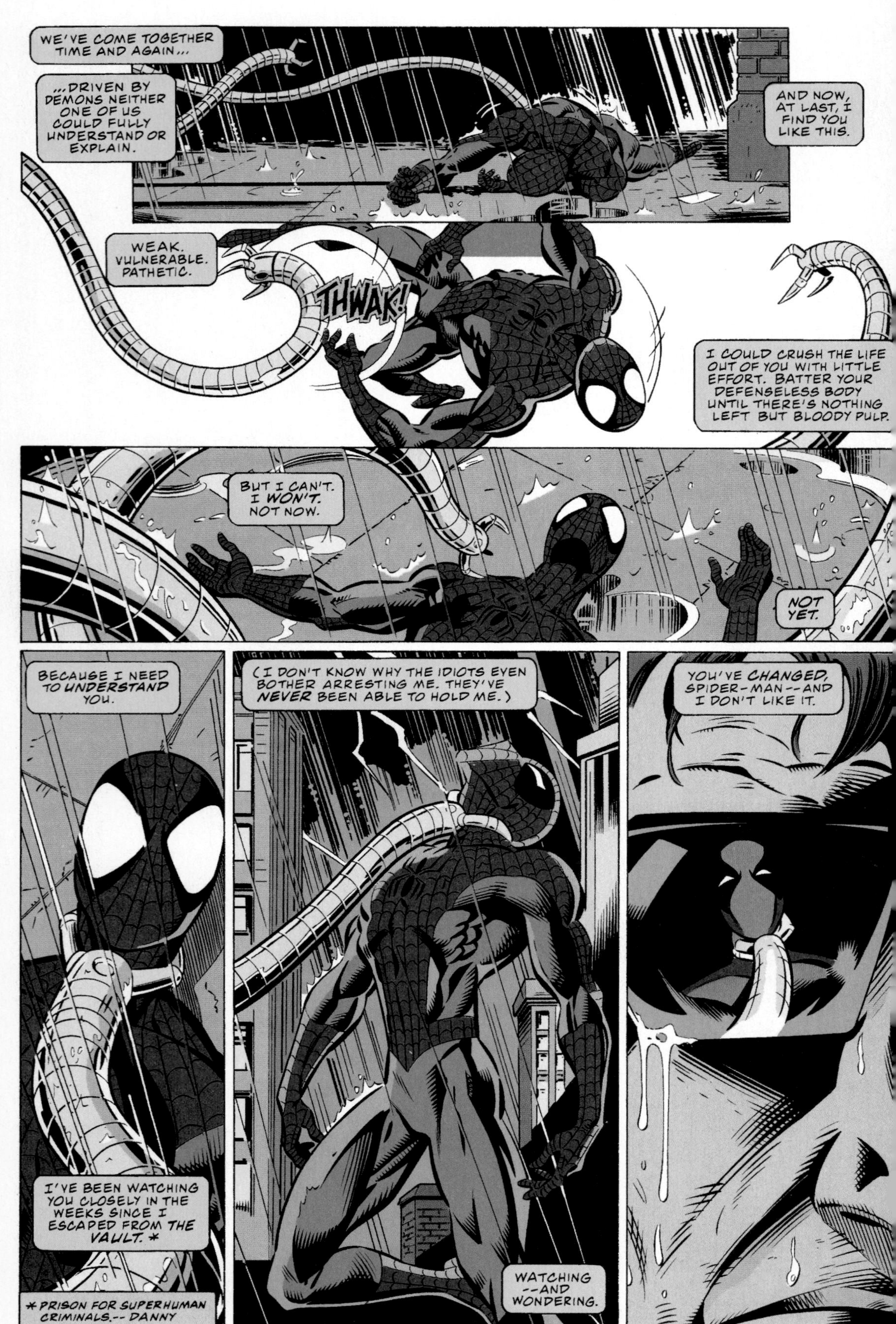
WE'VE COME TOGETHER TIME AND AGAIN...
...DRIVEN BY DEMONS NEITHER ONE OF US COULD FULLY UNDERSTAND OR EXPLAIN.
AND NOW, AT LAST, I FIND YOU LIKE THIS.
WEAK. VULNERABLE. PATHETIC.
THWAK!
I COULD CRUSH THE LIFE OUT OF YOU WITH LITTLE EFFORT. BATTER YOUR DEFENSELESS BODY UNTIL THERE'S NOTHING LEFT BUT BLOODY PULP.
BUT I CAN'T. I WON'T. NOT NOW.
NOT YET.
BECAUSE I NEED TO UNDERSTAND YOU.
I'VE BEEN WATCHING YOU CLOSELY IN THE WEEKS SINCE I ESCAPED FROM THE VAULT. *
* PRISON FOR SUPERHUMAN CRIMINALS.-- DANNY
(I DON'T KNOW WHY THE IDIOTS EVEN BOTHER ARRESTING ME. THEY'VE NEVER BEEN ABLE TO HOLD ME.)
WATCHING --AND WONDERING.
YOU'VE CHANGED, SPIDER-MAN--AND I DON'T LIKE IT.

I DON'T LIKE IT ONE BIT.
WEB OF DEATH PART ONE:
TENTACLES
J. M. DEMATTEIS WRITER
MARK BAGLEY PENCILER
LARRY MAHLSTEDT INKER
BILL OAKLEY LETTERER
BOB SHAREN COLORIST
DANNY FINGEROTH EDITOR
TOM DEFALCO EDITOR IN CHIEF

I'VE ALWAYS LOOKED UPON YOU AS THE LAST DECENT MAN : BRAVE, SELF-SACRIFICING. A BREED WE SEE FAR TOO LITTLE OF IN THESE CORRUPTED TIMES.
IS THAT WHY I'VE ENJOYED OUR ENCOUNTERS SO MUCH DOWN THROUGH THE YEARS?
DO YOU REMIND ME OF A PART OF MYSELF THAT WAS LOST ...LONG AGO... IN THE EXPLOSION THAT TRANSFORMED OTTO OCTAVIUS INTO THE CREATURE THE MEDIA CALLS...
...DOCTOR OCTOPUS?
OR WAS IT LOST LONG BEFORE THAT--BEATEN DOWN BY AN ABUSIVE FATHER... SMOTHERED BY A MOTHER WHO REFUSED TO ALLOW ME TO--
Hmmmm.
WEARY OF THE CONSTANT ROUNDS OF SCHEMING AND FIGHTING, INCARCERATION AND ESCAPE?
I SEEM TO BE GROWING ALARMINGLY REFLECTIVE THESE DAYS. A MID-LIFE CRISIS, PERHAPS? OR AM I SIMPLY... WEARY?
YOU, AT LEAST, HAVE ALWAYS MADE THE GAME WORTHWHILE. BUT, AS OF LATE, YOU SEEM TO HAVE CHANGED. BECOME AS MUCH THE BLOOD-THIRSTY VIGILANTE AS THOSE OTHER SO-CALLED "HEROES" OUT THERE.
AND IF WHAT I'VE HEARD ON THE STREETS IS TRUE ...IF THE VULTURE HAS SUCCEEDED WHERE THE REST OF US HAVE FAILED...
...IF YOU'RE DYING--!
YOU MAY LIVE...FOR NOW... MY OLD ADVERSARY. WHILE I CONTINUE TO WATCH. AND WONDER.
AND PLAN.
Oh, man.

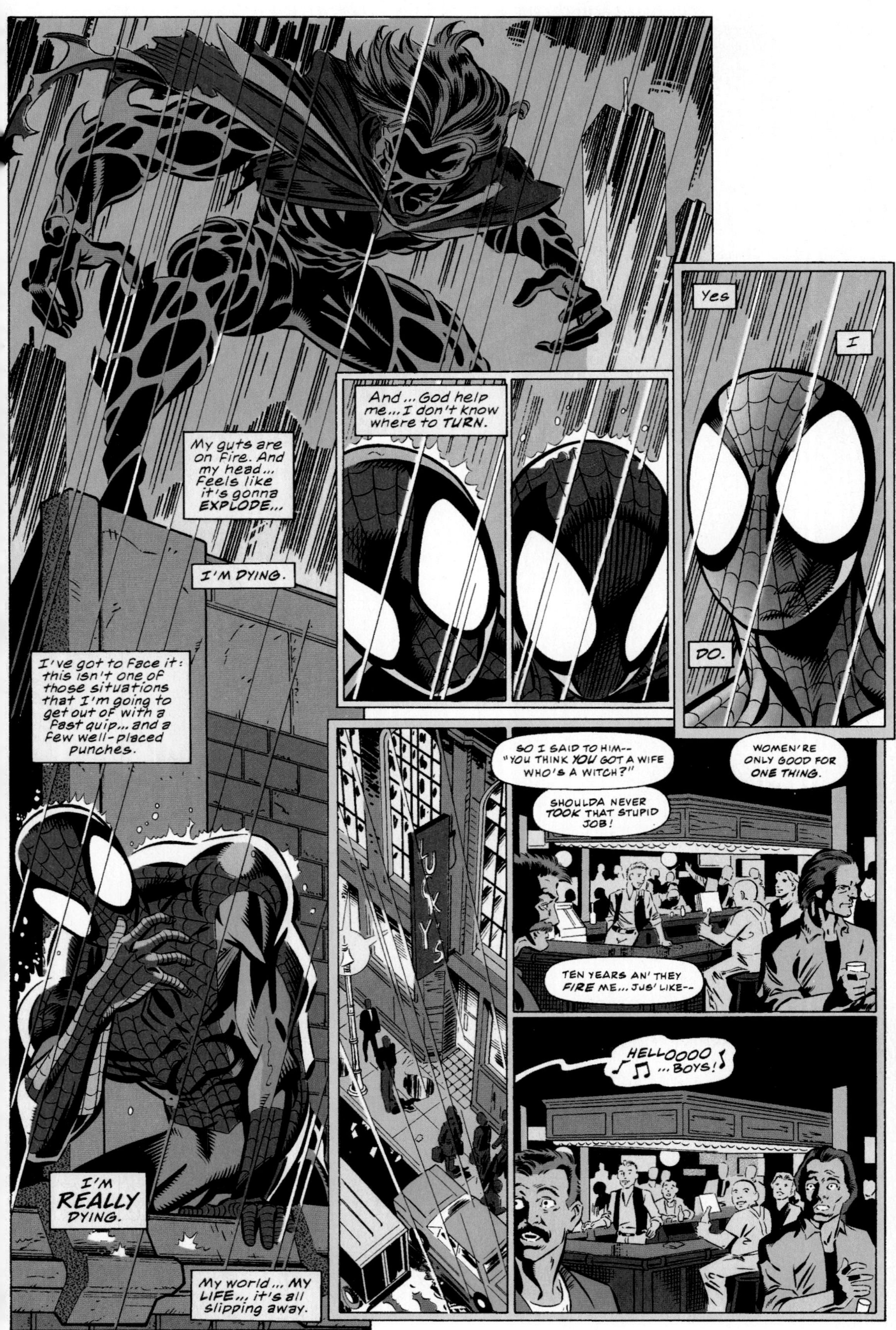
My guts are on Fire. And my head... Feels like it's gonna EXPLODE...
I'M DYING.
I've got to Face it: this isn't one of those situations that I'm going to get out of with a Fast quip... and a Few well-placed punches.
I'M REALLY DYING.
My world... MY LIFE... it's all slipping away.
And... God help me... I don't know where to TURN.
Yes
I
DO.
LUCKY'S
SO I SAID TO HIM-- "YOU THINK YOU GOT A WIFE WHO'S A WITCH?"
WOMEN'RE ONLY GOOD FOR ONE THING.
SHOULDA NEVER TOOK THAT STUPID JOB!
TEN YEARS AN' THEY FIRE ME... JUS' LIKE--
HELLOOOO ...BOYS!

HARD DAY AT THE OFFICE?
KIDS DRIVING YOU UP THE WALL?
HURT YOUR HAND BEATING THE WIFE?
NO CHOICE, IS THERE, BUT TO LOSE YOURSELF IN BEER AND FANTASY.
WELL, GET ON YOUR KNEES AND THANK THE LORD, BOYS--'CAUSE YOUR FANTASIES HAVE ALL COME ***TRUE***.
STUNNER'S HERE.

I'M EVERY WOMAN YOU'VE EVER DREAMED ABOUT AND DROOLED OVER.
BIG AND BUILT... READY, WILLING, AND ABLE.

I DON'T ASK A LOT OF STUPID QUESTIONS. I DON'T EXPECT TOO MUCH. I JUST WANT TO ***PLEASE*** YOU.
SO WHADDAYA SAY, BOYS? WHO'S GONNA BE FIRST?
WHO'S ***MAN*** ENOUGH FOR ME?

WELL, COME ON... SPEAK UP! STEP FORWARD! PUT YOUR MONEY WHERE YOUR MACHO MOUTHS ARE!
NO ONE?

Y'KNOW, THAT WAS MORE FUN THAN I *THOUGHT* IT WAS GONNA BE!

FUN?

FUN?!

YOU TRASH MY BAR... BEAT UP ON MY CUSTOMERS--

--AND YOU CALL THAT **FUN?!**

LADY... I AM GONNA BLOW YOU FROM HERE TO--

...TO...

PUT THE GUN DOWN, IDIOT, AND BACK AWAY FROM HER-- BEFORE I *DISEMBOWEL* YOU.

GOOD.
NOW TAKE THIS. IT SHOULD COVER THE DAMAGES--TO YOUR ESTABLISHMENT, AT LEAST.
YOUR PATRONS, I'M AFRAID, WILL HAVE TO FEND FOR THEMSELVES.
YEAH. SURE. W-WHATEVER YOU SAY--
SIR?
SIR.
TIME T'GO HOME, DOC?
YES, MY DEAR. IT'S LONG PAST TIME...
"...TO GO HOME."
WHATCHA THINKIN' ABOUT?
TOO MANY THINGS, I'M AFRAID.
THINKING'S A DEAD END. I KNOW THAT FROM EXPERIENCE.
DOING, ON THE OTHER HAND--
--IS THE KEY T' LIFE.

OTTO-- WHAT IS IT?
ARE YOU MAD AT ME ABOUT WHAT HAPPENED BACK AT THE BAR?
ANGRY? AT YOU?
MY DEAR, YOU'RE THE BEST THING THAT'S HAPPENED IN MY LIFE SINCE--
WELL... IN FAR TOO LONG.
AND WHY WOULD I BE UPSET ABOUT WHAT YOU DID? HEAVEN KNOWS, YOU HAVE GOOD REASON TO TREAT THOSE TROGLODYTES THAT WAY.
THEN WHAT IS IT?
IT'S... HIM.
SPIDER-MAN.
I DON'T GET IT. HE'S JUST ANOTHER MUSCLE-FLEXING SHOW-OFF, RIGHT?
YOU DON'T KNOW HIM THE WAY I DO. I DOUBT IF ANY-ONE DOES.
A VIBRANT, INTELLIGENT OPPONENT. SO FULL OF LIFE AND HUMOR. AND NOW, IT SEEMS, HE'S BECOME A GRIM AND HUMORLESS THUG--

--NO BETTER THAN **MYSELF**.

DON'T **SAY** THAT, OTTO! YOU--

TRUTH IS TRUTH, MY DEAR.

I'VE ALWAYS FELT THAT, BENEATH HIS MASK, SPIDER-MAN WAS THE SAME DECENT AND SELF-SACRIFICING SOUL HE WAS IN COSTUME.

WHILE I, ON THE OTHER HAND, HAVE BEEN HIDDEN BEHIND THE DARK GLASSES AND TENTACLES OF DOCTOR OCTOPUS FOR SO LONG--

--THAT I'VE LOST ALL SENSE OF WHO AND WHAT **OCTAVIUS** TRULY IS!

I'VE BECOME MY **PERSONA**. NOT A MAN...

...BUT A WARPED **IMAGE** OF ONE!

AND SO, APPARENTLY, HAS **HE**.

IT'S SLIGHTLY **EMBARRASSING**... HOW DEEPLY I FEEL ABOUT HIM. I'M ACTUALLY **SHOCKED** BY HOW MUCH SPIDER-MAN HAS **CHANGED**.

I NEVER REALIZED HOW MUCH I **DEPENDED** ON HIM TO MAINTAIN A LEVEL OF HUMANITY--

--THAT **I** NEVER COULD.

Y'KNOW--I CAN'T BELIEVE SOMEONE AS SMART AS YOU ARE--CAN BE SO UNBELIEVABLY **STUPID**.

ALL THOSE THINGS YOU THINK YOU SEE IN **HIM**--

--YOU ALREADY **ARE**.

BUT **DOCTOR OCTOPUS**--

IS THE **FAKE**. YOU'RE OTTO. ALWAYS WERE. ALWAYS **WILL** BE.

AND I **LOVE** YOU, OTTO. WITH ALL MY...

...HEART--?!

S-SORRY, DOC... GOTTA **GO** NOW! BUT DON'T WORRY, LOVER... IT'LL JUST BE FOR--

--A LITTLE WHILE...
NO!
COME BACK!
COME BACK!!
COME BACK.
PETER...?
PETER-- I'M BACK!

Who're you kidding, Mary Jane?

When you left to go to Pittsburgh, your husband was treating you like a leper; hiding behind the Spider's mask ...webbing himself up so tightly that you couldn't possibly get close to him.

And still you expect him to be here, waiting for you. Just like you always expected your father to be there... even after he abandoned--

No! Enough of that! The whole point of my trip was to lay the past to rest. I've made a peace... however tenuous... with my father.*
Now it's time to make peace with my husband.
God, look at this kitchen.
MILK
Guess he was home... long enough to trash the place.
*SPEC. #219. --Danny

I should clean it up. After all, I've been cleaning up the wreckage of Peter's life for months now.

But I can't.
I'm just too tired.

All this stress... it's starting to take its toll.

No energy left. Can hardly look at food. I'm so edgy I'd snap at Mother Teresa.

Oughta call the hospital. See how May is.

But I'm just

so

tired...

Only one thing to do.

Only one place to go:
HOME.
The masks are off. The walls are down. I'm scared. I'm alone...
...and I need my WIFE beside me. My partner. My BEST FRIEND.
How long can I keep running from the person I love most in the--

AYEEE!

GET OUT OF MY HEAD, BLAST YOU!
GET OUT OF MY--
--HEAD!!
EASY DOES IT, BIG FELLA!
YOU OKAY?
YEAH... YEAH, I THINK SO.
BUT... WHO ARE YOU?
LI'L OL' ME? WHY, I'M THE BIG BAD MAMA--

--WHO'S GONNA BELT YOU FROM HERE TO BOMBAY!!
KA-THOOM!!
AND YOU CAN BET I'M GONNA HAVE A GREAT TIME DOING IT!

KRASSH!
Y'KNOW, WHEN I WAS A LITTLE GIRL, I ALWAYS WANTED TO GO OUT AND MIX IT UP LIKE THE BOYS DID--
--CLIMB TREES, PLAY PIRATES, ROLL AROUND IN THE MUD, WRESTLE AND BOX AND KICK!
BUT MY FATHER ALWAYS TOLD ME IT WASN'T LADYLIKE-- A SWEET, SENSITIVE CHILD LIKE ME HAD TO STAY INSIDE--
--PLAY WITH HER DOLLIES... READ BOOKS... COOK AND SEW!
NOW, DON'T GET ME WRONG... I'M NOT AGAINST THOSE THINGS--
--IN FACT, I CAN COOK JULIA CHILD UNDER THE TABLE... AND SEW RINGS AROUND BETSY ROSS!
BUT I'VE WAITED MY WHOLE LIFE TO GET DOWN AND DIRTY, OUT IN THE OPEN AIR!
SO... WHADDAYA SAY, MISTER SUPER HERO?
WANNA PLAY?
PLAY?
YOU... YOU THINK THIS IS SOME KIND OF GAME?!
WELL-- ISN'T IT?!
I'VE WATCHED YOU HYPO-THYROID JERKS GO AT IT FOR YEARS!
RAM
YOU DROP BUILDINGS ON EACH OTHER... TEAR UP ENTIRE CITY BLOCKS--

--AND NO ONE EVER GETS HURT! YOU DUST YOURSELVES OFF... GO HOME--
--AND COME BACK TO PLAY ANOTHER DAY!
LADY... I DON'T KNOW WHO YOU ARE--OR WHY YOU PICKED ME TO MESS AROUND WITH--
--BUT YOU'VE JUST MADE THE BIGGEST MISTAKE OF YOUR LIFE!
WHAT I DO IS NO GAME!
THOOOM!
WHAT I DO TAKES A MAN AND TURNS HIM INSIDE OUT--
--BREAKS HIS SPIRIT... SHATTERS HIS WORLD--
--POISONS EVERYONE HE CARES ABOUT!
CHOOOM!
I THOUGHT YOU WERE THE GUY WITH THE INCREDIBLE SENSE OF HUMOR! SO HOW COME ALL I'M HEARING IS WHINE, WHINE, WHINE?
WHAT ARE YOU, ANYWAY-- SPIDER-MAN OR SPIDER-INFANT?
K-KOW!
TELL YOU WHAT--AFTER I'M FINISHED BEATING THE STUFFING OUT OF YOU, I'LL DROP YOU OFF AT THE YMCA--
--MAYBE THEY'RE RUNNING A TWELVE-STEP PROGRAM FOR SELF-PITYING SUPER-HEROES!
She's RIGHT!
I've wasted so much precious time... feeling SORRY for myself... HIDING from the world-- when I should have been REACHING out... EMBRACING it!
KOW!
But now... when I want life-- all the love and struggle... all the pleasure and pain-- more than EVER...

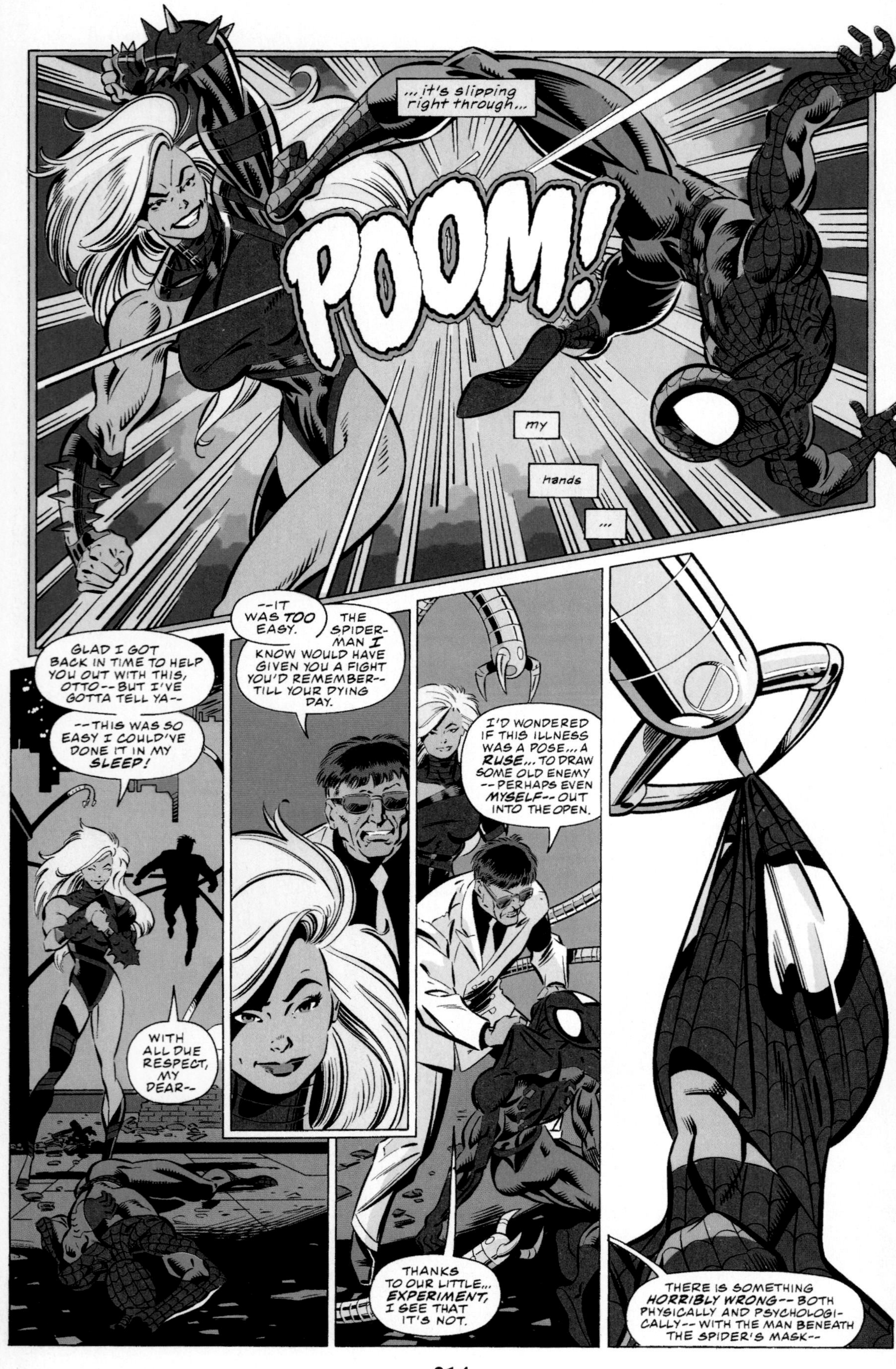
...it's slipping right through...
POOM!
my
hands
...
GLAD I GOT BACK IN TIME TO HELP YOU OUT WITH THIS, OTTO--BUT I'VE GOTTA TELL YA--
--THIS WAS SO EASY I COULD'VE DONE IT IN MY SLEEP!
--IT WAS TOO EASY.
THE SPIDER-MAN I KNOW WOULD HAVE GIVEN YOU A FIGHT YOU'D REMEMBER--TILL YOUR DYING DAY.
WITH ALL DUE RESPECT, MY DEAR--
I'D WONDERED IF THIS ILLNESS WAS A POSE... A RUSE... TO DRAW SOME OLD ENEMY--PERHAPS EVEN MYSELF--OUT INTO THE OPEN.
THANKS TO OUR LITTLE... EXPERIMENT, I SEE THAT IT'S NOT.
THERE IS SOMETHING HORRIBLY WRONG--BOTH PHYSICALLY AND PSYCHOLOGICALLY--WITH THE MAN BENEATH THE SPIDER'S MASK--

--AND I INTEND TO FIND OUT WHAT IT IS.
"WEB OF DEATH" CONTINUES IN SPECTACULAR SPIDER-MAN #220! (FEATURING THE MOST INCREDIBLE SURPRISE OF ALL!)
THEN BE BACK HERE NEXT MONTH FOR CHAPTER THREE: "...BEFORE I WAKE!"

MARVEL COMICS
GIANT-SIZED FLIP BOOK
THE SPECTACULAR SPIDER-MAN
WEB OF DEATH 2 OF 4
© 1994 MARVEL ENT. GROUP, INC.
$2.25 US
$3.05 CAN
220
JAN
02199
APPROVED BY THE COMICS CODE AUTHORITY
TIGER, DO I HAVE NEWS FOR YOU!

BITTEN BY A RADIOACTIVE SPIDER, STUDENT PETER PARKER GAINED THE PROPORTIONATE STRENGTH AND AGILITY OF AN ARACHNID! ARMED WITH HIS WONDROUS WEB-SHOOTERS, THE RELUCTANT SUPER HERO STRUGGLES WITH SINISTER SUPER-VILLAINS, MAKING ENDS MEET, AND MAINTAINING SOME SEMBLANCE OF A NORMAL LIFE!

STAN LEE PRESENTS: THE SPECTACULAR SPIDER-MAN

WEB OF DEATH PART 2
A TIME TO LIVE!
THE PRISON PSYCHIATRISTS MAY BE RIGHT AFTER ALL.
EMPLOYED BY THE STATE (PROBABLY BECAUSE THEY LACK THE NECESSARY SKILLS OR STOMACHS FOR PRIVATE PRACTICE) THOSE POMPOUS CRETINS HAVE OFTEN RENDERED THE SOMEWHAT ANNOYING OPINION THAT I AM CRAZY.
HARDLY A SURPRISING VERDICT FOR THE MAN WHOM THE PUBLIC KNOWS AS DOCTOR OCTOPUS!
AND YET, CONSIDERING THE PRESENT CIRCUMSTANCES, I AM FORCED TO CONCEDE THEIR POINT.
BY ALL RIGHTS, THIS SHOULD BE THE HAPPIEST DAY OF MY LIFE!
MY GREATEST ENEMY IS COMPLETELY AT MY MERCY!
SPIDER-MAN IS DYING!

TOM DeFALCO WRITER · SAL BUSCEMA BREAKDOWNS · BILL SIENKIEWICZ FINISHES · CLEM ROBINS LETTERER · JOHN KALISZ COLORIST · MARK POWERS EDITOR · DANNY FINGEROTH GROUP EDITOR

AND YET INSTEAD OF REVELING IN HIS AGONY, I SPEND HOURS --THOUGH IT SEEMS MORE LIKE DAYS--IN THE FRANTIC PURSUIT OF AN ANTIDOTE TO THE CHEMICAL VIRUS THAT IS KILLING HIM!
BUT, AS MY DEAR STUNNER CAN READILY ATTEST, FINDING SUCH A CURE IS PROVING TO BE FAR MORE ELUSIVE THAN ORIGINALLY ANTICIPATED!
HURRY, OTTO! HE SEEMS TO BE GROWING WEAKER WITH EACH PASSING SECOND!
I DOUBT HE CAN SURVIVE MUCH LONGER!
I WISH I HAD KNOWN HIM IN HIS PRIME...
IT'S SO HARD TO IMAGINE THAT THIS PALE AND FEVER-RAVAGED YOUNG MAN USED TO BE ONE OF THE MOST POWERFUL SUPER-JOCKS OF ALL!
A SAVAGE CONVULSION CHOOSES THAT EXACT MOMENT TO CLAW THROUGH PETER PARKER'S BODY--
--AS HIS MIND IS SUDDENLY PIERCED WITH THE JAGGED SLIVER OF A MEMORY!
AN INCIDENT FROM A PAST WHICH SHOULD NOT BE HIS TO REMEMBER!

THE FORMULA--!
IT ISN'T REACTING AS PREDICTED!
BUT I WILL NOT ACCEPT FAILURE!
NOT HERE!
NOT NOW!
NOT--
--AGAIN!
WHOA, DOC--! SLOW DOWN! YOU'RE PUTTING WAY TOO MUCH PRESSURE ON YOURSELF!
YOU DON'T OWE THIS CLOWN ANYTHING! HE'S ONLY A MACHO VIGILANTE WHO USED TO GET HIS JOLLIES BY TRYING TO POUND THE DAYLIGHTS OUT OF YOU!
NO! OUR RELATIONSHIP GOES MUCH DEEPER!

SPIDER-MAN HAS ALWAYS BEEN MY PERFECT FOIL: COURAGEOUS, DECENT, AND SELF-SACRIFICING!
IN SO MANY WAYS, HE WAS THE MAN I COULD HAVE BEEN...
MIGHT HAVE BEEN...
IF ONLY...
PLEASE DON'T PUT YOURSELF DOWN, DOC!
I LOVE YOU JUST THE WAY YOU ARE!

AND I LOVE YOU, MY DEAR!
JUST AS THERE ARE THOSE WHO LOVE THE MAN BENEATH THE SPIDER'S MASK--

--AND WHO MUST BE WORRIED SICK ABOUT HIM!
RINGGG!
I WONDER WHO COULD BE CALLING--?
I ONLY STOPPED BY MAY'S HOUSE TO PICK UP A FEW NICE NIGHTGOWNS FOR HER!
MAYBE NO ONE ELSE CARES, BUT I KNOW THAT SHE'D CERTAINLY PREFER HER OWN CLOTHES TO A HOSPITAL GOWN!
RINGGG!

GOOD AFTERNOON, DEAR LADY. IS MAY PARKER HOME?
I AM A... BUSINESS ASSOCIATE... OF HER NEPHEW... AND AN OLD FRIEND OF HERS.
WHAT--?!

I'M SORRY TO GIVE YOU SUCH BAD NEWS! MAY RECENTLY SUFFERED A MASSIVE STROKE--

--AND SHE STILL HASN'T REGAINED CONSCIOUSNESS!

FORGIVE ME FOR NOT INTRODUCING MYSELF. I'M ANNA WATSON. I USED TO BE MAY'S NEIGHBOR, AND YOU --HELLO? ARE YOU THERE?!

FROM YOUR EXPRESSION, IT'S SAFE TO ASSUME THAT YOUR CALL TO REASSURE THE FAMILY DID NOT GO AS EXPECTED!

HARDLY.

A VERY DECENT WOMAN I ONCE KNEW IS APPARENTLY DYING.

I SUSPECT THAT THERE IS LITTLE I CAN DO FOR HER--

--ASIDE FROM RENEWING MY EFFORTS TO SAVE THE LIGHT OF HER LIFE!

HOWEVER, I WOULD LIKE TO PAY MY RESPECTS...!

OTTO IS SUCH A CLASS ACT!
HE ASKED ME TO ORDER A LARGE BOUQUET FROM THE LOCAL FLORIST FOR THAT POOR WOMAN!
THAT'S JUST THE KIND OF GALLANT GESTURE I LOVE ABOUT HIM!
SHE IS SO BEAUTIFUL.
A SHAME SHE KEEPS SUCH BAD COMPANY.
I AM KAINE--
--AND I CANNOT... WILL NOT... ALLOW THE LIKES OF OTTO OCTAVIUS TO INTERFERE WITH THE PATH I MUST BLAZE FOR SPIDER-MAN!
THE JOURNEY WE ARE DESTINED TO TAKE WILL BE FRAUGHT WITH TRAGEDY.
MANY WILL SUFFER.
AND EVEN MORE WILL SURELY DIE.

Please don't die!

We need you, May!
Maybe now... more than ever!

Peter has always looked upon you as his rock. His pillar of strength!
You can't imagine how many times you've inspired him to keep fighting in the face of overwhelming adversity.
You're the reason he used to be so wonderful, so responsible.
He's changed recently... and not for the better.

I need the old Peter back! The loving and supportive man I married.
I'm desperate, May. And you're the only one who can help me!
I recently learned something, May. Something which fills me with both joy and terror.
Something which will change our lives forever!

I have no idea how Peter will react to the news.
I don't even know how he feels about me... or our marriage anymore.
Help me, May!
Please help me!
I mustn't lose him.
Especially not now.
I can't lose him!

I WON'T LOSE HIM!
I SWEAR I WON'T!
OTTO! ARE YOU SURE THAT COMPOUND'S GONNA WORK?
NOT COMPLETELY!
BUT THERE'S NO TIME TO TEST IT!
SPIDER-MAN IS ABOUT TO GO INTO CARDIAC ARREST! HE'LL BE DEAD WITHIN THE MINUTE UNLESS I ACT!
SLAMMING INTO PARKER'S BLOODSTREAM WITH ALL THE SUBTLETY OF A NUCLEAR STRIKE, THE RESULTS ARE AS INSTANTANEOUS--
--AS THEY ARE DRAMATIC!
AAAARRGGH!
HIS BODY SPASMS, ERUPTING IN A FIREBALL OF UNRELENTING PAIN--

--AS SEARING IMAGES KALEIDOSCOPE WITHIN HIS EQUALLY TORMENTED MIND.
IMAGES OF ANOTHER LABORATORY.
ANOTHER ESCAPE.
LOOK OUT!
HE BURST FREE OF HIS BONDS--AND HE'S LITERALLY RICOCHETING OFF THE WALLS!
THE PAIN IS DRIVING HIM NUTS!
HE'S REACTING ON INSTINCT ALONE!

STAY BACK, OTTO! HE'S MUCH TOO DANGEROUS IN THIS STATE!
HE'S A MASS OF NAKED AGGRESSION!
ONLY I HAVE THE NECESSARY PHYSICAL STRENGTH TO CORNER HIM, AND--
INTUITIVELY ANSWERING STUNNER'S ATTACK, RESPONDING TO THE WARNING BUZZ OF HIS AMAZING SPIDER-SENSE, PETER PARKER BLINDLY LASHES OUT, AND--
KAWAKK!
URRRGH
STUNNER! MY DARLING--!
EVEN AS DOCTOR OCTOPUS RACES TO THE SIDE OF HIS FALLEN LOVER--
--PETER PARKER MAKES A MAD BOLT FOR FREEDOM!

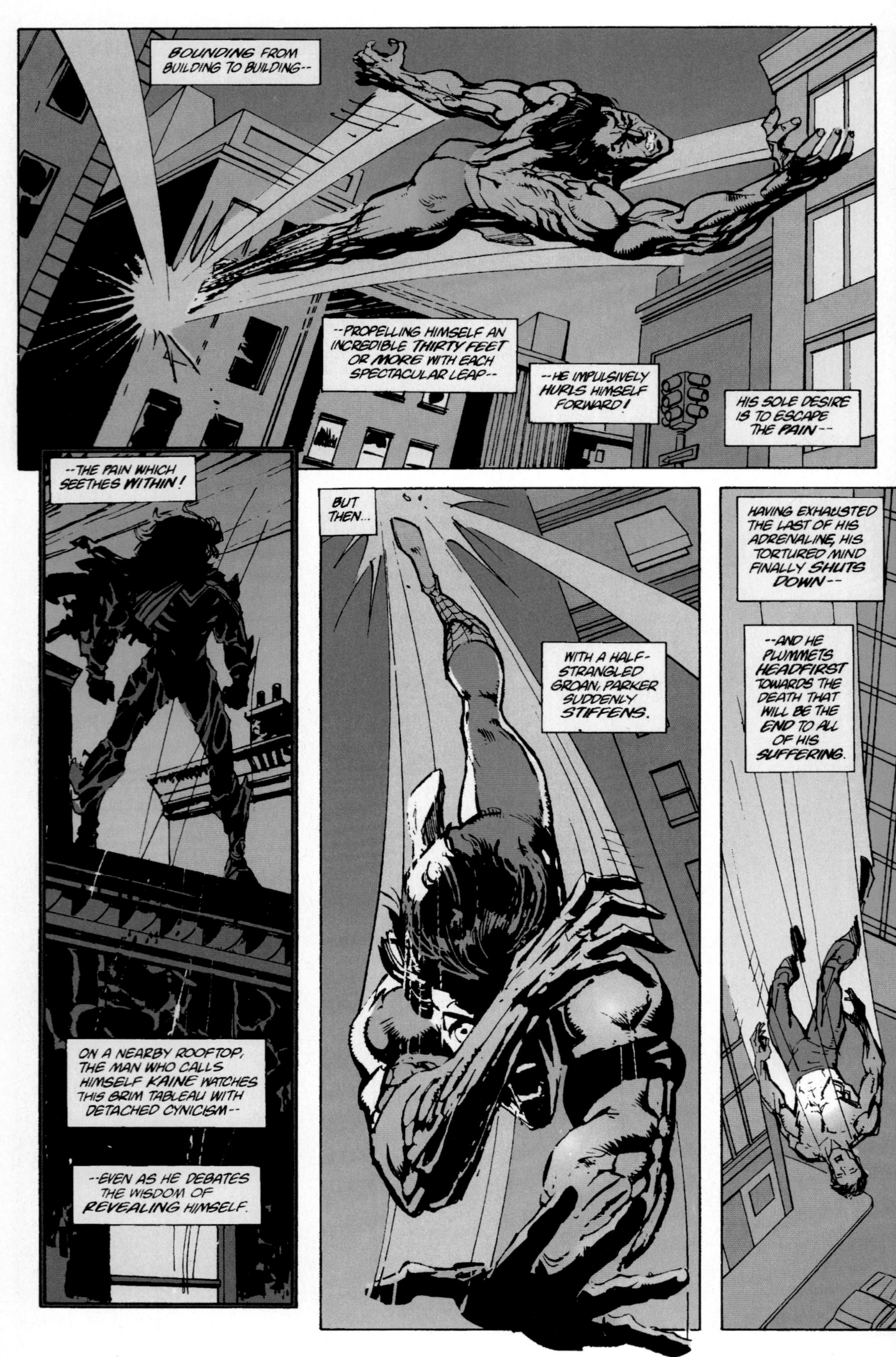
BOUNDING FROM BUILDING TO BUILDING--
--PROPELLING HIMSELF AN INCREDIBLE THIRTY FEET OR MORE WITH EACH SPECTACULAR LEAP--
--HE IMPULSIVELY HURLS HIMSELF FORWARD!
HIS SOLE DESIRE IS TO ESCAPE THE PAIN--
--THE PAIN WHICH SEETHES WITHIN!
ON A NEARBY ROOFTOP, THE MAN WHO CALLS HIMSELF KAINE WATCHES THIS GRIM TABLEAU WITH DETACHED CYNICISM--
--EVEN AS HE DEBATES THE WISDOM OF REVEALING HIMSELF.
BUT THEN...
WITH A HALF-STRANGLED GROAN, PARKER SUDDENLY STIFFENS.
HAVING EXHAUSTED THE LAST OF HIS ADRENALINE, HIS TORTURED MIND FINALLY SHUTS DOWN--
--AND HE PLUMMETS HEADFIRST TOWARDS THE DEATH THAT WILL BE THE END TO ALL OF HIS SUFFERING.

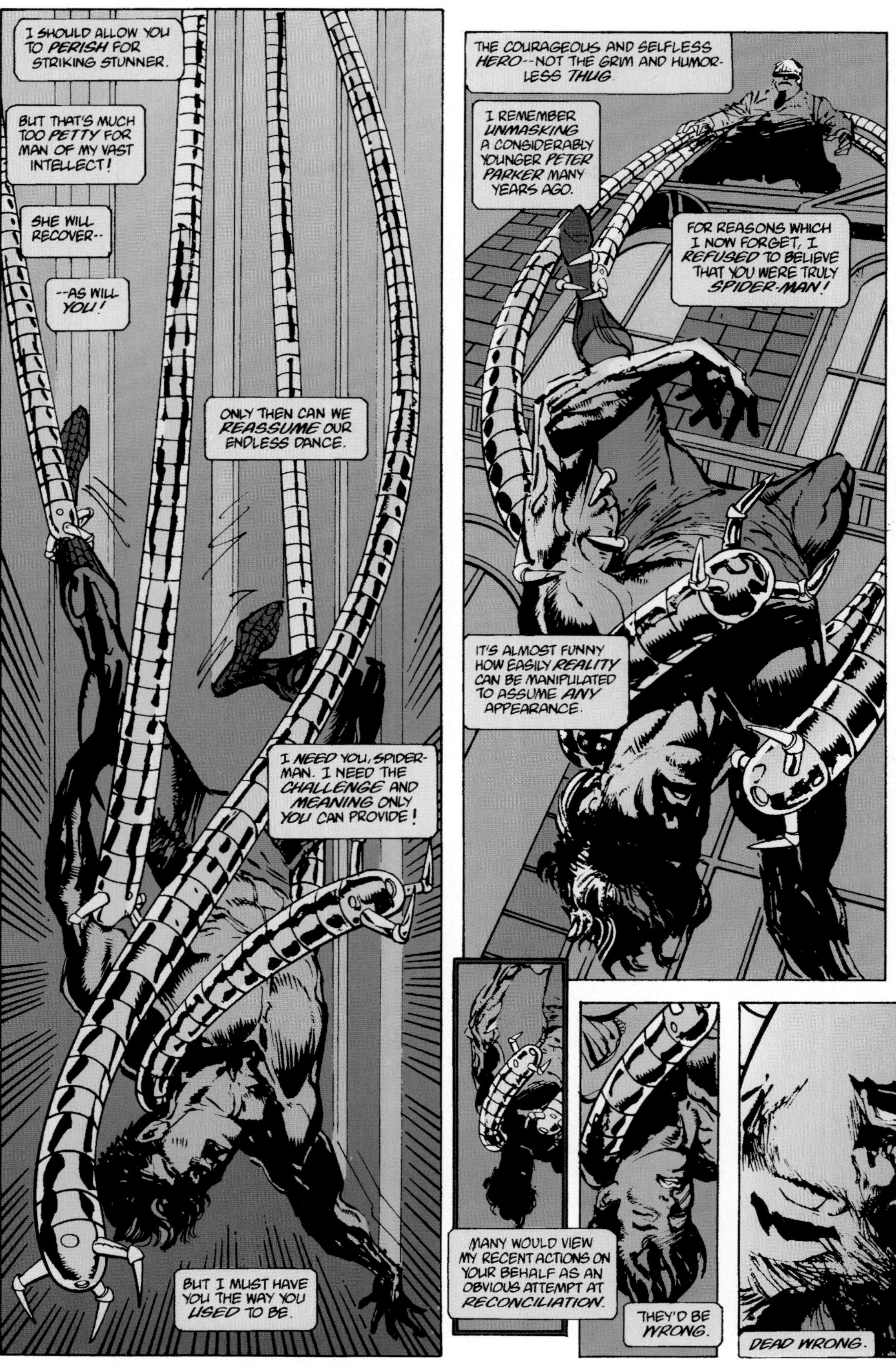

I SHOULD ALLOW YOU TO PERISH FOR STRIKING STUNNER.
BUT THAT'S MUCH TOO PETTY FOR MAN OF MY VAST INTELLECT!
SHE WILL RECOVER--
--AS WILL YOU!
ONLY THEN CAN WE REASSUME OUR ENDLESS DANCE.
I NEED YOU, SPIDER-MAN. I NEED THE CHALLENGE AND MEANING ONLY YOU CAN PROVIDE!
BUT I MUST HAVE YOU THE WAY YOU USED TO BE.
THE COURAGEOUS AND SELFLESS HERO--NOT THE GRIM AND HUMORLESS THUG.
I REMEMBER UNMASKING A CONSIDERABLY YOUNGER PETER PARKER MANY YEARS AGO.
FOR REASONS WHICH I NOW FORGET, I REFUSED TO BELIEVE THAT YOU WERE TRULY SPIDER-MAN!
IT'S ALMOST FUNNY HOW EASILY REALITY CAN BE MANIPULATED TO ASSUME ANY APPEARANCE.
MANY WOULD VIEW MY RECENT ACTIONS ON YOUR BEHALF AS AN OBVIOUS ATTEMPT AT RECONCILIATION.
THEY'D BE WRONG.
DEAD WRONG.

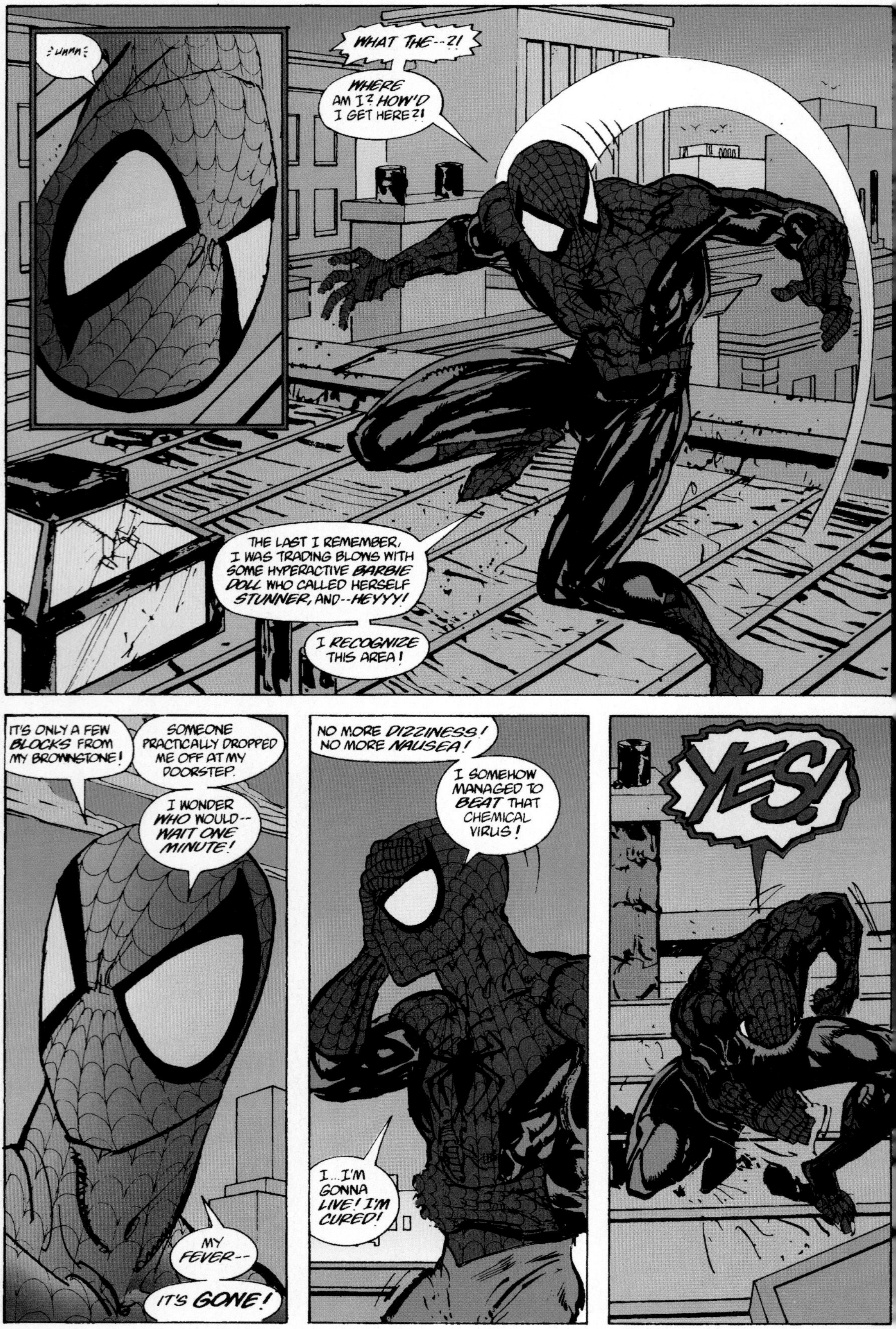

UHNN
WHAT THE--?!
WHERE AM I? HOW'D I GET HERE?!
THE LAST I REMEMBER, I WAS TRADING BLOWS WITH SOME HYPERACTIVE BARBIE DOLL WHO CALLED HERSELF STUNNER, AND--HEYYY!
I RECOGNIZE THIS AREA!

IT'S ONLY A FEW BLOCKS FROM MY BROWNSTONE!
SOMEONE PRACTICALLY DROPPED ME OFF AT MY DOORSTEP.
I WONDER WHO WOULD-- WAIT ONE MINUTE!
MY FEVER--
IT'S GONE!

NO MORE DIZZINESS! NO MORE NAUSEA!
I SOMEHOW MANAGED TO BEAT THAT CHEMICAL VIRUS!
I...I'M GONNA LIVE! I'M CURED!

YES!

YAHOO!
♪ HE FLOATS THROUGH THE AIR WITH THE GREATEST OF EASE-- ♫
♪ THAT DARING YOUNG MAN IN HIS WEBBED UP JAM-EES! ♪
I'M BACK!
I'M REAL-LEE BACK!
NO MORE DOUBTS! NO MORE REGRETS!
THE DARK AND MOODY SPIDER IS FINALLY GONE
--AND ONLY THE FRIENDLY NEIGHBORHOOD WEB-SLINGER REMAINS!

AND EVEN AS THE EVER-AMAZING ONE FROLICS IN HIS NEWFOUND HEALTH--
--A SOMEWHAT MORE SEDATE AND PENSIVE MARY JANE LIKEWISE HEADS FOR HOME!
HOW WILL PETER REACT TO MY ANNOUNCEMENT?
WILL HE BE HAPPY? SAD?! THRILLED OR PANICKED?!
WHY AM I EVEN WORRYING? WHO KNOWS WHEN I'LL EVER GET THE CHANCE TO TELL HIM?!
YOU ARE ALSO QUITE BEAUTIFUL, MRS. PARKER.
UNFORTUNATELY, I ALSO HAVE AN ISSUE WITH THE COMPANY YOU KEEP.
SEEING YOU IN THIS FASHION...SO FRAGILE, SO VULNERABLE...!
KNOWING THE MIRACULOUS SECRET WHICH YOU SHALL SOON REVEAL--!
I TRULY WISH I COULD GUARANTEE YOUR SURVIVAL.
ALAS...
I CANNOT!

Home sweet home!
It's GREAT to be alive, but I still wish I could RECALL what happened!
My mind keeps FLASHING to these weird images--
--I see someone (who IS he?!) floating within a big VAT...
Me, I'm strapped to an OPERATING TABLE, and the attending physician is none other than DOCTOR OCTOPUS!
DOCTOR OCTOPUS?!
HA! Like he WOULDN'T take total advantage of my helplessness!
But...
NAH! It must have been an HALLUCINATION caused by the virus!
whew! I desperately need a HOT SHOWER and some CLEAN CLOTHES.
I've been LIVING in this costume so long ...it's almost like I'm SHEDDING a second skin.
Much better!
I'd almost forgotten how good it feels to be plain ol' PETER PARKER.
I just hope I can find a way to SALVAGE the remnants of my personal life.
Should I start by visiting AUNT MAY at the hospital--
--or do I try to track down my errant WIFE?
Poor MARY JANE! Do I even have the nerve to beg her FORGIVE-NESS after the way I've acted?!
WAIT! Someone's at the door--!

Ohmigosh! I never expected to find Peter here!
What should I say to him? How can I even begin to repair the rift between us?!
That LOOK in her eyes--!
Is she just SURPRISED to see me--
--or have I hurt her so DEEPLY that she can't even bear the sight of me?!
He... he's turning away!
He hates me! It's my own fault for deserting him when he most needed me!
Maybe I should go. There's no need to prolong his agony.
No reason he should suffer for my mistakes.
And yet...
Do we have any hope of getting past all the hurts and disappointments?
Isn't there ANY WAY we can excuse the words spoken in hasty ANGER... without THOUGHT or MERCY?!
Isn't there any possibility of forgiveness--
--or any CHANCE of rebuilding our love?!

Oh, God...
YES!!

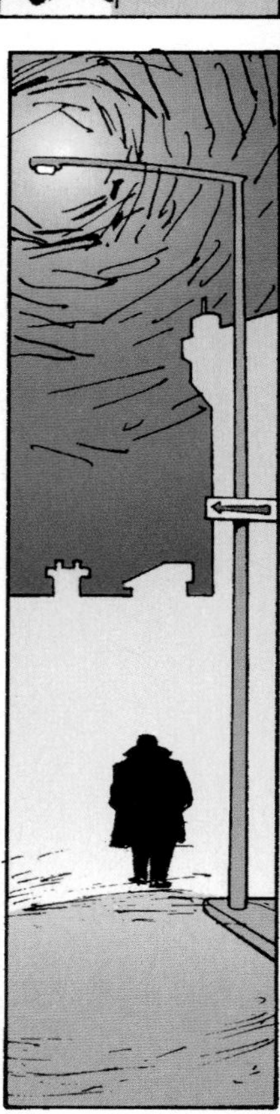

The Food may not rank HIGHLY as a gourmet Feast...
The same can easily be said for our libation of choice...
But the LIGHTS are soft and low...
...and the music is SINATRA at his moody best!
ORANGE JUICE
ORANGE JUICE
The JOURNEY has been hard and costly.
We have each stared into our own ABYSS.
But the WORST is Finally over!
Tonight we'll DANCE into the wee hours, LUXURIATING in wonder of our love!
Tonight we'll renew our VOWS, strengthening the TIES which bind us so closely!
And maybe...
Just MAYBE...
We'll Finally Find a way to live happily ever after!

NO!
IT ISN'T POSSIBLE! IT ISN'T FAIR!
OTTO--!
WHAT'S WRONG, MY DARLING? WHY ARE YOU SO UPSET?!
I JUST FINISHED TESTING MY ANTIDOTE!
THE FINAL RESULTS CANNOT BE DENIED!
I...
...FAILED!
MY SERUM WILL ONLY MASK THE SYMPTOMS FOR A FEW HOURS...
I DOUBT IT WILL CARRY ALL THE WAY UNTIL MORNING!
I don't get it! My head's POUNDING like a hyperactive drummer!
Why would I WAKE to such a hangover unless... THE VIRUS!
It's BACK... and SO is my memory!
DOCTOR OCTOPUS did this to me!
He somehow managed to give me a new LEASE on life... even if it was only temporary!
I'll never know if he really TRIED to cure me... or if I hallucinated the whole thing.

The FACT remains that I'm DYING!
I'm still DYING!
I've got to tell Mary Jane ...but HOW?
HOW?!

HOW do I break the news to him?
HOW do I make my announcement?
HOW?!

MARY JANE...
THERE'S SOMETHING YOU SHOULD KNOW!
SOMETHING REAL IMPORTANT!
FUNNY YOU SHOULD SAY THAT, TIGER...

...I'VE SPENT THE LAST FEW MINUTES ...SCREWING UP MY COURAGE... SO THAT I COULD SHARE SOME PRESSING NEWS WITH YOU AS WELL!

WHO SHOULD SPEAK FIRST?
THE FLOOR IS ALL YOURS, PRETTY LADY!
OKAY, HERE GOES...

CONGRATULATIONS, TIGER! YOU HIT ANOTHER JACKPOT!
YOU'RE ABOUT TO BECOME A FATHER!
WE'RE HAVING A BABY!
"WEB OF DEATH" CONTINUES IN AMAZING SPIDER-MAN #398! (FEATURING A STARTLING SHOCK ENDING!)
THEN IT CONCLUDES HERE NEXT MONTH AS WE BID A FINAL FAREWELL TO A CHARACTER YOU HAVE KNOWN FOR OVER THIRTY YEARS! TRUST US, YOU WON'T WANT TO MISS... "A TIME TO DIE!"

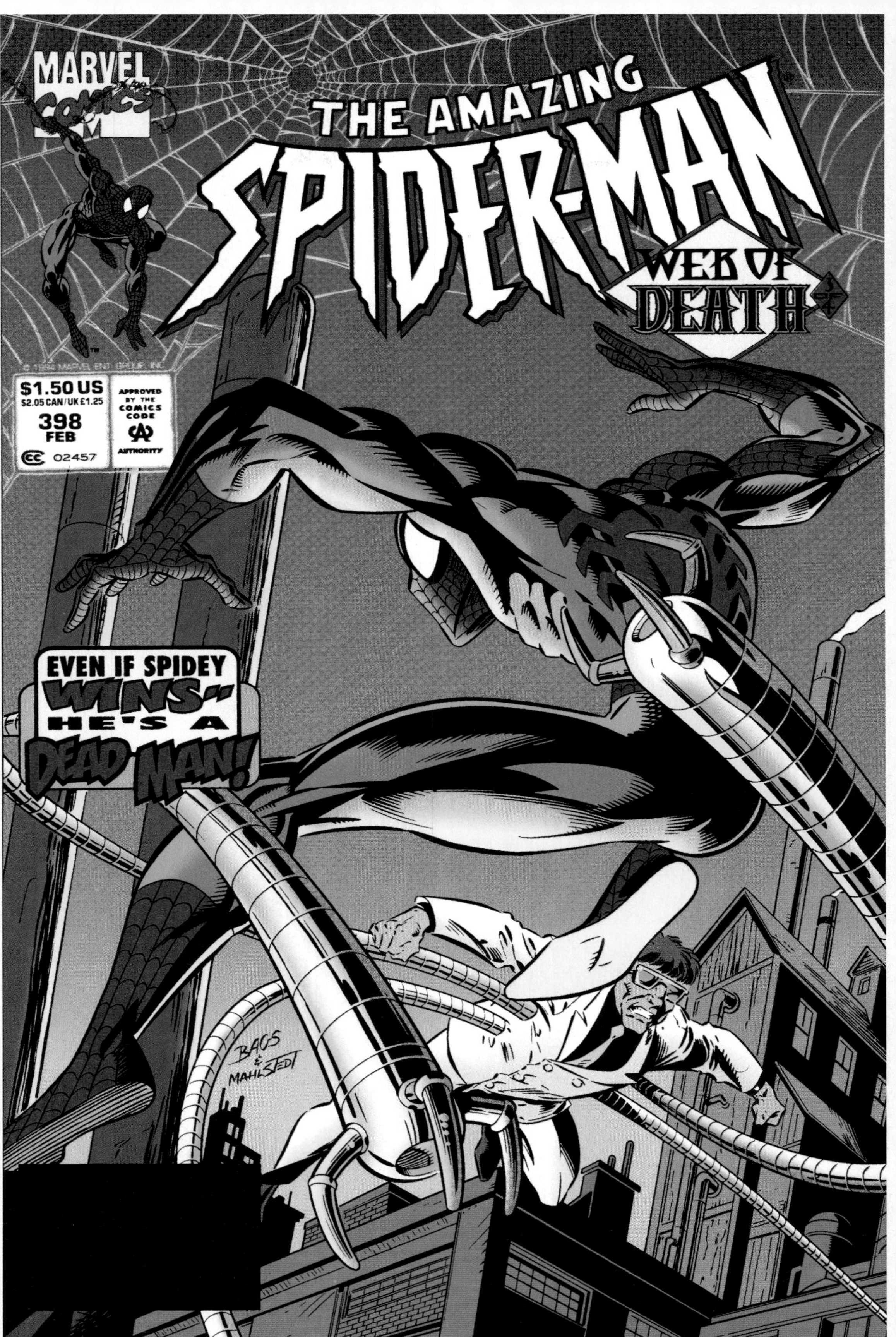

MARVEL COMICS
THE AMAZING
SPIDER-MAN
WEB OF DEATH
3 of 4
© 1994 MARVEL ENT. GROUP, INC.
$1.50 US
$2.05 CAN/UK £1.25
398
FEB
02457
APPROVED BY THE COMICS CODE AUTHORITY
EVEN IF SPIDEY WINS..
HE'S A
DEAD MAN!
BAGS & MAHLSTEDT

BITTEN BY A RADIOACTIVE SPIDER, STUDENT **PETER PARKER** GAINED THE PROPORTIONATE STRENGTH AND AGILITY OF AN ARACHNID! ARMED WITH HIS WONDROUS WEB-SHOOTERS, THE RELUCTANT SUPER HERO STRUGGLES WITH SINISTER SUPER-VILLAINS, MAKING ENDS MEET, AND MAINTAINING SOME SEMBLANCE OF A NORMAL LIFE!

Stan Lee PRESENTS: THE AMAZING SPIDER-MAN®

Manhattan's Upper East Side...
YOU'VE DONE WELL FOR YOURSELF, PARKER.
A BEAUTIFUL HOME. A GORGEOUS WIFE.
IT'S AN EXISTENCE MOST MEN WOULD ENVY. AND YET IT'S NOT ENOUGH FOR YOU, IS IT?
YOU NEED THE MASK, THE MISSION. YOU NEED SPIDER-MAN...
...ALMOST AS MUCH AS I NEED...
...DOCTOR OCTOPUS.
OF COURSE, THAT'S WHERE THE SIMILARITY BETWEEN US ENDS. TIME AND AGAIN, YOU'VE PROVEN YOUR DEDICATION TO--ONE MIGHT EVEN SAY OBSESSION WITH--DOING WHAT'S RIGHT.
MINDLES SCRIBBLIN IGNORE IT.
A TRUE HERO--READY TO SACRIFICE YOURSELF AND THIS PRECIOUS LIFE OF YOURS. READY TO DIE--IN THE NAME OF SIMPLE HUMAN DECENCY.
IS IT DEATH YOU TRULY WANT, MY OLD ENEMY? BECAUSE, IF IT IS... THEN THE DAY MAY HAVE FINALLY ARRIVED...

...WHEN YOUR WISH COMES TRUE.
WE'RE GOING TO HAVE A WHAT?!!
WEB OF DEATH PART THREE:
BEFORE I WAKE
J. M. DEMATTEIS WRITER • MARK BAGLEY PENCILER • LARRY MAHLSTEDT INKER • BILL OAKLEY LETTERER • BOB SHAREN COLORIST • DANNY FINGEROTH EDITOR • TOM DEFALCO EDITOR IN CHIEF

A BABY.
A BABY--?!
YA-
HOOOO!!
A baby!
New life! New HOPE!
After all these months of pain... this is the best news I could have ever ASKED for.
A BABY!
Finally! A whole new beginning for the Parkers! Even AUNT MAY...
...she can't die... she WON'T die! She's got to live to see our child! She--

SHE'S got to live?
What about ME?
For a little while there, it seemed as if I'd shaken off the effects of that VIRUS the Vulture infected me with... *
* IN AMAZING #396.-Danny
...but I'm feeling it all coming back again: the fever. The chills. The tightness in my throat, the aching in my muscles.
I'M the one who's dying. Now...
...when I want SO MUCH to live!
What am I going to do? What am I going to tell MARY JANE?
PETER--?
WHAT IS IT, HON? WHAT'S WRONG?
I KNOW THINGS HAVE BEEN HARD LATELY... AND WE'RE CERTAINLY NOT IN THE BEST SHAPE FINANCIALLY, BUT--
THAT DOESN'T MATTER, SWEETHEART.
WE'RE GOING TO HAVE A BABY.
YOU AND I... WE CREATED A LIFE. WE MADE A MIRACLE!
AND NOTHING'S GOING TO TAKE THAT JOY AWAY FROM US, DO YOU HEAR ME?
NOTHING!

PETER...? YOU FEEL WARM, HONEY.
ARE YOU RUNNING A *FEVER*?
Nah... I'M FINE. NEVER BEEN BETTER.

THINK I'LL JUMP IN THE SHOWER AND THEN WE CAN HEAD OVER TO THE HOSPITAL AND SEE AUNT MAY.
THEY SAY PEOPLE CAN ACTUALLY *HEAR* YOU WHEN THEY'RE IN A COMA... AND WE'VE JUST *GOT* TO TELL HER THE GOOD NEWS.

I LOVE YOU, MARY JANE. WITH ALL MY HEART.
WITH EVERY CELL IN MY BODY.
AND I'LL LOVE YOU TILL THE DAY I DIE.

He's so happy. After all he's been through, he's finally free!
And I'm happy, too. I really am.

But I can't help wondering... worrying...
...about our child.

When that irradiated spider bit Peter and gave him his incredible powers...
...it somehow mutated his metabolism.
It doesn't seem to have harmed my husband in any way...

...but what about my baby?

What about my baby?
YOU CAN HEAR ME, AUNT MAY.

I BELIEVE THAT WITH ALL MY HEART.
SO YOU LISTEN TO ME. YOU LISTEN TO EVERY WORD.
Forest Hills Hospital.

YOU'VE GOT TO COME BACK TO US. YOU'VE GOT TO BE WITH YOUR FAMILY.
OUR BABY... OUR BABY HAS TO KNOW YOU--

I WON'T TAKE NO FOR AN ANSWER, MAY PARKER. I REFUSE TO LET YOU SLIP AWAY FROM US.
SO WHEREVER YOU ARE... YOU JUST FOLLOW MY VOICE... AND COME HOME. PLEASE, AUNT MAY... I'M BEGGING YOU--

--COME HOME.
Peter...?

It's good to hear your voice. Sweet... comforting.
But you're so distant... so far away from...

...HERE?
WHERE AM I?

Not a place, really. Just warmth and light and memory.
Time and feeling, faces and events, drifting lazily around me.

I LIKE it here, Peter. No weight on my shoulders. No struggle. No pain. I've had ENOUGH pain in my life... don't you think?
Oh, I could drift here forever... cocooned in these warm yesterdays.

But your VOICE--!
It's got such a HOLD on me. TETHERS me to the world.

Keeps me from drifting too far.
I don't know what to do, Peter: come back to you or pass on.
Slip down, into the world --or sail off...

...INTO FOREVER.

TO US.
KLINK
TO US.
WHEN'S THE LAST TIME WE DID THIS? GOT ALL DRESSED UP AND CAME TO DECARLO'S FOR A ROMANTIC DINNER?
TOO LONG, LOVER. MUCH TOO--
Manhattan.
uhhhhh...
KRAAK
PETER...?!
I... I'M ALL RIGHT. JUST GOT... A LITTLE DIZZY THERE FOR A SECOND...
Yeah. Right. Lie to your wife without missing a beat.
SIR...? ARE YOU ALL RIGHT, SIR?
Truth is, I feel like every atom in my body's on fire. It's all I can do not to SCREAM from the pain.
GET THIS MAN SOME WATER... QUICK! AND GET SOMEONE TO CLEAN UP THIS BROKEN GLASS--
RIGHT AWAY--
Getting a buzz from my spider-sense... very slight. But the way I'm feeling right now, it might just be a reaction to the VIRUS or...
WEIRD.
MA'AM... I THINK YOU'D BETTER GET YOUR HUSBAND HOME. HE'S NOT LOOKING VERY WELL.
I THINK I WILL. THANK YOU FOR YOUR CONCERN.
YOU KNOW, WE'VE BEEN COMING TO DECARLO'S FOR YEARS. WE KNOW THE WHOLE STAFF... BUT I DON'T THINK I'VE EVER SEEN YOU BEFORE.

GOOD NIGHT TO YOU, MRS. PARKER. AND GOD BLESS YOU BOTH.
MRS. PARKER...? HOW DOES HE--?
SPIDER-SENSE going again...
WHEN DID YOU START WORKING HERE?
OH, NO, MA'AM... YOU'RE MISTAKEN. I DON'T WORK HERE.
BUT...?
NOW GET YOUR HUSBAND RIGHT HOME.
...more INTENSE this time.
And THERE'S the reason why!
OCTOPUS!
I wasn't sure if I'd REALLY encountered him earlier... if he'd really UNMASKED me... or if it was just a Fever-dream.*
BUT THAT'S NO DREAM.
*SPECTACULAR SPIDER-MAN #220--Danny.
MJ-- DARLIN'--I'VE GOT TO GO--
WHAT? WHERE?
THERE'S SOMETHING I HAVE TO TAKE CARE OF. I WON'T BE LONG.
I SWEAR.
PETER... YOU'VE JUST COME BACK TO ME--
--YOU CAN'T RUN AWAY AGAIN--!
I HAVE TO.

I'VE BEEN THROUGH THIS BEFORE.

VENOM... PUMA... THE GREEN GOBLIN--

--INVADING MY PERSONAL LIFE... THREATENING THE PEOPLE I LOVE!

I'M NOT GOING TO GO THROUGH IT AGAIN.

NOW-- MORE THAN EVER-- I WANT MY FAMILY--

--I WANT MY LIFE--

--AND I WON'T SEE IT DESTROYED BY THE LIKES OF YOU!!

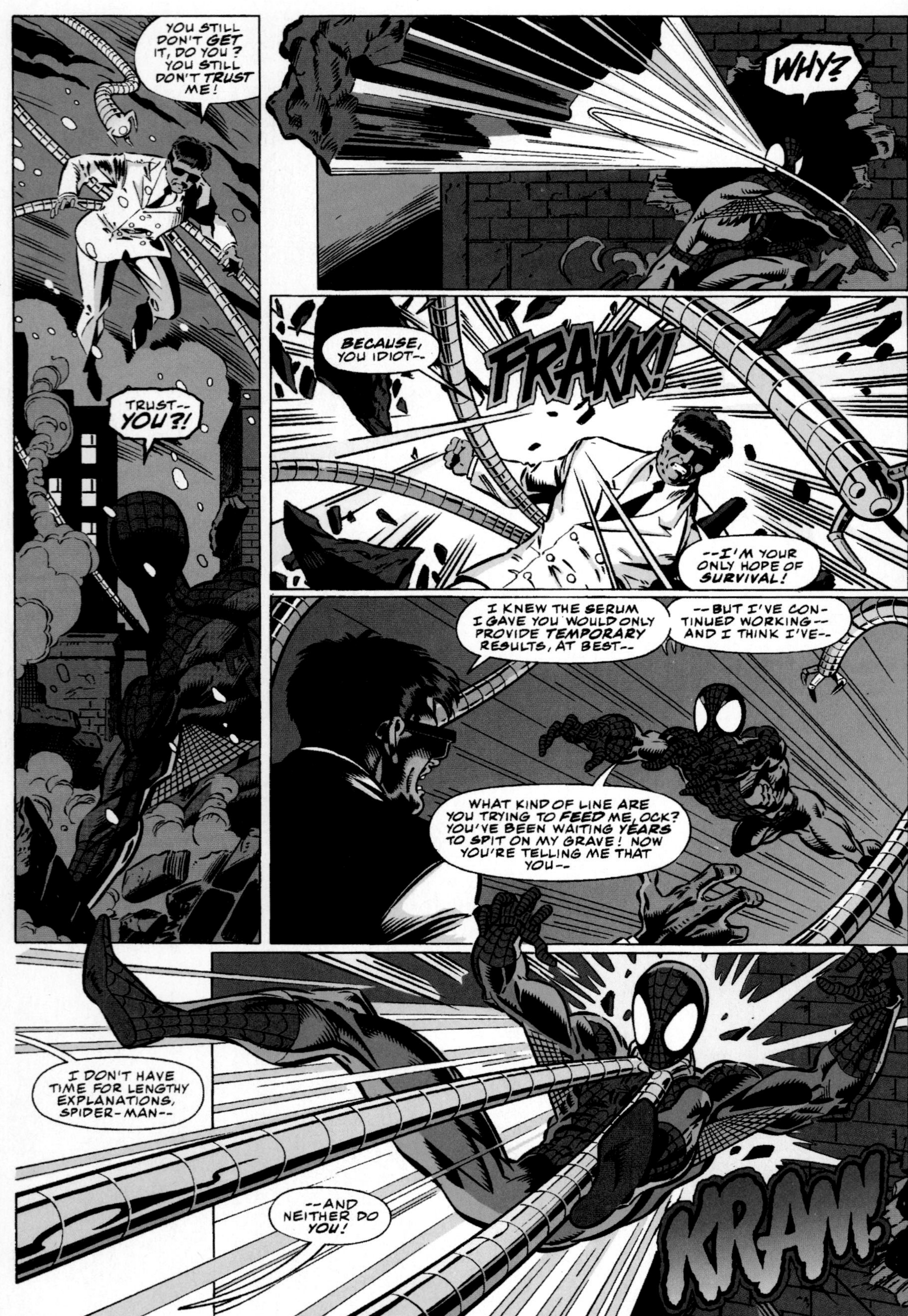
YOU STILL DON'T GET IT, DO YOU? YOU STILL DON'T TRUST ME!
TRUST-- YOU?!
WHY?
BECAUSE, YOU IDIOT--
FRAKK!
--I'M YOUR ONLY HOPE OF SURVIVAL!
I KNEW THE SERUM I GAVE YOU WOULD ONLY PROVIDE TEMPORARY RESULTS, AT BEST--
--BUT I'VE CONTINUED WORKING-- AND I THINK I'VE--
WHAT KIND OF LINE ARE YOU TRYING TO FEED ME, OCK? YOU'VE BEEN WAITING YEARS TO SPIT ON MY GRAVE! NOW YOU'RE TELLING ME THAT YOU--
I DON'T HAVE TIME FOR LENGTHY EXPLANATIONS, SPIDER-MAN--
--AND NEITHER DO YOU!
KRAM!

YOU'VE ONLY GOT DAYS--
--PERHAPS HOURS--
--LEFT TO LIVE!
NOW LISTEN TO ME!

I'M NOT HERE TO HURT YOU... I'M HERE TO SAVE YOU!
DON'T YOU UNDER-STAND?
I'VE FOUND THE CURE!!

your lab... I--I REMEMBER... I WAS in your lab, wasn't I? and you were trying to--
BUT I DON'T UNDERSTAND. WHY WOULD YOU WANT TO HELP ME?

BECAUSE YOU'VE PROVIDED A CERTAIN... CONTINUITY IN MY LIFE. A CERTAIN CHALLENGE. A CERTAIN--
--INSPIRATION.

I NEED YOU, PARKER.
NOT THE GRIM AND RELENTLESS SPIDER, BUT THE MAN WHO'S DANCED WITH ME ON THE EDGE OF A PRECIPICE... DOWN THROUGH THE LONG AND EVENTFUL YEARS.

NOW, COME--LET'S GET TO WORK--
--SO WE CAN BEGIN THE DANCE ANEW.

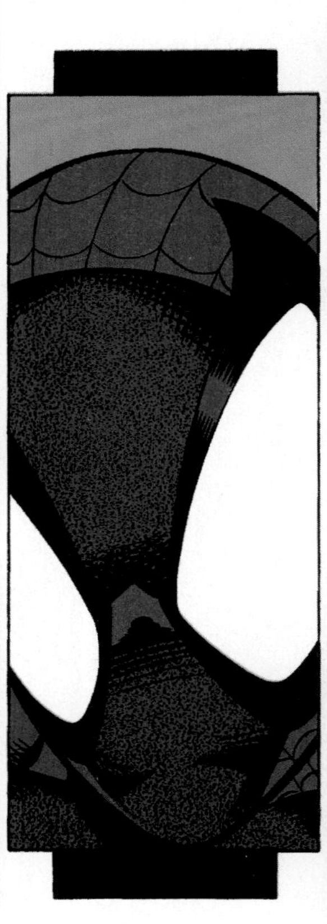

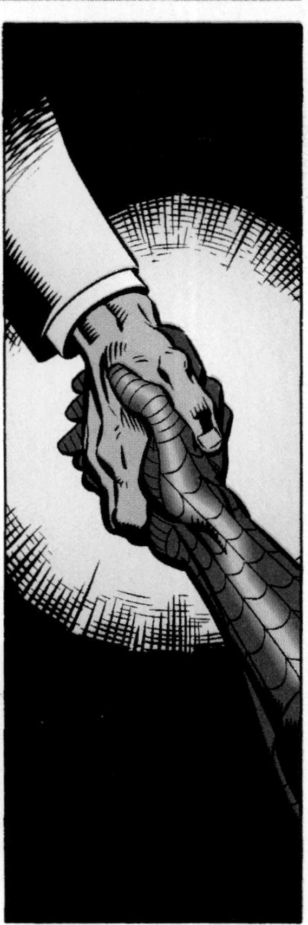

Central Park.
I'M NOT THE KIND OF WOMAN WHO SMOTHERS A MAN... WON'T GIVE HIM SPACE. OTTO CAN HAVE ALL THE SPACE HE WANTS...
...AS LONG AS IT'S ME HE SNUGGLES UP WITH AT THE END OF THE DAY.
OTTO NEEDS TIME ALONE TO WORK OUT THIS SPIDER-MAN THING. HE CAN HAVE IT.
BESIDES, WHY WOULD I WANT TO BE COOPED UP IN THAT STUFFY LAB WHEN I CAN BE OUT HERE...
...BREATHING IN COLD, FRESH AIR... FEELING THE SNOW ON MY SKIN... TESTING MY BOUNDARIES...
...PUSHING MY LIMITS?
RAK!
IS THIS FUN OR WHAT?

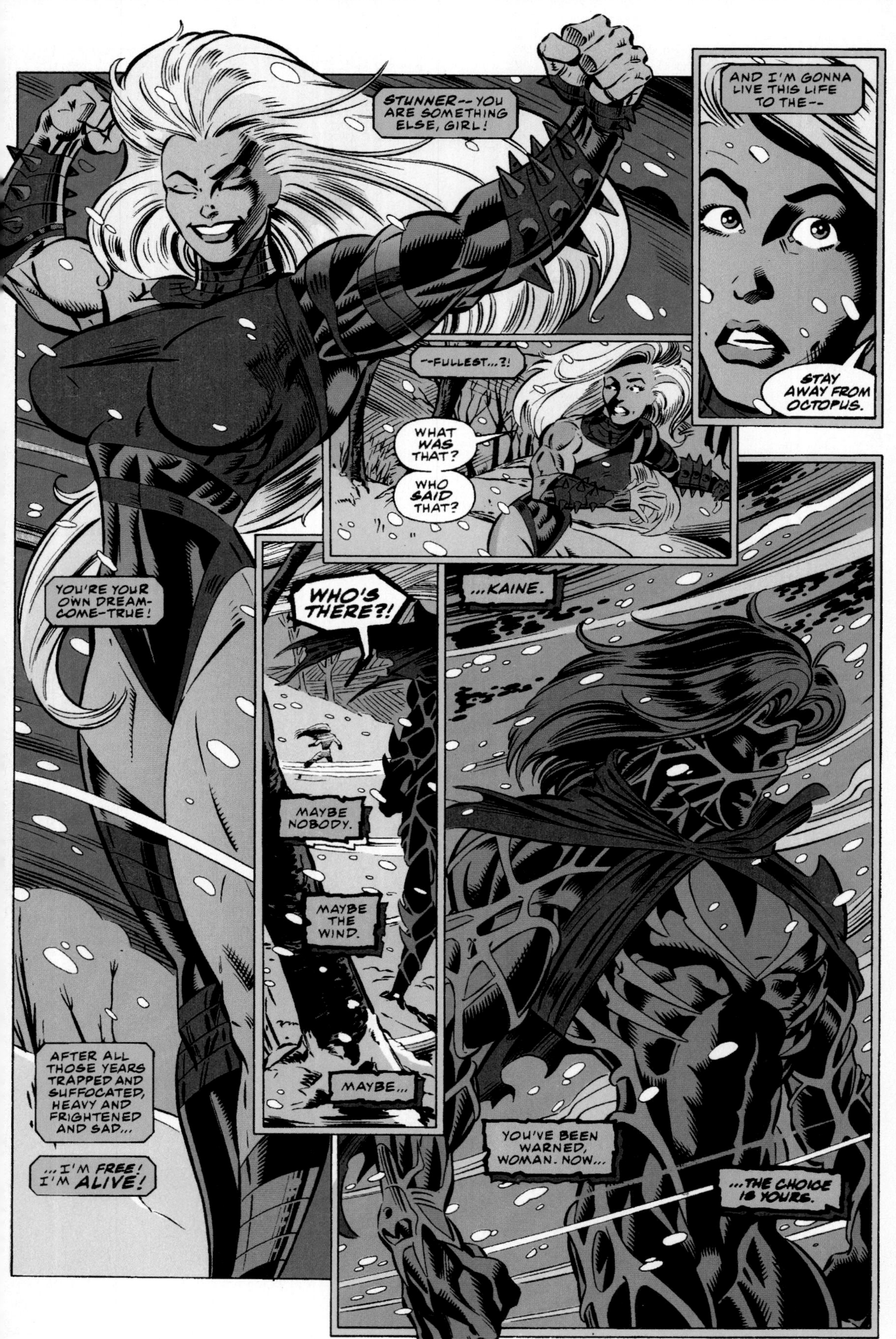
STUNNER-- YOU ARE SOMETHING ELSE, GIRL!
YOU'RE YOUR OWN DREAM-COME-TRUE!
AFTER ALL THOSE YEARS TRAPPED AND SUFFOCATED, HEAVY AND FRIGHTENED AND SAD...
...I'M FREE! I'M ALIVE!
AND I'M GONNA LIVE THIS LIFE TO THE--
--FULLEST...?!
STAY AWAY FROM OCTOPUS.
WHAT WAS THAT?
WHO SAID THAT?
WHO'S THERE?!
MAYBE NOBODY.
MAYBE THE WIND.
MAYBE...
...KAINE.
YOU'VE BEEN WARNED, WOMAN. NOW...
...THE CHOICE IS YOURS.

Somewhere beneath Manhattan.
THE VIRAL CELL STRUCTURE IS BREAKING DOWN. THE BLOOD SAMPLE HAS BEEN PURIFIED.
RUN THE TEST AGAIN.
WE'VE RUN IT A DOZEN TIMES.
BUT THE TEST IS JUST THAT. THE ONLY WAY WE'LL KNOW FOR CERTAIN IF THE ANTIDOTE IS SUCCESSFUL--
--IS IF YOU INGEST IT.
BUT YOU DON'T WANT TO DO THAT-- DO YOU?--
--BECAUSE YOU STILL DON'T TRUST ME.
I CAN'T SAY THAT I BLAME YOU. AFTER ALL, IF I WERE IN YOUR SHOES, I'D REACT IN EXACTLY THE SAME MANNER.
BUT THEN, YOU'RE A BETTER MAN THAN I AM, PETER PARKER... OR AT LEAST YOU WERE ONCE.
HAVE YOU FALLEN THAT FAR? DON'T YOU HAVE MORE FAITH IN YOUR FELLOW MAN THAN OTTO OCTAVIUS DOES?
Ah, WELL--
--I SUPPOSE I HAVE NO CHOICE BUT TO DESTROY THIS--AND LEAVE YOU TO YOUR OWN DEVICES.

A SUDDEN BURST OF FAITH--
--OR PERHAPS JUST... DESPERATION?
I SUPPOSE IT DOESN'T MATTER-- SINCE ONE GROWS OUT OF THE OTHER.
HERE, MY DEAR ENEMY--
--DRINK LONG. DRINK WELL.
I KNOW YOU DON'T BELIEVE THIS--
--BUT I WISH YOU NOTHING BUT THE BEST.
NO!

HEY... Y'KNOW SOMETHING? I THINK I'M STARTING TO FEEL BETTER ALREAD--
EEEEEEE

WHERE AM I?!
I feel like I've been sucked up... out of my body... into...
Into WHAT?
That's the city down there... but up here... the wind... screaming with a human voice... light and color, pulsing and swirling all around me...
...and over there--

PEOPLE...?
No. They're SOULS. I know it. (I don't know HOW I know it, but I DO!)
Souls of the DEAD.
But... if THEY'RE dead... then I must be--

NO!
This can't be real! (Can it?) This isn't happening! (Is it?)
All these years... I've faced death dozens of times... and I've always cheated it! I've always ESCAPED!
THIS CAN'T BE HAPPENING!!
OH, PLEASE, PARKER--SPARE US THE HISTRIONICS.

NICK KATZENBERG?!
THE LATE, GREAT NICK KATZENBERG.
GET THAT SHOCKED LOOK OFF YOUR FACE, PARKER. BEING DEAD'S NO BIG DEAL. Y' HANG AROUND THE LOWER ASTRAL PLANE FOR A WHILE... ADJUSTING TO YOUR NEW, NON-CORPOREAL STATUS--THEN UP Y'GO--
--WELL, Y'HOPE YOU'RE GOIN' UP--
--INTO THE LIGHT.
NO! I CAN'T DIE NOW! I'VE GOT TOO MUCH TO LIVE FOR!
Y'THINK THE REST OF US DIDN'T?
LOOK, KID, WE COME, WE GO... IT'S THE NATURE OF THE GAME.
EVERYONE'S GOTTA DIE SOMETIME.
WHAT MAKES YOU THINK YOU'RE ANY BETTER'N THE REST OF US?
I'M NOT DEAD!
I'M NOT!
I'M NOT!
Somebody... please... HELP me!
Help me make sense of this before I go insane!
PETER...?
THIS WAY, PETER.
That VOICE--!

AUNT MAY...?
No. It couldn't have been her. She's still in the COMA. Still beyond my reach.
Oh, but if only you WERE here, Aunt May.
You've guided me through the best of times... carried me through the worst.
I CAN SAY THE SAME OF YOU.
AND THAT'S WHY--
--I CAN'T TURN AWAY FROM YOU NOW!
AUNT MAY! IT WAS YOU!
YOU SHOULDN'T BE HERE, PETER.
BUT I DON'T KNOW WHERE ELSE TO TURN.
YOU HAVE A DESTINY. A JOURNEY TO MAKE.
A JOURNEY I CAN'T TAKE WITH YOU... MUCH AS I'D LIKE TO.
WHERE, AUNT MAY? WHERE AM I SUPPOSED TO GO?
REMEMBER WHEN YOU WERE LITTLE, PETER... SO UPSET, SO WOUNDED AFTER HAVING LOST YOUR PARENTS?
REMEMBER HOW YOU LOVED HEARING THE TALE OF THAT OTHER LOST BOY NAMED PETER... AND HIS ADVENTURES IN NEVERLAND?
I... I DO. BUT-- I DON'T UNDERSTAND WHAT--

"SECOND TO THE RIGHT--
"--AND STRAIGHT ON TILL MORNING."

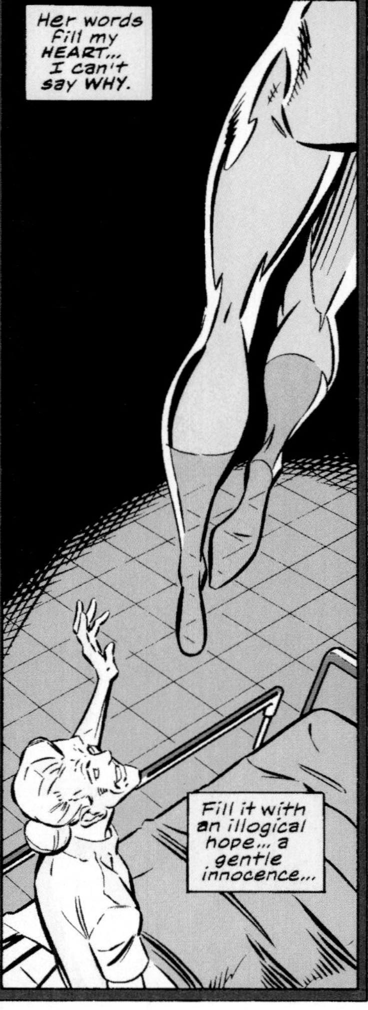
Her words fill my HEART... I can't say WHY.
Fill it with an illogical hope... a gentle innocence...

...a FAITH in life...
...and all that lies BEYOND it.

So I wave farewell and I let the soul winds carry me up.
And I let Aunt May's words lead me on --to my final DESTINATION.

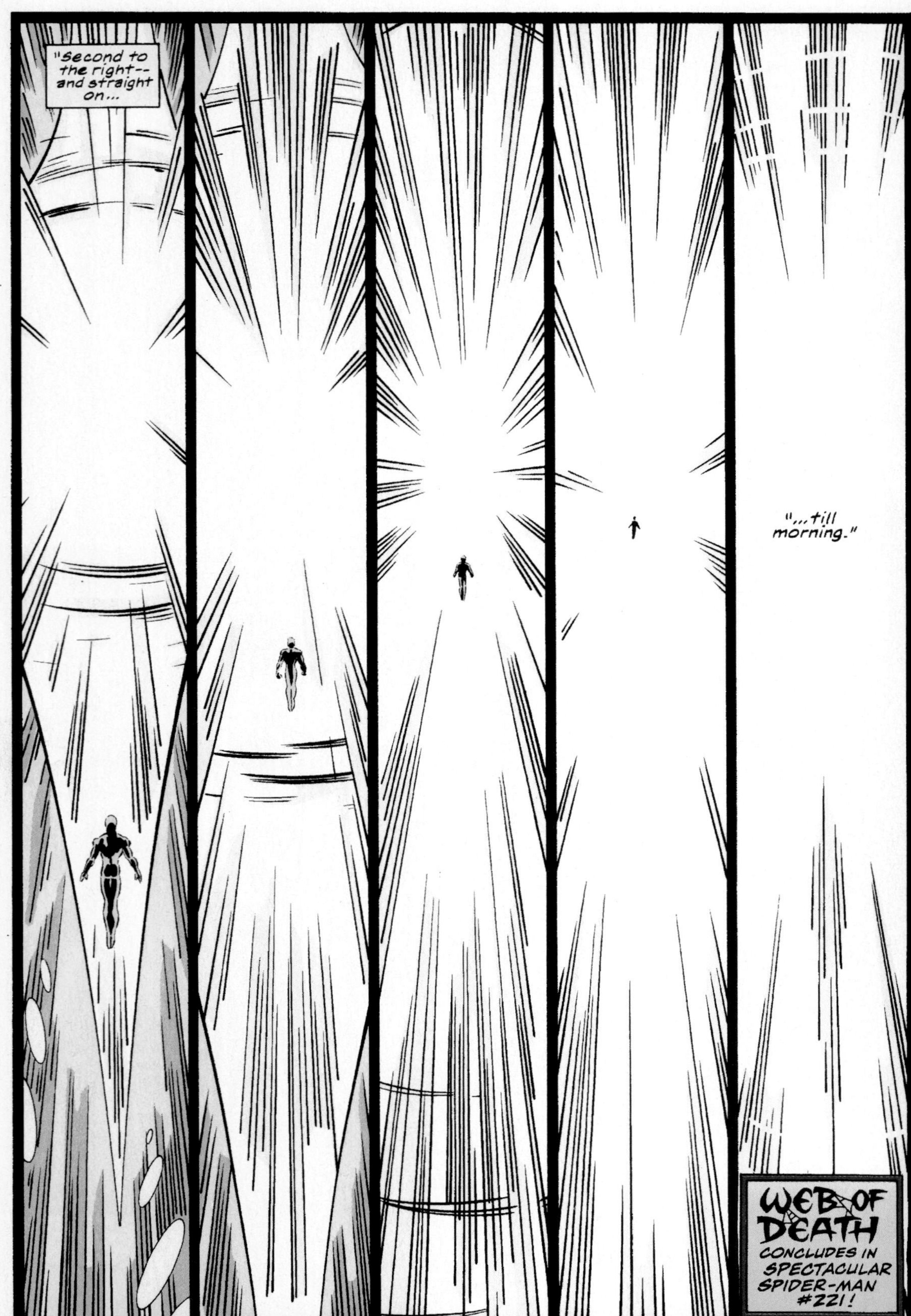
"Second to the right-- and straight on...
"...till morning."
WEB OF DEATH CONCLUDES IN SPECTACULAR SPIDER-MAN #221!

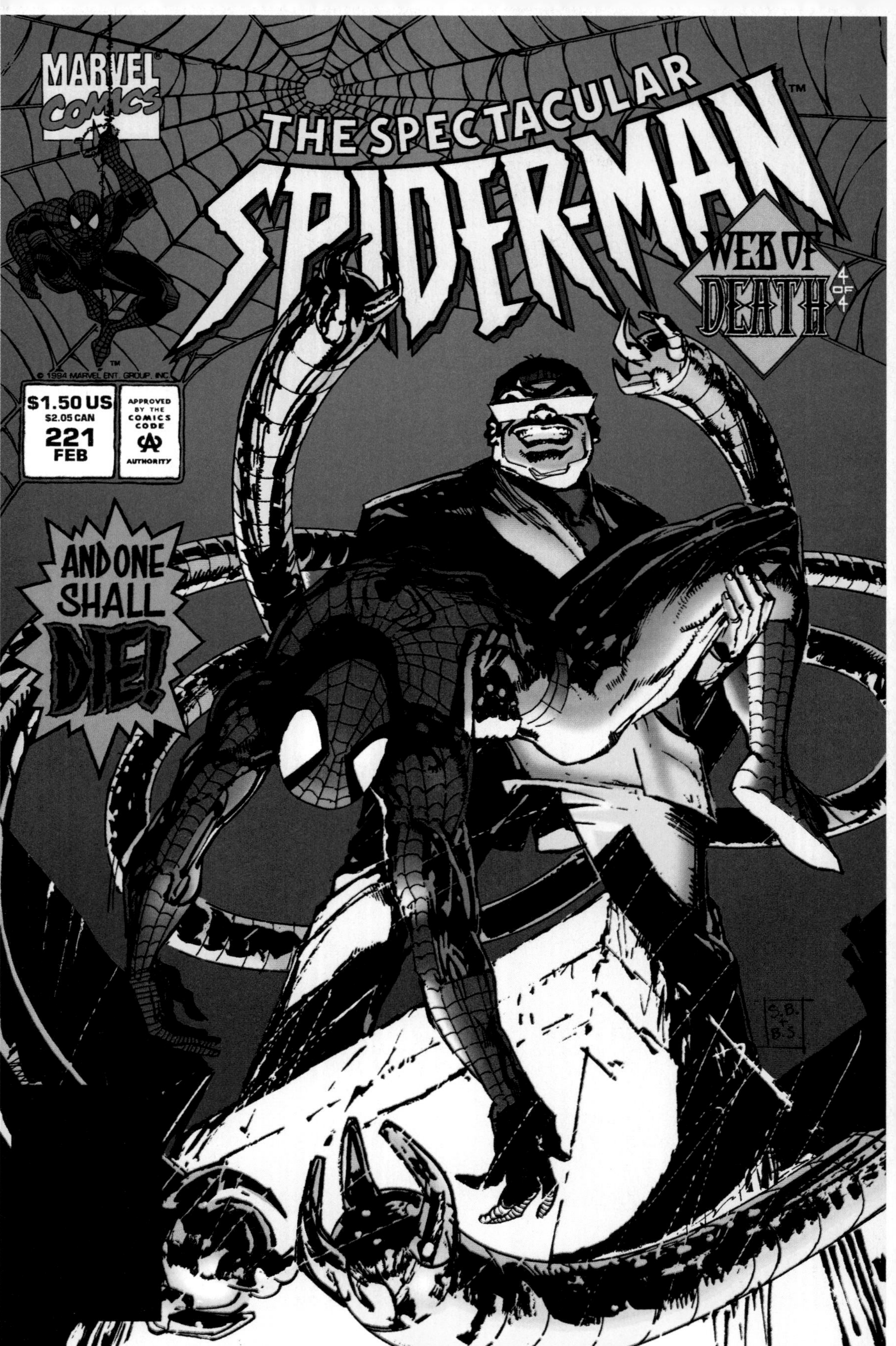
MARVEL COMICS
THE SPECTACULAR
SPIDER-MAN™
WEB OF DEATH 4 OF 4
© 1994 MARVEL ENT. GROUP, INC.
$1.50 US
$2.05 CAN
221
FEB
APPROVED BY THE COMICS CODE AUTHORITY
AND ONE SHALL DIE!
S.B. + B.S.

BITTEN BY A RADIOACTIVE SPIDER, STUDENT PETER PARKER GAINED THE PROPORTIONATE STRENGTH AND AGILITY OF AN ARACHNID! ARMED WITH HIS WONDROUS WEB-SHOOTERS, THE RELUCTANT SUPER HERO STRUGGLES WITH SINISTER SUPER-VILLAINS, MAKING ENDS MEET, AND MAINTAINING SOME SEMBLANCE OF A NORMAL LIFE!

STAN LEE PRESENTS: **THE SPECTACULAR SPIDER-MAN**

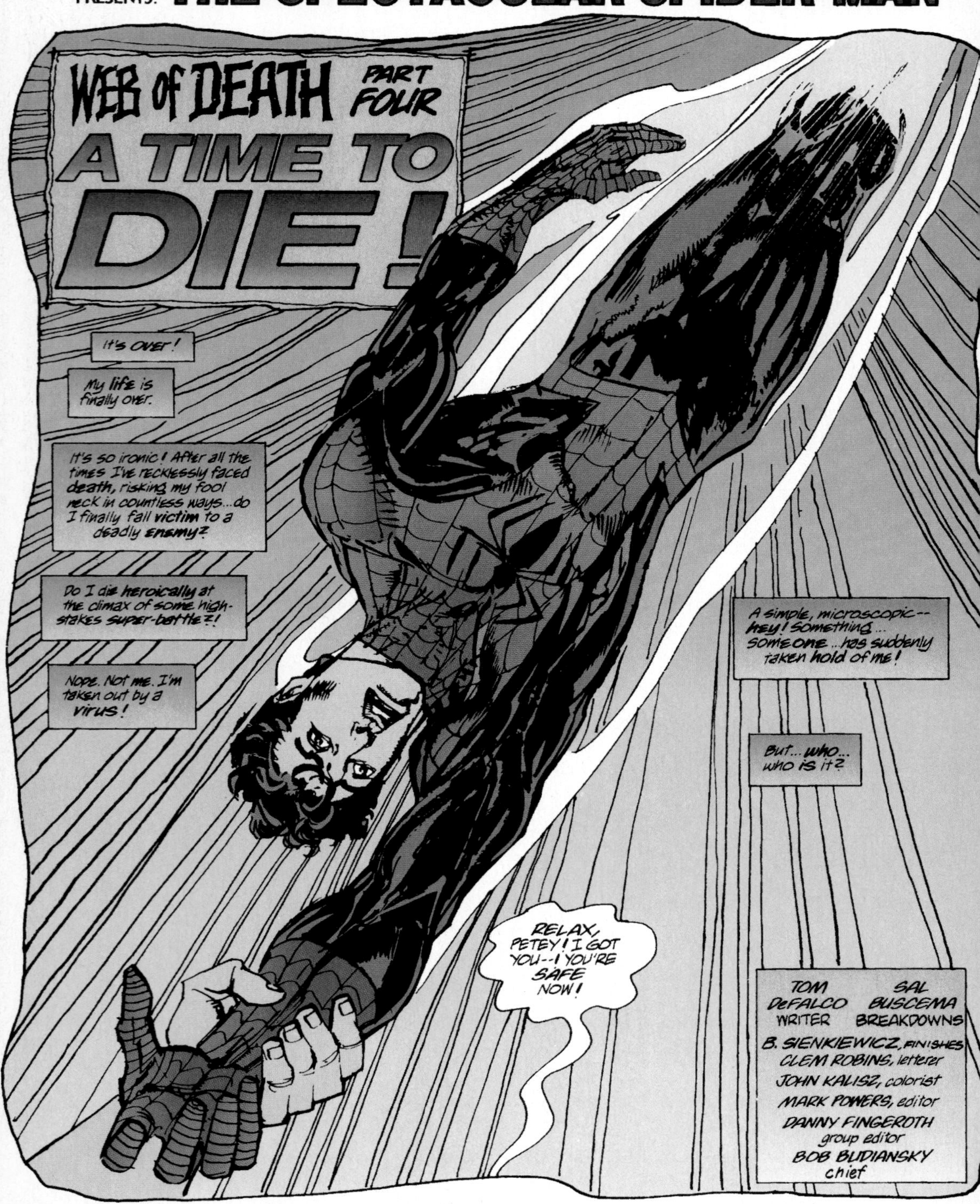

WEB of DEATH PART FOUR
A TIME TO DIE!
It's over!
My life is finally over.
It's so ironic! After all the times I've recklessly faced death, risking my fool neck in countless ways...do I finally fall victim to a deadly enemy?
Do I die heroically at the climax of some high-stakes super-battle?!
Nope. Not me. I'm taken out by a virus!
A simple, microscopic-- hey! Something... someone...has suddenly taken hold of me!
But...who... who is it?
RELAX, PETEY! I GOT YOU--I YOU'RE SAFE NOW!
TOM DeFALCO WRITER
SAL BUSCEMA BREAKDOWNS
B. SIENKIEWICZ, FINISHES
CLEM ROBINS, letterer
JOHN KALISZ, colorist
MARK POWERS, editor
DANNY FINGEROTH group editor
BOB BUDIANSKY chief

EASY DOES IT! I WON'T LET YOU DOWN! I'LL NEVER FAIL YOU!
YOU CAN ALWAYS COUNT ON YOUR OLD UNCLE BEN!
U-UNCLE BEN--?
IS IT REALLY YOU?
SURE IS, PETEY!
JUST LOOK AT YOU, BOY! YOU'VE GROWN INTO SUCH A STRONG AND HEALTHY YOUNG MAN!
I'D HAVE MY HANDS FULL TRYING TO OUT-WRESTLE YOU NOW!
I'M NOT SO SURE ABOUT THAT!
DON'T DAWDLE, BOY! THERE ARE SOME OTHERS WHO'VE BEEN ANXIOUSLY AWAITING YOUR ARRIVAL!
PETER--!
I CAN'T TELL YOU HOW MUCH WE'VE MISSED YOU!
HELLO, SON! IT'S SO GOOD TO SEE YOU AGAIN!
TH-THOSE...ARE MY PARENTS!
MY REAL PARENTS!
YEP!

WE ALL WISH WE COULD HAVE FOUND A WAY TO WARN YOU ABOUT THOSE FAKES ...BUT THAT'S THE PAST!
THERE AIN'T NO SIMULCRA, NO DOPPELGANGERS OR IMPOSTERS HERE!
I'LL BET THERE AREN'T ANY CLONES, EITHER!
WELL...UH...THAT'S SOMETHING YOU DON'T HAVE TO WORRY ABOUT, ANYMORE!
WE'RE ALL SO PROUD OF YOU, PETER! YOU'VE LED SUCH A RESPONSIBLE, EXEMPLARY LIFE! YOU'VE EARNED YOUR REST!
LISTEN TO YOUR MOTHER, SON!
ALL OF YOUR PAIN...YOUR FEARS...YOUR INSECURITIES... AND FAILINGS... ARE FINISHED!
NO ONE... AND NOTHING...CAN EVER HURT YOU AGAIN!
I DON'T KNOW WHAT TO SAY OR HOW TO--
AARGGK
WHAT IS IT, PETER?
WHAT'S HAPPENING TO YOU?

AGAIN!
I MUST JOLT HIM AGAIN!
MY ANTIDOTE WAS A SUCCESS!
THE VIRUS IS IN FULL REMISSION! THE HEALING PROCESS HAS BEGUN!
BUT TOO MUCH TIME HAS ALREADY PASSED! PARKER IS IN HEART FAILURE!
HELP ME, PARKER! IT'S ALL UP TO YOU! YOU'RE THE ONLY ONE CAN MAKE A DIFFERENCE!
YOU NEVER KNEW WHEN TO QUIT IN THE PAST! NO MATTER WHAT THE ODDS! NO MATTER WHAT THE COST!
DON'T QUIT ON ME NOW!
I CANNOT... I MUST NOT... LOSE YOU!

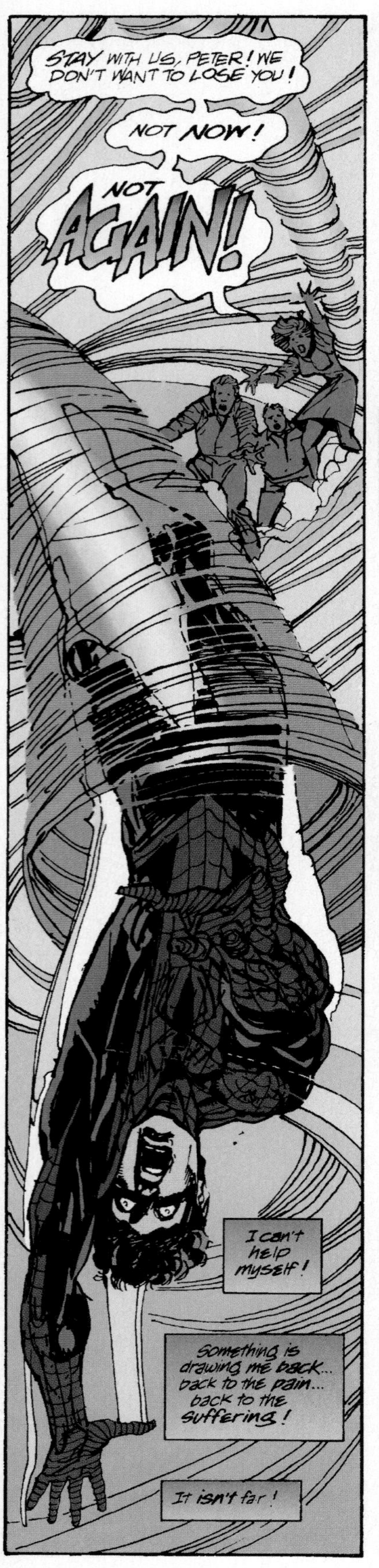
STAY WITH US, PETER! WE DON'T WANT TO LOSE YOU!
NOT NOW!
NOT AGAIN!
I can't help myself!
Something is drawing me back... back to the pain... back to the suffering!
It isn't far!

I've done my bit! I've earned my rest!
I should have the right to choose my own fate!
There's got to be some way to slow my fall! To stop my descent!

GOTCHA!

HANG ON, BUDDY!
I WON'T FAIL YOU! I WON'T ALLOW YOU TO PLUMMET ANY FARTHER!
HARRY--?
HARRY OSBORN?!

THE OTHERS LACK THE NECESSARY MOTIVATION TO KEEP YOU HERE!
THEY LOVE YOU TOO MUCH TO HOLD YOU AGAINST YOUR WILL!
THEY AREN'T FULLY CONVINCED ...THAT THIS IS WHERE YOU TRULY BELONG!

I HAVE NO SUCH CONSTRAINTS!
YOUR LIFE HAS BEEN PURE MISERY SINCE I DIED!

YOU HAVE NO JOY! NO HAPPINESS!
AND IT'S ALL MY FAULT!
THIS IS THE GREEN GOBLIN'S LAST CHANCE TO MAKE AMENDS!

I CAN EASE YOUR TORMENT, OLD FRIEND! I CAN ALLEVIATE YOUR GUILT, AND PUT AN END TO YOUR REGRETS...
...FOR ALL ETERNITY!

No!
No!
Death is not the refuge I imagined!
I can't hide here!
I know what I must do... and where I must go!

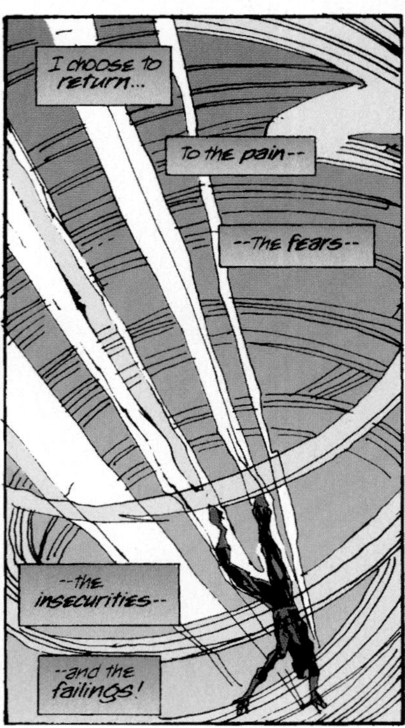
I choose to return...
To the pain--
--The fears--
--the insecurities--
--and the failings!

I choose LIFE!
BREATHE, PARKER!
ANYONE CAN WIN AN EASY FIGHT! ONLY A TRUE HERO SURVIVES IN THE FACE OF CERTAIN DEFEAT!
YOU WERE ONCE A MAN WHO ROUTINELY FACED OVERWHELMING ODDS... AND FREQUENTLY DARED TO BATTLE UNBEATABLE FOES!
I NEED YOU TO BE THAT MAN AGAIN!
PLEASE BREATHE!
IT'S WORKING, OTTO! HE'S STARTING TO RESPOND!
HE'S GOING TO MAKE IT!
BRAVO, MISTER PARKER...
BRAVO!

THE TIME HAS COME, MY DEAR...
YOU HAVE A MOST IMPORTANT DUTY TO PERFORM!
AND YOU MUST BE GONE...BEFORE HE FULLY REGAINS CONSCIOUSNESS!
ALL RIGHT, OTTO! I KNOW YOU WORKED OUT ALL THE DETAILS SO I'LL DO AS YOU ASK--
--EVEN THOUGH I REALLY HATE TO LEAVE YOU!
TRUST ME, MY DARLING STUNNER! WE WILL SOON BE REUNITED. NOTHING CAN POSSIBLY GO WRONG!
I HAVE NEVER BEEN SO HAPPY!
THIS IS LIFE AS I ALWAYS DESIRED IT TO BE.
I POSSESS THE LOVE OF A BEAUTIFUL WOMAN--
--AND MY OLD ADVERSARY WILL SOON BE HALE AND HEARTY, READY TO RESUME OUR ENDLESS DANCE!
AND YET...SOMETHING NAGS AT ME...
CAN IT BE THAT I MUST SUBCONSCIOUSLY QUESTION MY RIGHT TO EXPERIENCE SUCH UNRESTRAINED JOY--

--OR DO I INSTINCTIVELY SENSE SOME OUTSIDE MALEVOLENCE AT WORK?!
POOR, BEAUTIFUL STUNNER...
SO NAIVE, SO BLISSFULLY IGNORANT--
--OF THE GRIM TRAGEDY RUSHING TO GREET HER...
Still a little WOOZY, but my fever's definitely HISTORY!
He did it! DOCTOR OCTOPUS really came through for me!
So... WHAT happens now?!
IS THAT ANXIETY I SEE WELLING WITHIN HIS EYES?
DO I ALSO DETECT CONFUSION AND UNCERTAINTY?!
DELICIOUS!

YOU ARE PUZZLED, PARKER. CURIOUS AS TO THE FUTURE COURSE OF OUR RELATIONSHIP!
BE AT EASE! THERE IS NO NEED TO TAX YOUR WEARY MIND!
WE HAVE KNOWN EACH OTHER FOR MANY--PERHAPS TOO MANY YEARS! OUR FATES ARE INTIMATELY ENTWINED, MY FRIEND!
I HAVE LONG ADMIRED YOUR WIT, YOUR SELF-SACRIFICING HEROISM, YOUR VERY HUMANITY...
YOU HAVE ALWAYS BEEN MY MOST WORTHY FOE.
AND YOU SHALL BE AGAIN!
YOU ACTUALLY WANT ME TO FIGHT YOU?!
YOU CAN'T BE SERIOUS, DOC! YOU CAN'T HONESTLY EXPECT EVERYTHING TO GO BACK TO THE WAY IT WAS!
NOT AFTER ALL THAT'S HAPPENED!

DON'T BE SO SHOCKED! I DID NOT AID YOU TO BECOME YOUR BOSOM BUDDY!
NOR WILL I SUDDENLY BEGIN PATROLLING THE CITY IN THE NAME OF TRUTH, JUSTICE, OR--
OPEN UP! THIS IS THE POLICE--!
COME RIGHT IN, GENTLEMEN! THE DOOR IS UNLOCKED.
OH, MAA-ANN! OUR ANONYMOUS TIP WAS RIGHT ON THE MONEY!
IT'S HIM-- DOCTOR OCTOPUS HIMSELF!
FREEZE, MISTER! YOU'RE UNDER ARREST!
YOU MAY DISPENSE WITH THE MELODRAMATICS, GENTLEMEN. I INTEND A PEACEFUL SURRENDER.
WOULD ANYONE CARE FOR A REFRESHMENT?
YOU--! YOU DID THIS! YOU HAD YOUR LADY FRIEND CALL THE COPS--BUT WHY? WHY?!

I DIDN'T WANT TO PUT ANY UNDUE PRESSURE UPON YOU, MY FRIEND.
YOU NEED SUFFICIENT TIME TO FULLY RECOVER FROM YOUR RECENT MALADY.

I EXPECT YOU TO BE IN PEAK CONDITION FOR OUR NEXT ENCOUNTER!

OTTO OCTAVIUS HAS NO FEAR OF PRISON.

I WILL EVENTUALLY FIND A WAY TO ESCAPE!

POL

AND I TAKE A CERTAIN DEGREE OF COMFORT IN THE KNOWLEDGE THAT MY VALIANT AND VIBRANT OPPONENT WILL BE WAITING FOR ME WHEN I DO!

SPIDER-MAN WILL ALWAYS BE WAITING FOR ME!

S'funny...
I'd normally be going BATTY with paranoia right now.
My greatest NIGHTMARE has become a reality. My deadliest, most ruthless enemy KNOWS my secret identity.
Doc Ock could strike at MARY JANE or AUNT MAY at his leisure.
And yet... I don't think he ever WOULD!
Maybe I'm only deluding myself, but I honestly can't see Otto Octavius CROSSING that line.
NYPD
Ah, well... I CAN'T worry about that now!
It's just so gosh-darn glorious to be ALIVE!
I've stared deeply into the cold, numbing eyes of DEATH--
--But the WORST is now behind me!
The virus is out of my system--and my HEAD is finally screwed on right!
And the best news is that my wife and I are going to have a BABY!
A BABY!

This calls for a major CELEBRATION!
Peter and I should be out celebrating somewhere--
--rejoicing in the fact that we're about to start a family.
Fat chance!
Instead, I'm scrubbing away the filth and mold which has built up over the past few months.
What's wrong with us?
This is our home! How could we have allowed it to become so disgusting?
--so chaotic--
--so cluttered with dirt and debris?
There! The place is already beginning to take shape...
...and it didn't take anywhere near the time or effort I was afraid it would.
I wonder if Peter and I will be able to put our lives back in order as quickly and neatly as our house?
We still have so much old baggage hanging over us.
And the baby will present so many new problems --and responsibilities
How can we possibly cope with it all, and--
Wait! I hear someone at the door--

GREETINGS, PRETTY LADY! I COME BEARING GIFTS TO COMMEMORATE THIS JOYOUS OCCASION!
TODAY IS THE VERY FIRST DAY OF THE REST OF OUR LIVES!
UH... SURE, WHATEVER YOU SAY!
ALTHOUGH I WISH I HAD A BIT MORE NOTICE. I'M HARDLY DRESSED OR PREPARED FOR FESTIVITIES...
DON'T GIVE IT A THOUGHT! ASIDE FROM THE SWEAT AND GRIME--YOU'RE PERFECT!
I EVEN LIKE THE SCENT YOU'RE WEARING!
FLATTERER! YOU ALWAYS WERE PARTIAL TO EAU DE LYSOL.
DARE I ASK WHAT'S IN THE BOX?
JUST A LITTLE HOME "BUILD IT YOURSELF" PROJECT!
BABY CRIB
ACME
WHAT DO YOU SAY, SWEETHEART? SHALL WE UNPLUG THE PHONE, DISCONNECT THE TV, AND BREAK OUT THE POWER TOOLS?
LET'S GO FOR IT, TIGER! JUST SO LONG AS YOU PROMISE TO ACT MORE LIKE BOB VILLA THAN TIM ALLEN!
It's going to work!
I don't know why, but I'm suddenly convinced Peter and I will make everything work out just fine...

YES...
...THE PLAN IS PERFECT.
OTTO DESIGNED IT HIMSELF...AND HE DOESN'T MAKE MISTAKES!
I DON'T KNOW WHY I'M SO NERVOUS--WE'LL SOON BE REUNITED.

NOTHING CAN KEEP US APART!

WHAT THE--?!

GAS!
IT CAUGHT ME COMPLETELY BY SURPRISE!
DOC! SOMEONE DOESN'T WANT HIM RESCUED!
BUT... WHO?
AND... WHY?
WHY?
...

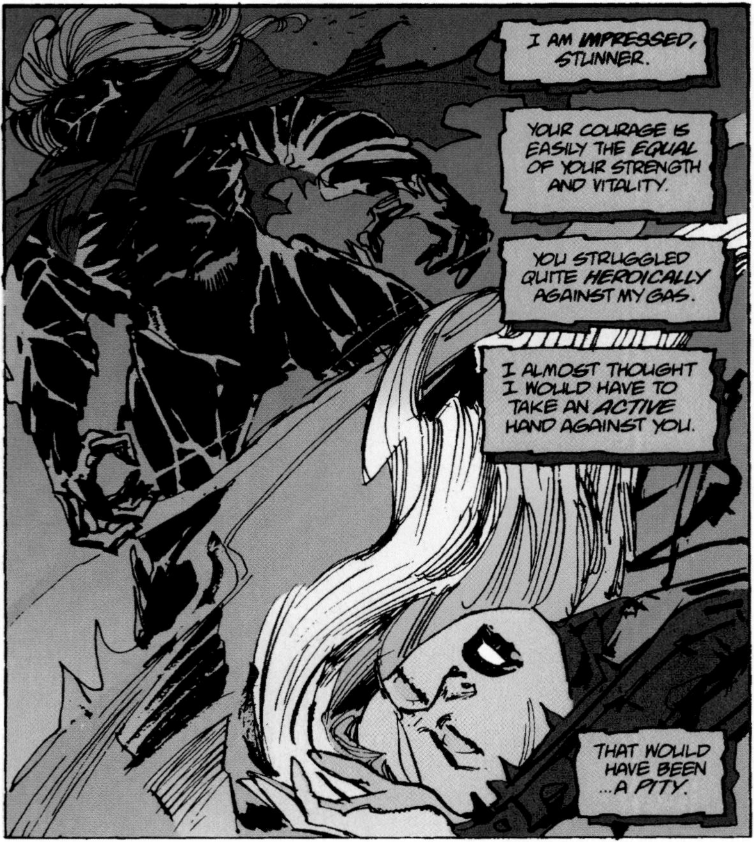
I AM IMPRESSED, STUNNER.
YOUR COURAGE IS EASILY THE EQUAL OF YOUR STRENGTH AND VITALITY.
YOU STRUGGLED QUITE HEROICALLY AGAINST MY GAS.
I ALMOST THOUGHT I WOULD HAVE TO TAKE AN ACTIVE HAND AGAINST YOU.
THAT WOULD HAVE BEEN ...A PITY.

YOU SEEM AWFULLY SMUG FOR A GUY HEADED FOR A LONG LOCK-UP!
TELL ME, OFFICERS ...DO ANY OF YOU TRULY BELIEVE YOUR PITIFUL WEAPONS HOLD ANY THREAT TO ME?
uh... OF COURSE... WHY ELSE WOULD YOU BE HERE?
YOU PROVIDED AN EXPEDIENT EXIT!
ALTHOUGH I AM FRANKLY SURPRISED YOU EVEN BOTHERED TO TAKE ME INTO CUSTODY.
MY ESCAPE IS AS INEVITABLE--
--AS MY NEXT BATTLE WITH SPIDER-MAN!
NY
HEADS UP! SOMETHING JUST HIT THE ROOF, AND--
--WHO IS THIS FREAK?!
TAKE HIM DOWN! HE'S OBVIOUSLY WITH OCTOPUS!
SOMETHING'S WRONG!
THAT'S
NOT
STUNNER!

WHERE IS SHE?
WHAT HAS HAPPENED TO STUNNER?!
IF YOU DARED HARM HER--!
SHE IS SAFE.
YOU, HOWEVER, ARE NOT!
DO YOU HAVE A DEATH WISH, MY FRIEND? OR ARE YOU MERELY IMPUDENT TO THE POINT OF INSANITY?

I AM OTTO OCTAVIUS...
KNOWN AS DOCTOR OCTOPUS TO THE GREAT UNWASHED AND UNEDUCATED!
DO NOT BE LULLED INTO A FALSE SENSE OF SECURITY BY THE EXTRA POUNDAGE I CARRY!
SPIDER-MAN, DAREDEVIL AND EVEN CAPTAIN AMERICA HIMSELF HAVE SUFFICIENT REASON TO RESPECT MY BATTLE PROWESS!
I AM KAINE!
MY ACTIONS WILL SPEAK FOR ME!
It is truly amazing how certain TASKS and SITUATIONS can bring two people--
--SO CLOSE together.
I HAVE NO PATIENCE FOR THIS GAME, KAINE!
I NEITHER KNOW NOR CARE ABOUT THE POINT YOU WISH TO MAKE!
I ONLY WANT STUNNER! MY SOLE DESIRE IS TO BE REJOINED WITH HER!
WHERE IS SHE?!

MARY JANE and I had been on such DIVERGENT paths the past few months--
--I honestly didn't know if our LOVE would survive.
I WILL NOT ALLOW YOU TO KEEP ME FROM THE WOMAN I LOVE!
I WILL NOT PERMIT YOU TO INTERFERE WITH OUR HAPPINESS!
YOU CANNOT STOP ME!
I HARBOR NO PERSONAL ANTAGONISM-- NO MALICE-- TOWARD YOU, DOCTOR!
But we MADE it.
We found a way to BEAT the odds!
YOUR WOMAN IS ONLY A PAWN IN THIS GAME.
HOWEVER, FOR REASONS OF MY OWN--

--YOU MUST
DIE!
KRAKKK

HEAD'S STILL SPINNING--!
FEELS LIKE SOMEONE USED IT FOR A TRAMPOLINE.
I NEVER REALIZED IT WAS POSSIBLE FOR ME TO--OH, MY GOD!
DOC!
DOC!!

It's days like this that can almost CONVINCE you it IS possible for FAIRY TALES to come true--
--and for a few people to live HAPPILY ever after!
But only a FEW people--
--A very chosen FEW...
NEXT: PLAYERS AND PAWNS

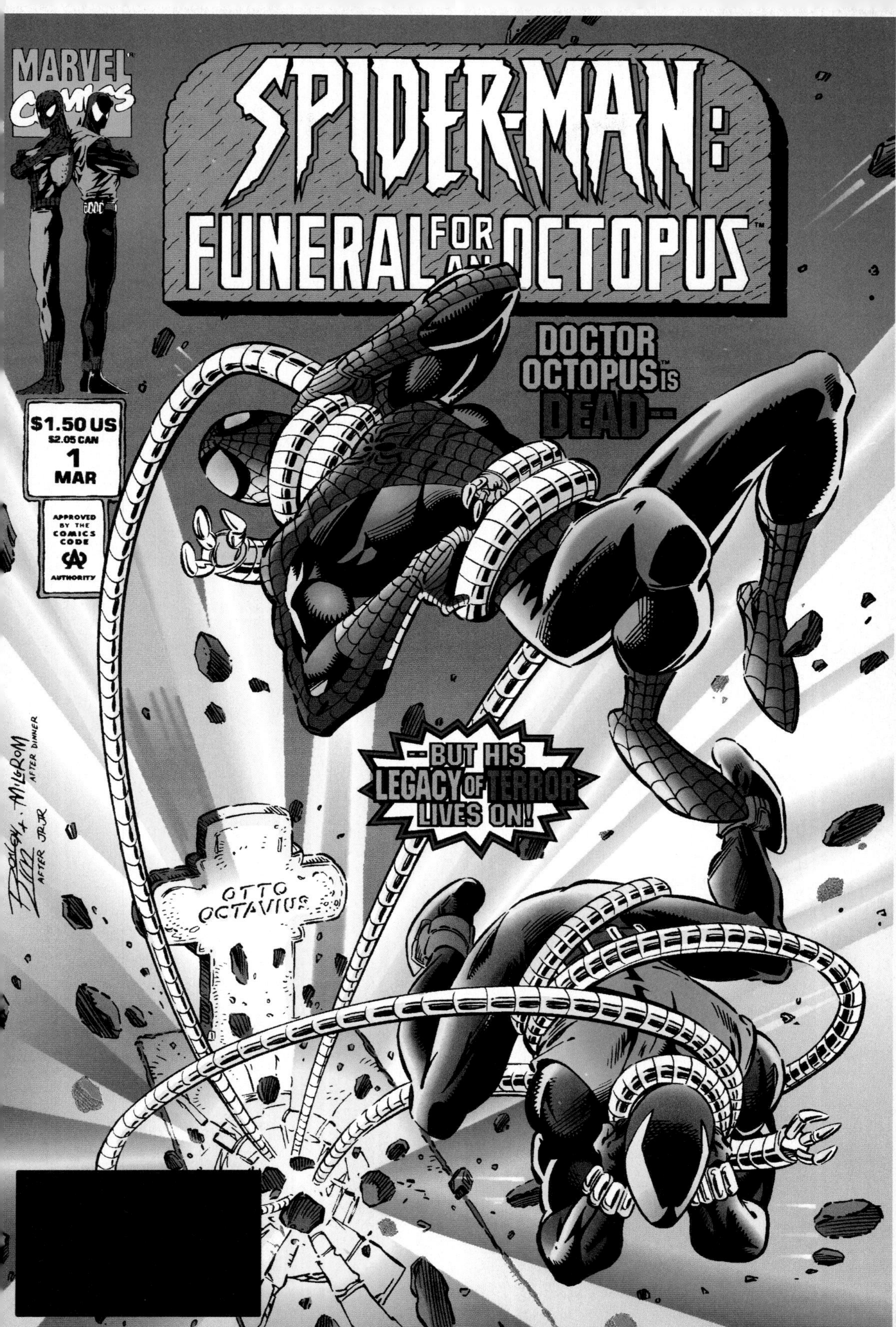
MARVEL COMICS
SPIDER-MAN:
FUNERAL FOR AN OCTOPUS
$1.50 US
$2.05 CAN
1
MAR
APPROVED BY THE COMICS CODE AUTHORITY
DOCTOR OCTOPUS IS DEAD--
--BUT HIS LEGACY OF TERROR LIVES ON!
OTTO OCTAVIUS

STAN LEE PRESENTS: SPIDER-MAN AND THE SCARLET SPIDER!

A GLOOMY OLD WAREHOUSE NOT FAR FROM THE WATER-FRONT.
"IT WAS AT A PLACE LIKE THIS THAT IT ALL BEGAN...
"...WHEN A SHY TEEN-AGED BOY FACED OFF AGAINST AN ARMED GUNMAN... AND LEARNED A VALUABLE LESSON THAT WOULD LAST A LIFETIME!
"IT WAS IN A PLACE LIKE THIS THAT SPIDER-MAN WAS REALLY BORN!"
EH...?

AND NOW...
...THANKS TO DR. OTTO OCTAVIUS, MORE POPULARLY REFERRED TO BY THE MASSES AS DOCTOR OCTOPUS...
...IT'S WHERE IT ALL BEGAN ANEW!
NOTE: THIS STORY TAKES PLACE IMMEDIATELY FOLLOWING SPECTACULAR SPIDER-MAN #221. --ERIC

LOOKS LIKE THE FEDS GAVE THE LAB A GOOD ONCE-OVER!
TOOK EVERYTHING THAT WASN'T NAILED DOWN!
WELL...
...ALMOST EVERYTHING!
A SAMPLE OF THE TOXIN!
THIS STUFF WAS NEARLY MY FINISH!
WHO'D HAVE BELIEVED I'D OWE MY FUTURE--MY VERY LIFE...
...TO MY OWN WORST ENEMY!
WHEN THE VULTURE'S BIRD TAGGED ME--RAKED ME WITH THOSE POISON-TIPPED TALONS--I THOUGHT THAT WAS ALL SHE WROTE!*
* SEE AMAZING SPIDER-MAN #396. --ERIC
BUT OCK HAD OTHER PLANS.
OTHER IDEAS!

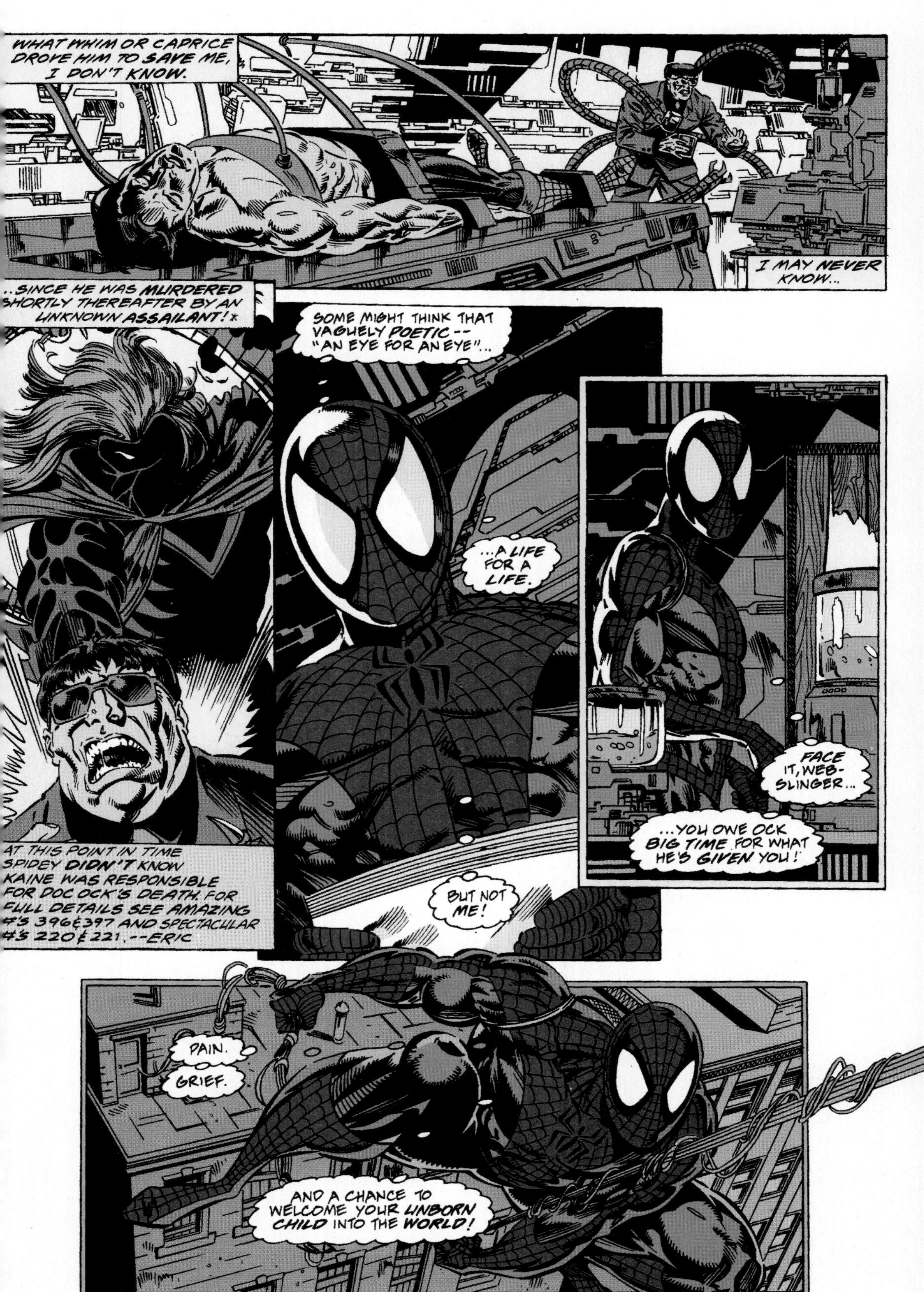

WHAT WHIM OR CAPRICE DROVE HIM TO SAVE ME, I DON'T KNOW.
I MAY NEVER KNOW...
...SINCE HE WAS MURDERED SHORTLY THEREAFTER BY AN UNKNOWN ASSAILANT! *
AT THIS POINT IN TIME SPIDEY DIDN'T KNOW KAINE WAS RESPONSIBLE FOR DOC OCK'S DEATH. FOR FULL DETAILS SEE AMAZING #'S 396 & 397 AND SPECTACULAR #'S 220 & 221. --ERIC
SOME MIGHT THINK THAT VAGUELY POETIC -- "AN EYE FOR AN EYE"...
...A LIFE FOR A LIFE.
BUT NOT ME!
FACE IT, WEB-SLINGER...
...YOU OWE OCK BIG TIME FOR WHAT HE'S GIVEN YOU!
PAIN.
GRIEF.
AND A CHANCE TO WELCOME YOUR UNBORN CHILD INTO THE WORLD!

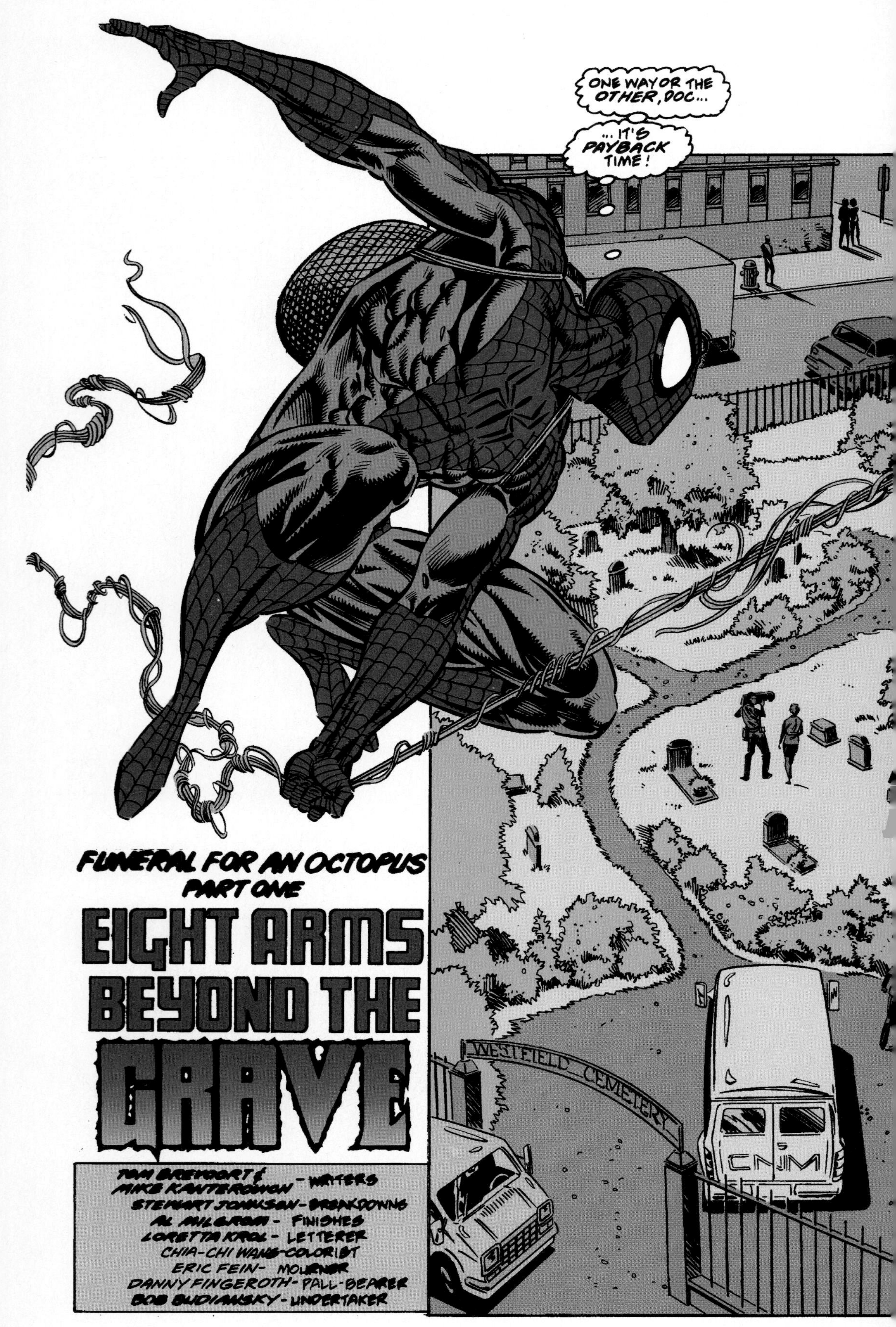
ONE WAY OR THE OTHER, DOC...
...IT'S PAYBACK TIME!
FUNERAL FOR AN OCTOPUS
PART ONE
EIGHT ARMS BEYOND THE GRAVE
TOM BREVOORT & MIKE KANTEROVICH - WRITERS
STEWART JOHNSON - BREAKDOWNS
AL MILGROM - FINISHES
LORETTA KROL - LETTERER
CHIA-CHI WANG - COLORIST
ERIC FEIN - MOURNER
DANNY FINGEROTH - PALL-BEARER
BOB BUDIANSKY - UNDERTAKER
WESTFIELD CEMETERY
CNJM

KXB N

LOOKS MORE LIKE A CIRCUS THAN A FUNERAL DOWN THERE!
STILL, WHAT DID I EXPECT?
OCK WAS ONE OF THE MOST NOTORIOUS CRIMINAL MASTERMINDS SINCE AL CAPONE...
...AND ONLY SLIGHTLY LESS PHOTOGENIC!
WOULDN'T FEEL RIGHT STIRRING UP ANY MORE OF A COMMOTION BY SWINGING IN UNINVITED!
FORTUNATELY...
...I CAME PREPARED!
SINCE DOC'S FINAL ACT ULTIMATELY BENEFITED PETER PARKER...
...HE'S THE ONE WHO SHOULD PAY HIS LAST RESPECTS!
HEY! WATCH IT, FELLA!
THIS IS NEWS!
NEWS? HARDLY.
TRY EXPLOITATION... AND SENSATIONALISM!
AND SPEAKING OF SENSATION-ALISM...

...THERE'S THE GUY WHO MADE IT A HOUSEHOLD WORD!
THAT'S THE TROUBLE WITH THESE TV NEWS-CASTERS, ROBBIE: NO INTEGRITY!
THEY'RE LIKE A PACK OF HUNGRY WOLVES... DISRUPTING THE DIGNITY OF THIS SOLEMN OCCASION FOR THE SAKE OF A FEW SOUND BYTES!
NOT LIKE THAT FULL-COLOR INSERT YOU WANTED IN THIS MORNING'S BUGLE, EH, JONAH?
HRRMPH! THAT'S DIFFERENT. THAT'S JOURNALISM!
GLAD YOU CAME, PETER. YOU CAN DO US BOTH A FAVOR...
...AND PASS ME A BARF BAG WHEN I START TO RETCH!
YOU'RE HERE AS A REPORTER, BETTY. TRY TO JUST DO YOUR JOB.
RIGHT. OCTOPUS NEVER DID A DECENT THING IN HIS LIFE! THE MAN WAS A MONSTER...
...YET HERE WE ARE ABOUT TO PAY HOMAGE TO HIS MEMORY!
AS FAR AS I'M CONCERNED, THEY CAN'T BURY OTTO OCTAVIUS DEEP ENOUGH! IF NOT FOR HIM...
...MY BROTHER BENNETT WOULD STILL BE ALIVE! *
* SEE AMAZING SPIDER-MAN #11 FOR THE DEATH OF BENNETT BRANT. --ERIC
DEAR FRIENDS...
...I AM ELIAS HARGROVE...
...AND WE ARE GATHERED HERE, UNDER GREY SKIES, TO BID FAREWELL TO MY COUSIN, DOCTOR OTTO OCTAVIUS.
HIS TIME AMONG US WAS ALL TOO BRIEF...
...BUT TO THOSE WHOSE LIVES HE TOUCHED...
...HE SHALL REMAIN... A MOST PROFOUND INFLUENCE.

WHEN I LOOK BACK, I PREFER NOT TO THINK OF HIM AS DOCTOR OCTOPUS, BUT RATHER AS THE BENEVOLENT... THE SENSITIVE... SOUL HE ONCE WAS.
THE SON OF A MIGRANT LABORER, GIFTED WITH A RESTLESS INTELLECT BEYOND HIS STATION.
A MAN OF SCIENCE, WHOSE GIFT BROUGHT HOPE TO OTHERS...
...BUT ONLY PAIN AND SUFFERING UPON HIMSELF.
HIS PATH... WAS SELDOM AN EASY ONE...
...WITH THIS, ITS ULTIMATE DESTINATION.
"THOU PREPAREST A TABLE BEFORE ME, IN THE PRESENCE OF MINE ENEMIES..."
SUCH A WASTE.
IF ONLY I COULD HAVE FREED HIM FROM HIS PSYCHOSES!
YOU WERE ONE SORRY, MANIPULATIVE PIECE OF WORK, DOC...
...BUT EVEN YOU RATED BETTER!
WELL, WELL, WELL...
...LOOKS LIKE I'LL HAVE THE CHANCE TO USE THAT OCTAVIUS OBITUARY AFTER ALL!
"THOU ANOINTEST MINE HEAD WITH OIL...
"MINE CUP RUNNETH OVER.

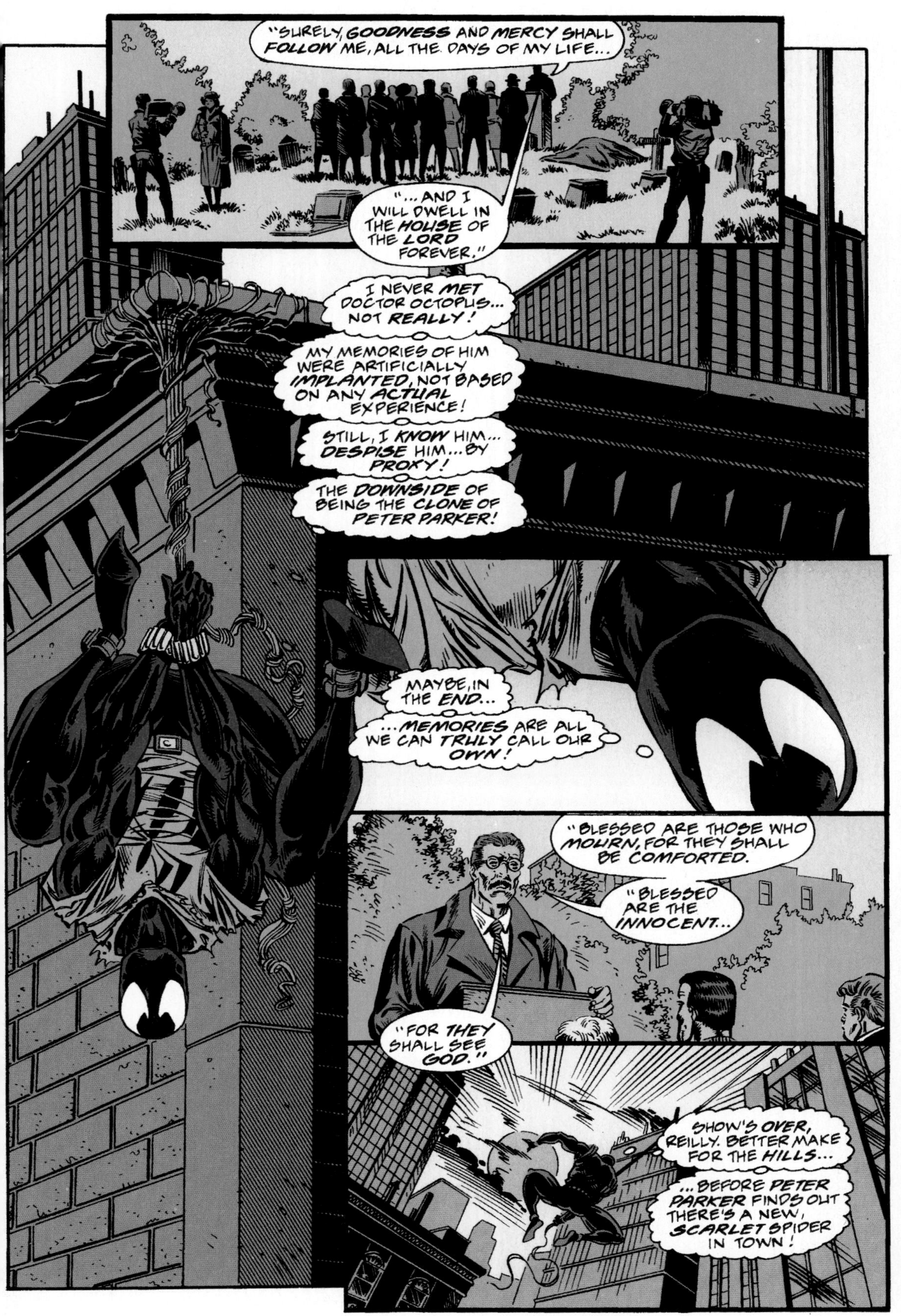
"SURELY, GOODNESS AND MERCY SHALL FOLLOW ME, ALL THE DAYS OF MY LIFE...
"...AND I WILL DWELL IN THE HOUSE OF THE LORD FOREVER."
I NEVER MET DOCTOR OCTOPUS... NOT REALLY!
MY MEMORIES OF HIM WERE ARTIFICIALLY IMPLANTED, NOT BASED ON ANY ACTUAL EXPERIENCE!
STILL, I KNOW HIM... DESPISE HIM... BY PROXY!
THE DOWNSIDE OF BEING THE CLONE OF PETER PARKER!
MAYBE, IN THE END...
...MEMORIES ARE ALL WE CAN TRULY CALL OUR OWN!
"BLESSED ARE THOSE WHO MOURN, FOR THEY SHALL BE COMFORTED.
"BLESSED ARE THE INNOCENT...
"FOR THEY SHALL SEE GOD."
SHOW'S OVER, REILLY. BETTER MAKE FOR THE HILLS...
...BEFORE PETER PARKER FINDS OUT THERE'S A NEW, SCARLET SPIDER IN TOWN!

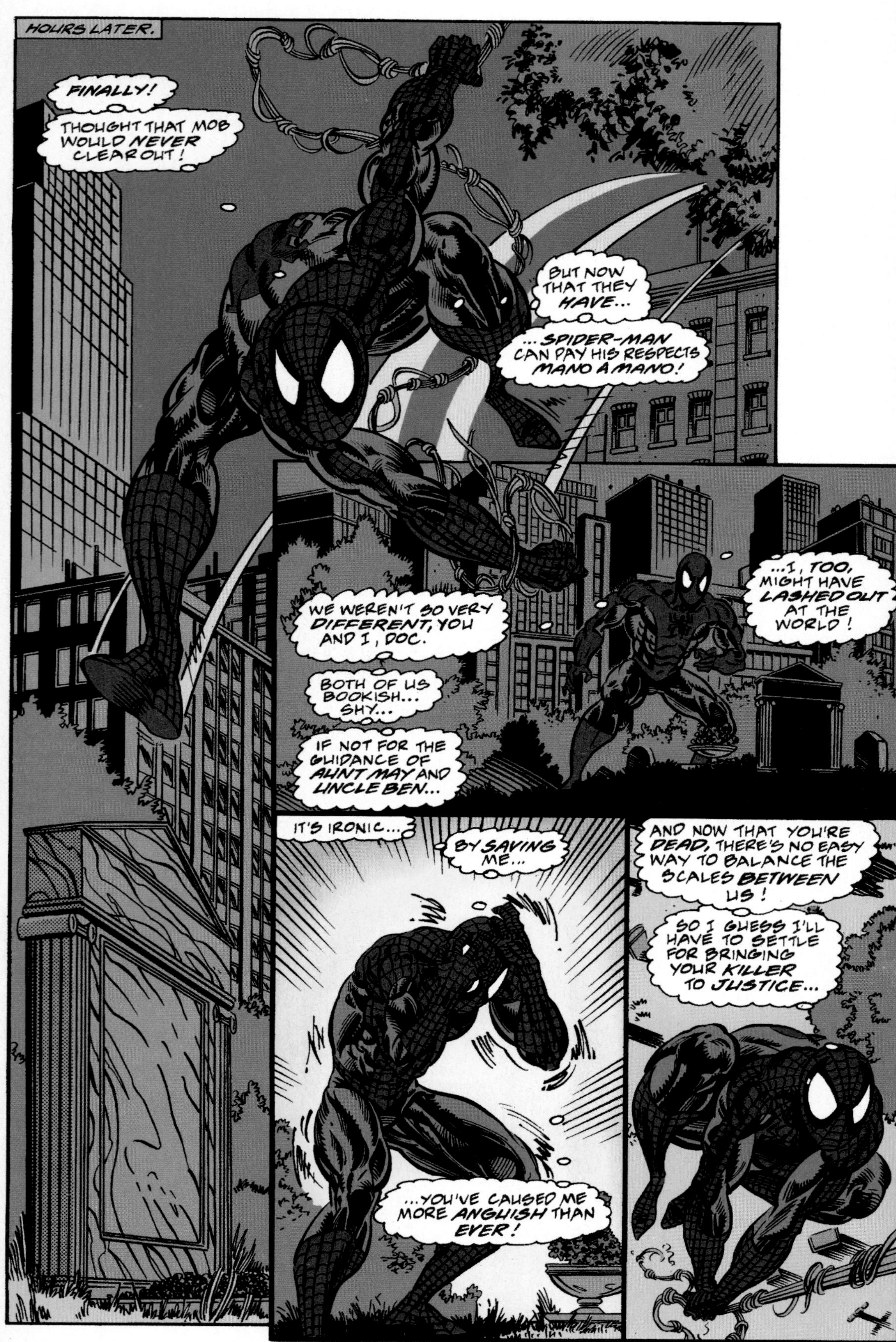
HOURS LATER.
FINALLY!
THOUGHT THAT MOB WOULD NEVER CLEAR OUT!
BUT NOW THAT THEY HAVE...
...SPIDER-MAN CAN PAY HIS RESPECTS MANO A MANO!
WE WEREN'T SO VERY DIFFERENT, YOU AND I, DOC.
BOTH OF US BOOKISH... SHY...
IF NOT FOR THE GUIDANCE OF AUNT MAY AND UNCLE BEN...
...I, TOO, MIGHT HAVE LASHED OUT AT THE WORLD!
IT'S IRONIC...
BY SAVING ME...
...YOU'VE CAUSED ME MORE ANGUISH THAN EVER!
AND NOW THAT YOU'RE DEAD, THERE'S NO EASY WAY TO BALANCE THE SCALES BETWEEN US!
SO I GUESS I'LL HAVE TO SETTLE FOR BRINGING YOUR KILLER TO JUSTICE...

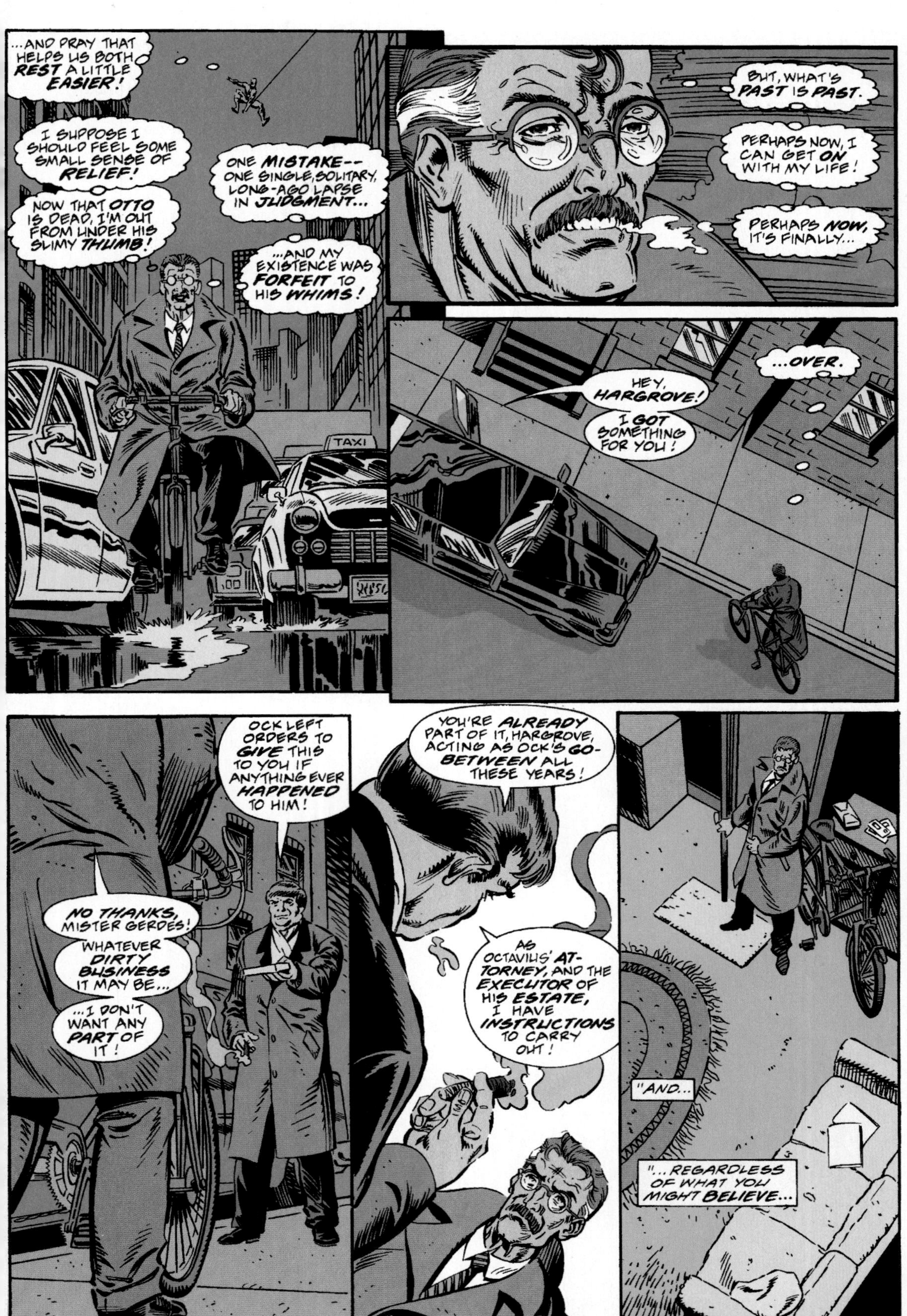
...AND PRAY THAT HELPS US BOTH REST A LITTLE EASIER!
I SUPPOSE I SHOULD FEEL SOME SMALL SENSE OF RELIEF!
NOW THAT OTTO IS DEAD, I'M OUT FROM UNDER HIS SLIMY THUMB!
ONE MISTAKE-- ONE SINGLE, SOLITARY, LONG-AGO LAPSE IN JUDGMENT...
...AND MY EXISTENCE WAS FORFEIT TO HIS WHIMS!
TAXI
BUT, WHAT'S PAST IS PAST.
PERHAPS NOW, I CAN GET ON WITH MY LIFE!
PERHAPS NOW, IT'S FINALLY...
...OVER.
HEY, HARGROVE!
I GOT SOMETHING FOR YOU!
OCK LEFT ORDERS TO GIVE THIS TO YOU IF ANYTHING EVER HAPPENED TO HIM!
NO THANKS, MISTER GERDES!
WHATEVER DIRTY BUSINESS IT MAY BE...
...I DON'T WANT ANY PART OF IT!
YOU'RE ALREADY PART OF IT, HARGROVE, ACTING AS OCK'S GO-BETWEEN ALL THESE YEARS!
AS OCTAVIUS' ATTORNEY, AND THE EXECUTOR OF HIS ESTATE, I HAVE INSTRUCTIONS TO CARRY OUT!
"AND...
"...REGARDLESS OF WHAT YOU MIGHT BELIEVE...

"...IT AIN'T OVER...
"...UNTIL THE DOC HAS SAID A FEW LAST WORDS!"
ELIAS HARGROVE... IF YOU ARE WATCHING THIS, IT IS SAFE TO ASSUME THAT I AM DEAD.
WE HAVE NEVER BEEN WHAT ONE WOULD CONSIDER "CLOSE," COUSIN...
...BUT, AS MY LAST SURVIVING RELATION, I FEEL I OWE YOU SOMETHING!
THEREFORE, I HEREBY BESTOW UPON YOU LEGAL AND MORAL RIGHT TO ALL MY PATENTS, INVENTIONS AND WORLDLY GOODS!
IT FALLS TO YOU TO CARRY THE OCTAVIUS LEGACY FORWARD!
I HAD CONSIDERED YOU A WEAK MAN, COUSIN, BUT OF LATE, YOU HAVE DEMONSTRATED A HERETOFORE UNSUSPECTED RESOLVE!*
*IN THE LETHAL FOES OF SPIDER-MAN LIMITED SERIES. -- ERIC
THIS IS PROMISING, FOR, IF I'VE LEARNED ONLY ONE LESSON...
...IT'S THAT NONE BUT THE STRONG THRIVE IN THIS LIFE!
YOU HAVE PROVEN THAT YOU HAVE IT WITHIN YOURSELF TO BE STRONG!
THINK OF ALL YOU MIGHT ATTAIN...
...WITH THE FRUITS OF MY CEASELESS TOIL AND LABOR AT YOUR FINGERTIPS!
THE POWER TO FORGE YOUR OWN DESTINY!
LISTEN CLOSELY NOW, ELIAS HARGROVE!
HERE IS WHAT YOU NEED DO...

"...TO CLAIM YOUR RIGHTFUL HERITAGE!"
THE LOCATION OF MY SECRET DROP-BOX IS KNOWN TO ONLY A SELECT FEW...
...AND YET, I HAVE BEEN SUMMONED!
CURIOUS.
THOUGH I HAVE NO INKLING AS TO EITHER THE WHY OR THE HOW OF THIS IMPROMPTU GATHERING...
...ANYONE WITH THE RESOURCE-FULNESS MY MYSTERIOUS HOST DEMONSTRATES...
...IS WORTHY OF THE VULTURE'S ATTENTION!
WELL, HI-DIDDILY-HO, NEIGHBOR!
HEY! IT'S THE ALL-NEW VULTURE!
THOUGHT YOU WERE IN THE PEN, GUY!
SPIDER-MAN?!
NO! SOME SECOND-RATE IMPOSTER!
THOKK
THE ONE THE BUGLE CALLS "THE SCARLET SPIDER"!

UNMITIGATED BUFFOON!
KRAK
HEY, BIRDFACE--
-- I MIGHT NOT BE THE ORIGINAL WALL-CRAWLING WONDER...
...BUT I LIKE TO THINK THAT, AS #2, I TRY A WHOLE LOT HARDER!
TAKE THIS IMPACT WEBBING, F'RINSTANCE!
THOOP
IT SLICES, DICES, TRAPS AIR-BORNE REFUSE AND COMES IN THESE ENVI-RONMENTALLY FRIENDLY CANNISTERS!
PRETTY SPIFFY, HUH?
ARROGANT...
...INSECT!
PHOOM
PHOOM
PHOOM
PHOOM
PHOOM
HEY!
CAREFUL WHERE YOU POINT THAT THING, TEX...

FTAK
...IT MIGHT GO OFF!
AARGH!
FTAK
FTAK
THESE STINGER DARTS SHOULD KEEP YOU ON YOUR BEST BEHAVIOR...
...WHILE I CIRCLE 'ROUND...
...AND REVISIT THIS PROBLEM FROM A FRESH PERSPECTIVE!
NAMELY...
...UP CLOSE AND PERSONAL!
BRAKK
I HAVE NO QUARREL WITH YOU, SPIDER!
NOR HAVE I TIME TO WASTE IN FRUITLESS CONTENTION!
THUS...

PHOOOOOM
K-RRMMMBL
BLAST YOU, VULTURE!
ENDANGERING INNOCENTS TO SAVE YOUR OWN WORTHLESS HIDE! JUST LIKE OCK ONCE DID...
...AND GWEN'S DAD, CAPTAIN GEORGE STACY, PAID THE PRICE! *
NO!
WELL, HISTORY WON'T REPEAT ITSELF!
THRUUK
I... ...WON'T... ...LET IT!
UHNFH!
* AMAZING SPIDER-MAN #90.--ERIC
ADIEU, YOU WOULD-BE WALL-CRAWLER!
A PITY YOURS IS SUCH A HEAVY LOAD TO BEAR!
GLOAT WHILE YOU CAN, LAUGHING BOY...
PAF
THIPT
...'CAUSE ONCE I CATCH UP TO THIS MINI-DOT TRACER'S SIGNAL...

"...YOU'RE GONNA CHOKE DOWN EVERY LAST ONE OF THOSE WORDS!"
KLIKT
WHIRRRRR
YOU'RE LATE, TOOMES!
I WAS... UNAVOIDABLY DETAINED, HOBGOBLIN!
WHATSA-MATTER, VULTURE? SOMEONE SPRINKLE SALT ON YOUR TAIL?
IT MATTERS LITTLE WHO OR WHAT DELAYED HIM, ELECTRO! NOW THAT HE IS HERE...
...THE REMNANTS OF THE SINISTER SIX STAND REUNITED!

INTERLUDE.
A NONDESCRIPT FACTORY IN NASSAU COUNTY, LONG ISLAND...
...CAN'T FORCE THIS, REINHOLDT!

WE HAVE ONLY THE ONE WORKING MODEL, AND IF WE WRECK IT--
YOU, MORETTI, WERE CONTRACTED FOR THIS ASSIGNMENT BECAUSE YOU'RE THE FINEST CYBER-JOCK MONEY CAN BUY!
WE ENDURED NO SMALL DIFFICULTY WRESTING THIS EQUIPMENT FROM OUR "SISTER" AGENCIES!
OCTAVIUS' ARMS ARE A MASTERWORK OF MULTIPURPOSE ORDINANCE ENGINEERING!
YOUR JOB IS TO REPLICATE 'EM. PLAIN AND SIMPLE.

I'VE REQUISITIONED THE COMPUTER FILES AND EQUIPMENT WE EXPROPRIATED FROM THE GOOD DOCTOR'S LAB.
MAYBE YOU CAN BUY A CLUE AMONG THE REFUSE!
BUT THESE ENCEPHALOGRAPHIC READOUTS DON'T MAKE ANY SENSE!
NEITHER DO BUMBLEBEES, MORETTI!
THEY CAN'T FLY--NOT ACCORDING TO EVERY AERO-DYNAMIC PRINCIPLE IN THE BOOK!
DOESN'T STOP 'EM FROM ZIPPIN' UP AND ZAPPIN' YOU ON THE KEESTER!
IF THERE ARE SECRETS TO BE HAD, WE'LL HARVEST THEM!
ONE WAY OR THE OTHER!

PETER!
YOU'RE BACK!
THANK HEAVENS!
WITH THE BABY ON THE WAY, IT'S MORE IMPORTANT THAN EVER THAT WE--
NOTHING.
NO SIGN.
NO TRACE.
IT'S AS THOUGH OCK'S KILLER SLIPPED THROUGH THE CRACKS SOMEHOW--FELL OFF THE FACE OF THE EARTH!
BUT HE'S OUT THERE SOMEWHERE!
AND IF I DON'T STOP HIM--
--HE'LL KILL AGAIN.
HEY, TIGER, YOU'RE STARTING TO SCARE ME!
NO ONE--NOT EVEN YOU--CAN BE RESPONSIBLE FOR EVERYONE!
BAD THINGS HAPPEN EVERY DAY, WITHOUT REASON...
...AND SPIDER-MAN CAN'T BE EVERYWHERE AT ONCE!
I'M JUST GLAD YOU'RE HOME, HONEY.
I'M JUST GLAD YOU'RE HERE.

...GLAD YOU'RE HERE, GENTLEMEN!
I AM ELIAS HARGROVE, AND I HAVE CHOSEN TO CONDUCT THIS MEETING IN THIS FASHION FOR... OBVIOUS REASONS!
THE MISSION FOR WHICH I HAVE SUMMONED YOU IS A STRAIGHT-FORWARD ONE.
OTTO OCTAVIUS' NOTES AND EQUIPMENT HAVE BEEN CONFISCATED BY THE GOVERNMENT!
YOU FOUR ARE GOING TO HELP ME RETRIEVE THEM!
IF YOU DON'T MIND MY ASKIN', POPS...
...WHY SHOULD WE BOTHER WITH OCK'S STUFF...
...OR WITH YOU, FOR THAT MATTER?
BECAUSE, DEAR FELLOW, THERE IS BOOTY ENOUGH FOR ALL...
...AND YOUR TIME AND EFFORTS SHALL BE RECOMPENSED ACCORDINGLY!

IN ADDITION, OTTO LEFT ME ENOUGH INFORMATION ON THE LOT OF YOU TO MAKE YOUR LIVES VERY, VERY UNCOMFORTABLE, SHOULD I SO CHOOSE!
I'VE NO INTENTION OF USING SAID INFORMATION, UNLESS MY HAND IS FORCED.
ALL I WANT IS WHAT'S COMING TO ME, NO MORE, NO--
THWAPP
SURE IS NICE THAT YOU CLOWNS ARE ALL TOGETHER!
WHO--?!
SAVES ME THE TROUBLE OF HAVING TO LOOK YOU UP ONE AT A TIME!
OVER THERE!
THWAP
THWAP
THWAP

I WOULDN'T WORRY ABOUT OL' DOC OCK'S BOOTY IF I WERE YOU!
YOU'VE GOT MORE PRESSING CONCERNS...
...NAMELY ME!
AND THE SCARLET SPIDER IS GONNA TAKE GREAT PLEASURE...
...IN TAKING YOU OUT...
...PERMANENTLY!
NEXT: THE RACE FOR DOC OCK'S ARMS IS ON! IT'S GOT SPIDEY, THE SCARLET SPIDER, A GAGGLE OF VILLAINS AND A SURPRISE OR TWO, ALL IN JUST THIRTY SHORT DAYS!

MARVEL COMICS
SPIDER-MAN:
FUNERAL FOR AN OCTOPUS
$1.50 US
$2.05 CAN
2
APR
APPROVED BY THE COMICS CODE AUTHORITY

ENTER:
THE OCTO-SPIDER!

THE SECRET HIDEOUT OF THE SINISTER SIX...
...IS SECRET NO MORE!
I WOULDN'T WORRY ABOUT RECOVERING DEAR, DEPARTED DOC OCK'S LOOT IF I WERE YOU!
YOU'VE GOT MORE PRESSING CONCERNS...
...NAMELY ME!
AND I'M GONNA TAKE GREAT PLEASURE...
...IN TAKING YOU CLOWNS OUT, PERMANENTLY!
SPIDER-MAN?!
NO, ELECTRO, YOU FOOL! IT'S THE OTHER ONE!
THE SCARLET SPIDER!
STAN LEE PRESENTS:
FUNERAL FOR AN OCTOPUS
PART II
ARMED AND DANGEROUS
TOM BREVOORT & MIKE KANTEROVICH WRITERS
STEWART JOHNSON BREAKDOWNS
AL MILGROM FINISHES
LORETTA KROL LETTERER
CHIA-CHI WANG COLORIST
ERIC FEIN EDITOR
DANNY FINGEROTH GROUP EDITOR
BOB BUDIANSKY EDITOR IN CHIEF
THIS STORY TAKES PLACE PRIOR TO THE EVENTS OF WEB OF SPIDER-MAN #123.--ERIC

GOSH, IT'S GREAT TO BE NOTICED!
GUESS MY PRESS AGENT REALLY DOES KNOW HIS STUFF!
BUT I WONDER, WILL SUCCESS SPOIL AMERICA'S FAVORITE SWEAT-SHIRTED SENSATION?
FRA-Z
ZZZZZZAWUTTT
CEASE YOUR STRUGGLES, VULTURE...
...AND ALLOW THE SOLVENTS WITHIN MY ACIDIC MISTS TO DO THEIR WORK!
YOU MADE A BIG MISTAKE CHALLENGING US, INSECT!
NO ONE CAN STAND AGAINST THE SINISTER SIX!
FASTER, MYSTERIO!
I'VE A MARKER TO SETTLE WITH THAT CRIMSON BUFFOON!
SHREEE
PHOOM
PHOOM
FRAZZ
SINISTER SIX, HUH? LOOKS LIKE YOU COULD USE A REFRESHER IN REMEDIAL MATH, SPARKY--ESPECIALLY SUBTRACTION!

FORTUNATELY THE EQUIVALENCY PROGRAM AT RYKER'S ISLAND IS TORNOTCH!
THOKK
SPIDER-SENSE-- TINGLING!
BETTER MOVE IT, BEN...
...BEFORE THERE'S ONLY ONE PETER PARKER LEFT IN THE WORLD...
..AND IT AIN'T THE CLONE!

IN CASE YOU HAVEN'T BEEN FOLLOWING THE TABLOIDS...
...I'M THE GUY WHO PUT THE HURT ON VENOM!*
EH...?
* SPIDER-MAN #53. --FIN FANG FEIN
COMPARED TO 'OL SLACK-JAW, YOUR LITTLE COFFEE KLATCH IS STRICTLY SECOND-RATE!
I MEAN, IT TAKES SIX OF YOU TO SCREW IN A LIGHT BULB...
...AND NOW YOU'RE DOWN BY TWO!
WHUMP

THINK YOU'RE PRETTY CLEVER, DON'T YOU?
YOU'RE NOTHING MORE THAN A CHEAP FACSIMILE OF THE TRUE WALL-CRAWLER!
AND EVEN HE IS SCARCELY WORTHY OF MY ATTENTIONS!
FSSSSSSSS
HEY, LOOK WHO'S CALLIN' THE KETTLE BLACK!
MISTER, I KNEW THE GREEN GOBLIN...
I FOUGHT THE GREEN GOBLIN...
PHOOM
...AND, BELIEVE ME...
THOKK
...YOU'RE NO GREEN GOBLIN!

YOU... INSOLENT... LITTLE... UPSTART...
PHOOOM
NO ONE MOCKS THE HOBGOBLIN!
ELECTRO! VULTURE! PIN HIM DOWN WITH A CROSSFIRE!
NO MATTER HOW AGILE THAT NIGGLING ANNOYANCE MIGHT BE...
...NOT EVEN HE...
...CAN AVOID THE ENTIRE CEILING!
K-RRRRMMMBLLLL
WHAT WERE YOU THINKING, MACENDALE? YOU COULD'VE CRUSHED US ALL!
AH, BUT I DIDN'T, ELECTRO!
IF YOU NO LONGER POSSESS THE STONES FOR THIS SORT OF THING...
...PERHAPS YOU SHOULD GO BACK TO BEING A POWER COMPANY LINEMAN!
HA HA HA

ELSEWHERE, IN AN APARTMENT OWNED BY ELIAS HARGROVE, LAST LIVING RELATIVE OF DOCTOR OCTOPUS...
WHAT AN UNMITIGATED DISASTER-- JUST AS I'D FEARED!
I ONLY HOPE THAT SPIDER CHARACTER DIDN'T CATCH A GLIMPSE OF MY FACE ON THE VIEWSCREEN...
...AND THAT THE SINISTER SIX'S REPUTATION FOR DISCRETION IS WELL-EARNED!

IN ANY EVENT, THE WHEELS OF MY LATE COUSIN'S PLAN FOR ME TO RECLAIM HIS POSSESSIONS HAVE BEEN SET INTO MOTION...
KLIK
...AND I MAY RESUME PLAYBACK OF OTTO'S LIVING WILL TO RECEIVE MY NEXT SET OF INSTRUCTIONS!

IF YOU ARE VIEWING THIS PORTION OF THE TAPE, ELIAS, IT IS SAFE TO ASSUME THAT YOU HAVE SUCCESSFULLY COMPLETED PHASE ONE.
VERY GOOD. NOW...
...THIS IS WHAT YOU MUST DO NEXT.

THESE INSTRUCTIONS MUST BE FOLLOWED TO THE LETTER. IF--
WHA--!
IT'S... UNBELIEVABLE!
NO NEED TO GO ANY FURTHER, DEAR COUSIN...
...I ALREADY KNOW WHAT NEEDS TO BE DONE!

A SECRET GOVERNMENT BASE IN NASSAU COUNTY, LONG ISLAND...
...DONE AS YOU'VE ASKED, REINHOLDT!
IF OUR PRELIMINARY TESTS HOLD WATER, THAT ENCEPHALO-HELMET SHOULD RECONFIGURE THE WEARER'S BRAIN WAVE PATTERNS TO MATCH THOSE OF OCTAVIUS, ALLOWING HIM TO MANIPULATE THE ARMS!
OCK'S FILES YIELDED A VERITABLE CORNUCOPIA OF DATA!
THE MAN WAS DECADES AHEAD OF HIS TIME!
YOU'RE NOT TOO SHABBY YOURSELF, MORETTI!
THE AGENCY SHOULD BE VERY PLEASED. REMIND ME TO PUT YOU IN FOR A--
EEOOEEEOOEEEOOE
INTRUDER ALERT! WE'VE GOT A PERIMETER BREACH!
SCRAMBLE ALL UNITS -- ASAP!
REINHOLDT TO SECURITY!
WHAT THE DEVIL'S GOING ON DOWN THERE?
THIS INSTALLATION'S SUPPOSED TO BE TOP SECRET!
I KNOW, SIR...

"...BUT SOMEBODY FORGOT TO TELL THEM!"
HA! HA! HA! HA! HA! HA!
THE SIGNAL ON THE TRACKING DEVICE WHICH HARGROVE SO KINDLY SUPPLIED EMANATES FROM WITHIN THIS WAREHOUSE!
FWAASH
FWAASH
PHOOM
PHOOM
PHOOM
PHOOM
PHOOM
ELECTRO! MYSTERIO!
SHRA-ZAAKK
DON'T GET YER PINFEATHERS IN AN UPROAR--
--WE'RE RIGHT BEHIND YOU!
BY ALL MEANS, MY FRIENDS, STAY CLOSE...

"...AND MAKE MY TASK ALL THE EASIER!"
HEY! WHO DIED AND MADE YOU KING OF THE HILL?
NOW TOGETHER, ON MY ORDER!
I WOULD THINK THAT TO BE OBVIOUS, ELECTRO!
THEY'RE THROUGH!
KRA-KOOOOM!
QUICKLY! SALVAGE THE DOCUMENTATION...
...BEFORE OUR WORK IS LOST!
ROSS! ANDREW!
GET THOSE ARMS ON A TRANSPORT!
WE'LL KEEP THEM OFF YOUR BACK, UNTIL--

THINK SO, HUH?
PHOOOM
FRA-ZAAAT
WELL, I'VE GOT A NEWSFLASH FOR YOU! G-MAN...
...YOU DON'T KNOW WHO YOU'RE DEALING WITH!
YEEE-ARGGGHHH!

PRETTY SMOOTH, HUH?
WE SHOULD DO THIS MORE OFTEN!
SPARE US YOUR CHEST-THUMPING, DILLON! YOU IMPRESS NO ONE!
LET'S SEEK OUT WHAT WE CAME FOR AND BEGONE!
OVER THERE! LOOK!
OCTAVIUS' ARMS. HARDLY THE PRIZE WE SOUGHT...
...BUT STILL--
UH-UH, BOYCHIK!
THWAPP
YOU CAN LOOK...
...BUT YOU BETTER NOT TOUCH!
BESIDES, THOSE GARISH ACCESSORIES WOULD CLASH WITH YOUR SHINY NEW WARDROBE!
SPIDER-MAN?
WELL, IT AIN'T THE JERKY BOYS!

I WAS LOOKING FOR OCK'S KILLER, NOT HIS CRONIES, BUT THAT STRANGE BLIP I PICKED UP WITH MY SPIDER-SENSE DREW ME STRAIGHT TO 'EM!*
AND FAR BE IT FROM ME NOT TO PUNCH A GIFT HORSE IN THE MOUTH!
KILL HIM!
SQUASH THAT INSECT LIKE--
*FROM THE MINIDOT TRACER THE SCARLET SPIDER ATTACHED TO THE VULTURE LAST ISSUE! --ERIC
TSK TSK!
HOW MANY TIMES I GOTTA TELL YOU GUYS...
...IT'S ARACHNID! ARACHNID!
YOU KNOW...
...THEY SAY THAT VIOLENCE...
...IS THE FIRST REFUGE OF THE INCOMPETENT!

OOPS!
FORGOT WHO I WAS TALKING TO FOR A MINUTE!
PHOOM
PHOOM
PHOOM
STILL, I'M SURE YOU'LL FORGIVE THE FAUX PAS...
"...I CAN SURREPTITIOUSLY SECURE THE ITEM OF INTEREST! AND LEAVE JUST AS I ARRIVED-- UNSEEN!"
MY STRATEGY IS WORKING PERFECTLY!
WHILE THOSE FOUR IMBECILES KEEP THE WEB-SLINGER AND THE DEFENSE FORCES OCCUPIED...
THINK AGAIN, SPIDER-MAN!
OH-HO, THE OLD "MIST-UP-THE-SLEEVE" BIT, EH?
I AM SO-OOOO SCARED!
LISTEN UP, MYSTY...
THESE ARE THE BIG LEAGUES, NOT "STAR SEARCH '95!"
SO YOU MIGHT WANNA RETIRE THAT BUBBLE, BEFORE YOU GET SERIOUSLY HURT... LIKE OCK!
OR...
...IN WORDS OF ONE SYLLABLE FOR THE INTELLECT-UALLY CHALLENGED...

...DON'T DO THE CRIME...
...IF YOU CAN'T DO THE TIME!
WHUMP
GET THE IDEAAAAAAAA--
FRAAZ
ZZZKRRRRRRKKLL
THAT WAS ONLY A HYPER-STATIC BURST TO GET YOUR ATTENTION, WALL-CRAWLER!
I WANT TO SEE YOUR EXPRESSION WHEN YOU DIE!
THAT'D BE A PRETTY GOOD TRICK, ELECTRO.
...SINCE I'M WEARING A FULL FACE-MASK!
YOU WON'T BE TALKING SO SMART...
...ONCE I REALLY POUR ON THE JUICE!
SHA-RAAAKT
YOW!

WHATEVER HAPPENED TO THE TOUCHY-FEELY MAX DILLON I KNEW AND LOVED?
FRA-ZAAAK!
EITHER ELECTRO'S BEEN FOLLOWING A TWELVE-STEP SELF-ESTEEM PROGRAM...
...OR HE ATE HIS WHEATIES FOR BREAKFAST!
MAYBE OCK CAN SAVE MY BACON TWICE IN ONE LIFETIME!
USE HIS ARMS AS A LIGHTNING ROD TO ATTRACT--
CAN'T LET HIM GET THE ARMS...
A BARAGE OF PUMPKIN BOMBS SHOULD STOP HIM.
THAT'S...
...FAR...
SKA-REEEEEEEEEEEEEE
WA-THOOOOOOOOOOOOM
...ENOUGH!

IS THE WALL-CRAWLER--?
FINISHED!
I-I CAN'T SEE--
STAY ALERT IN CASE--
WHOK
THOKK
KRAKK
THUDD

DON'T BAIL OUT NOW, GUYS!
THE PARTY'S JUST GETTING STARTED!
AND...
...IN CASE YOU COULDN'T TELL...
...SOMETHING NEW HAS BEEN ADDED TO THE MIX!
SAY HELLO... TO THE AMAZING OCTO-SPIDEY!

GET BACK!
HE'S GOT THE HELMET AND OCTOPUS' ARRRRR--!
THROKK
MY, BUT AREN'T YOU THE BRIGHT BOY!
BUT BETWEEN THEIR REACH...
...AND MY HANDY-DANDY SPIDER-SENSE...
I COULD GET TO LIKE THIS!
STILL A LITTLE SHAKY ON THESE FOUR NEW PINS...
WHOK

"...I'D SAY THE TIDE'S ABOUT TO TURN IN MY FAVOR!"
H-HE'S UNSTOPPABLE!
UNSTOPPABLE? HARDLY!
THE ARACHNID MAY NOW MORE RESEMBLE HIS NAME-SAKE...
...BUT A WELL-AIMED PLASMA-BOLT WILL STILL MAKE SHORT WORK OF HIM!
TRUE ENOUGH, BIRD-BRAIN...
...BUT YOU'VE GOTTA TAG ME FIRST!
WHAT'S YOUR HURRY, FELLAS? I COULD KEEP THIS UP ALL NIGHT!

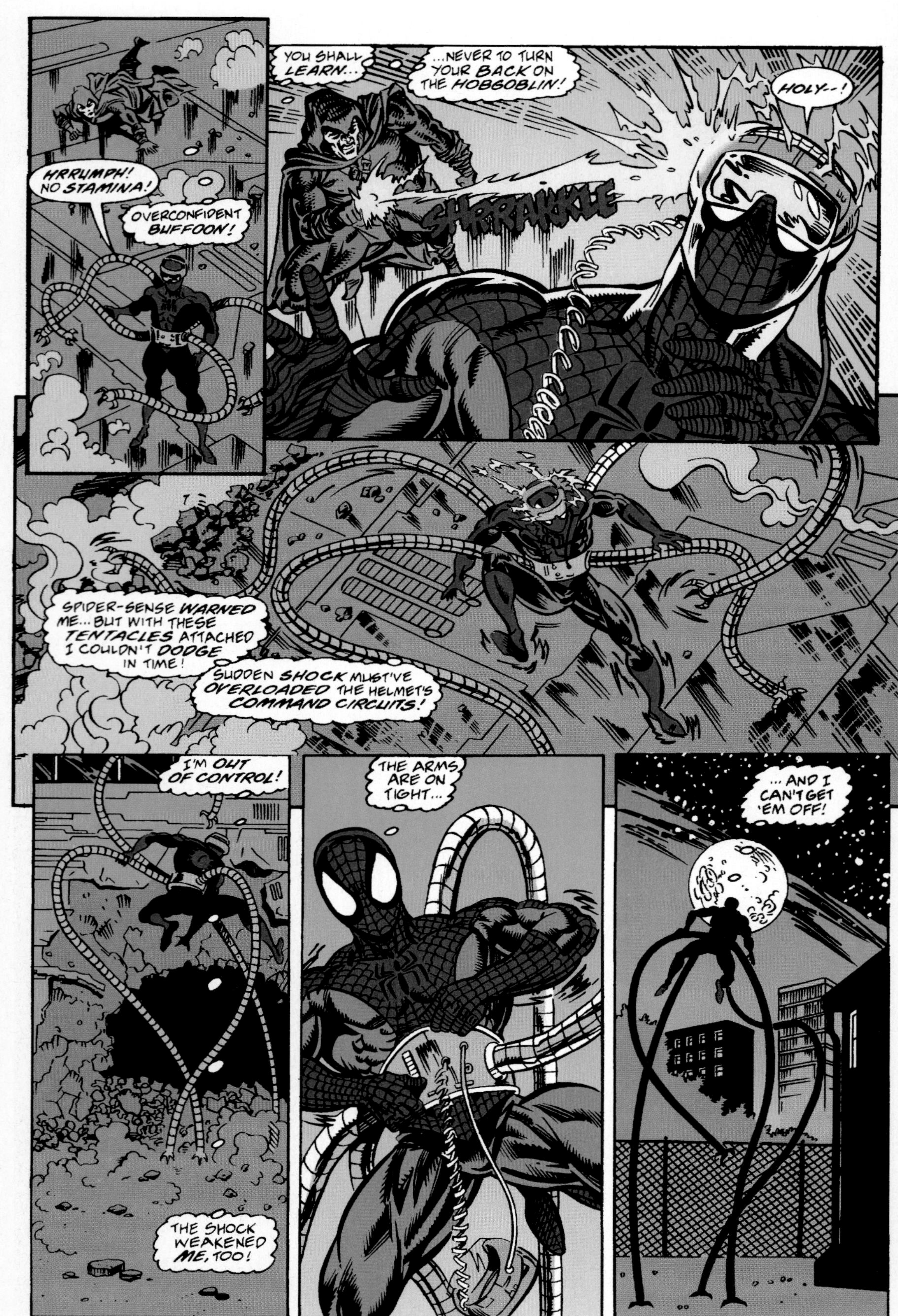
HRRUMPH! NO STAMINA!
OVERCONFIDENT BUFFOON!
YOU SHALL LEARN...
...NEVER TO TURN YOUR BACK ON THE HOBGOBLIN!
SHRRAKKLE
HOLY--!
SPIDER-SENSE WARNED ME... BUT WITH THESE TENTACLES ATTACHED I COULDN'T DODGE IN TIME!
SUDDEN SHOCK MUST'VE OVERLOADED THE HELMET'S COMMAND CIRCUITS!
I'M OUT OF CONTROL!
THE SHOCK WEAKENED ME, TOO!
THE ARMS ARE ON TIGHT...
... AND I CAN'T GET 'EM OFF!

LET THE OTHERS TAKE THE FALL, MYSTERIO!
AT LEAST WE'RE SAFE!
"SAFE?"
K-RUUKT
THERE IS NO SAFETY...
KER-RAAKT
...WHILE YOUR ILK ROAMS THE NIGHT!
THOOM
W-WHO-- WHO ARE YOU...?
PATIENCE, MAXWELL DILLON! YOU'LL HAVE YOUR TURN...
...ONCE I'VE BESTOWED UPON YOUR COMPANION...

...THE MARK... ...OF KAINE!
NEXT: THE CONCLUSION!

MARVEL COMICS
SPIDER-MAN:
FUNERAL FOR AN OCTOPUS
REST IN PIECES
$1.50 US
$2.05 CAN
3
MAY
APPROVED BY THE COMICS CODE AUTHORITY
RON LIM '95 AFTER JRJR + MILGROM

SMOOTH MOVE, "HERO"!
THOUGHT YOU WERE SOOO SMART--USING DOC OCK'S ARMS TO NAIL HIS CRONIES IN THE SINISTER SIX!
WELL, WHO'S SORRY NOW, PARKER?
THESE CRAZY THINGS'VE RUN AMOK...
...AND THEY'RE TAKING YOU ALONG FOR THE RIDE!
STAN LEE PRESENTS:
FUNERAL FOR AN OCTOPUS PART III
A FAREWELL TO ARMS!
TOM BREVOORT & MIKE KANTEROVICH--WRITERS
TOD SMITH-- BREAKDOWNS
MILGROM, S.BUSCEMA & HUDSON--FINISHES
DAVE SHARPE-- LETTERER
CHAI-CHI WANG-- COLORIST
ERIC FEIN-- UNDERTAKER
DANNY FINGEROTH-- OVERTAKER
BOB BUDIANSKY-- CRYPT-KEEPER

PULL BACK!
HE'S OUT OF CONTROL!
GOT THAT RIGHT, PAL!
TENTACLES ARE FLAILING WILDLY-- THROWING ME OFF-BALANCE!
CAN'T GET ENOUGH LEVERAGE TO--
WHOA! SPIDER-SENSE GOING CRAZY!
KRA-KOW!
LOOKS LIKE THE CAVALRY'S ARRIVED...
...ONLY THEY THINK I'M THE BAD GUYS!
KEEP FIRING! THE ARMS MUST NOT BE ALLOWED TO ESCAPE!
WITH THE ENCEPHALO-HELMET INOPERATIVE, OCTAVIUS' APPENDAGES ARE SCRAMBLING THE WEB-SLINGER'S MENTAL COMMANDS!
TAKE HIM DOWN AND THEY SHOULD DROP LIKE A STONE!

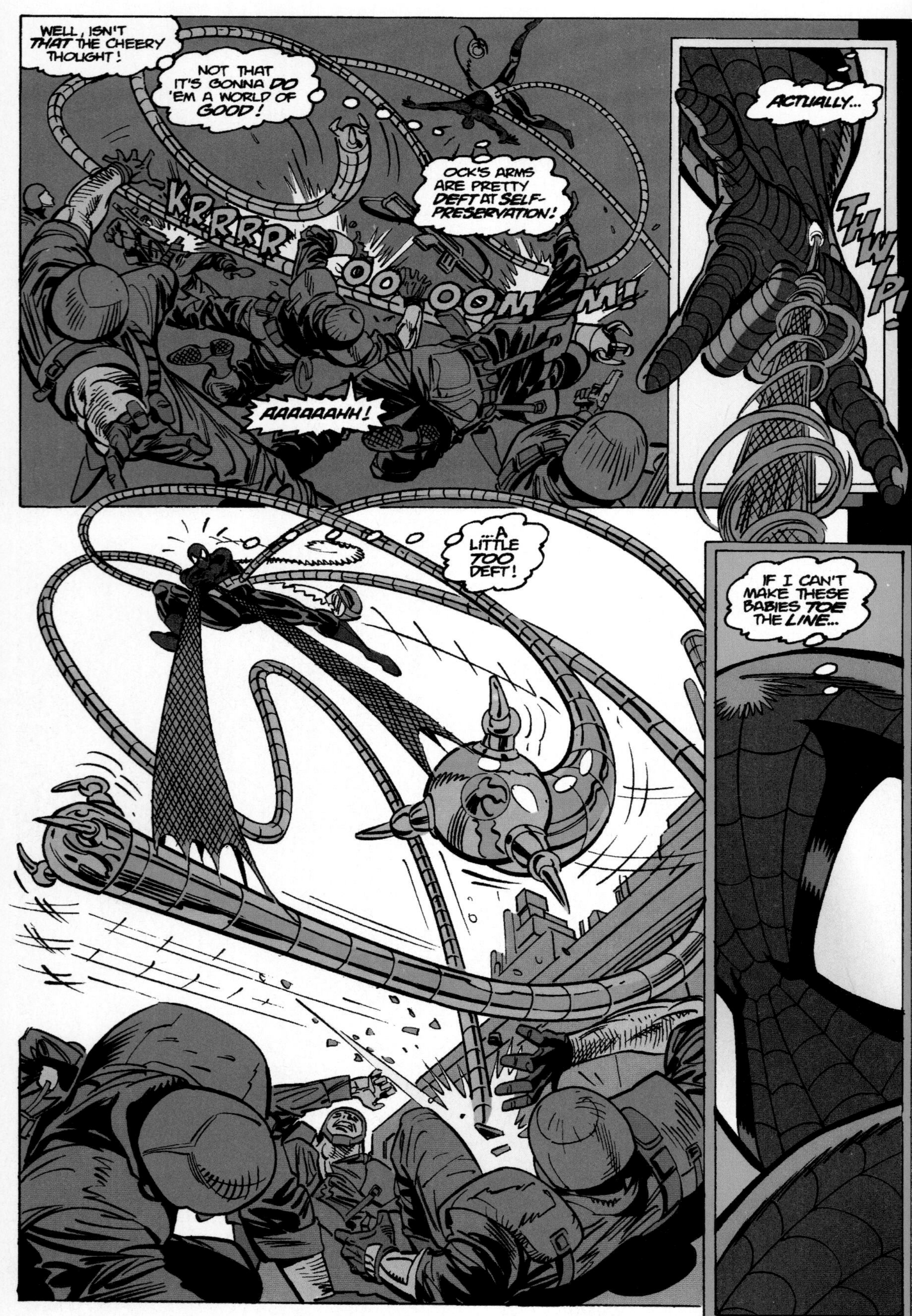
WELL, ISN'T THAT THE CHEERY THOUGHT!
NOT THAT IT'S GONNA DO 'EM A WORLD OF GOOD!
OCK'S ARMS ARE PRETTY DEFT AT SELF-PRESERVATION!
KRRRR
OOOOOOMM!
AAAAAAHH!
ACTUALLY...
THWIP!
...A LITTLE TOO DEFT!
IF I CAN'T MAKE THESE BABIES TOE THE LINE...

"...SOMEONE'S GONNA WIND UP DEAD!"
KRKK!
K-RULK!
I'M FREE!
SPIDER-SENSE LET ME ROLL WITH THE BLOW--EVADE THE LARGER CHUNKS OF RUBBLE!
EVEN SO, THE IMPACT REALLY KNOCKED ME FOR A LOOP!*
THROOM!
THAT'S WHAT I GET FOR TAKING THE SINISTER SIX SO LIGHTLY!
ALMOST ENOUGH TO MAKE A CLONE WANT TO HANG UP HIS WEBS--ALMOST!
DON'T KNOW WHAT THEY'RE PLANNING...
*THE SCARLET SPIDER WAS BURIED BENEATH FALLING RUBBLE LAST ISSUE, REMEMBER?--ERIC
...BUT I'D LAY DOLLARS TO DOUGHNUTS THAT MOUSY GUY I SAW ON THEIR VIEW-SCREEN DOES!
REMEMBER HIM FROM OCTOPUS' FUNERAL--ELIAS HARGROVE, DOC'S LAST LIVING RELATION!
AND...
...ONCE I'VE FINISHED MY LITTLE TÊTE-À-TÊTE WITH THE DIVINE MISTER HARGROVE...

"...IT'S PAYBACK TIME!"
PATIENCE, ELECTRO! YOU'LL HAVE YOUR TURN...
...ONCE I'VE BESTOWED UPON YOUR COMPANION, MYSTERIO...
...THE MARK...
OF KAINE!
SUCH IS THE FATE AWAITING ALL YOUR ILK!
MY GRIM VISIONS OF TOMORROW MUST BE AVERTED!
WHA--?!

AN AUTOMATON!
THEN BECK WAS NEVER TRULY PRESENT!
KLIK!
FSSSS!
WHRRR!
I... ...HAVE... ...BEEN... ...DENIED!
SKA-RASH!
AW... ...NOW AIN'T THAT TOO FREAKIN' BAD!!
MYSTERIO MAY BE A LITTLE ON THE RUSTY SIDE...

...BUT AT LEAST THAT COWARD'S ROBOT GAVE ME A CHANCE TO TURN UP THE JUICE!
THIS NIGHT IS NOT A TOTAL LOSS!
I YET HAVE THE OPPORTUNITY TO ELIMINATE YOU!
FRA-ZAAKKT!
FRA-ZAAKKT
YOU'RE STILL STANDING?!
WH-WHAT ARE YOU?
ALL YOU NEED KNOW OF ME...
...IS THAT I AM...
...YOUR DEATH!
KRAKK!

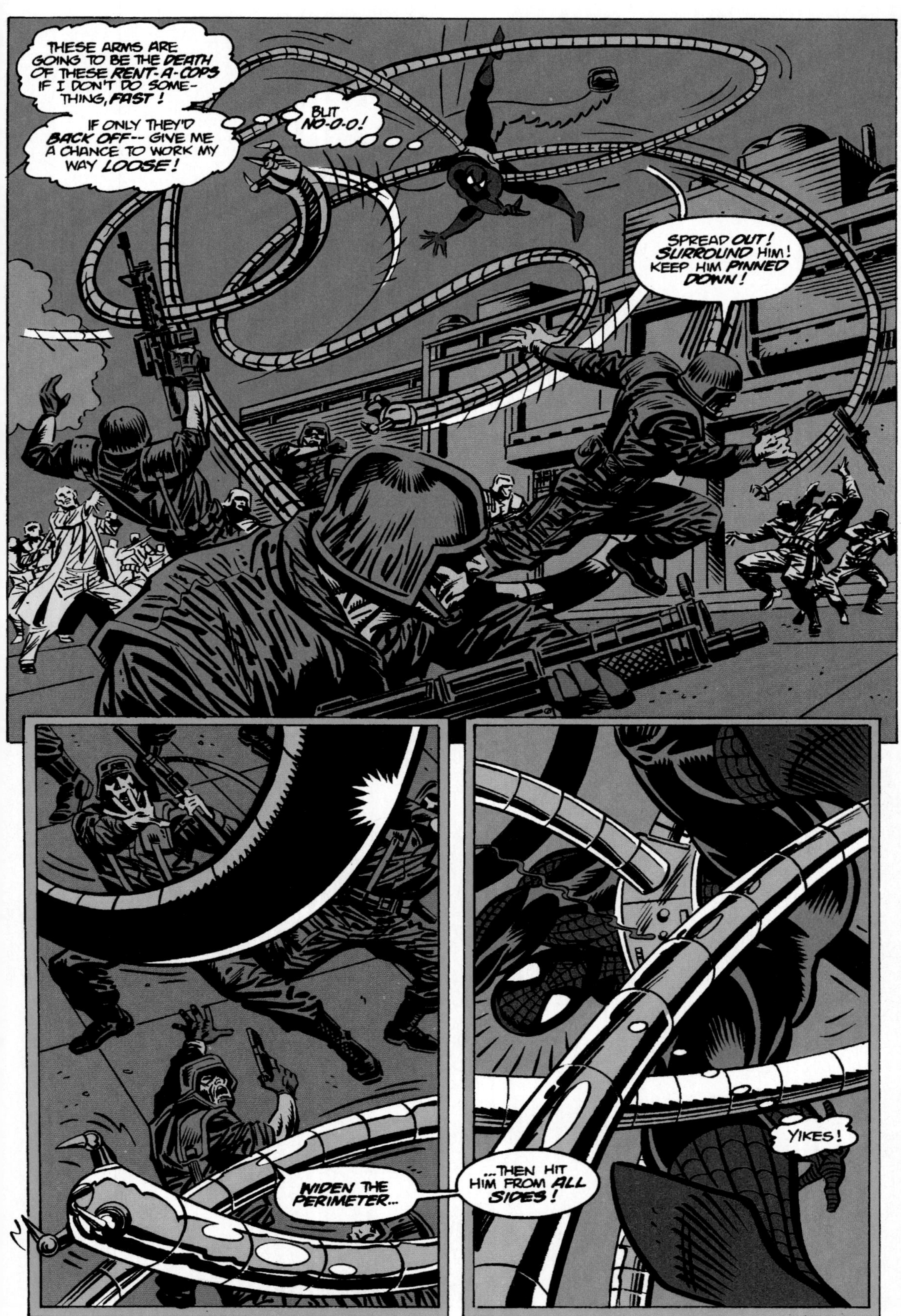
THESE ARMS ARE GOING TO BE THE DEATH OF THESE RENT-A-COPS IF I DON'T DO SOMETHING, FAST!
IF ONLY THEY'D BACK OFF-- GIVE ME A CHANCE TO WORK MY WAY LOOSE!
BUT NO-O-O!
SPREAD OUT! SURROUND HIM! KEEP HIM PINNED DOWN!
WIDEN THE PERIMETER...
...THEN HIT HIM FROM ALL SIDES!
YIKES!

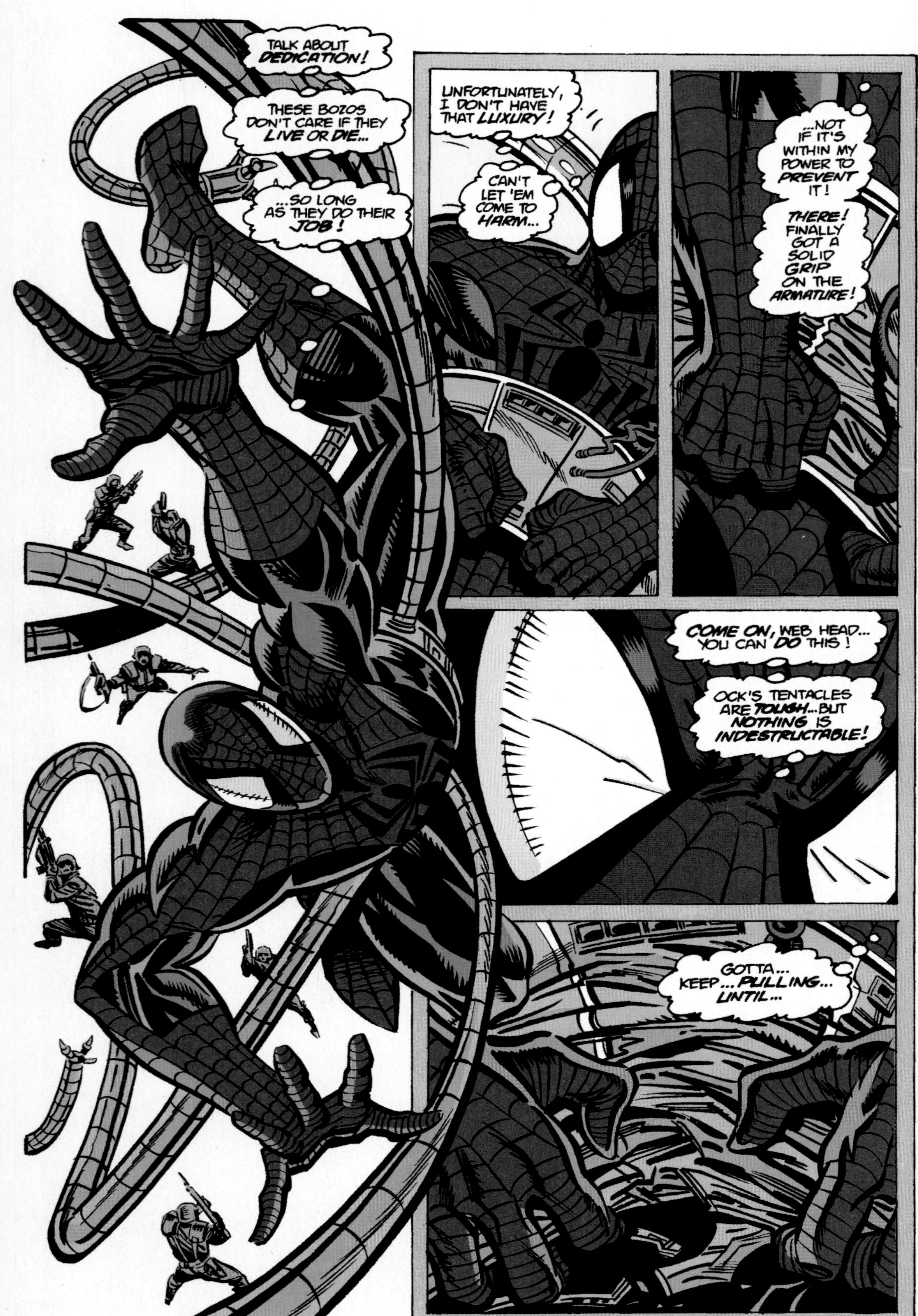
TALK ABOUT DEDICATION!
THESE BOZOS DON'T CARE IF THEY LIVE OR DIE...
...SO LONG AS THEY DO THEIR JOB!
UNFORTUNATELY, I DON'T HAVE THAT LUXURY!
CAN'T LET 'EM COME TO HARM...
...NOT IF IT'S WITHIN MY POWER TO PREVENT IT!
THERE! FINALLY GOT A SOLID GRIP ON THE ARMATURE!
COME ON, WEB HEAD... YOU CAN DO THIS!
OCK'S TENTACLES ARE TOUGH...BUT NOTHING IS INDESTRUCTABLE!
GOTTA... KEEP... PULLING... UNTIL...

SKA AAN NGG!

WHEW! NOW THAT'S MORE LIKE IT!
FSSS
FSSS
FSSS
DO YOU REALIZE WHAT YOU'VE DONE?
THOSE ARMS WERE THE VERY PINNACLE OF ENCEPHALO-RESPONSIVE PROSTHETICS TECHNOLOGY!
NOW THEY'RE NOTHING BUT SCRAP METAL!
OUR RESEARCH WAS GOVERNMENT SANCTIONED, YOU VANDAL! UNCLE SAM'S GOING TO HAVE YOUR HIDE FOR--
THWIP!!
MRRPH!
HEY, DON'T BOTHER TO THANK ME, CURLY...
...JUST REMEMBER ME COME CHRISTMAS!
CAN'T WASTE ANY MORE TIME ON SOCIAL NICETIES...

"...NOT WHILE THE SIXERS ARE STILL ON THE LOOSE!"
FAREWELL, MISCREANT! I SEND YOU TO JOIN YOUR FALLEN LEADER, OCTAVIUS...
...IN OBLIVION!
EH?
SPIDER-MAN?!
THE TIME IS NOT YET RIGHT FOR HIM TO UNCOVER THE TRUTH OF MY EXISTENCE!*
I MUST WITHDRAW!
* THIS STORY TAKES PLACE SHORTLY BEFORE SPIDEY MET UP WITH KAINE. --ERIC

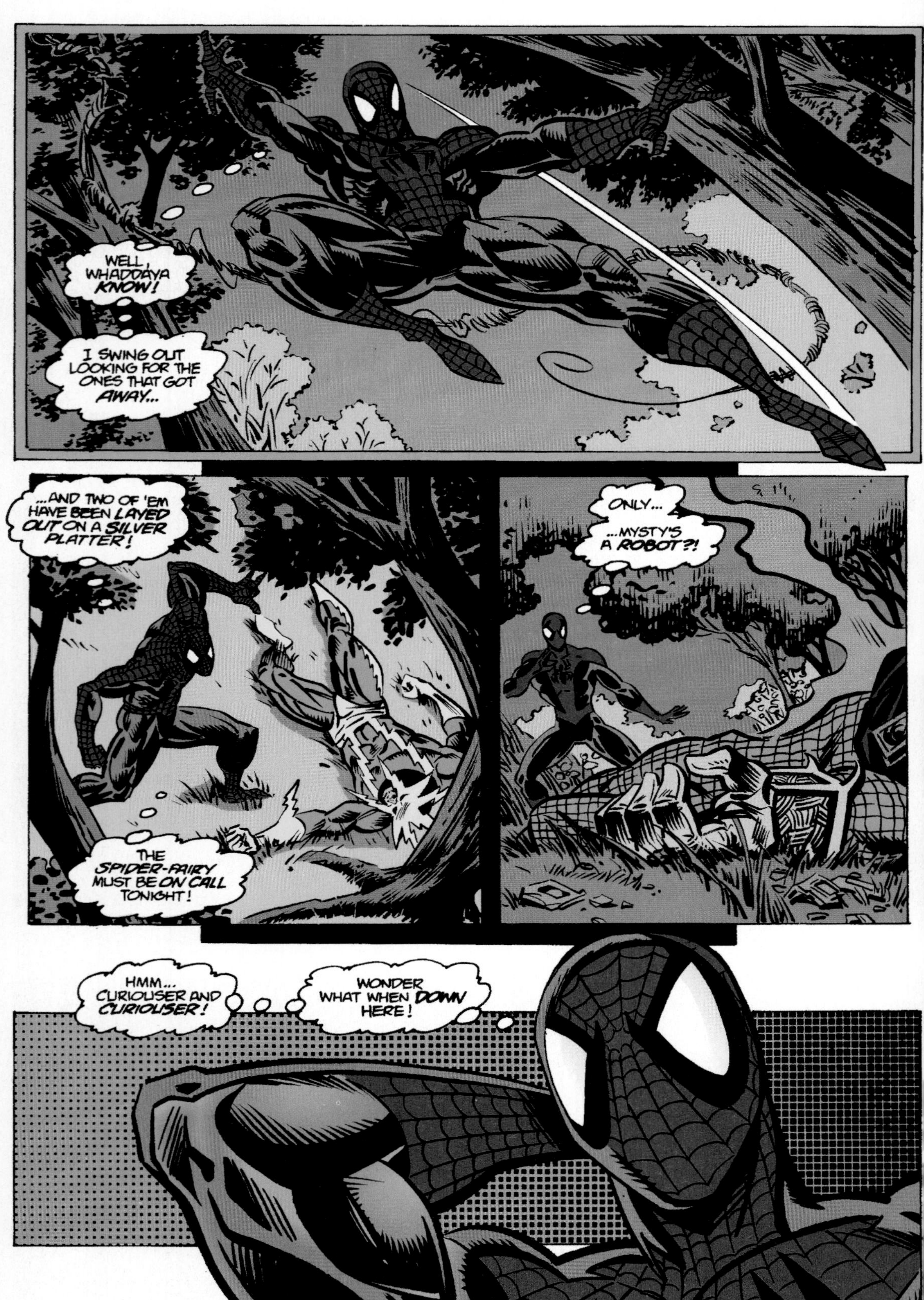
WELL, WHADDAYA KNOW!
I SWING OUT LOOKING FOR THE ONES THAT GOT AWAY...
...AND TWO OF 'EM HAVE BEEN LAYED OUT ON A SILVER PLATTER!
THE SPIDER-FAIRY MUST BE ON CALL TONIGHT!
ONLY...
...MYSTY'S A ROBOT?!
HMM... CURIOUSER AND CURIOUSER!
WONDER WHAT WHEN DOWN HERE!

"COULD HE AND ELECTRO HAVE HAD A FALLING OUT?"
OUT WITH IT, GERDES!
YOU WON'T MAKE A FOOL OF ELIAS HARGROVE ANY LONGER!
WHAT'S YOUR ANGLE?
WHUMP
ANGLE?
DON'T PLAY THE INNOCENT WITH ME, LAWYER!
YOU KNOW FULL WELL WHAT'S ON MY MIND!
THIS TAPE YOU GAVE ME-- OTTO'S LIVING WILL...
...IS A FRAUD!
WHOEVER COMPUTER-COMPOSITED THE IMAGERY KNEW A GREAT DEAL ABOUT MY COUSIN!..
...BUT APPARENTLY LITTLE ABOUT THE LAWS OF OPTICS!
I NOTICED CERTAIN REFLECTIONS IN OTTO'S GLASSES WERE INVERTED-- A PATENT IMPOSSIBILITY!
THE CULPRIT NEARLY HAD ME FOOLED, BUT HIS OWN SENSE OF PANACHE PROVED HIS UNDOING!
YOU POSSESS A DISCERNING EYE, MY FRIEND. IT SEEMS UNCOMMON INTELLIGENCE RUNS IN YOUR FAMILY!

I'LL NEED TO PAY MORE ATTENTION TO SUCH FINE DETAILS...
...THE NEXT TIME I HURRIEDLY DOCTOR A VIDEOTAPE!
S-STAY BACK!
BLAM!
BLAM!
ENOUGH GUNPLAY, ELIAS! AS YOU CAN SEE IT'S ENTIRELY FUTILE!
THERE'S SIMPLY NO HARM YOU CAN DO TO A MAN...
...WHO IS NO MORE THAN A HOLOGRAPHIC PROJECTION!
MYST-- MYSTERIO?!

K-RUKT!
YOU SEE, OVER THE YEARS, YOUR LATE COUSIN HAD ACCRUED A VAST STOREHOUSE OF INFORMATION ON THE CITY'S MAJOR UNDERWORLD FIGURES!
INFORMATION WHICH COULD PROVE QUITE--DAMAGING--SHOULD IT EVER COME TO LIGHT...
...OR INVALUABLE IN THE RIGHT HANDS!
THUS, I ARRANGED TO RELIEVE THE AUTHORITIES OF IT--ALBEIT IN A DELIGHTFULLY BYZANTINE MANNER!
AH, BUT EVEN THE BEST LAID PLANS OFT CONTAIN A FATAL FLAW!
OCTAVIUS HAD CONFIGURED THE DISK IN SUCH A WAY THAT, WITHOUT THE PROPER DECRYPTION SEQUENCE...
...THE CONTAINMENT VESSEL WOULD SPONTANEOUSLY SELF-DESTRUCT!
THAT'S THE OTHER REASON I ENGINEERED YOUR INVOLVEMENT! AS OCTOPUS' CLOSEST LIVING RELATIVE, SURELY YOU MUST BE PRIVY TO THIS CODE!
QUITE SO, HARGROVE!
I SHOULD THANK YOU FOR JOINING ME!
YOU'VE SAVED ME THE EFFORT OF PAYING A PERSONAL CALL!
I HID IN PLAIN SIGHT WHILE I SURREPTITIOUSLY ACCRUED THE SOUGHT-AFTER DATA-DISK DURING THE MELEE AT THAT GOVERNMENT RESEARCH CENTER! *
ONCE IN MY POSSESSION, I HOPED TO PUT THAT INFORMATION TO FULL AND EFFECTIVE USE!
AND IF ANY MISHAPS WERE TO OCCUR, YOU WOULD BE THE ONE TO TAKE THE FALL!
* FUNERAL #2, PAGE 19.--KNEW IT ALL ALONG ERIC
TELL ME...
...AND YOU MAY YET LIVE TO SEE TOMORROW!
B-BUT I DON'T--
--I DON'T KNOW ANYTHING!

WHERE'S YOUR SENSE OF HOSPITALITY, MYSTERIO?
YOU'RE REQUIRED TO SERVE COGNAC AND BRIE AT THESE SOIREES BEFORE YOU MANHANDLE THE GUESTS!
SK
RAASH!
SPIDER-MAN?!
JUST AS I SUSPECTED-- YOU REALLY CAN'T SEE THROUGH THAT DESIGNER FISHBOWL, CAN YOU?
THE MONIKER'S SCARLET SPIDER. TWO ESSES. ACCENT ON THE FIRST!
MAYBE I SHOULD HAND OUT BUSINESS CARDS!
BUT... HOW--??
WOULDJA BELIEVE THE PHONE BOOK?
AFTER I DUG MYSELF OUT OF THE RUBBLE, I LET MY FINGERS DO THE WALKING... AND SCOPED OUT THE ADDRESS OF HARGROVE'S APARTMENT!
JUST AS I'D HOPED...
...HE LED ME STRAIGHT TO WHERE THE ACTION IS!!!

PERHAPS...
...MORE ACTION...
...THAN YOU BARGAINED FOR IMPOSTER!
OH, GET REAL, QUENTIN! DON'T YOU EVER UPDATE YOUR MATERIAL?
HOLOGRAPHIC PROJECTORS? HALLUCINOGENIC GAS?
BEEN THERE, DONE THAT!
SAVE THE DAVID COPPERFIELD ACT FOR SOMEONE WHO--
UNGH!
KRAK!

THUPT THUPT THUPT
FORGOT HIS BUILT-IN JAMMERS COULD BLOCK MY SPIDER-SENSE!
BETTER PLAY THIS BY THE NUMBERS!
PEPPER THE LOT OF 'EM WITH IMPACT WEBBING!
NO DICE! EVERY ONE OF EM'S AS PHONY AS...WELL, AS A FIVE-YEAR OLD CLONE!
SO WHERE'S--
HEY, WAITAMINUTE!
THE ANSWER'S BEEN STARING ME RIGHT IN THE FACE!
THUPT
THWAAPT

EXCELLENT, MY ERZATZ OPPONENT!
YOU'VE CORRECTLY REASONED THAT...
...ALL IS SELDOM AS IT APPEARS
YES!
A PITY YOU UNCOVERED MY DECEPTION, SPIDER!
BIG SURPRISE, GIVEN WHO I'M FIGHTING!
FIGURED YOU'D PULLED A FAST ONE-- MADE THE SWITCH WITH HARGROVE WHEN YOU RELEASED YOUR MIST...
...AND THE PROOF IS CATCHING FORTY WINKS BEHIND THAT DESK!
YOU'VE FORCED ME TO TAKE MEASURES I'D SOONER HAVE AVOIDED...

...TO ENSURE THAT YOU TROUBLE ME NO FURTHER!
KLIK!
TH-THE DATA-DISK!
WITHOUT THE DECRYPTION CODE--!
KLIK!
I GET THE PICTURE, HARGROVE!
HANG TIGHT...
BA-WHROOOM!
...'CAUSE WE ARE OUTTA HERE!
NO TIME TO GRAB MYSTERIO, TOO!

EPILOGUE

NOT MUCH POINT GOING BACK *IN* AFTER *MYSTERIO*-- THE *BLAST* TOOK OUT THE ENTIRE *FLOOR!*

HE *COULDN'T* HAVE SURVIVED...

...ASSUMING THAT WAS REALLY *HIM* IN THE *FIRST* PLACE!

MISDIRECTION ALWAYS *WAS* HIS *STRONG SUIT!*

≷KOFF≷ ≷KOFF≷

I IMAGINE YOU'LL BE ESCORTING ME TO THE *AUTHORITIES* NOW.

NAH.
MAYBE I'M JUST GETTING SOFT IN MY OLD AGE...
...BUT...
...JUDGING BY WHAT I HEARD OUTSIDE GERDES' OFFICE...
...YOU WERE A DUPE...
...IF NOT ENTIRELY AN INNOCENT ONE!

WHATEVER HOLD YOUR COUSIN HAD OVER YOU ENDED WITH HIS DEATH!
YOU'RE FREE TO MAKE YOUR OWN CHOICES-- WITHOUT YOUR LINEAGE FORCING YOU
BUT IF I HEAR YOU'VE CHOSEN TO PURSUE THE FAMILY VOCATION...
...YOU'LL SEE ME AGAIN -- AND IT WON'T BE PRETTY!

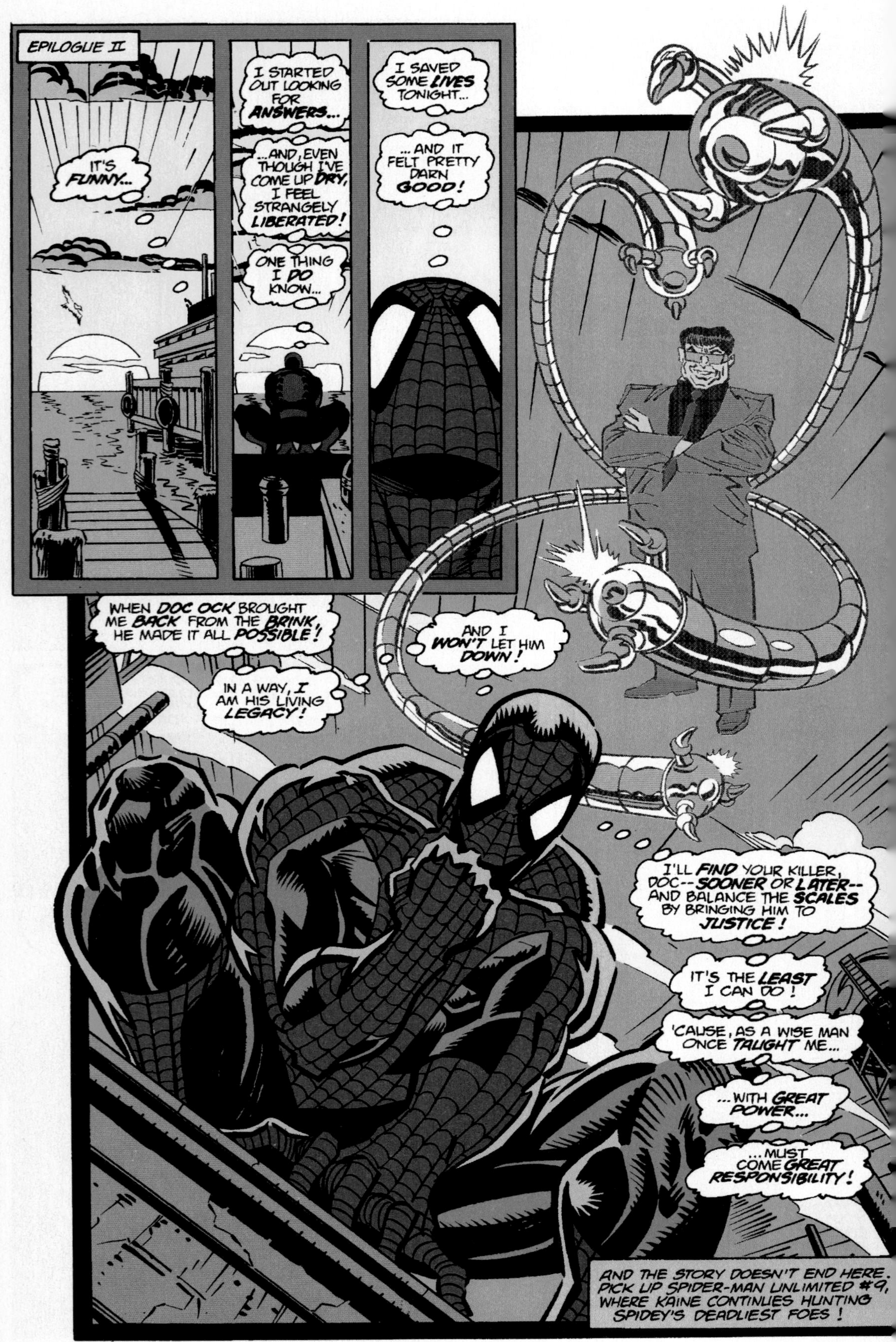
EPILOGUE II
IT'S FUNNY...
I STARTED OUT LOOKING FOR ANSWERS...
...AND, EVEN THOUGH I'VE COME UP DRY, I FEEL STRANGELY LIBERATED!
ONE THING I DO KNOW...
I SAVED SOME LIVES TONIGHT...
...AND IT FELT PRETTY DARN GOOD!
WHEN DOC OCK BROUGHT ME BACK FROM THE BRINK, HE MADE IT ALL POSSIBLE!
IN A WAY, I AM HIS LIVING LEGACY!
AND I WON'T LET HIM DOWN!
I'LL FIND YOUR KILLER, DOC--SOONER OR LATER--AND BALANCE THE SCALES BY BRINGING HIM TO JUSTICE!
IT'S THE LEAST I CAN DO!
'CAUSE, AS A WISE MAN ONCE TAUGHT ME...
...WITH GREAT POWER...
...MUST COME GREAT RESPONSIBILITY!
AND THE STORY DOESN'T END HERE. PICK UP SPIDER-MAN UNLIMITED #9, WHERE KAINE CONTINUES HUNTING SPIDEY'S DEADLIEST FOES!

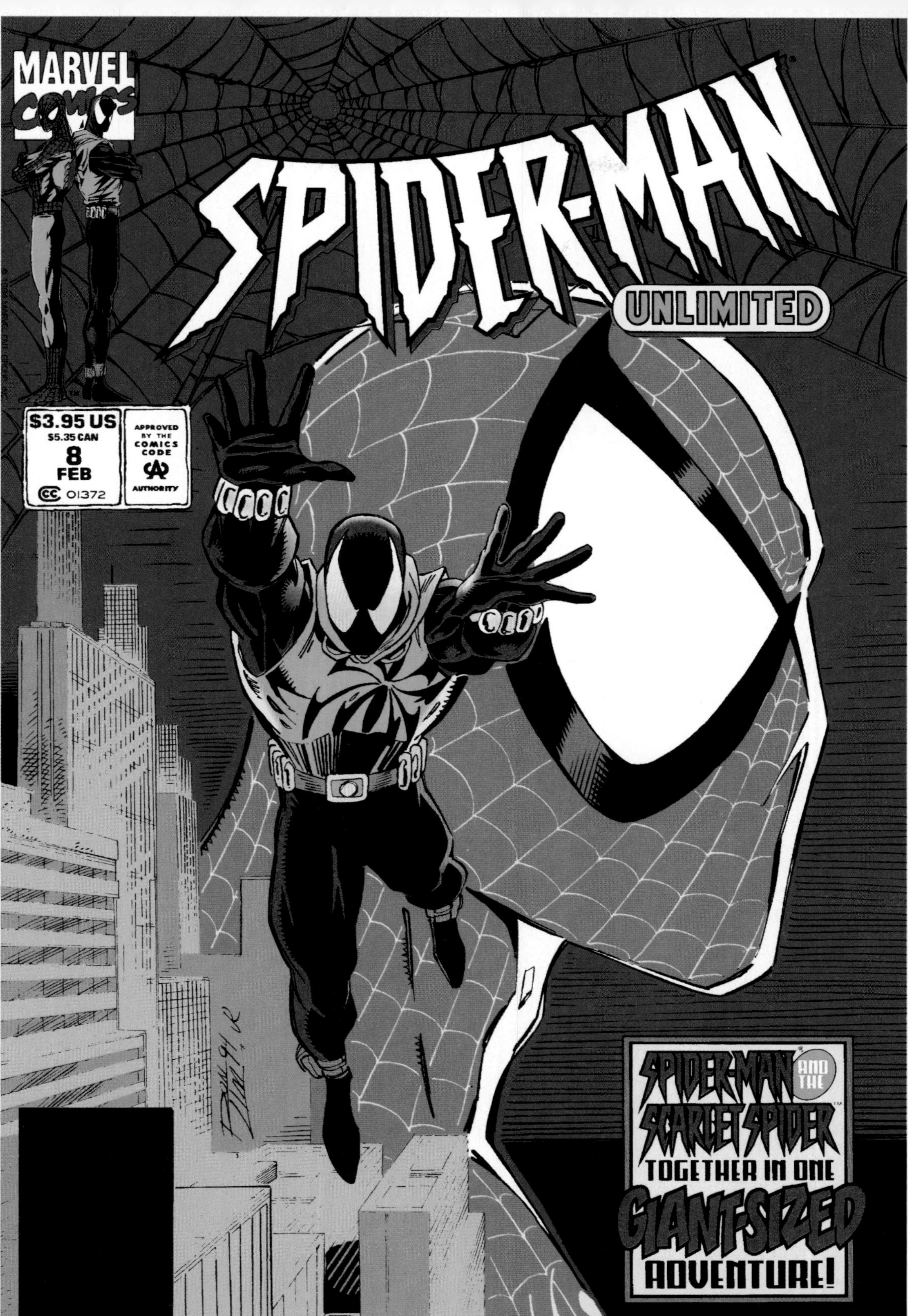
MARVEL COMICS
SPIDER-MAN
UNLIMITED
$3.95 US
$5.35 CAN
8
FEB
01372
APPROVED BY THE COMICS CODE AUTHORITY
SPIDER-MAN AND THE SCARLET SPIDER
TOGETHER IN ONE
GIANT-SIZED
ADVENTURE!

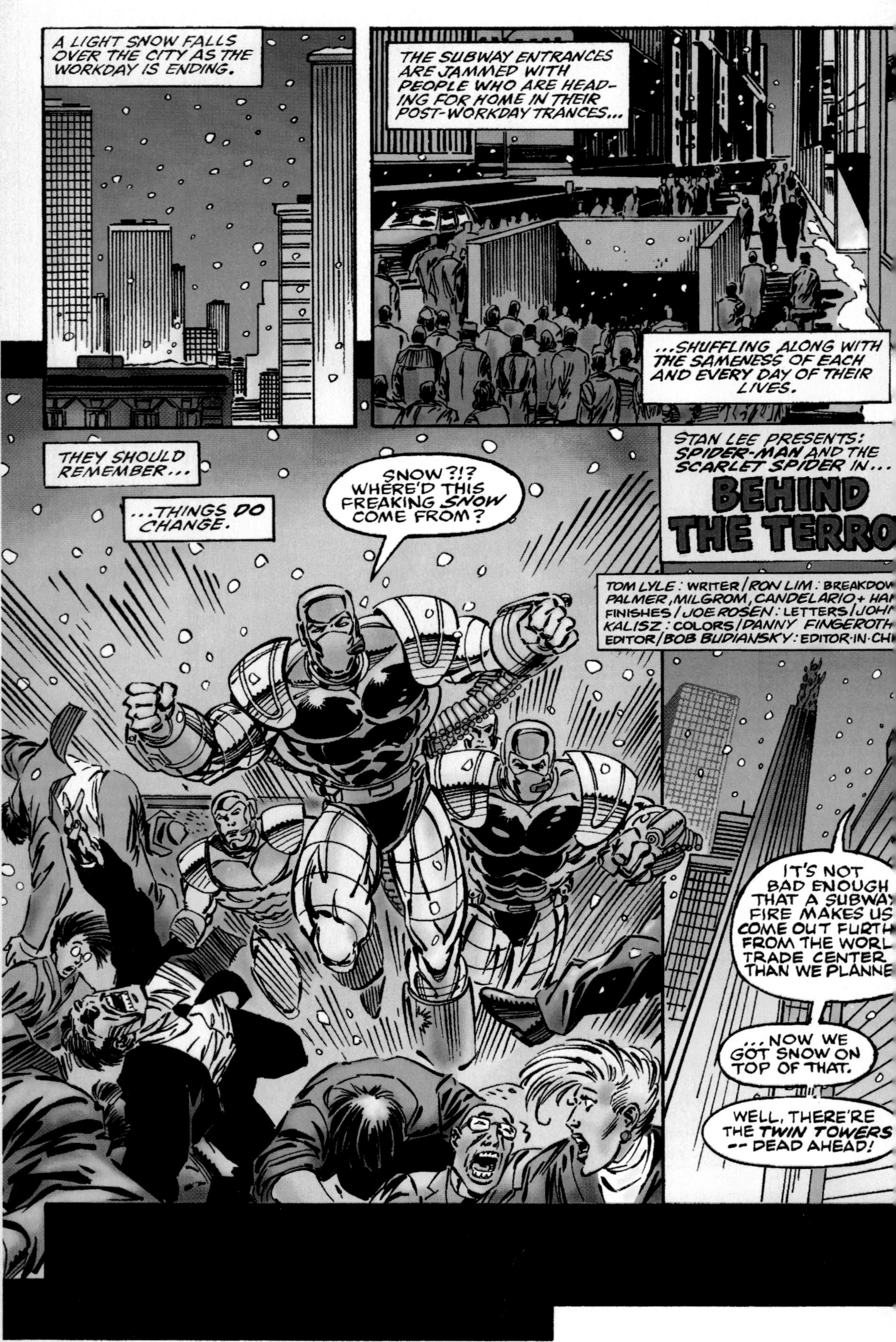
A LIGHT SNOW FALLS OVER THE CITY AS THE WORKDAY IS ENDING.
THE SUBWAY ENTRANCES ARE JAMMED WITH PEOPLE WHO ARE HEADING FOR HOME IN THEIR POST-WORKDAY TRANCES...
...SHUFFLING ALONG WITH THE SAMENESS OF EACH AND EVERY DAY OF THEIR LIVES.
THEY SHOULD REMEMBER...
...THINGS DO CHANGE.
SNOW?!? WHERE'D THIS FREAKING SNOW COME FROM?
STAN LEE PRESENTS: SPIDER-MAN AND THE SCARLET SPIDER IN...
BEHIND THE TERRO
TOM LYLE : WRITER / RON LIM : BREAKDOW
PALMER, MILGROM, CANDELARIO + HA
FINISHES / JOE ROSEN : LETTERS / JOHN
KALISZ : COLORS / DANNY FINGEROTH
EDITOR / BOB BUDIANSKY : EDITOR-IN-CH
IT'S NOT BAD ENOUGH THAT A SUBWA FIRE MAKES US COME OUT FURTH FROM THE WORL TRADE CENTER THAN WE PLANNE
...NOW WE GOT SNOW ON TOP OF THAT.
WELL, THERE'RE THE TWIN TOWERS -- DEAD AHEAD!

AT THE TOP OF THE WORLD TRADE CENTER...THE SKY-LINE RESTAURANT. THE PATRONS WITHIN ARE OBLIVIOUS TO THE EVENTS TRANSPIRING OUTSIDE... FOR NOW.
ONE OF THOSE PATRONS... MARY JANE WATSON PARKER...IS DINING HERE THIS EVENING WITH HER FRIEND...
CARLY...
...YOU DON'T KNOW WHAT A CHANGE I'VE SEEN IN PETER EVER SINCE HE FOUND OUT THAT I WAS PREGNANT.
WELL, I'M SURE IT MUST BE IMPORTANT TO BOTH OF YOU. THINK OF ALL THE CHANGES IT WILL...
WHA--?
"WHAT'S GOING ON?"
DOWN! EVERYBODY DOWN!
GOT ONE! DID YOU SEE?
KA-BLAM
BLAM
LOOK AT 'EM SCRAMBLE.
OH, MAN, THIS IS GREAT!
VIP

HOLD IT! BACK OFF!!
WE NEED SOME OF THESE PEOPLE ALIVE TO USE AS HOSTAGES.
YEAH! HOSTAGES. GOOD THINKING, DON. THIS IS ALL SO DIFFERENT FROM WHAT WE HAD PLANNED. I GUESS I'M NOT ADJUSTING TO THE CHANGES AS WELL AS YOU ARE.
CARLY, WAIT. THERE'S GOING TO BE A LOT OF PEOPLE HURT IF WE ALL RUN FOR THE EXITS.
I THINK WE'D BE BETTER OFF STAYING WHERE WE ARE.
NO WAY! NOT ME!
EVERYBODY, HOLD IT RIGHT THERE. IF NO ONE WANTS TO GET SHOT, THEN I'D ADVISE YOU ALL TO GET BACK INSIDE THE RESTAU-RANT... NOW!
BUG ONE TO THE TWIN MEN...
EVERYTHING HERE IS SECURE. OPERATION: SHAKEDOWN IS READY TO ROLL.

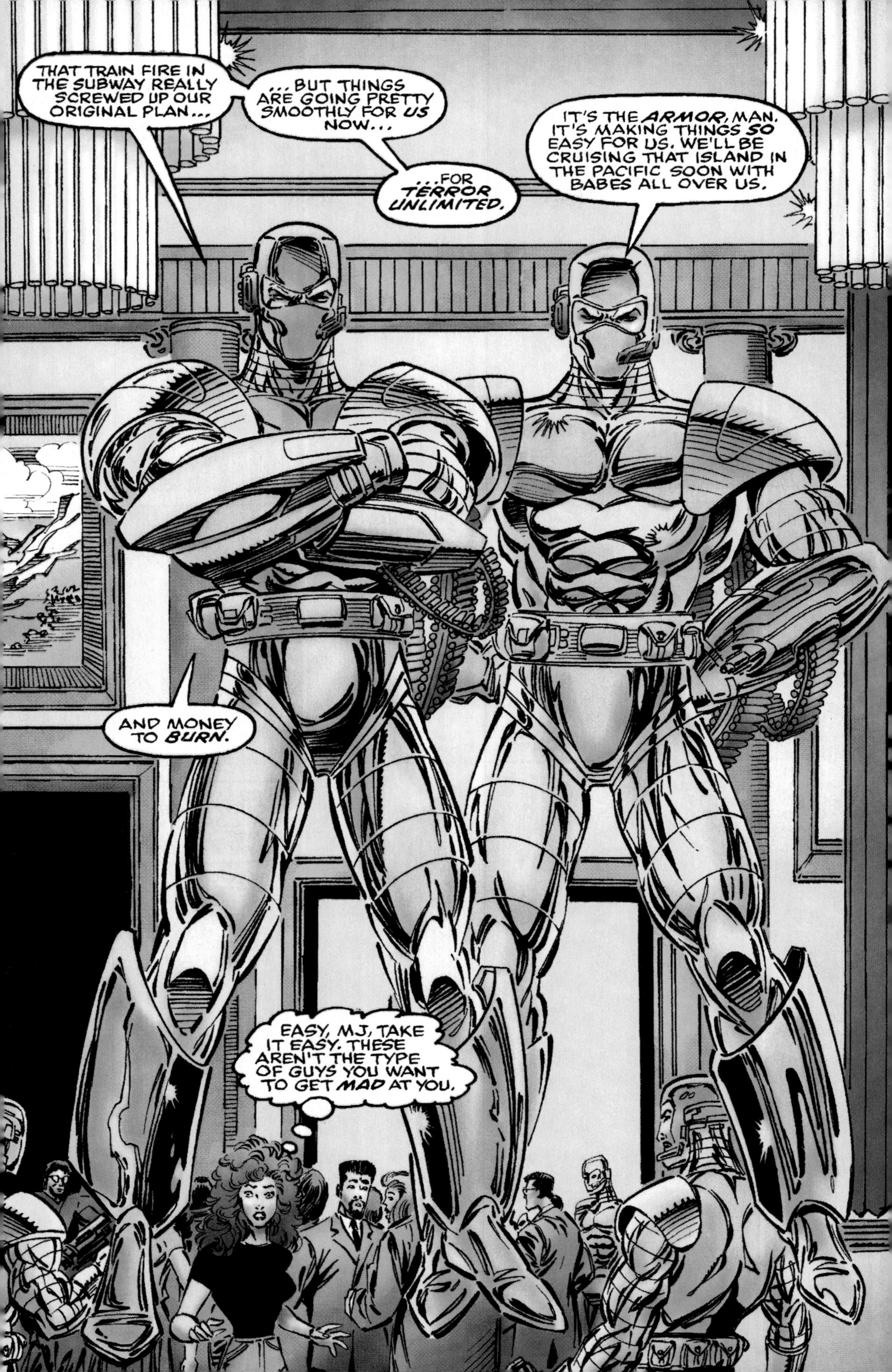
THAT TRAIN FIRE IN THE SUBWAY REALLY SCREWED UP OUR ORIGINAL PLAN...
...BUT THINGS ARE GOING PRETTY SMOOTHLY FOR US NOW...
...FOR TERROR UNLIMITED.
IT'S THE ARMOR, MAN. IT'S MAKING THINGS SO EASY FOR US. WE'LL BE CRUISING THAT ISLAND IN THE PACIFIC SOON WITH BABES ALL OVER US.
AND MONEY TO BURN.
EASY, MJ, TAKE IT EASY. THESE AREN'T THE TYPE OF GUYS YOU WANT TO GET MAD AT YOU.

NOT FAR FROM THE WORLD TRADE CENTER...
WOW! IT'S YOU. I'VE WANTED TO FIND YOU AND THANK YOU.
YEAH? DO I KNOW YOU?

RICH GANNON. YOU KNOW...
...YOU TRIED TO HELP ME WHEN I WAS GETTING ROUSTED BY THAT DARRYL AND HIS BULLY BOYS.*
OH, YEAH! I'M AFRAID I WASN'T MUCH HELP, THOUGH.
*LAST ISSUE.--DANNY

NO...YOU DON'T KNOW HOW IMPORTANT WHAT YOU TRIED TO DO WAS TO ME.
IT MEANT THAT SOMEONE CARED. I REALLY NEEDED THAT.
WELL, I STILL DON'T THINK I DID ANYTHING.
LOOK...YOU STARTED THE BALL ROLLING THAT IS HELPING TO GET MY LIFE BACK ON TRACK.
I GOT MY OLD JOB BACK AT STARK ENTERPRISES I'M OFF THE STREETS AND LIVING IN THIS HOTEL... MY WHOLE LIFE IS LOOKING UP.
IF YOU'RE LIVING HERE, THEN YOU SHOULD COME AND HAVE A CUP OF COFFEE WITH ME SOMETIME. I'M REILLY. BEN REILLY.
LOVE TO. GOTTA GO NOW, THOUGH. TODAY, I'M STARTING MY VOLUNTEER WORK AT THE SOUTH STREET MISSION UP THE STREET, NOW THAT I'M GETTING BACK ON MY FEET AGAIN.
GOOD LUCK, SEE YA SOON.

DOC OCK!?! OH, MAN, THIS IS TOO WEIRD.
BEN REILLY IS A MAN WHOSE WHOLE LIFE IS BASED ON MEMORIES.
THE MEMORIES OF PETER PARKER. THE MAN HE WAS CLONED FROM.
THE NEWS BEN REILLY IS READING HAS JUST SHATTERED ONE OF THOSE MEMORIES.
A MEMORY THAT REACHES BACK TO HIS BEGINNINGS.
OR, RATHER, TO HIS BEGINNINGS... PETER PARKER'S.
GOT TO GET OUT OF HERE.
THE WAY I'M FEELING THE ONLY THING THAT WILL HELP...
...IS TO GO SLING SOME WEBBING AROUND TOWN.
MAYBE FIND SOME EASY PURSE SNATCHER TO TAKE IT OUT ON.

MAN, I FEEL BETTER ALREADY!
CAN'T BELIEVE ABOUT OCK*--!
*FOR THE AWESOME DETAILS ON OCK, SEE SPEC. SPIDER-MAN #221, ON SALE NOW--AND A VERY SPECIAL SERIES FEATURING SCARLET SPIDER AND SPIDER-MAN THAT DEBUTS NEXT MONTH --DANNY

THE SKYLIGHT OF A FAMILIAR BROWNSTONE ON THE UPPER EAST SIDE OF MANHATTAN.

SPIDER-MAN IS RETURNING HOME.
WHOA. I'M REALLY TIRED. THESE LONG DAYS AND NIGHTS ARE GOING TO BE EVEN TOUGHER WHEN THE BABY COMES.

I GOTTA GET SOME SLEE-- WHAT'S THIS?
A NOTE FROM MARY JANE.

WELL, WHILE SHE'S OUT TO DINNER, I'M GOING TO JUST CRASH.

AT LEAST WHEN I KNOW THAT MARY JANE'S SOMEWHERE SAFE AND WITH FRIENDS, I CAN REST EASY.

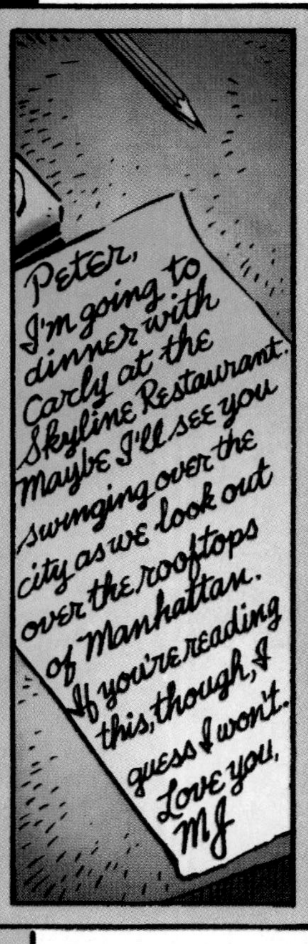
Peter,
I'm going to dinner with Carly at the Skyline Restaurant. Maybe I'll see you swinging over the city as we look out over the rooftops of Manhattan. If you're reading this, though, I guess I won't.
Love you,
MJ

THIRTEEN-HUNDRED ODD FEET BELOW THE **SKYLINE RESTAURANT** AND THE TERROR THAT HAS JUST BEGUN INSIDE OF IT...

...THE NEW YORK CITY POLICE ARE GATHERING THEIR FINEST TO DEAL WITH THE CRISIS OF **TERROR UNLIMITED!**

LIEUTENANT **CARR**... THEY'RE ON THE CELLULAR LINKUP, SIR.

FINE. LET ME FIND OUT WHAT THESE JOKERS WANT.

GENTLEMAN... THIS IS DAN CARR.
WHAT DO YOU WANT OUT OF THIS? FIRST, I'D LIKE TO MAKE SURE THAT NO ONE ELSE GETS HURT, BUT I'M HERE MAINLY TO HELP RESOLVE THIS... SITUATION.
SWAT
SWAT
POLICE
LOOKIE, DAN... WE'RE TERROR UNLIMITED AND WE AND THE DRONES... WELL, WE'RE LOOKING FOR CASH...

...LOTS OF CASH! AND...
...WE NEED A CONCORDE OUT OF THE COUNTRY!!

THAT'S ALL DO-ABLE, BUT I'M GOING TO NEED SOME TIME TO GET THIS ALL TOGETHER. I GOT A LOT OF RED TAPE I GOT TO GET THROUGH ON THIS ONE.
NO DELAYS! WE WANT IT NOW!!
I'LL GET IT FOR YOU AS FAST AS POSSIBLE... I...
THAT'S NOT FAST ENOUGH, HUMP!!

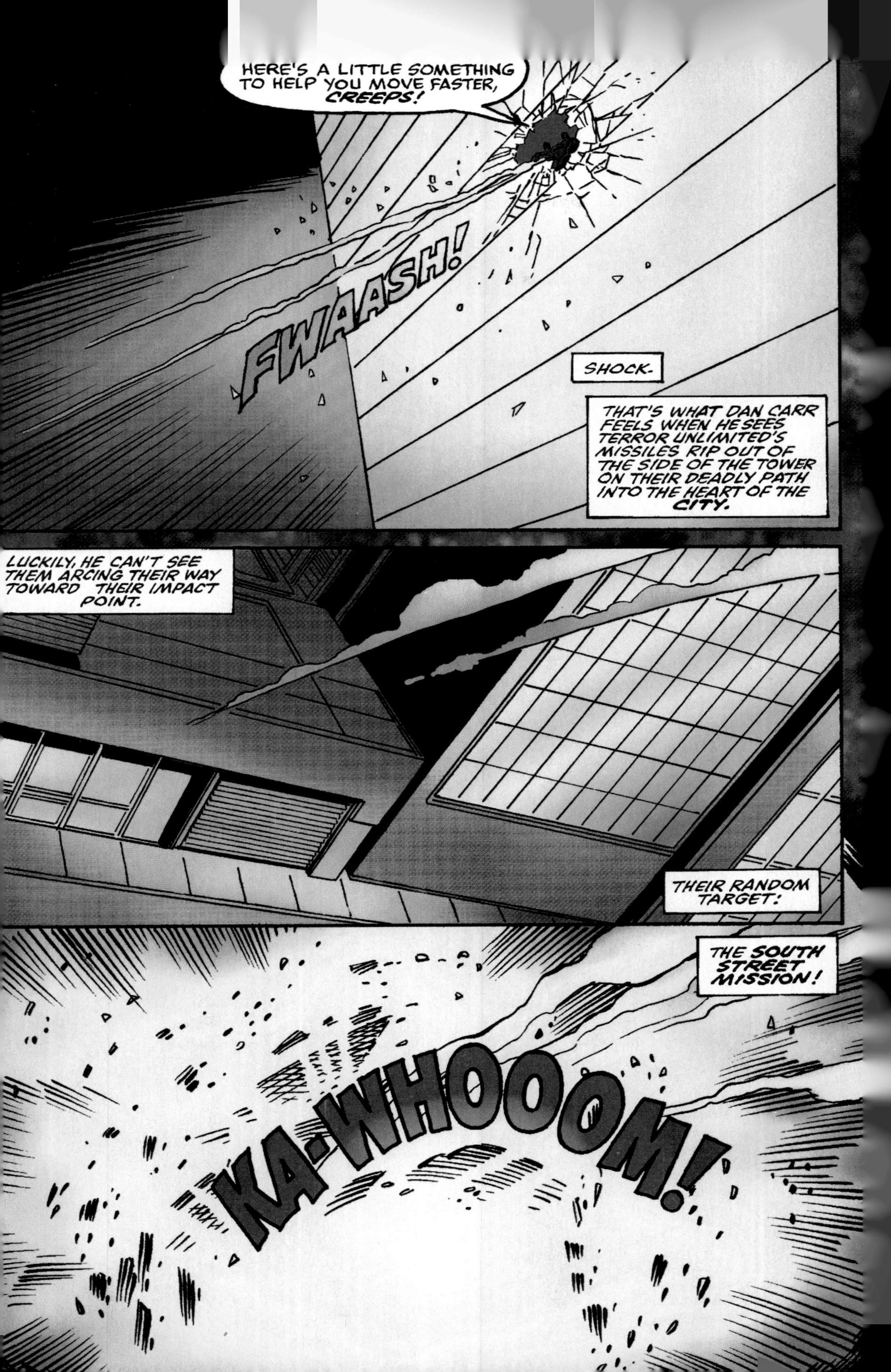
HERE'S A LITTLE SOMETHING TO HELP YOU MOVE FASTER, CREEPS!
FWAASH!
SHOCK-
THAT'S WHAT DAN CARR FEELS WHEN HE SEES TERROR UNLIMITED'S MISSILES RIP OUT OF THE SIDE OF THE TOWER ON THEIR DEADLY PATH INTO THE HEART OF THE CITY.
LUCKILY, HE CAN'T SEE THEM ARCING THEIR WAY TOWARD THEIR IMPACT POINT.
THEIR RANDOM TARGET:
THE SOUTH STREET MISSION!
KA-WHOOOM!

WHY? WHY'D YOU DO THAT?
I TOLD YOU YOU'D GET WHAT YOU WANT... AND THAT I'D GET IT AS FAST AS POSSIBLE.
WELL, DANNY, WE JUST DON'T FEEL YOU'RE TAKING US SERIOUS ENOUGH.
DO YOU WANT TO KNOW HOW SERIOUS WE ARE?
WE'RE TALKING NUCLEAR BOMB HERE, DAN-MY-MAN.
W-W-WHAT?

A FEW MOMENTS BEFORE THAT SHOCKING REVELATION...
WHAT A RIP! CAN'T FIND ANY BAD GUYS TO LET ME BLOW OFF STEAM!
MAYBE I'LL JUST SWING ON OVER TO FOREST HILLS AND SEE HOW AUNT MAY IS DOING THIS EVENING.
SHE'S BEEN... WHOA!
KA-WHOOM!!
AUNT MAY'S GOING TO HAVE TO WAIT!
I'VE GOT TO SEE WHAT THE HECK IS GOING DOWN OVER THERE.

THE END OF THE DAY AT THE DAILY BUGLE OFFICES...
BUT, ROBBIE, I KNOW I CAN COVER THAT WORLD TRADE THING BETTER THAN URICH CAN.
I'M NOT GOING TO AGREE OR DISAGREE WITH YOU, BUT I DO KNOW THAT BEN URICH HAS MORE EXPERIENCE AT COVERING THE BIG STORIES THAN KEN ELLIS DOES.
YOU'LL LEARN, KID. YOU'LL LEARN.

THE TERROR THAT IS TAKING PLACE AT THE WORLD TRADE CENTER HAS WIDENED ITS SCOPE AS WE SEE IN THESE LIVE PICTURES FROM THE BLASTED REMAINS OF THE SOUTH STREET MISSION...
THAT'S IT...

ROBBIE, LET ME FIND MY ANGLE ON TERROR UNLIMITED BY DOING THE HUMAN INTEREST SIDE OF THE STORY. I CAN START AT THE MISSION...YOU KNOW... PAIN AND SUFFERING AND ALL THAT STUFF.
OKAY, ELLIS, THAT'S YOUR BABY... NOW DELIVER IT.

AND DELIVER IT I WILL...

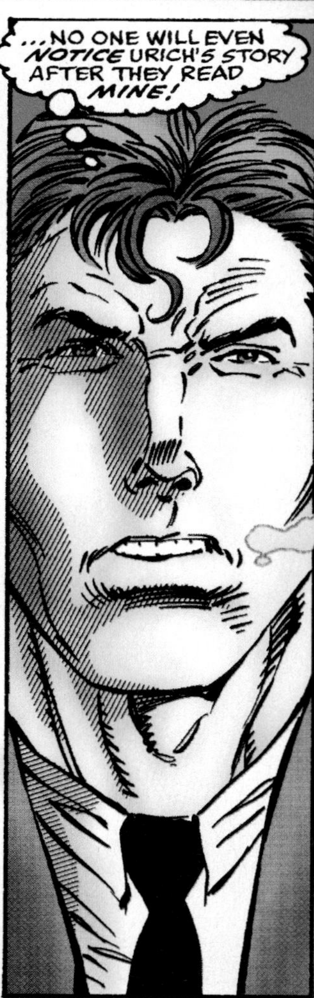
...NO ONE WILL EVEN NOTICE URICH'S STORY AFTER THEY READ MINE!

OKAY...YOU FOUR BOMB SQUAD DRONES ARE HEADING OVER TO THE OTHER TOWER WITH ME.
THE NEW PLAN THAT DON AND I CAME UP WITH...
...HAS THE FIVE OF US SETTING UP THE NUCLEAR BOMB IN ONE OF THE ELEVATORS OF THE OPPOSITE TOWER.
DON AND I BOTH HAVE REMOTE TRIGGERS FOR THE DETONATOR, SO IT'LL BE HARDER FOR THE POLICE TO STOP US IF WE'RE NOT IN THE SAME TOWER TOGETHER.
COLD CASH AND HOT BABES... HERE WE COME!
HIT!
I'M HIT!!
THE SICKENING SOUND OF THE DEAD DRONE'S BODY SLAMMING INTO THE ROOFTOP IS EASILY HEARD IN THE COLD, WINTRY AIR.

COPS?
NO, THEY'RE NOT *THAT* STUPID.
AN OVERZEALOUS SECURITY GUARD.
BRRRT
HE *IS* STUPID.
BUT HE'S *PAID* FOR HIS INTERFERENCE WITH HIS *LIFE*.

KER-RASH!
NO!
OH, *YES!* READY OR NOT... HERE WE COME.

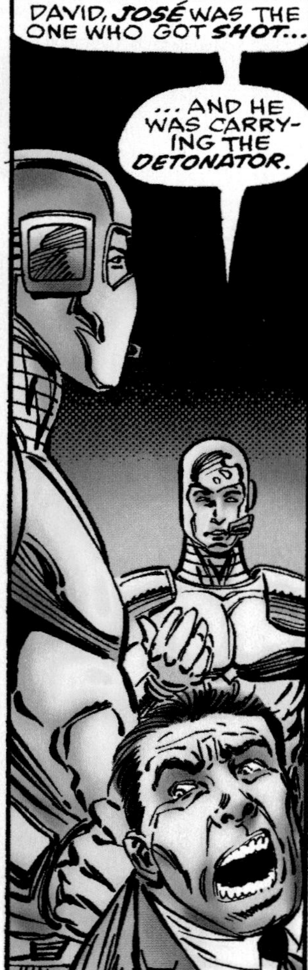

DAVID, *JOSÉ* WAS THE ONE WHO GOT *SHOT*...
...AND HE WAS CARRYING THE *DETONATOR*.

HEY, *CARR*, THIS ONE'S FO
LETTING *ANYTHING* INTERFE
WITH OUR PLA

WHILE...
MY GOD! IT'S THE MISSION THAT RICH GANNON WAS HEADED FOR THAT'S BEEN BLOWN UP.
HOW? WHY?

GOT TO GET THIS RUBBLE OUT OF THE WAY...
...SEE IF ANYONE NEEDS HELP.

THIS OLD MAN... HE'S STILL ALIVE. MAYBE NO ONE WAS KILLED AFTER ALL.

AS THE SCARLET SPIDER WORKS FURIOUSLY TO CLEAR AWAY THE DEBRIS, ONE QUESTION BURNS BRIGHTLY IN HIS THOUGHTS...
..."WHERE IS RICH GANNON?"

THE ANSWER COMES ALL TOO SOON.
RICH!
DEAD. HE'S DEAD.

WHY!?!
WHY THIS MAN? WHY THIS MISSION? WHAT'S GOING ON HERE--
OOOOH, HELP. SOMEONE HELP.

SOMEONE'S ALIVE DOWN THERE.

A YOUNG GIRL. SHE'S UNHURT.
NO MORE DISTRACTIONS UNTIL I'VE CHECKE EVERYWHERE FOR SURVIVORS.

AFTER THE SCARLET SPIDER HAS SEARCHED THE RUBBLE COMPLETELY...
CAN YOU TELL ME WHAT HAPPENED HERE?
SOME SORT OF... MISSILES...

...THEY CAME FROM ONE OF THE TRADE CENTER TOWERS.

HEY! SPIDER! IT'S KEN ELLIS. HELP ME OUT HERE. WHAT'S GOING ON?
#%#%! GUESS HE DIDN'T HEAR ME.

THE SCARLET SPIDER DOESN'T HEAR KEN ELLIS' PLEA.
HE CAN'T HEAR ANYTHING...
...EXCEPT FOR RICH GANNON'S VOICE...
...AND HIS OWN VOICE... BOTH DEMANDING JUSTICE FOR THIS SENSELESS DEATH.
KEN ELLIS, DAILY BUGLE.
THE SCARLET SPIDER SEEMED TO REALLY TAKE THAT ONE MAN'S DEATH HARD. ANYONE HERE KNOW IF THERE'S SOMETHING PERSONAL FOR HIM WITH THIS GUY...THIS RICH GANNON?
MAN...HE WAS REALLY M-A-D MAD...

BACK INSIDE THE SKYLINE RESTAURANT...
WHAT'S THAT MAN DOING?
UH...EXCUSE ME, SIR, BUT I WAS WONDERING IF MY SON MIGHT BE ABLE TO USE THE RESTROOM. IT'S GETTING KIND OF URGENT.
DON'T BOTHER ME, BUD!
BLAM!
UNGH!
HE SHOT HIM!! HE JUST SHOT HIM!
THIS MAN NEEDS A DOCTOR... IS ANYONE HERE A DOCTOR?
WHY'D HE SHOOT ME?!?

ONE OF YOUR BULLYING DRONES JUST SHOT A HELPLESS MAN OVER THERE. HE NEEDS MEDICAL ATTENTION... NOW!
WHOO! SCARY! AND YOU WANT WHAT FOR WHO?
DON'T PLAY GAMES WITH ME. THERE'S A MAN DYING OVER THERE AND IT'S YOUR FAULT. YOU SHOULD GET HIM TO A DOCTOR SOON.
I DON'T THINK THAT'S GOING TO BE POSSIBLE, MY DEAR.
BUT WOULD YOU SETTLE FOR...
...THIS?!?
KA-POW!

NOW! THAT SHOULD EVEN THINGS OUT. EVERYONE SHOULD BE HAPPY.
HAPPY? I SUPPOSE I SHOULD BE HAPPY THAT HE DIDN'T SHOOT ME!

I'M BEGINNING TO WONDER IF ANY OF US ARE GOING TO GET OUT OF THIS ALIVE.

OH!

THAT FIGURE CLIMBING THE OTHER TOWER! IT'S PETER!
HE'LL GET US OUT OF HERE!
NOW, MAYBE I CAN CONCENTRATE ON HELPING THAT POOR GUY WHO WAS SHOT.

BACK AT THE *PARKER* RESIDENCE...

OH, *MAN*, THAT ONE HOUR NAP JUST BARELY *DENTED* THE SURFACE OF HOW *TIRED* I'M FEELING.

THE TERRIBLE MENACE OF TERROR UNLIMITED CONTINUES TO PLAY ITSELF OUT AS YET *ANOTHER* HOSTAGE HAS BEEN REPORTEDLY KILLED BY GUNFIRE FROM THE TERRORISTS.

NOW, *LIVE* FROM THE WORLD TRADE CENTER IS OUR ON-THE-SCENE REPORTER... *CARMEN DIAZ*.

THANKS, ERIC. POLICE *HAVE* CONFIRMED THAT YET ANOTHER HOSTAGE HAS BEEN MURDERED BY THE TERRORISTS CALLING THEMSELVES... TERROR UNLIMITED.

BEGINNING A MERE TWO HOURS AGO IN THE *SKYLINE RESTAURANT* ATOP TOWER ONE OF THE WORLD TRADE CENTER...

...THE DEATH TOLL IS NOW KNOWN TO BE AT LEAST *TEN PEOPLE* WITH MORE LIKELY TO BE CONFIRMED LATER.

"ON TOP OF THAT, THE POLICE HAVE NOW RELEASED INFORMATION THAT THERE MAY BE A NUCLEAR BOMB IN ONE OF THE TWO TOWERS OF THE WORLD TRADE CENTER.
"THEY ARE ASKING THE PUBLIC TO REMAIN CALM ABOUT THIS. TELL ME, ERIC, CAN YOU STAY CALM KNOWING THIS?"
MARY JANE.

WITH ALMOST AS MUCH DETERMINATION AS SPIDER-MAN, KEN ELLIS HAS TRACKED DOWN RECENT EVENTS IN THE LIFE OF THE NOW-DECEASED RICH GANNON. THE TRAIL HAS TAKEN HIM TO...

CARL AND ME, HERE... WE TREATED RICH WITH NOTHIN' BUT RESPECT. HE WAS ALWAYS WELCOME HERE, KNOWING WHAT A HARD LIFESTYLE HE WAS LEADIN'.

YEP, STEVE, I'D HAVE BEEN PROUD TO HAVE OL' RICHIE FOR MY SON.

WELL, WE TRIED TO TREAT HIM LIKE ONE.

WELL, CARL... STEVE... THAT'S NOT THE WAY I HEARD IT.
I HEARD THAT YOU TWO CHASED HIM OUT OF HERE EVEN THOUGH HE HAD MONEY TO SPEND.
HEY, YOU MIKE WALLACE OR SOMETHIN'?

I DON'T THINK WE'LL BE TALKING TO YOU ANYMORE, MIS-TER ELLIS.
YEAH. IT'S TIME TO CLOSE.
FUNNY, I THOUGHT THIS WAS A 24-HOUR MARKET.

JERKS.
BUT THEY JUST GAVE ME SOME GREAT MATERIAL FOR THE 'TRAGIC LIFE OF RICH GANNON' OR WHATEVER I CALL THIS PIECE.

YOU TWO. I WANT THAT DETONATOR BACK NOW. SO... GO GET IT.

HEY, LOOK. THE COPS ARE TRYING TO GET TO JOSÉ'S BODY BEFORE US.

I THINK THERE'RE GOING TO BE SOME DIS-APPOINTED COPS...
...'CAUSE WE GOT THE DETONATOR NOW AND THEY DON'T.

THAT NEWS CHOPPER... PROBA-BLY GOT COPS IN IT TO TRY AND STOP US.
20 NEWS

I'M SICK OF THEIR INTERFERENCE AND DELAYS.
TAKE THIS, LIEUTENANT DAN CARR.

OH, MAN. BAD GUYS AT FIVE O'CLOCK AND A MISSILE HEADED FOR THAT NEWSCHOPPER.
GREAT WAY TO START.

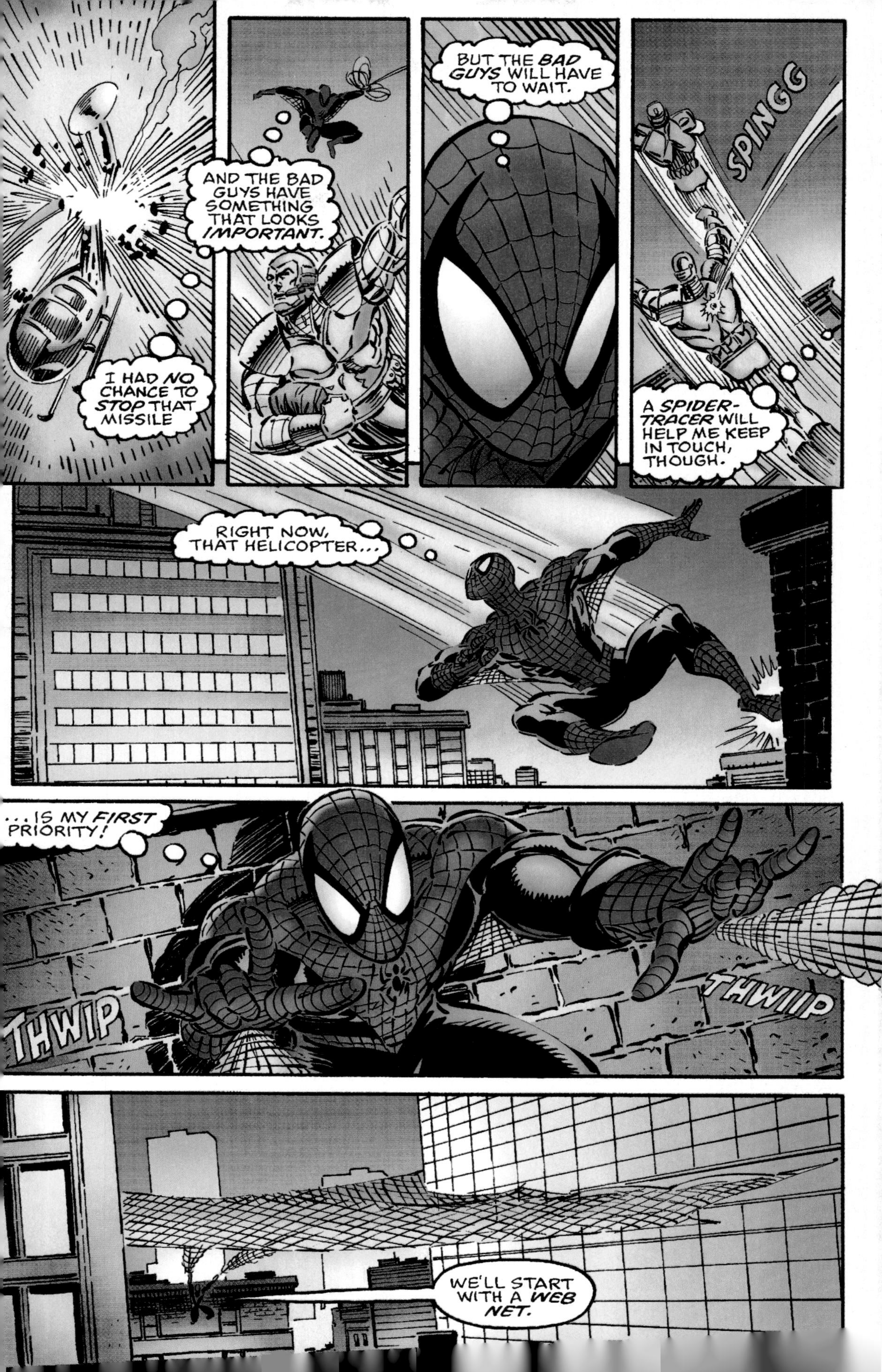
I HAD NO CHANCE TO STOP THAT MISSILE
AND THE BAD GUYS HAVE SOMETHING THAT LOOKS IMPORTANT.
BUT THE BAD GUYS WILL HAVE TO WAIT.
SPINGG
A SPIDER-TRACER WILL HELP ME KEEP IN TOUCH, THOUGH.
RIGHT NOW, THAT HELICOPTER...
...IS MY FIRST PRIORITY!
THWIP
THWIIP
WE'LL START WITH A WEB NET.

I'VE GOT TO STOP THOSE ROTORS SO THEY DON'T JUST SLICE RIGHT THROUGH THE WEBBING.
HOPE THE WEBLINE CAN HOLD THEM.
THWIP

ALL RIIIGHT!

SOON...
EVERYONE IN THE CHOPPER SEEMS OKAY.
LIEUTENANT CARR IS OVER HERE, SPIDEY. HE WANTS TO SEE YOU.

THANKS FOR THE HELP, WALL-CRAWLER.
WE'RE IN IT REALLY DEEP, HERE. THIS TERROR UNLIMITED HAS GOT BETWEEN THIRTY TO FORTY HOSTAGES IN THERE.

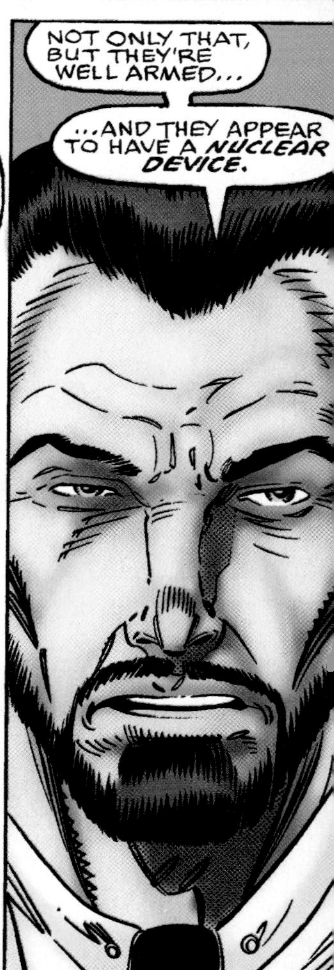

NOT ONLY THAT, BUT THEY'RE WELL ARMED...
...AND THEY APPEAR TO HAVE A NUCLEAR DEVICE.

"FOR NOW, THAT BOMB IS OUR FIRST PRIORITY. WE'RE HANDLING THE TOWER THOSE 'DRONES' JUST FLEW INTO.
"OUR EXPERTS FEEL THAT IT'S THE MOST LIKELY CANDIDATE TO HAVE THE BOMB INSIDE. STAY OUT OF THEIR WAY.
"THE HOSTAGES IN THE OTHER TOWER APPEAR TO BE CONGREGATED IN THE SKYLINE RESTAU-RANT...
"BUT DON'T DO ANYTHING TO ENDANGER THEM!"
THE SKYLINE?
MARY JANE.

INSIDE THE MAIN ELEVATOR SHAFT OF THE TOWER OPPOSITE TO SPIDER-MAN'S.
THE SCARLET SPIDER IS MAKING DECISIONS.
WATCH IT!
MY SPIDER-SENSE LET ME KNOW THESE "DRONES" WERE IN THAT ELEVATOR CAR. NOW I'VE JUST GOT TO LISTEN AND FIGURE OUT WHAT THEY'RE UP TO.
YOU JUST ABOUT SOLDERED MY ARM AND NOT THE WIRES, YOU JERK!
DON'T BE SO NERVOUS, MAN. THIS BOMB AIN'T DANGEROUS UNTIL WE GET THAT DETONATOR.
WE'VE JUST GOT A LITTLE MORE TO DO...
THERE! THAT'S CONNECTED. THAT'S IT FOR NOW.
ME. ASSEMBLING A NUCLEAR BOMB. WHO'D HAVE THOUGHT IT?

GUYS? THE BOMB IS READY TO ROCK AND ROLL. ALL WE NEED IS JOSÉ'S DETONATOR AND YOU'RE IN BUSINESS.
MESSAGE RECEIVED. YOUR MISSING-IN-ACTION PART IS ON ITS WAY UP TO YOU RIGHT NOW.
WE'LL MEET THEM ON THE ROOF...
...RIGHT AFTER WE CATCH A QUICK SMOKE... UH.
DIDN'T YOUR MOTHERS TEACH YOU THAT...
AAH, I ALREADY USED THAT ONE RECENTLY.
HOW ABOUT...?
SMOKING'S BAD FOR YOU... AND I AM TOO!

HEY! WHAT DO YOU...?
DO YOU READ ME?! WE GOT...
EAT IMPACT WEBBING, BOYS.
THWIPP
THWIPP
...TROUB-UNGH.
GIVE ME THOSE!
HEY, NUMBER 7? NUMBER 12? WE'LL BE THERE IN A MINUTE WITH A DETONATOR.
WE'LL COME DOWN THE SHAFT AND MEET YOU THERE.
ANYBODY THERE?
I'M HERE. YOU JUST GET THAT DETONATOR HERE.

DOWN ON THE STREET BELOW...
OKAY, DETECTIVE, YOU CAN PASS.
FACE IT, ELLIS...THAT WAS WAY TOO EA-SY!!
WILL I GET THE WHOLE STORY THAT I NEED WHEN THIS ELEVATOR OPENS?
I KNOW URICH IS DOWN THERE DOING HIS JOB, BUT I WANT MORE INFORMATION THAN HE'LL BE ABLE TO GET THERE DOWN AMONG THE MASSES.
IN THE LOBBY...
WHO IS IN THE ELEVATOR? I DIDN'T KNOW ANYONE WHO WAS AUTHORIZED TO GO UP THERE.
ME NEITHER.
I GOTTA STOP THAT THING... NOW!
HEY!
WHO STOPPED THE ELEVATOR?
WELL...THAT WORKED.
NOW...WHICH ONE OF US GETS TO TELL CARR ABOUT THIS?

THIS ELEVATOR SHAFT SEEMS TO BE THE BEST WAY TO GET TO THESE CREEPS UNDETECTED.

I SHOULD BE JUST OUTSIDE THE SKYLINE RESTAURANT IF I REMEMBER CORRECTLY FROM WHEN MJ AND I CAME HERE.

WAIT!
THAT'S KEN ELLIS. WHAT'S HE DOING HERE?

I DON'T KNOW WHAT HE'S GOT GOING ON IN THAT OVERZEALOUS BRAIN OF HIS, BUT HE COULD REALLY MUCK THINGS UP HERE.

IT'S HIM! ONE OF THE T. U. LEADERS!

I DON'T KNOW... SHOULD I GO IN AND TRY TO TALK TO HIM...OR NOT?

DON'T THINK SO MUCH, ELLIS. JUST DO IT!

IF I HURRY, MAYBE I CAN BEAT THOSE GUYS TO THE ROOF.
THERE'S THE ELEVATOR SHAFT. LET'S GET DOWN THERE AND GET RID OF THIS CREEPY DETONATOR.
TOO LATE! SPIDER-SENSE SAYS...
...THEY'RE HERE!
I'LL BE GLAD TO GET RID OF THAT THING, TOO.
THIS NUCLEAR BOMB ANGLE IS THE ONLY PART OF THIS WHOLE DEAL THAT REALLY CREEPS ME OUT.
NOTHING ELSE COULD BE AS SPOOKY AS THAT.

I SUPPOSE I SHOULD SAY, "I'M YOUR WORST NIGHTMARE"...
...OR "BOO!"... OR SOME SUCH HOOEY...
...BUT I THINK I'LL STICK TO JUST KICKING THE STUFFING OUT OF YOU TWO.
THE DETONATOR... HE LET GO OF IT!

GOT IT!
THWIPP
THWAPP

CAN'T JAR IT-- EVEN THOUGH DANGER-SENSE IS SCREAMING--!

THWACK

YE-E-O-OOWW!
COULDN'T STOP THE PUNCH-- BUT I ROLLED WITH THE IMPACT...!

OH, MAN. WHY DIDN'CHA FINISH HIM OFF?

YOU GUYS ARE IN BIG TROUBLE NOW!

MEANWHILE...
I'VE GOT TO GET THESE *HOSTAGES* SAFELY OUT OF HERE BEFORE I TRY TO CONFRONT THIS GUY.
LOOK! IT'S...
SSSHHH!
EVERYONE HEAD FOR THE ELEVATORS AS QUIETLY AS POSSIBLE AND GET OUT OF HERE... *NOW!*
LET'S ALL STAY AS QUIET AS POSSIBLE AND MOVE AS QUICKLY AS WE CAN TO THE ELEVATORS.
WHAT ABOUT MY DADDY?
WE'RE GOING TO HAVE TO LEAVE YOUR DADDY HERE FOR NOW, DARLING, BUT *I'VE* GOT YOU.
BE CAREFUL.
I WILL.
THANK YOU.
I *LOVE* YOU.
"*PLEASE...* COME HOME SAFELY TO US."

NOW THAT I'VE STASHED THAT DETONATOR WHERE THESE TERRORISTS WILL NEVER FIND IT...
...I CAN SEE ABOUT TAKING CARE OF THESE CREEPS.
BRRRT POW KA-POW
WHAT'S GOING ON IN THERE?
THERE'S ONLY TWO OF THEM HERE, GUYS! TAKE 'EM OUT... FAST!
PIECE O' CAKE, LIEUTENANT.
HATE TO DISAPPOINT, BOYS-IN-BLUE...
...BUT I'M NOT GOING DOWN EASY.
THAT'S FOR SHOOTING ONE OF MY MEN.
THESE COPS MUST HAVE COME UP AN ELEVATOR WHILE I WAS DEALING WITH THOSE DRONES WITH THE DETONATOR.

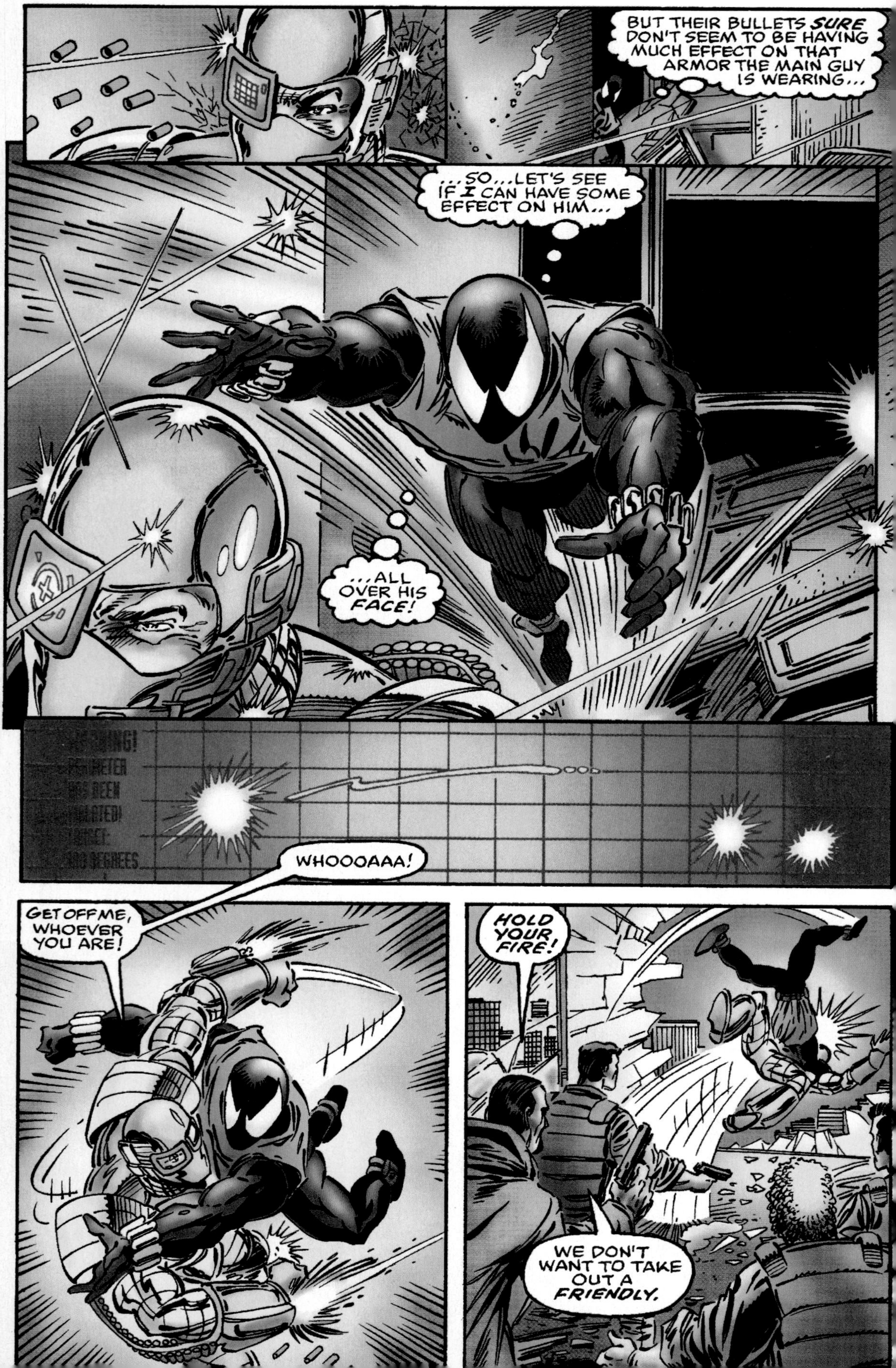

BUT THEIR BULLETS *SURE* DON'T SEEM TO BE HAVING MUCH EFFECT ON THAT ARMOR THE MAIN GUY IS WEARING...

...SO...LET'S SEE IF *I* CAN HAVE SOME EFFECT ON HIM...

...ALL OVER HIS *FACE!*

WHOOOAAA!

GET OFF ME, WHOEVER YOU ARE!

HOLD YOUR FIRE!
WE DON'T WANT TO TAKE OUT A *FRIENDLY.*

OKAY, GENIUS, THE BOOTJET THING IS FUN FOR A WHILE...
...BUT I THINK IT'S TIME TO LAND, NOW.
AIM THESE SUCKERS UP, BUD. I DON'T WANT YOU HURTING ANYONE ELSE.
AARRRGH!
GET OFF MY BACK!
WELL...THAT TIGHT LOOP GOT YOU WHAT YOU WANTED...
LET'S SEE WHAT I CAN DO TO DIS-APPOINT YOU.
THWIIP

I CAN'T JUST JUMP IN THERE AS SPIDER-MAN... ELLIS MIGHT GET KILLED.
SO YOU SAY THIS TECNO-TRAN FIRM MADE YOU INTO WHAT YOU ARE?
SURE! AND MY TWIN BROTHER, DAVID, TOO. WE...

HEY!
WHERE ARE THE FREAKIN' HOSTAGES?

WHAT DID YOU DO WITH THE HOSTAGES?
I DON'T -GNN-L-URG!-
TELL ME OR YOU'RE DEAD MEAT!

THIS IS THE TRIGGER FOR A NUCLEAR BOMB. IF YOU DON'T TELL ME WHAT'S GOING ON, RIGHT NOW, THERE'S GONNA BE A LOT OF UNHAPPY PEOPLE IN NEW YORK CITY TONIGHT.
THAT'S IT!
THERE'S TOO MUCH AT STAKE HERE. I CAN'T JUST SIT BAC AND WAIT FOR THE RIGHT MOMENT ANYMORE.

FIRST... I USE SOME WEBBING TO *NEUTRALIZE* THE DETONATOR TRIGGER...

THWIPP

...THEN WE GET THE *EVER* OVERZEALOUS MISTER ELLIS OUT OF HARM'S WAY.

WHA-A-T??

PRETTY NEAT *TRICK* WITH THE WEBLINE, SPIDER-*CREEP!*

ELLIS... *RUN* FOR IT... *NOW!!*

YOU'RE GOING TO PAY FOR *THA-A-A-T...*

WHOOMPH

KA-POW

THWAP

I HAVE HAD *JUST* ABOUT ENOUGH OF YOU AND YOUR *THREATS.*

I THINK YOU SHOULD FOLLOW KENNY ROGERS' ADVICE...
BRRRT
...AND KNOW WHEN TO FOLD 'EM!
BRAAAT
POW
POW
POW
POW
POW
ENOUGH!!
MISTER--
--I'VE HAD A BELLYFUL OF YOU.
WHA-TAANG

AND...
...I...
...THINK...
...IT'S TIME...
WHANNG
...TO PACK UP ALL YOUR TOYS...
THWIIP
WHOOOMP
...AND GO HOME!!
ESPECIALLY SINCE YOU CAN'T SEEM TO PLAY NICE WITH OTHERS.

WHAT DRIVES A MAN?
THREATEN HIS LOVED ONES AND YOU WILL FIND OUT.
THIS ONE'S FOR MARY JANE!
NOT SO TOUGH AFTER ALL-- EH, CHUMP?!?

BACK WITH THE SCARLET SPIDER...
YOU CAN SHOOT ALL YOU WANT, BUT YOU'RE STILL GIVING ME ENOUGH MOMENTUM...
...TO SWING UP AND USE MY IMPACT WEBBING AND A STINGER ON YOU!
EEAARR...
WHA-A...?
AND, NOW... FOR MY FINAL ACT...
...I'M BRINGING THE CURTAIN DOWN ON YOU.
THE PLAY'S OVER, BAD BOY.

A WEBLINE TO THAT TRADE CENTER TOWER AND THEN... UH, OH...
MY WEB-SHOOTER'S EMPTY!
I'M FALLING AND I'VE GOT TO TRY TO SWITCH THIS PIECE OF CRUD TO MY OTHER SIDE WITHOUT DROPPING HIM.
I HOPE YOU APPRECIATE THE THINGS I DO FOR YOU, ARMOR-BOY.
WELL, AT LEAST THIS WEB-SHOOTER WORKS.
THWIP
HOPE YOU LIKE BUNGEE-JUMPING.
'CAUSE YOU'RE GOING ON THE WILDEST RIDE OF YOUR LIFE.

NO...
NO NEED TO THANK ME.
YOUR CONTINUED UNCONSCIOUSNESS IS THANKS ENOUGH.
HEY, SPIDER, NEED SOME HELP WITH THAT HUMP!?!
NO THANKS. I'LL BRING HIM UP TO YOU... C.O.D.

WELL, YOU STOP A NUCLEAR TERRORIST... SAVE A REPORTER FROM HIMSELF... YOU DO ALL THIS FOR NOTHING.

SO? WHAT'S YOUR POINT?
WHAT'S YOUR MOTIVATION, SPIDER-MAN? WHY RISK YOUR NECK FOR US?

BECAUSE I CARE. THAT'S ALL.

THANKS, GUYS. YOU CAN HAVE HIM.
BY THE WAY, THE DETONATORS ARE WEBBED UP AND HIDDEN IN THE AIR VENT JUST OUTSIDE IN THE HALL.

THANKS FOR YOUR HELP, SPIDER.
I DON'T KNOW WHY YOU DO THIS STUFF, BUT I GUESS WE ALL HAVE OUR REASONS FOR WHAT WE DO.

I RISK MY NECK BECAUSE I CARE. THAT'S ALL THERE IS TO IT.

IT MADE THE FRONT PAGE.
"Behind the Terror" by Ken Ellis
"When you look at this day's events, the Terror Unlimited crisis and how everyone handled it--it all seems so simple.
"But nothing could be further from the truth.
"Everyone who was involved in stopping these urban terrorists was a hero.
"Behind these individual heroes was their motivation... and that's when you realize...
"...nothing in life is simple, no matter who you are."
END.

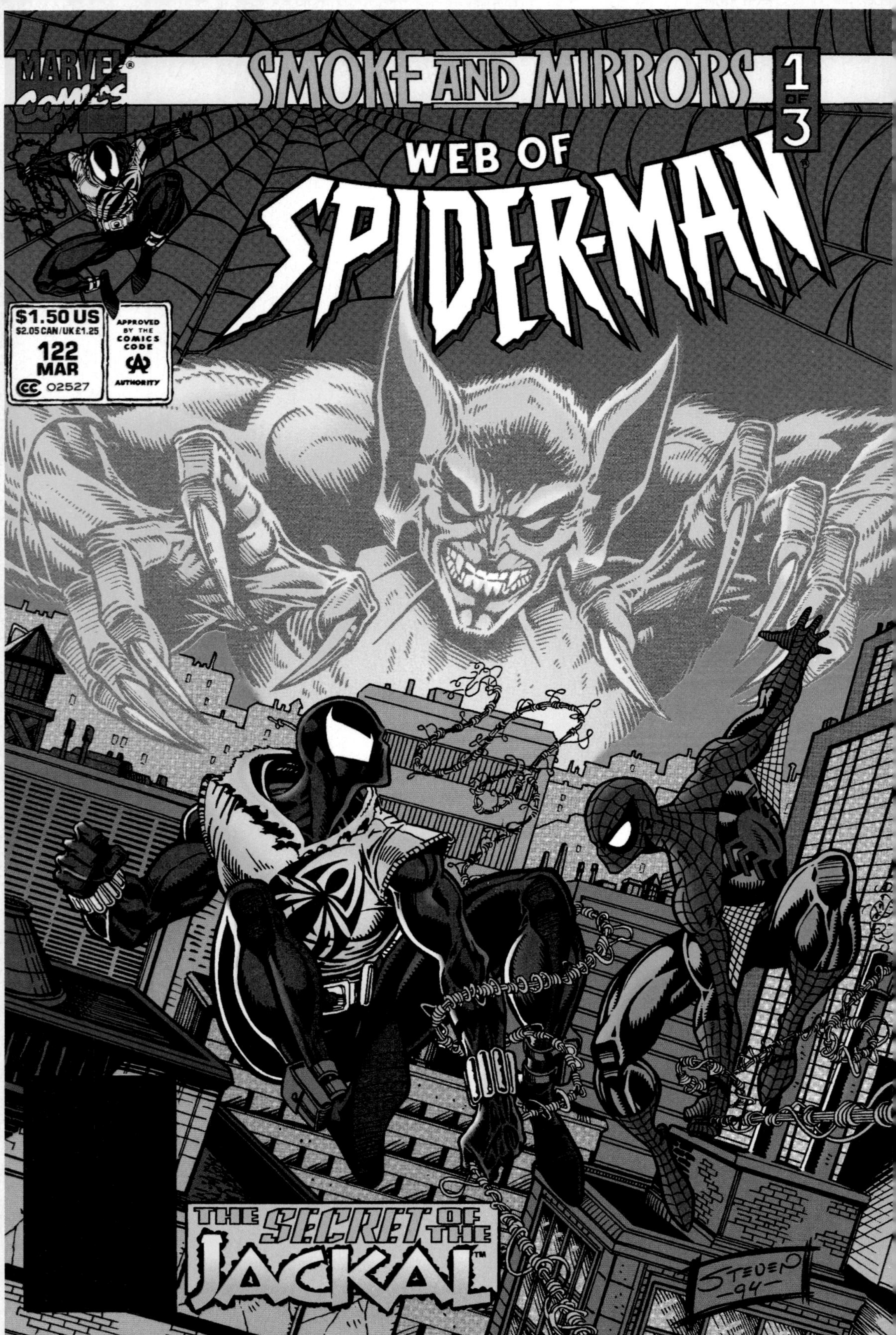
MARVEL COMICS
SMOKE AND MIRRORS 1 OF 3
WEB OF SPIDER-MAN
$1.50 US
$2.05 CAN/UK £1.25
122
MAR
02527
APPROVED BY THE COMICS CODE AUTHORITY
THE SECRET OF THE JACKAL™
STEVEN -94-

BITTEN BY A RADIOACTIVE SPIDER, STUDENT PETER PARKER GAINED THE PROPORTIONATE STRENGTH AND AGILITY OF AN ARACHNID! ARMED WITH HIS WONDROUS WEB-SHOOTERS, THE RELUCTANT SUPER HERO STRUGGLES WITH SINISTER SUPER-VILLAINS, MAKING ENDS MEET, AND MAINTAINING SOME SEMBLANCE OF A NORMAL LIFE! AND NOW HE'S GOT HIS RETURNED CLONE TO CONTEND WITH!

Stan Lee PRESENTS: WEB OF SPIDER-MAN™

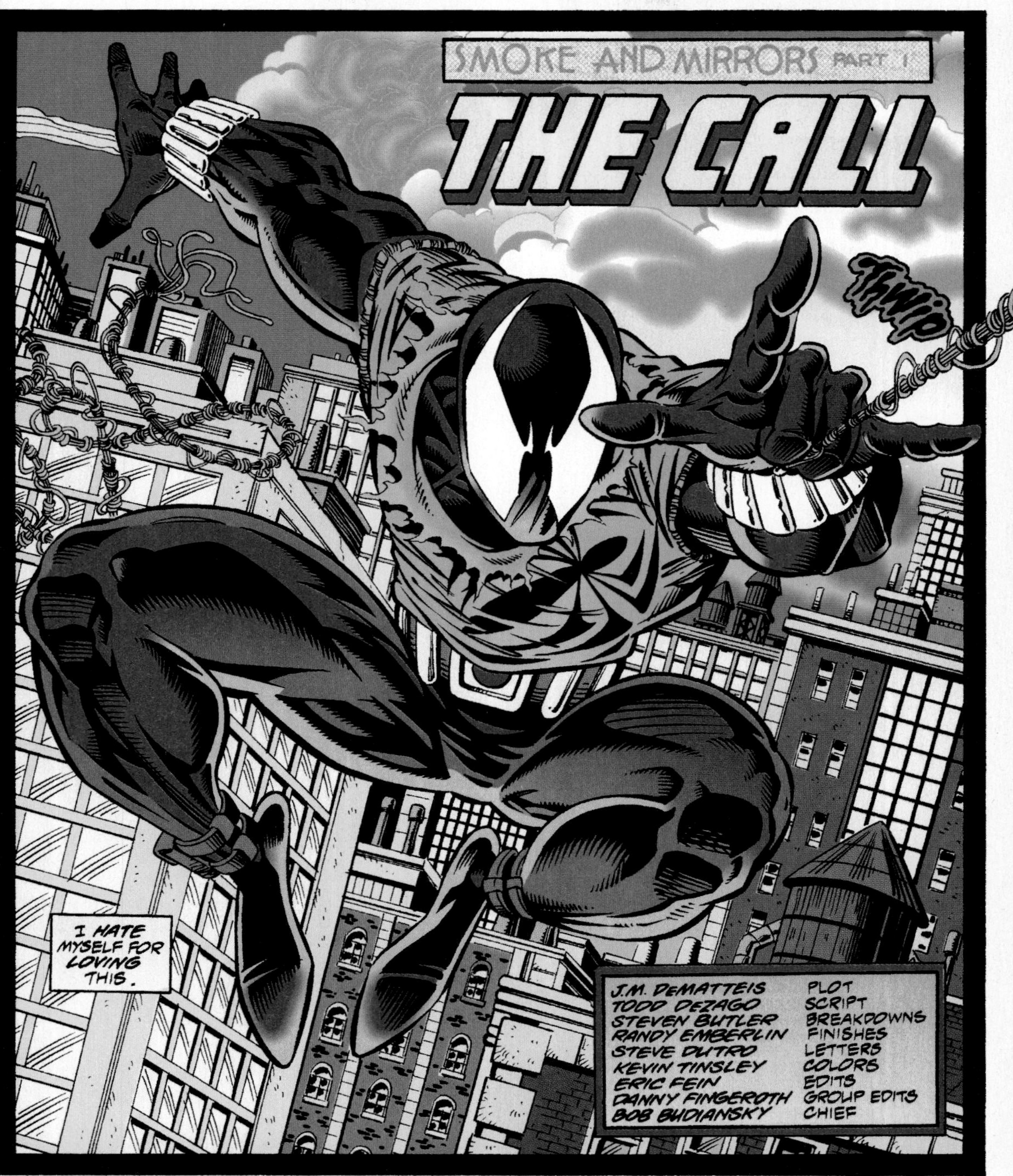

SMOKE AND MIRRORS PART 1
THE CALL
THWIP
I HATE MYSELF FOR LOVING THIS.
J.M. DEMATTEIS PLOT
TODD DEZAGO SCRIPT
STEVEN BUTLER BREAKDOWNS
RANDY EMBERLIN FINISHES
STEVE DUTRO LETTERS
KEVIN TINSLEY COLORS
ERIC FEIN EDITS
DANNY FINGEROTH GROUP EDITS
BOB BUDIANSKY CHIEF

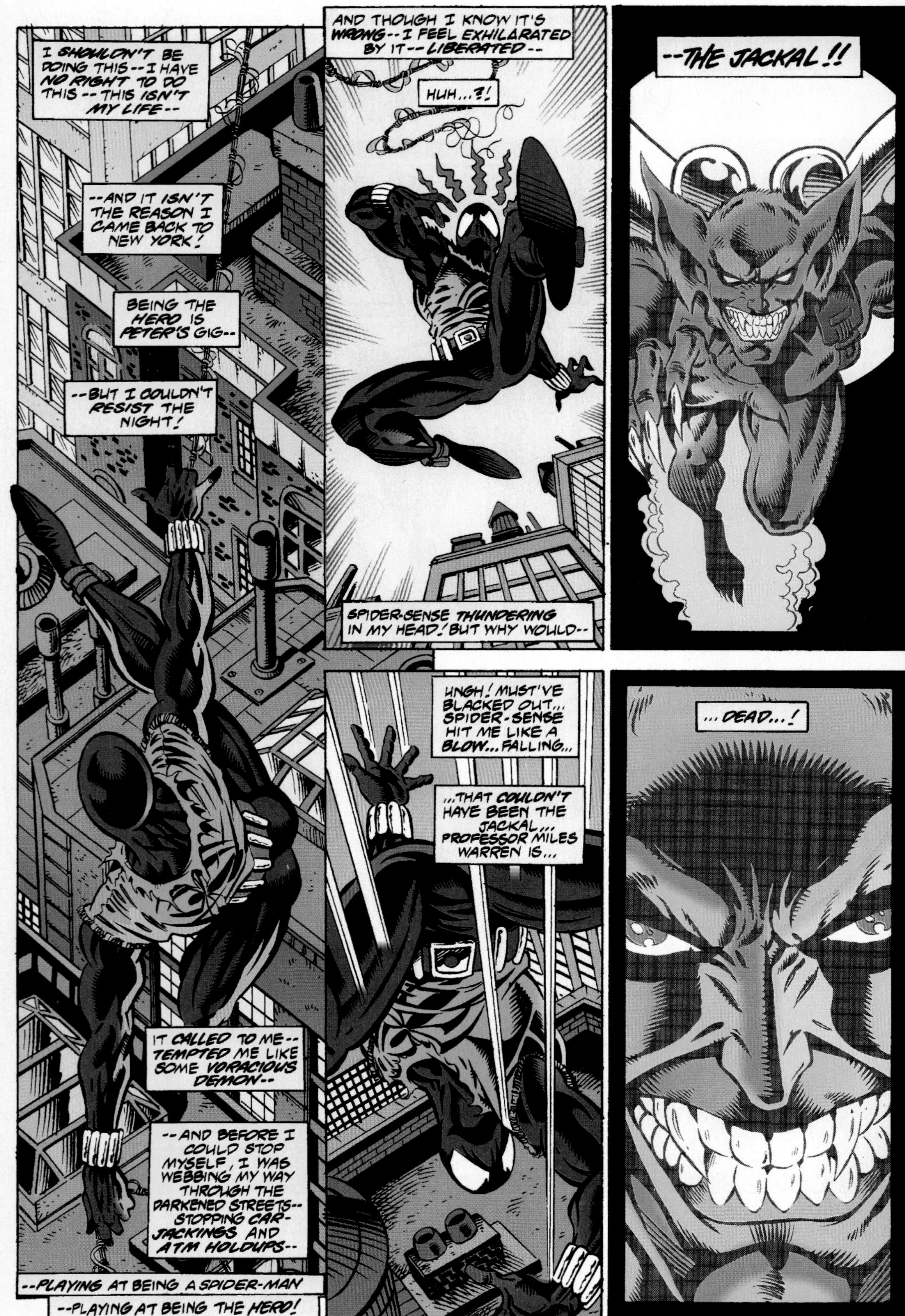
I SHOULDN'T BE DOING THIS--I HAVE NO RIGHT TO DO THIS--THIS ISN'T MY LIFE--
--AND IT ISN'T THE REASON I CAME BACK TO NEW YORK!
BEING THE HERO IS PETER'S GIG--
--BUT I COULDN'T RESIST THE NIGHT!
IT CALLED TO ME--TEMPTED ME LIKE SOME VORACIOUS DEMON--
--AND BEFORE I COULD STOP MYSELF, I WAS WEBBING MY WAY THROUGH THE DARKENED STREETS--STOPPING CAR-JACKINGS AND ATM HOLDUPS--
--PLAYING AT BEING A SPIDER-MAN
--PLAYING AT BEING THE HERO!
AND THOUGH I KNOW IT'S WRONG--I FEEL EXHILARATED BY IT--LIBERATED--
HUH...?!
SPIDER-SENSE THUNDERING IN MY HEAD! BUT WHY WOULD--
--THE JACKAL!!
UNGH! MUST'VE BLACKED OUT... SPIDER-SENSE HIT ME LIKE A BLOW... FALLING...
...THAT COULDN'T HAVE BEEN THE JACKAL... PROFESSOR MILES WARREN IS...
...DEAD...!

...DISORIENTED... CAN'T SHOOT WEB IN TIME...

...HAVE TO ROLL WITH IT

UNGH!

WHY DO THESE VISIONS --MEMORIES-- WHATEVER THEY ARE-- FEEL LIKE THEY'RE TUGGING AT THE DEEPEST PART OF ME--
--GUIDING ME TOWARDS SOMETHING I SHOULD KNOW--SOMEPLACE I SHOULD GO?! BUT I DON'T KNOW WHAT OR WHERE IT IS!

YOU'VE HAD ME VERY WORRIED, YOUNG MAN. I'VE SCOURED THIS ENTIRE CITY LOOKING FOR YOU--

--BUT EVERYTHING'S GOING TO BE FINE, NOW--
--PETER.

...PETER?
--WHA?!
...PETER?!
TH-THE JACKAL?! IT MUST BE A LINGERING EFFECT OF THE VIRUS--I--
SHAKE A LEG, LOVER.
I MUST BE HALLUCINATING.
BUT WHY WARREN? AFTER ALL THESE YEARS.
YOU KNOW HOW CROWDED DECARLO'S GETS--
--AND WE DON'T HAVE RESERVATIONS.
SO BE PERFECTLY HONEST, MR. PARKER--HOW DO I LOOK?
...HUH? OH...UM, FINE, HONEY--
--YOU LOOK GREAT.
YOUR HAIR LOOKS GOOD PINNED UP LIKE THAT.
TRY TO TONE DOWN THE ENTHUSIASM, TIGER--YOUR COMPLIMENTS ARE GOING TO MAKE MY HEAD SWELL.

HEY...I'M SORRY
YOU ARE THE MOST WONDERFUL... THE MOST BEAUTIFUL... THE MOST MAGNIFICENT WIFE A MAN EVER HAD. NOT A DAY GOES BY THAT I DON'T THANK GOD FOR BRINGING YOU INTO MY LIFE!
I'VE MISSED YOU SO... I'VE MISSED US!
NOW THAT--IS MORE LIKE IT!

I DO LOVE YOU SO--NOW AND FOREVER WITH ALL MY HEART--

--GWEN--
--HUH?!

HUH?!
PETER--WHAT'S WRONG? WHAT IS IT?

I--I GUESS I'M STILL A BIT SHAKY FROM THAT VIRUS, MJ--IT MUST'VE KNOCKED ME FOR MORE OF A LOOP THAN I THOUGHT.
BUT IS THAT IT? IS IT THE VIRUS...? OR ARE THESE VISIONS... THESE MIND-FLASHES... SOMETHING ELSE ENTIRELY...?
AND WHY DO I HAVE THE FEELING THAT THEY'RE PULLING AT ME--LEADING ME SOMEWHERE...?
WELL, I UNDERSTAND. IF YOU'D RATHER NOT GO OUT FOR LUNCH...

MRS. PARKER, THERE IS NOTHING IN THE WORLD I WANT MORE THAN TO HAVE LUNCH WITH YOU.
AND AFTER THAT, DINNER.
AND AFTER THAT, BREAKFAST.
AND THEN LUNCH AGAIN... YOU GET THE PICTURE!

I WANT TO SPEND EVERY MINUTE WITH YOU -- FOR THE REST OF OUR LIVES! I DON'T WANT ANYTHING TO EVER COME BETWEEN US.

I HAVE SO MUCH FAITH -- IN US -- IN OUR LOVE!
WE'RE GOING TO BE PARENTS!* WE'RE GOING TO BE A FAMILY! AND OUR BABY WILL BE THE MOST LOVED CHILD ON THE ENTIRE PLANET!
M.J. GAVE PETER THE GOOD NEWS IN SPEC. SPIDEY #220. --ERIC
AND AUNT MAY IS GOING TO GET BETTER. I KNOW SHE WILL. SHE HAS TO.
SHE HAS TO LIVE TO SEE OUR CHILD.

OUR FUTURE IS OUT THERE, MJ. IT'S RIGHT THERE ON THE HORIZON. AND I COULDN'T IMAGINE FACING THAT FUTURE--
--OF SPENDING THE REST OF MY LIFE--
--WITHOUT YOU.
OH, PETER, I LOVE YOU.

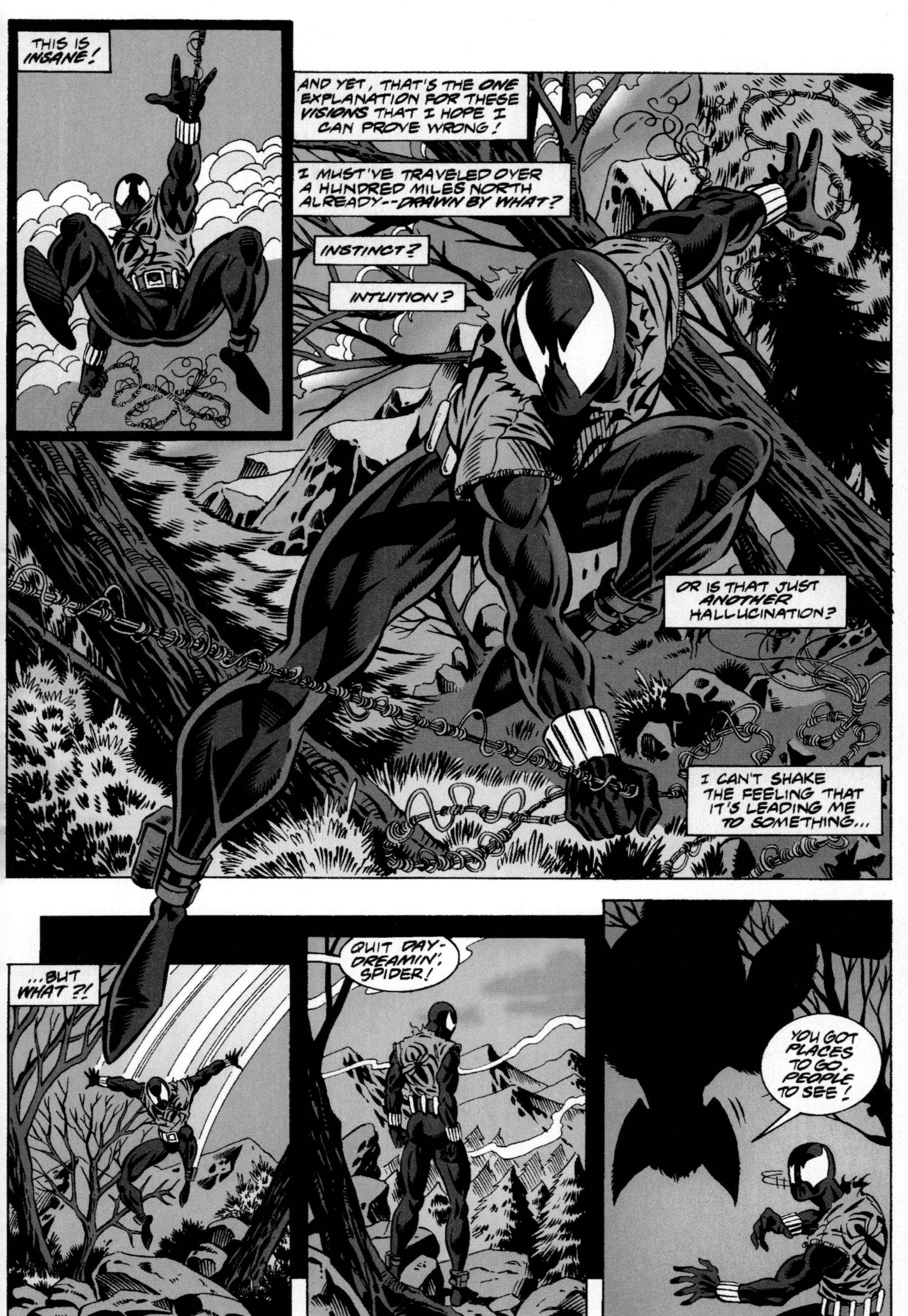

THIS IS INSANE!
AND YET, THAT'S THE ONE EXPLANATION FOR THESE VISIONS THAT I HOPE I CAN PROVE WRONG!
I MUST'VE TRAVELED OVER A HUNDRED MILES NORTH ALREADY--DRAWN BY WHAT?
INSTINCT?
INTUITION?
OR IS THAT JUST ANOTHER HALLUCINATION?
I CAN'T SHAKE THE FEELING THAT IT'S LEADING ME TO SOMETHING...
...BUT WHAT?!
QUIT DAY-DREAMIN', SPIDER!
YOU GOT PLACES TO GO. PEOPLE TO SEE!

NICE T'SEE YA, PAL! IT'S BEEN A LOOONG TIME!
PROFESSOR WARREN?!
AFTER A FASHION--
--YOU CAN CALL ME JACK!
HAHAHAHEHE
GONE. BUT WHERE COULD--
HEY, SPIDER. COME ON DOWN!
WHA?
WOULD YOU LIKE TO TAKE WHAT'S BEHIND THE CURTAIN OR WHAT'S BEHIND DOOR NUMBER ONE?
TAKE THE DOOR! TAKE THE DOOR!
AFTER ALL, THE JACKAL HAD THIS PLANNED FOR YOU YEARS AGO, AND THE ANSWERS TO ALL YOUR QUESTIONS ARE RIGHT BEHIND THIS DOOR!
SO GET A MOVE ON, LITTLE SPIDER, THE METER'S RUNNIN'!

I DON'T GET IT... WHERE DID THAT DOOR COME FROM? AND HOW DID HE GET UP THERE SO FAST?
IT'S ALL DONE WITH MIRRORS, KID. DON'T LET ANYBODY TELL YOU OTHERWISE!
OF COURSE, THERE'S NO GUARANTEE THAT I'M NOT LYIN' TO YA RIGHT NOW!
I WANT SOME ANSWERS NOW, "JACK".
LIKE--WHAT'S GOING ON? WHERE ARE YOU TAKING ME?
IS THE JACKAL ALIVE?
YA BETTER LET GO O'ME, PETE, OR YER GONNA MAKE HIM EVEN MADDER!
GRAARR!
HIM? HIM WHO?
HIM HIM!

THE OFFICES OF THE DAILY BUGLE.
...JUST GREAT, PETER. WITH ALL THE NEWS THAT'S CONSTANTLY COMING IN AND OUT OF THIS PLACE, YOUR IMPENDING PARENTHOOD IS THE BEST NEWS I'VE HEARD IN A LONG TIME.
YOU JUST CALL GAIL ON THE ELEVENTH FLOOR IF YOU HAVE ANY OTHER QUESTIONS ABOUT YOUR FREELANCER'S INSURANCE COVERAGE.
THANKS, ROBBIE...A LOT! OH, AND I'D REALLY APPRECIATE IT IF YOU DIDN'T SAY TOO MUCH TO ANYONE ELSE ABOUT THE BABY.
IT'S STILL SO EARLY IN THE PREGNANCY. THERE'S SO MUCH THAT COULD GO WRONG...

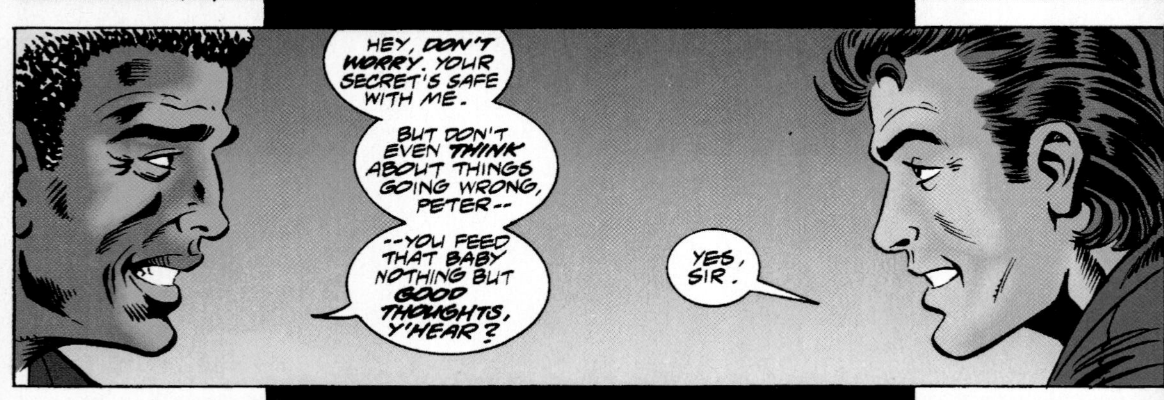

HEY, DON'T WORRY. YOUR SECRET'S SAFE WITH ME.
BUT DON'T EVEN THINK ABOUT THINGS GOING WRONG, PETER--
--YOU FEED THAT BABY NOTHING BUT GOOD THOUGHTS, Y'HEAR?
YES, SIR.

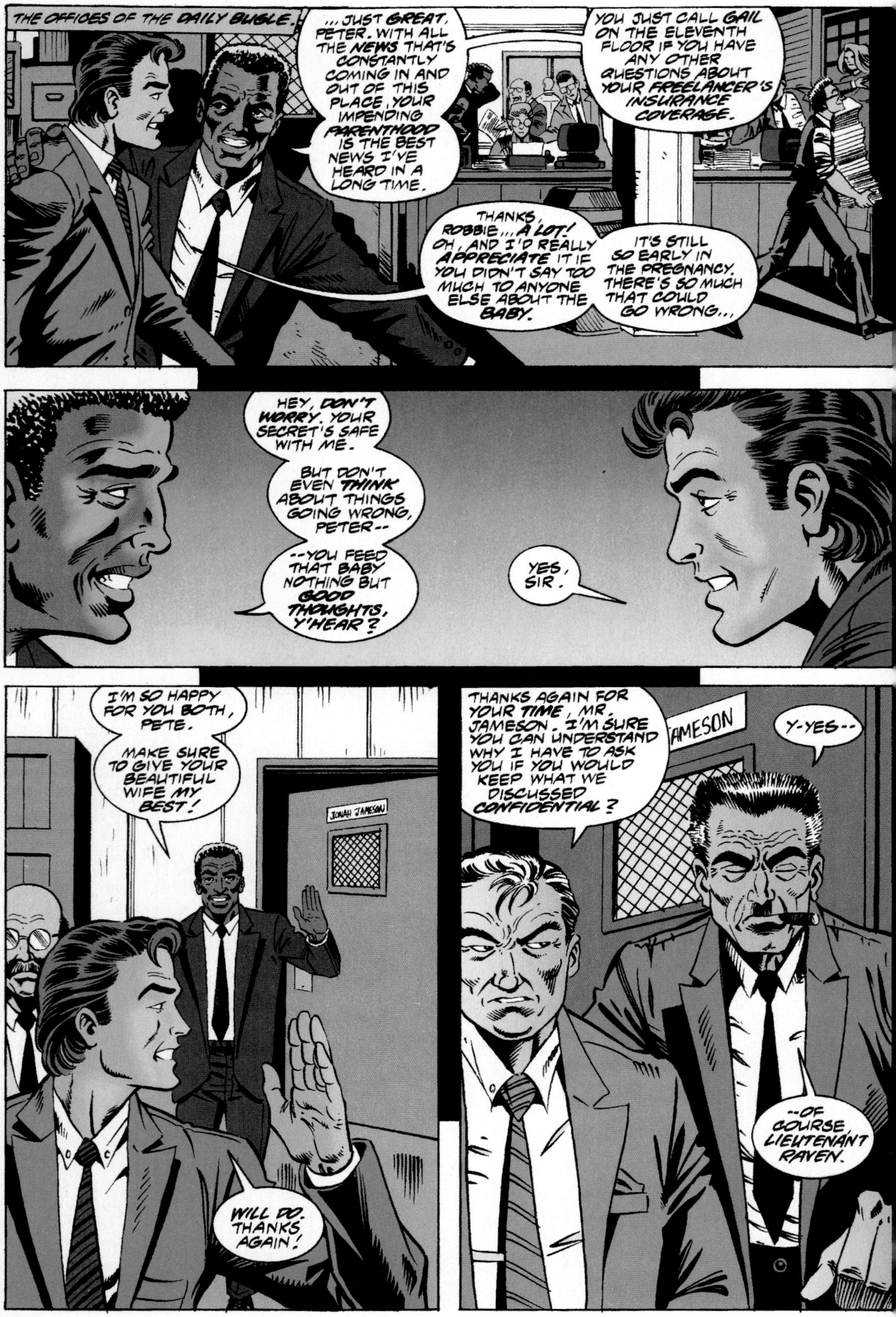

I'M SO HAPPY FOR YOU BOTH, PETE.

MAKE SURE TO GIVE YOUR BEAUTIFUL WIFE MY BEST!

JONAH JAMESON

WILL DO. THANKS AGAIN!

THANKS AGAIN FOR YOUR TIME, MR. JAMESON. I'M SURE YOU CAN UNDERSTAND WHY I HAVE TO ASK YOU IF YOU WOULD KEEP WHAT WE DISCUSSED CONFIDENTIAL?

JAMESON

Y-YES--

--OF COURSE, LIEUTENANT RAVEN.

WHO'S YOUR FRIEND?
BELIEVE ME, ROBBIE...

...YOU DON'T WANT TO KNOW!
J. JONAH JAMES
PUBLISHER
WHAM

HOW ABOUT "GRETCHEN" FOR A GIRL AND "HANK" FOR A BOY...
...NAH!
I CAN'T BELIEVE IT! WE'RE GOING TO HAVE A BABY! I'M GOING TO BE A FATHER!
"JAKE" IS A NICE NAME...

I'VE ALWAYS BEEN AWARE OF WHAT HAVING THESE POWERS MEANS. THE RESPONSIBILITY OF BEING SPIDER-MAN--

--BUT THIS--THIS RESPONSIBILITY WILL BE BIGGER THAN ANYTHING I'VE EVER FACED--
--AND IT WILL BE WONDERFUL!

AARRGH!

NOOOO!
NO MORE!

HAHAHA!
I'VE COME FOR YOU, PETER--

UNGH.
M-MINDFLASH-- THE JACKAL AGAIN.
WHAT'S GOING ON?
I'VE COME TO TAKE YOU HOME!
ARE YOU ALL RIGHT, SON?
YOU LOOK LIKE YOU COULD USE A HAND...

SPIDER-SENSE IS BUZZING LIKE A HORNET'S NEST...
...MUST'VE BEEN SHORTED OUT BY THESE HALLUCINATIONS.
LET'S GET YOU SOMEPLACE WHERE YOU CAN SIT DOWN AND REST FOR A MINUTE.

NO... NO, I'M FINE... REALLY...
...MAYBE JUST A TOUCH OF THE FLU... THANKS, MISTER, BUT REALLY...
...I'M OKAY!

I WONDER... PETER--

"--ARE YOU?"
DAILY BUG
FOREST HILLS HOSPITAL, QUEENS.
IT'S AS IF SHE'S STEPPING ASIDE--
--MOVING ON TO MAKE ROOM IN THE WORLD FOR THE BABY.
NO, I DON'T BELIEVE THAT.
SHE'S GOING TO MAKE IT, AUNT ANNA. I KNOW SHE WILL. I DON'T THINK I BELIEVED IT TILL NOW. BUT PETER CONVINCED ME.
THERE'S TOO MUCH FOR HER TO LIVE FOR.
...AND AUNT MAY'S GOING TO BE WITH US TO SHARE THE JOY OF OUR CHILD.

OH, SWEETHEART, I'D LOVE TO BELIEVE THAT WITH ALL MY HEART.
BUT I'VE BEEN THROUGH THIS ONE TOO MANY TIMES.
YOU KNOW BETTER THAN ANYONE THAT I'M THE ETERNAL OPTIMIST! I BELIEVE IN MIRACLES.

BUT THIS IS ONE TIME WE HAVE TO ACCEPT REALITY.
WE HAVE TO LET GO.

EACH DAY, MAY SLIPS FARTHER AND FARTHER AWAY FROM US.

WE SHOULD THANK GOD FOR HER WONDERFUL LIFE AND FOR THE NEW LIFE THAT'S ON THE WAY--

--AND ASK HIM TO HELP MAY ALONG ON HER JOURNEY.

IN HIS ENTIRE LIFE, HE HAS KNOWN ONLY PAIN--

--GNAWING--

--BLINDING--

--EXCRUCIATING--

GRRR

--PAIN!!

RRAHR!!

IN SEARING AGONY, IT HAS HELD HIM FOREVER IN ITS SWAY-- RULING HIM--

--USING HIM.

FORCED--
--MANIPULATED--
--PROGRAMMED--
--HE HAS BEEN INSTILLED WITH BUT ONE OBJECTIVE--
YARR
FOOM
SWAPP
--TO DEFEND THE DOORWAY WITH HIS LIFE!
GAAARRH!
IT IS THE PAIN THAT TELLS HIM TO DO THIS--
THOMP
--AND HE MUST EVER OBEY THE PAIN.
AND THIS LOOKS LIKE IT MIGHT BE IT, FOLKS.
THE GUARDIAN'S GOT THE KID ON THE ROPES AND HE'S NOT LETTIN' UP!

GAARR!
UNFF!
FOR AN INSTANT, HIS FEVERED MIND QUESTIONS HIS ACTIONS...
"WHY AM I DOING THIS?! WHY AM I--"
BUT THEN THE PAIN IS UPON HIM AGAIN--
THWAPT
--PUSHING--
THUNCH
--DRIVING--
--BURNING AT THE DEEPEST PART OF HIM!
AS THE BATTLE RAGES ON, A LONE FIGURE WATCHES AND WAITS.
AND WHEN KAINE FINALLY DOES STRIKE...
...THE LIVES OF SPIDER-MAN AND BEN REILLY WILL NEVER BE THE SAME!

THE DIRECTIVE SCREAMS THROUGH THE GUARDIAN'S MIND:
CHUD
"PROTECT THE DOORWAY.
SHUNTT
"PROTECT THE DOORWAY.
K'CHOK
"PROTECT THE DOORWAY!"

OH, WELL. LET'S GO.
I GOTTA SAY, THAT WASN'T AS MUCH FUN AS I EXPECTED.
I GUESS WE'LL JUST HAVE TO WAIT...
...FOR THE OTHER ONE.
I CAN'T DENY THESE VISIONS ANY LONGER. THEY'RE MUCH TOO STRONG--PULLING ME--TUGGING AT--
--MY SOUL...?

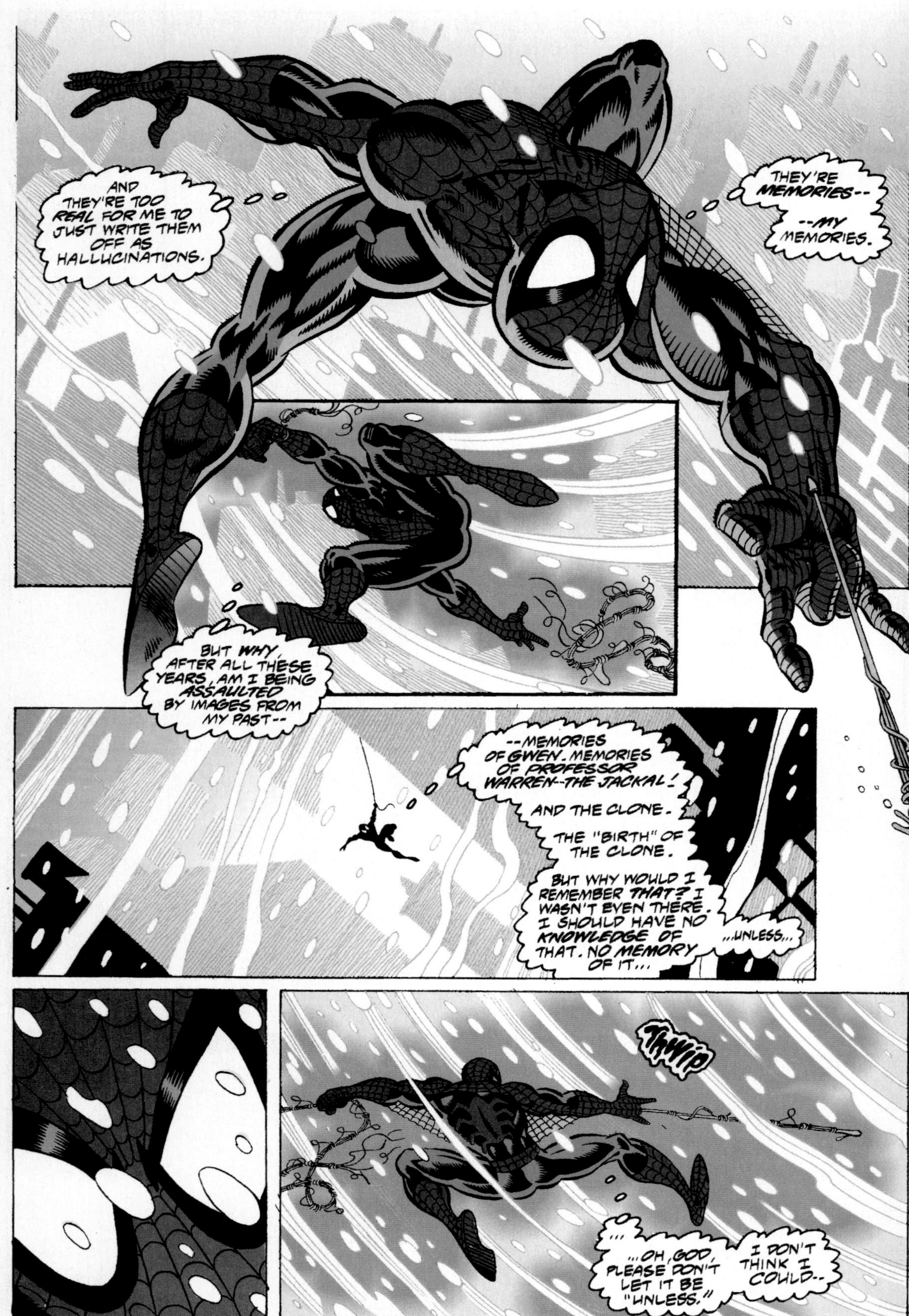
AND THEY'RE TOO REAL FOR ME TO JUST WRITE THEM OFF AS HALLUCINATIONS.
THEY'RE MEMORIES--
--MY MEMORIES.
BUT WHY, AFTER ALL THESE YEARS, AM I BEING ASSAULTED BY IMAGES FROM MY PAST--
--MEMORIES OF GWEN. MEMORIES OF PROFESSOR WARREN--THE JACKAL!
AND THE CLONE.
THE "BIRTH" OF THE CLONE.
BUT WHY WOULD I REMEMBER THAT? I WASN'T EVEN THERE. I SHOULD HAVE NO KNOWLEDGE OF THAT. NO MEMORY OF IT...
...UNLESS...
THWIP
...OH, GOD, PLEASE DON'T LET IT BE "UNLESS."
I DON'T THINK I COULD--

--UNGHH!
THAT WAS A BAD ONE. IT REALLY ROCKED ME!
MEMORY OF...

NO! NOT A MEMORY! THAT WAS REAL! THAT WAS NOW!
HE'S IN TROUBLE--THE SCARLET SPIDER! MY...
...MY...CLONE...?
MY OTHER SELF...

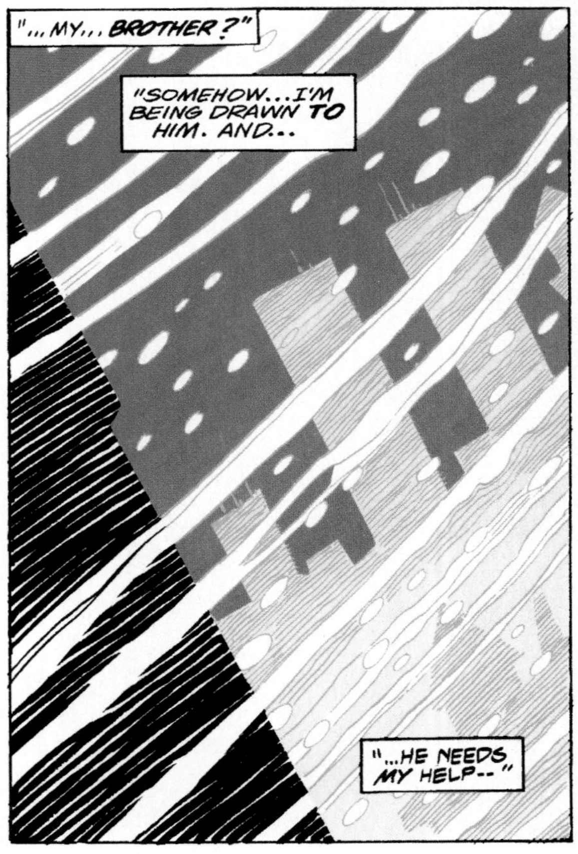
"...MY... BROTHER?"
"SOMEHOW...I'M BEING DRAWN TO HIM. AND...
"...HE NEEDS MY HELP--"

--AND THIS TIME I WON'T TURN MY BACK ON HIM!
THWIP
TO BE CONTINUED IN AMAZING SPIDER-MAN #399!
THE SCARLET SPIDER AND SPIDER-MAN FIGHT SIDE-BY-SIDE AGAINST THE MINIONS OF THE
JACKAL!
AND NEXT MONTH BE HERE AS THE JACKAL REVEALS A SHATTERING SECRET TO BEN REILLY!

MARVEL COMICS
SMOKE AND MIRRORS
PART 2 OF 3
THE AMAZING SPIDER-MAN
$1.50 US
$2.05 CAN/UK £1.25
399
MAR
02457
APPROVED BY THE COMICS CODE AUTHORITY
THE JACKAL REBORN!
BAG'S '94
MAHLSTEDT

SOMEWHERE IN THE CATSKILLS

HE'S NOT DEAD, IF THAT'S WHAT YOU'RE THINKING.
I'M DISAPPOINTED IN YOU, KAINE.
WHO...?
STILL HOUNDING HIM--

--AFTER ALL THESE LONG AND BITTER YEARS.
SCRIER?!
STAY AWAY... DO YOU HEAR ME? OR I SWEAR I'LL--
SO LIKE A CHILD, AREN'T YOU? YOU TREMBLE WITH FEAR--
--AND REACT WITH IMPOTENT THREATS.
DON'T WORRY. YOU HAVE NOTHING TO FEAR FROM ME. NONE OF YOU DO.
YET.

SCRIER...?
GONE.
MY GOD! IF HE'S INVOLVED IN THIS, THEN THERE'S EVEN MORE GOING ON THAN I REALIZED!
I'VE GOT TO BE CAREFUL. IF I CROSS SCRIER AGAIN I MAY NOT COME OUT OF IT WITH A WHOLE SKIN. THAT DEVIL'S GOT--
WHAT'S THAT?
SOMEONE ELSE COMING... AND I THINK I KNOW WHO IT IS.
TIME TO FADE BACK INTO THE SHADOWS...

BITTEN BY A RADIOACTIVE SPIDER, STUDENT **PETER PARKER** GAINED THE PROPORTIONATE STRENGTH AND AGILITY OF AN ARACHNID! ARMED WITH HIS WONDROUS WEB-SHOOTERS, THE RELUCTANT SUPER HERO STRUGGLES WITH SINISTER SUPER-VILLAINS, MAKING ENDS MEET, AND MAINTAINING SOME SEMBLANCE OF A NORMAL LIFE!

Stan Lee PRESENTS: THE AMAZING SPIDER-MAN®

My clone--he's HERE!
Exactly as I saw him in that VISION!
...uhhhh...
OH, MAN ...MY HEAD--!
YOU OKAY?
YEAH, I THINK SO, BUT I--
WAIT A MINUTE--
--WHAT ARE YOU DOING HERE?!
NO. DON'T TELL ME. YOU KEPT GETTING THESE FLASHES--DREAM IMAGES OF PETER PARKER FLOATING IN A TANK IN SOME WEIRD LABORATORY--
--AND YOU FELT LIKE THE ONLY WAY YOU WERE GONNA GET ANY ANSWERS WAS IF YOU CAME HERE--
YOU, TOO?
YEAH. AND WHEN I GOT HERE I RAN INTO SOME OVER-GROWN HULK WANNABE WHO CALLED HIMSELF THE GUARDIAN. WHOMPED ME PRETTY BAD.
I KNOW. I SAW YOU... IN MY MIND. LYING IN THE SNOW.*
THOUGHT I WAS DEAD, huh? ...SO YOU CAME TO MAKE SURE?
CHEAP SHOT... BUT NOT AS CHEAP AS THAT COSTUME.
HOW COULD MY CLONE HAVE SUCH A LOUSY DESIGN SENSE?
*SEE WEB #122, STILL ON SALE. --DANNY
YOU'RE JUST JEALOUS BECAUSE YOU'VE BEEN WEARING THAT OLD RAG FOR SO MANY YEARS THAT--!
LISTEN TO YOU TWO!
SO INSECURE AND UNCOMFORTABLE WITH EACH OTHER THAT YOU'RE REDUCED TO TRADING JUVENILE INSULTS!
YOU AGAIN!
AND AGAIN AND AGAIN AND AGAIN!

JUST WANTED TO LET YOU BOTH KNOW THAT I KNOW WHY YOU'RE HERE--
AND
I'M
NOT
TELLING!
At least not YET!
heeheeheehee!
A MIDGET-- IN THE JACKAL'S COSTUME?!
YEAH. AND HE'S BEEN BUSTING MY CHOPS EVER SINCE I GOT HERE!
WHO IS HE?
LET'S FIND OUT!
Funny. As soon as I saw the reports in the paper about the "Scarlet Spider," I KNEW it was him.
Knew he'd walked away from that explosion at Ravencroft.*
I just refused to deal with it... or even think about it, even after the World Trade Center crisis. ** My life was hard enough as it was.
But now, with these shared flashbacks... or WHATEVER they are... I can't close my eyes any longer.
* IN SPECTACULAR SPIDER-MAN #217.
** SPIDER-MAN UNLIMITED #8.--D
WHAT DOES IT ALL MEAN? Are those images memories of the clone's BIRTH?
And, if they are, am I somehow tuning in to his thoughts and feelings? Or has something unlocked a door...
...in my OWN head?
I don't want to think about it-- especially not now, when my life is finally back on track... When MJ and I have a CHILD on the way --but I HAVE to: What if they're NOT his memories...

...but MINE?
HEY! THE LITTLE GUY'S GONE!
AND WHAT HAVE WE HERE?
A DOOR--
--THAT LEADS NOWHERE!
OR APPEARS TO, ANYWAY!
MY FEELING IS THAT WHAT WE'RE SEEING-- ISN'T WHAT'S REALLY HERE!
SPIDER-MAN'S DIFFERENT.
THE LAST TIME WE MET HE WAS SO TWISTED INSIDE... SO ANGRY AND WOUNDED. BUT SOMETHING'S CHANGED. THERE'S A CONFIDENCE... A SENSE OF SECURITY AND POWER...
...THAT HE DIDN'T HAVE BEFORE. WHATEVER ABYSS HE WAS STARING INTO AT RAVENCROFT-- HE'S PULLED BACK FROM IT.
I SHOULD BE HAPPY ABOUT THAT...
CHECK THIS OUT. SOME KIND OF PALM-LOCK.
THIS WASN'T HERE A SECOND AGO...WAS IT?
...BUT I'M NOT.
SOMEBODY'S PLAYING GAMES WITH US--AND THE ONLY WAY WE'RE GONNA FIND OUT WHO IT REALLY IS--IS TO PLAY ALONG.
BEEPEEPEEPEEP!
I GUESS A PART OF ME WAS HOPING HE WOULD GO TOTALLY OVER THE EDGE.
THAT I'D HAVE NO CHOICE BUT TO STEP IN AND TAKE HIS PLACE.
TAKE BACK MY LIFE.
CHOOSH!
BUT IT'S NOT MY LIFE, IS IT?
NOW LET'S SEE WHO'S WAITING FOR US... ON THE OTHER SIDE.
IT'S HIS.

TWO FOR DINNER?
DO YOU HAVE RESERVATIONS?
HERE'S MY RESERVATION--
--YOU MANIPULATIVE LITTLE--!
KRAAAAK!
HEY... YOU GUYS REALLY OUGHTA LEARN HOW TO TAKE A JOKE!
A JOKE?!!
YOU THINK THIS IS A JOKE?!
THESE ARE OUR LIVES YOU'RE PLAYING WITH!
OUR LIVES!
WAM!
WE WANT SOME ANSWERS... NOW!
IS THE JACKAL BEHIND ALL THIS?
IS HE ALIVE ?!
AREN'T WE IN A FOUL MOOD TODAY! WHAT'S THE MATTER--GET UP ON THE WRONG SIDE OF THE WEB?
uh-oh.
THE DOOR!
HEY-- SCARLET--

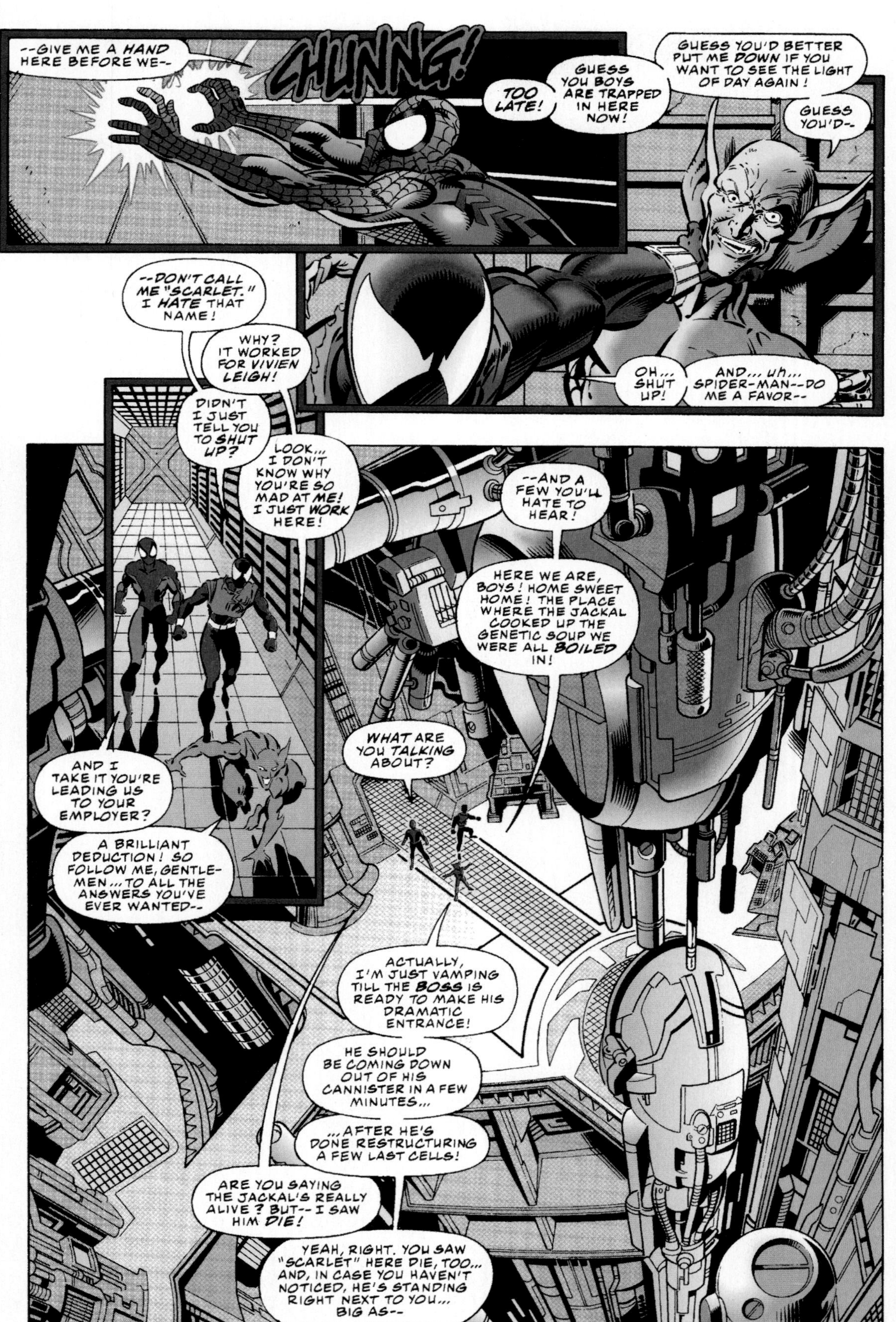

--GIVE ME A HAND HERE BEFORE WE--
CHUNNG!
TOO LATE!
GUESS YOU BOYS ARE TRAPPED IN HERE NOW!
GUESS YOU'D BETTER PUT ME DOWN IF YOU WANT TO SEE THE LIGHT OF DAY AGAIN!
GUESS YOU'D--
--DON'T CALL ME "SCARLET." I HATE THAT NAME!
WHY? IT WORKED FOR VIVIEN LEIGH!
OH... SHUT UP!
AND... uh... SPIDER-MAN--DO ME A FAVOR--
DIDN'T I JUST TELL YOU TO SHUT UP?
LOOK... I DON'T KNOW WHY YOU'RE SO MAD AT ME! I JUST WORK HERE!
--AND A FEW YOU'LL HATE TO HEAR!
HERE WE ARE, BOYS! HOME SWEET HOME! THE PLACE WHERE THE JACKAL COOKED UP THE GENETIC SOUP WE WERE ALL BOILED IN!
WHAT ARE YOU TALKING ABOUT?
AND I TAKE IT YOU'RE LEADING US TO YOUR EMPLOYER?
A BRILLIANT DEDUCTION! SO FOLLOW ME, GENTLEMEN... TO ALL THE ANSWERS YOU'VE EVER WANTED--
ACTUALLY, I'M JUST VAMPING TILL THE BOSS IS READY TO MAKE HIS DRAMATIC ENTRANCE!
HE SHOULD BE COMING DOWN OUT OF HIS CANNISTER IN A FEW MINUTES...
...AFTER HE'S DONE RESTRUCTURING A FEW LAST CELLS!
ARE YOU SAYING THE JACKAL'S REALLY ALIVE? BUT-- I SAW HIM DIE!
YEAH, RIGHT. YOU SAW "SCARLET" HERE DIE, TOO... AND, IN CASE YOU HAVEN'T NOTICED, HE'S STANDING RIGHT NEXT TO YOU... BIG AS--

ARRRR!
UH-OH! IT'S THE GUARDIAN--
AND HE DOESN'T LOOK VERY HAPPY!
SORRY, FELLAS-- YOU MIGHT NOT LIVE TILL THE BOSS'S ENTRANCE!
'CAUSE WHEN MY BIG BUDDY HERE GETS TICKED--
MAKE
IT
STOP!!
WAIT A MINUTE!
SOMETHING'S WRONG!
MAKE THE PAIN STOP!!

H-HIS BODY... IT'S MORE SCARRED... MORE DISTORTED... THAN EVER!
BIG GUY... WHAT'S THE MATTER? WHAT HAPPENED TO YOU?
JACKAL... DID THIS... TO ME...!

JUST LIKE... ALL THE...
...OTHERS--!

HE NEEDS HELP! WE'VE GOT TO DO SOMETHING!
NO. THERE'S NOTHING WE CAN DO. I'VE SEEN THIS HAPPEN BEFORE. BUT I NEVER THOUGHT THAT HE--
--THAT WE--?!

OH, JEEZ-- GUARDIAN... C'MON... TELL ME YOU'RE KIDDING!

IT'S A JOKE, RIGHT? AFTER ALL THIS TIME... YOU'VE FINALLY DEVELOPED A SENSE OF HUMOR?

C'MON, YOU BIG JERK-- DON'T DIE ON ME! PLEASE... I'M BEGGING YOU... DON'T--

--DIE...

HE'S GONE. AND... ONE WAY OR THE OTHER...
WHAT DO YOU--?
...SO AM I.
AND SO... ARE BOTH OF YOU.
DIDN'T YOU HEAR WHAT I SAID BEFORE?
WE'RE ALL FROM THE SAME GENETIC SOUP.
IT MAY TAKE A FEW DAYS... A FEW YEARS... A FEW DECADES--
--BUT THE SAME FATE'S WAITING FOR ALL OF US.
YOU'RE MISTAKEN, JACK.
TO EVEN MENTION YOURSELF IN THE SAME SENTENCE WITH THESE TWO IS THE HEIGHT OF ARROGANCE... AND STUPIDITY.
YOU AND THE GUARDIAN WERE TWO OF MY EARLIEST FAILURES--
--WHILE THESE TWO FINELY SCULPTED SPECIMENS--

--ARE THE JACKAL'S GREATEST TRIUMPHS!

HELLO, BOYS--
--DADDY'S BACK!
SHRAK!
KRAK!!

AND HE'S BETTER THAN EVER... IF I MUST SAY SO MYSELF!
CAN YOU BELIEVE IT? WIMPY OLD PROFESSOR WARREN-- AND LOOK AT ME! ABLE TO TAKE ON NOT ONE, BUT TWO SPIDER-MEN AT THE SAME TIME!
I'D LIKE TO SEE THOSE NITWITS AT ESU DENY ME TENURE NOW!
IS that creature Professor Warren... or is it just another CLONE?
Whoever... Whatever he is... he's right: he was strong enough, fast enough, to take the both of us down without breathing heavy.
This whole mess keeps getting weirder...

...and more DANGEROUS.
JACK... BE A GOOD BOY, WILL YOU, AND FETCH ME SOME CLOTHES?
YES, SIR, JACKAL! RIGHT AWAY, SIR!

WILL... ah... THIS BE SUITABLE, SIR?
YOU FETCH MY CLOTHES AND ASK IF IT'S SUITABLE? WHY JACK, YOU LITTLE DEVIL--WAS THAT A PUN?
IT, uh, DEPENDS, SIR. DID YOU FIND IT AMUSING?

NOT IN THE LEAST.
NO PUN INTENDED.
GOOD. NOW IF I MAY HAVE MY JACKET?

I HAD IT DRY-CLEANED WHILE YOU WERE IN THE CELLULAR REGENERATION TANK, SIR.
HOW CONSIDERATE. NOW IF YOU'D JUST--

OH, MY. I FORGOT ABOUT YOU TWO.
LOOK AT YOU-- FISTS AT THE READY... JAWS CLENCHED--
--YOU YOUNG SCALAWAGS JUST LIVE TO PUNCH AND HIT, DON'T YOU?

NOT HAPPY UNLESS THERE'S SOMEONE TO DROP A BUILDING ON OR WRAP A LAMP-POST AROUND!
WELL, I'M SORRY TO SAY THAT YOU MIS-UNDERSTAND ME. I HAVE NEITHER THE DESIRE NOR THE MOTIVATION TO FIGHT WITH YOU!
THAT LITTLE DEMON-STRATION WHEN I CAME OUT OF THE TANK WAS MORE FOR MY BENEFIT THAN YOURS!
YOU SEE, I'VE SPENT THE PAST FIVE YEARS IN THERE, GENETICALLY RE-STRUCTURING MY BODY. RE-GROWING IT, IF YOU WILL... FROM THE ORIGINAL CELLULAR MATRIX.
SO, NO... TO ANSWER YOUR UNSPOKEN QUESTION... I'M NOT A CLONE--
--I'M THE REAL McCOY... JUST NEW AND IMPROVED!
IT'S NOT POSSIBLE!
NOW THAT'S AN IDIOTIC STATEMENT--COMING FROM A FULLY-FUNCTIONING CLONE!
Y'KNOW, BOYS... I WAS MONITORING YOU THE WHOLE TIME I WAS TANKED UP.
WELL, WITH A LITTLE TIME OUT FOR CNN AND THE PLAYBOY CHANNEL!
QUITE AN INTERESTING HALF A DECADE YOU'VE HAD!
BUT I WANT TO HEAR ABOUT IT ALL IN DETAIL. THAT'S WHY I'VE SUMMONED YOU BACK HERE.
Y'SEE, WHEN LAST WE MET I SURREPTITIOUSLY PROGRAMMED YOU BOYS TO RETURN HERE WHEN I REAWAKENED.
THOUGHT WE COULD ENJOY A HEART-FELT LITTLE FAMILY REUNION! PROFESSOR WARREN AND HIS TWO SONS!
SWELL IDEA FOR A SIT-COM, DON'T YOU THINK? "MY TWO SONS"?
YOU'RE NOT WARREN! YOU CAN'T BE! WARREN IS--
WARREN IS DEAD? ⁘sigh⁘ DIDN'T JACK GO OVER ALL THIS WITH YOU?
Scarlet sounds angry... scared. And I don't blame him. I would be, TOO, if the Jackal had just told me, in no uncertain terms...

...that I was a CLONE.
For all the years of wandering, a part of him must have clung to the belief that it was a mistake. That HE was the real Peter Parker all along.
BEN, MY DEAR BOY, MY SPECIALTY IS CLONES... AS YOU WELL KNOW. THE JACKAL WHO DIED THAT MOMENTOUS NIGHT AT SHEA STADIUM--*
--WAS AS MUCH A GENETIC IMPOSTER AS YOU ARE!
*ISSUE #149 --D
LEAVE HIM ALONE!
KABOK!
KOOOM!
HE'S SUFFERED ENOUGH BECAUSE OF YOU, JACKAL--
--WE ALL HAVE!
EASY DOES IT, WEBS!
WHAT DO YOU THINK YOU'RE DOING?!
STOPPING YOU FROM MAKING A MISTAKE!
MUCH AS I'D LIKE TO BEAT HIS SMIRKING FACE IN--
--JACKAL'S THE ONLY ONE WHO'S GOT THE ANSWERS WE NEED! AND UNTIL WE GET THEM... WE PLAY IT HIS WAY--
--OR NOT AT ALL.
YOU--
YOU'RE--
YOU'RE RIGHT.
Much as I hate to admit it.

HOW NICE... MY BOYS ARE LEARNING FROM EACH OTHER-- JUST LIKE CHIP AND ERNIE! A SHAME MY OTHER CHILDREN AREN'T QUITE SO... ADAPTABLE.
ALAS, POOR GUARDIAN... I KNEW HIM WELL, HORATIO!
LOOK AT HIM... A MASSIVE, MISSHAPEN, MISUNDERSTOOD MONSTER--
I LOVE ALLITERATION, DON'T YOU?
--WHO MET HIS DEATH WITHOUT EVER ONCE FINDING THE ANSWER TO THAT MOST PRIMAL OF QUESTIONS:
WHO AM I?
THE JOKE OF IT IS-- WHO HE WAS... WAS PETER PARKER!
AND SO, BELIEVE IT OR NOT, IS HE!
BROTHERS, BOUND AT THE DNA! CLONES, ONE AND ALL!
WHAT ARE YOU BABBLING ABOUT?
WHAT I'M BABBLING ABOUT IS THIS: CREATION IS AN ONGOING PROCESS... FULL OF TRIAL AND ERROR. EVEN GOD HIMSELF DIDN'T MAKE THE WORLD IN A DAY.
JACK AND THE GUARDIAN WERE AMONG MY EARLIEST EXPERIMENTS. HORRIBLY BOTCHED ATTEMPTS TO BRING FORTH A PETER PARKER CLONE.
THEY SUFFERED PHYSICAL DEFORMITY, MENTAL IMPAIRMENT. I NEVER COULD INFUSE THEM WITH THE PROPER BALANCE OF EMOTION, INTELLECT, AND MEMORY--
--SO I WIPED THEIR MINDS CLEAN, REPROGRAMMED THEM AS THE PROTECTORS OF MY LITTLE MOUNTAIN RETREAT... THEN PUT THEM IN THE FREEZER--
--TO AWAIT THE RETURN OF MY MORE SUCCESSFUL EXPERIMENTS.
YOUR APPEARANCE ON THE MOUNTAIN, SCARLET SPIDER--
AND I MUST SAY I AGREE WITH YOU, THAT'S A PERFECTLY LUDICROUS NAME!
--REACTIVATED THEM.

--THEN DESTROYS THEM.
ARE YOU SAYING THAT MY CLONE IS GOING TO EVENTUALLY--
UNFORTUNATELY, THE POOR THINGS JUST AREN'T BUILT TO LAST.
ALL MY PROTOTYPES EVENTUALLY DEVEL-OP A DEGENERATION FACTOR THAT FIRST DETERIORATES--
YOUR CLONE? OH, THAT'S RICH! YOU REALLY HAVEN'T BEEN LISTENING, HAVE YOU?
OR MAYBE--YOU'VE CHOSEN NOT TO LISTEN!
STOP TALKING IN CIRCLES AND GET TO THE POINT!
DO YOU REALLY KNOW WHO YOU ARE... PETER?
DOES ANY MAN TRULY KNOW?
WHAT IF I WERE TO TELL YOU THAT, IN THE CHAMBER BEHIND ME, IS THE BODY OF THE TRUE PETER PARKER? PRE-SERVED, IN A STATE OF SUSPENDED ANIMATION, FOR FIVE LONG YEARS?
WHAT IF I WERE TO TELL YOU THAT NOT ONE, BUT BOTH OF YOU--
--ARE CLONES?!
BOTH OF US?
CAN IT BE TRUE?
IN A STRANGE WAY, IT ACTUALLY MAKES MY PREDICAMENT A LITTLE EASIER... LESS LONELY. BUT I DON'T THINK IT'S HAVING THE SAME EFFECT...

...ON HIM!
YOU LIAR!!
YOU'VE BEEN PLAYING WITH ME-- WITH MY MIND--SINCE THE MOMENT WE FIRST MET!
BUT I WON'T LISTEN TO YOUR LIES ANYMORE, DO YOU HEAR ME?! I WON'T--
HE'S SCARED TO DEATH. AND I CAN'T SAY I BLAME HIM.
SPIDER-MAN, HEAR ME OUT... EVEN IF IT IS TRUE, YOU CAN'T--
GET
YOUR
HANDS
OFF OF ME!!
CHOOOM!
YOU'RE A LIVING LIE! YOU'RE EVERYTHING I HATE! HOW DO I KNOW YOU'RE NOT A PART OF THIS--WORKING WITH THE JACKAL?!
FOR THE FIRST TIME IN MY LIFE, I'VE GOT HAPPINESS WITHIN MY REACH! I'VE FOUGHT MY WAY BACK FROM THE EDGE--
--MY WIFE AND I ARE EXPECTING A CHILD--
--AND I WON'T LET A GENETIC FRAUD LIKE YOU TAKE IT ALL AWAY FROM US!
A BABY?!

THEY'RE GOING TO HAVE A BABY?
YOU KNOW WHAT YOUR PROBLEM IS, WEBS? YOU'RE AFRAID TO FACE THE TRUTH!
AFRAID YOU MIGHT TURN OUT TO BE JUST AS MUCH OF A FAKE AS I AM!
I'M NOT AFRAID OF ANYTHING!
VENOM TRIED TO BREAK ME... AND I CAME BACK!

THE GREEN GOBLIN DRAGGED ME DOWN INTO MADNESS... AND I CAME BACK!
KRAVEN THE HUNTER BURIED ME ALIVE--
--AND I CAME BACK!
DO YOU REALLY THINK I'M AFRAID OF ANYTHING YOU TWO CAN DO?!
COME ON, JACKAL... OR WHOEVER YOU ARE... IF YOU'VE GOT PROOF-- LET'S SEE IT!
LET'S SEE IT!
I DIDN'T MEAN TO GOAD HIM ON LIKE THAT! BUT WHEN I HEARD HIM SAY THAT MARY JANE WAS EXPECTING HIS CHILD... I JUST LOST IT. THE IDEA THAT HE'S GOT EVERYTHING I'VE EVER WANTED... A FAMILY... CHILDREN--!

SO, IT'S PROOF YOU WANT, eh?
WELL, YOU SHALL HAVE IT!
BEHOLD! THE CRYOGENIC MISTS LIFT! THE SLEEPER AWAKENS! THE--
WHOOPS.
"WHOOPS"?

DADDY'S MADE A LITTLE MISTAKE HERE, BOYS. I OPENED UP THE WRONG CHAMBER.
THAT'S NOT PARKER IN THERE--
UNLESS, OF COURSE, HE HAD A SEX-CHANGE OPERATION WHILE I WASN'T LOOKING!
--THAT'S THE GIRL OF ALL OUR DREAMS!
MILES WARREN AND PETER PARKER'S "LATE", LAMENTED TRUE LOVE!

TRY TO KEEP THOSE HORMONES IN CHECK, KIDS--BECAUSE YOU'RE ABOUT TO GET THE SHOCK OF YOUR PSEUDO-LIVES!

GENTLEMEN, MAY I PRESENT, NOT A CLONE... BUT THE ONE, THE ONLY, THE ORIGINAL--
--GWEN STACY!!
WELL, DON'T JUST STAND THERE WITH YOUR TONGUES HANGING OUT-- WHERE ARE YOUR MANNERS?
SAY HELLO TO THE LADY!
"Smoke and Mirrors" CONCLUDES-- IN THE PAGES OF SPIDER-MAN #56!!
THEN BE HERE NEXT MONTH FOR AMAZING #400-- AND WHAT MAY VERY WELL BE THE SINGLE MOST POWERFUL TALE IN SPIDEY'S LONG AND DISTINGUISHED HISTORY:
THE GIFT!

MARVEL COMICS

SMOKE AND MIRRORS 3 OF 3

$1.95 US
$2.65 CAN/UK £1.25
56
MAR

APPROVED BY THE COMICS CODE AUTHORITY

SPIDER-MAN

THE TRIUMPH OF THE JACKAL™...

...AND THE RETURN OF GWEN STACY?!

Tom Lyle '94

Stan Lee presents
SPIDER-MAN and the SCARLET SPIDER in
SMOKE & MIRRORS
part THREE
TRUTHS & DECEPTIONS
Howard Mackie & Tom Lyle story&art
Scott Hanna inks
Starkings/ Comicraft lettering
Kevin Tinsley colors
Danny Fingeroth editor
Bob Budiansky ed. in chief
LIKE A MODERN VENUS, SHE EMERGES FROM THE SWIRLING MISTS OF A HIGH-TECH CAPSULE.
HER FACE IS FLAWLESS... BEAUTIFUL.
THE IMAGE OF HER STANDING THERE STIRS THE SHARED MEMORIES OF SPIDER-MAN AND THE MAN CALLED THE SCARLET SPIDER.
BUT THEY ARE PAINFUL MEMORIES.
FOR THE WOMAN STANDING BEFORE THEM IS GWEN STACY.
AND THEY BOTH KNOW THAT GWEN IS DEAD.
OR IS SHE?

BOTH MEN WERE LED TO THIS LABORATORY, SOMEWHERE BENEATH THE CATSKILL MOUNTAINS OF NEW YORK, BY STRANGE FLASHES OF SHARED DREAMS.*
NOW EVERYTHING THEY KNOW...
...EVERYTHING THEY THINK THEY KNOW...
...ABOUT THEMSELVES...
...AND ABOUT EACH OTHER...
...MAY ALL BE A LIE.
AND THE FUN HAS ONLY BEGUN.
SPIDER-MAN?
PETER?
WHAT'S HAPPENED TO ME?
HELP ME.
PLEASE?
*CHECK OUT WEB #122 & AMAZING #399. --D.F.
Ooh-HA! THAT WILL BE QUITE FAR ENOUGH, DEAR GWEN.

OUR TWO PETERS ARE LOOKING A BIT UNCOMFORTABLE, SO...
...PERHAPS YOU SHOULD DRESS BEFORE WE GO ANY FURTHER.
Oh, JAAAAACK!
COMING RIGHT AT YOU, JACKAL, SIR!
BOYS, SHALL WE ALL AVERT OUR EYES WHILE OUR BELOVED GWEN DRESSES?
Oh, BOYS!
I SAY... BOYS!
NO.

NO!
NO MORE OF YOUR LIES, JACKAL!
NO MORE PLAYING WITH MY HEAD!
I'M NOT BUYING IT!
GWEN DIED! I SAW HER DIE! I...
PETER...
...DON'T.
IT'S ME, PETER.
IT'S REALLY ME.
PLEASE, PETER...TALK TO ME...
...HOLD ME?

THERE'S A GOOD BOY, PETER.
DO GO TALK WITH YOUR DEAR SWEET GWEN!
MAYBE YOU CAN HELP HER FIND A NEW PAIR OF GO-GO BOOTS.
UGPH!
JACKAL!

FOREST HILLS HOSPITAL, QUEENS, NEW YORK...
CONGRATULATIONS, MRS. PARKER...

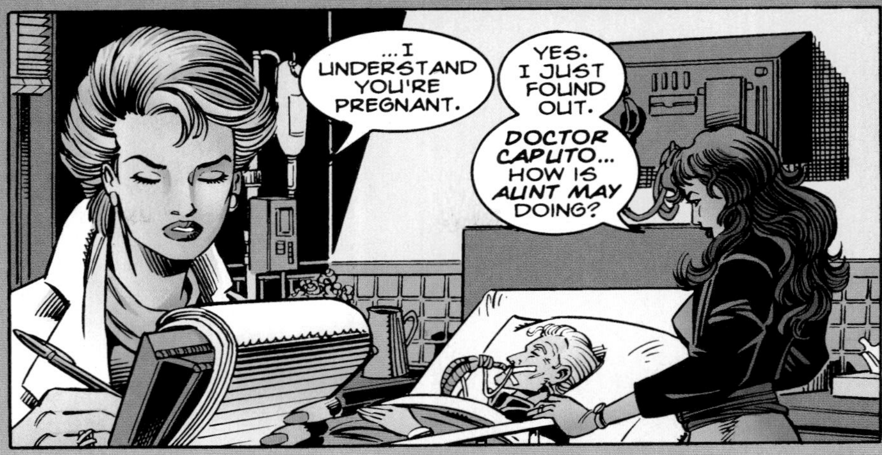
...I UNDERSTAND YOU'RE PREGNANT.
YES. I JUST FOUND OUT. DOCTOR CAPUTO... HOW IS AUNT MAY DOING?

SHE SEEMS TO HAVE STABILIZED.
BUT I'D APPRECIATE IT IF PETER WOULD COME BY AND SEE ME SOON. WE NEED TO DISCUSS OPTIONS.

OPTIONS.
PLEASE, AUNT MAY... WE NEED YOU... PLEASE...

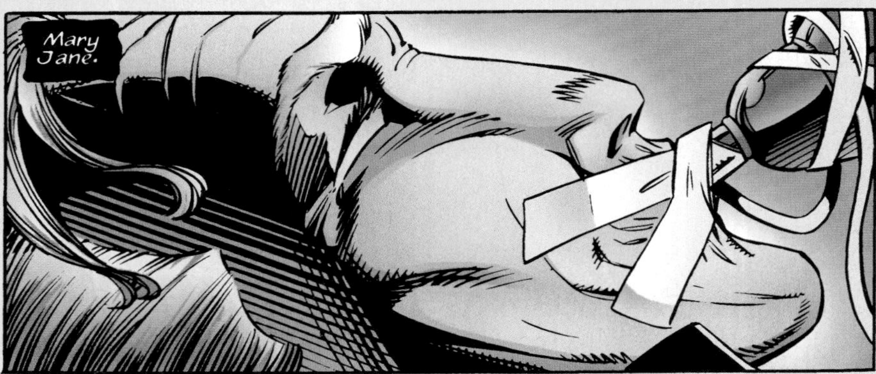
Mary Jane.

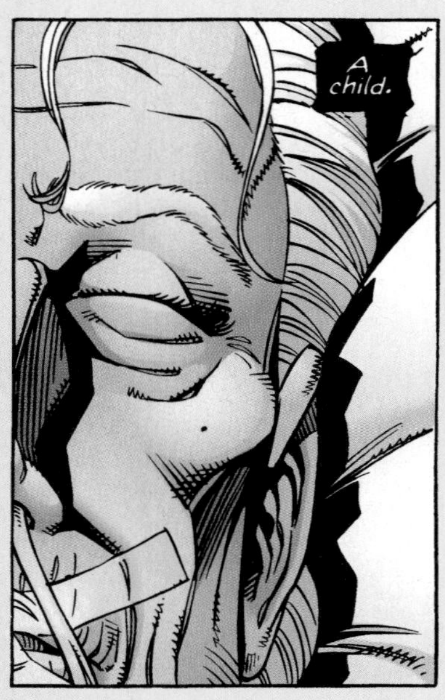
A child.
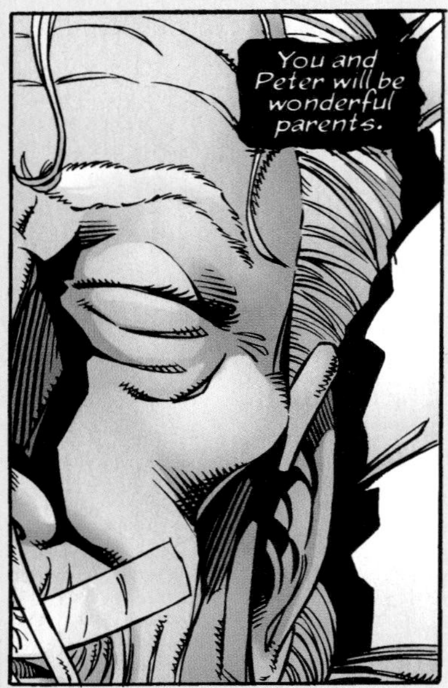
You and Peter will be wonderful parents.
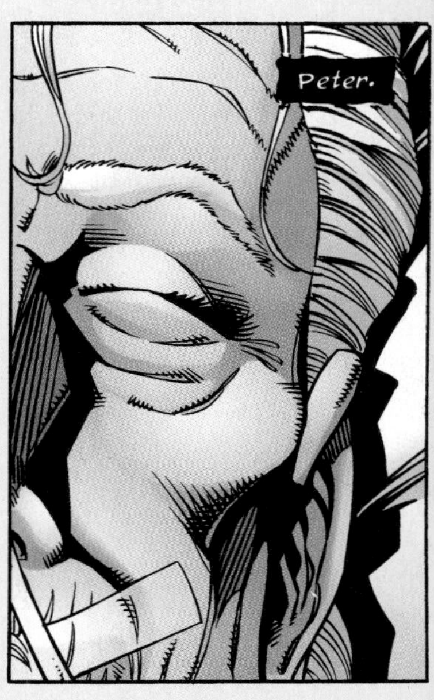
Peter.

I still worry about him so.
But now he has you, dear... and a child.

It would be nice to see the child when it's born. but...
...I'm so tired.

I've done so much...lived and loved so.
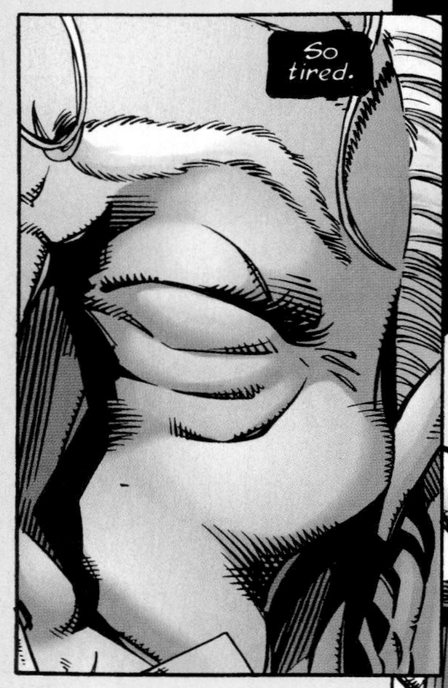
So tired.

DON'T DIE, MAY.
PLEASE.

LOOK AT THEM. GO AHEAD... LOOK.
SPIDER-MAN AND GWEN.
THAT COULD HAVE BEEN YOU AND MARY JANE...OR YOU AND GWEN... OR YOU AND THE WOMAN OF YOUR CHOICE.
INSTEAD, WHAT DID YOU GET? FIVE LONG YEARS ON THE ROAD.

EXCUSE ME, PROFESSOR? CAN WE TALK?
NOT NOW, JACK. I'M BUSY.
POOR BEN. IT'S JUST NOT RIGHT, WHAT I DID TO YOU.

I WAS ONLY WONDERING IF ALL YOUR PROTOTYPES HAVE TO DEGENERATE LIKE THE GUARDIAN DID?
NOT... NOW.

OKAY! I'LL DO IT. I'VE LIVED TOO LONG WITH THIS SIN.
COME AND LISTEN TO A STORY ABOUT A MAN NAMED BEN--

BECAUSE IF THE DEGENERATION WAS GOING TO HAPPEN TO ME...

NOT NOW!
WAP

NOW... WHERE WERE WE?
Oh, YES... THE TRUTH.

IS IT REALLY YOU, PETER, THE REAL YOU?
DON'T DO THIS TO ME. NOT AGAIN!
GWEN IS DEAD. I MADE MY PEACE WITH HER LONG AGO.
DON'T YOU DO THIS TO ME, PETER.
I'M CONFUSED. WHAT'S HAPPENED TO ME? WHAT'S HAPPENED TO US?
NO! YOU'RE NOT GWEN! YOU'RE A FAKE! ANOTHER CLONE!
HOW CAN YOU BELIEVE THAT, PETER? HOW CAN YOU LOOK ME IN THE EYES AND BELIEVE WHAT YOU'RE SAYING?
YOU DON'T. OTHERWISE YOU WOULDN'T STILL BE TALKING TO ME.
NO! NOT AGAIN!
NOT AGAIN!
I'M HAPPY WITH MY LIFE!
NOW, I'M GOING TO FIND A WAY OUT OF HERE!
THE REST OF YOU CAN PLAY THIS GAME IF YOU WANT!
I'M GETTING US OUT--AND TAKING THE JACKAL IN!
KRASSH

I DO HATE ALL THIS VIOLENCE... DON'T YOU, BEN?
OF COURSE YOU DO.
BUT I ONLY HAVE MYSELF TO BLAME FOR IT ALL.
THESE PLANS, I SET THEM IN MOTION SO LONG AGO...
WHAT WAS I THINKING?
ORCHESTRATING THE BATTLE BETWEEN YOU BOTH... THE ONE IN WHICH YOU APPEARED TO DIE!
I WAS A PATHETIC MAN SEARCHING... SEARCHING... FOR POWER... FOR LOVE.
I'M SORRY I DID IT TO YOU, SON. YOU DESERVED BETTER.
IT WAS ALL A GAME TO ME.
MIND CONTROL... CLONING...
CLONING MYSELF... GWEN... YOU!
ALL THOSE THINGS I TOLD YOU BEFORE*-- THEY WERE ALL LIES. THIS IS THE TRUTH.
*AMAZING #399. --D.
YES, BEN... OR SHOULD I CALL YOU PETER... YOU... YOU ARE THE REAL ONE!

IT'S WHY I COULDN'T LEAVE YOU IN THE SMOKESTACK TO REALLY DIE.
I HAD TO SAVE YOU THAT NIGHT. I HAD DONE SO MUCH TO YOUR LIFE IN THE NAME OF THIS WARPED EXPERIMENT...
...I JUST COULDN'T LET YOU DIE.
HOW? WHY DID HE THINK I WAS DEAD?
DO YOU THINK SOMETHING AS SIMPLE AS TEMPORARILY LOWERING YOUR BODY'S METABOLISM WOULD BE DIFFICULT FOR THE MAN WHO SUCCESSFULLY CLONED YOU?
I SAVED YOUR LIFE, PETER.
I IMPLANTED MEMORIES THAT MADE YOU BELIEVE YOU WERE THE CLONE AND SENT YOU ON YOUR WAY.
BUT NOW I WANT TO DO RIGHT BY YOU.
IT CAN ALL BE YOURS AGAIN, PETER. GWEN, THE BUGLE, THE WHOLE BALL OF WAX!
I'M GIVING IT ALL BACK TO YOU TONIGHT.

AND ABOVE IT ALL KAINE WATCHES...
...AND WAITS.
HE WANTS NOTHING MORE THAN TO JUMP DOWN INTO THE FRAY... TO KILL, BUT...
...HE WILL NOT... CANNOT!
SOMETHING DEEP INSIDE OF HIM PREVENTS HIM FROM LASHING OUT.
BUT THE TIME IS NEARING WHEN NOTHING WILL HOLD KAINE BACK.
SO HE PUSHES HIS ANGER DOWN DEEP INSIDE, AND...
...WATCHES.
ONLY TO BE WATCHED BY ANOTHER.
SCRIER.

WHAT ARE YOU WAITING FOR, BOY? JUST GO KILL HIM. HE'S NOTHING... A CLONE... A GENETIC MISTAKE. GO AHEAD--HE DID IT TO YOU ONCE.
TAKE BACK YOUR LIFE! DO IT NOW!
YOU KNOW, BOSS, I REEAALLY WANT TO TALK ABOUT THIS DEGENERATION THING.
GET...
...AWAY!
YOU'RE ANNOYING. ME...
...THE BOTH OF YOU!
WHY WON'T YOU JUST DO AS I TELL YOU?
WHY MAKE ME HAVE TO GET ALL VIOLENT?
I TOLD YOU, I HATE VIOLENCE!
I COULD JUST KILL YOU FOR MAKING ME DO THIS!
Oh, AND GIVE THE SPIDER-SENSE A REST ALREADY.
EVENTUALLY I'M GOING TO NAIL YOU.
JACK! WHERE ARE YOU?! GET OVER HERE NOW!
ASSIST ME!

RIGHT HERE, BOSS!
WOULD NOW BE A CONVENIENT TIME TO TALK, PROFESSOR?
NO!
I HAVE SOME UNFINISHED BUSINESS TO ATTEND TO HERE. NOW I'M GOING TO RID MYSELF OF THIS GENETIC MISTAKE!
YOU TRY TO DO SOMEONE A FAVOR... GIVE THEM A LIFE... AND DO THEY APPRECIATE IT? NO!
YOU HAD TO GO AND MAKE ME MAD.
AND LOOK AT YOU... CAN'T EVEN STRIKE BACK AT ME... CAN YOU?
OF COURSE NOT. YOU THINK I'M ABOVE PROTECTING MYSELF WITH THE HELP OF A FEW SIMPLE MENTAL IMPLANTS?!
WHAT ABOUT ME, PROFESSOR?
YOU? DEAR BOY, IT'S TIME YOU LEARNED THE TRUTH!
THOK

OKAY... MAYBE I DESERVED THAT! BUT THAT DOESN'T CHANGE THE TRUTH, PETER.
YOU ARE THE REAL ONE, BEN'S THE CLONE.
EVERY-THING ELSE IS JUST SMOKE AND MIRRORS.
WHY LIE? WHY TELL ME I WAS THE REAL ONE JUST NOW?
FOR FUN? I'VE GOT TO LEARN TO PROGRAM IN A SENSE OF HUMOR TO THE NEXT BATCH!
NO. I CAN'T ACCEPT THAT! I'M GOING TO POUND THE TRUTH OUT OF YOU.
NO...
...LET ME!
AH, THE REAL SPIDER-MAN COMES TO THE RESCUE!
SEE, BEN, THIS IS HOW A REAL MAN ACTS!
THAT'S IT, BOY, HANG YOUR HEAD IN SHAME.
PETER KNOWS HOW TO DEAL WITH OUR TYPE. A QUICK KILL AND THEN OFF TO THE SMOKE-STACKS FOR US!
ISN'T THAT HOW IT GOES, PETEY?
SHUT UP!
YOU'RE STILL LYING! YOU NEVER CLONED ANY-ONE!
I READ YOUR JOURNAL! THE HIGH EVOLUTIONARY TOLD ME... ABOUT ANTHONY SERBA... ABOUT JOYCE DELANEY...
HIGH EVOLUTIONARY? HOO-BOY! HANGING OUT WITH SOME PRETTY HEAVY HITTERS THERE, AREN'T YOU, PETEY OLD BOY?

SO NOW TELL ME, PETER... AND YOU ALWAYS WERE ONE OF MY TOP STUDENTS... EXACTLY WHAT PURPOSE WOULD TELLING THE TRUTH TO YOU HAVE SERVED THE HIGH EVOLUTIONARY?
Hmm? INTERESTING. CAN'T THINK OF A THING... CAN YOU? ME NEITHER!
THERE ARE POWERS AT WORK HERE THAT YOU'LL NEVER UNDERSTAND.
NOW TRUST ME... YOU'RE THE REAL McCOY, PETER.
YOU KNOW THAT IT'S THE TRUTH. BEN KNOWS IT'S THE TRUTH.
BELIEVE WHAT'S IN YOUR HEART.
TRUST ME. GO... TAKE GWEN.
HAVE THE LIFE YOU'VE ALWAYS DESERVED.
ALWAYS WANTED.
ALWAYS DESERVED.

COME ON, PETER... YOU KNOW YOU **WANT** TO.
KISS THE GIRL. THAT'LL **PROVE** IT TO YOU.
SEE IF THERE'S STILL A LITTLE **SPARK** LEFT IN THE RELATION-SHIP.
SURE YOU'RE MARRIED. BUT ONE LITTLE KISS? JUST FOR OLD TIMES SAKE?
I'LL NEVER TELL.

I KNOW IT'S NOT YOU.
PLEASE, PETER, DON'T SAY THAT, IT HURTS.
NO MATTER WHAT YOU SAY...**I** KNOW IT'S REALLY ME.

IT WOULDN'T MATTER IF YOU **WERE.** I HAVE MARY JANE... AUNT MAY... FRIENDS.
NO MATTER WHAT HE'S TRIED TO **DO** TO ME...WHAT HE'S **TAKEN** FROM ME...
...WHETHER I'M REAL OR A CLONE...
...I HAVE A LIFE!

PETER...
...I...
...FEEL...
...STRANGE.
PETER, WHAT'S HAPPENING TO...
...ME?
SHE'S DEGENERATING!
JUST LIKE THE OTHER ONE! *
PETER! I'M REALLY GWEN.
AREN'T I?
PETER...
...I... LOVE... YOU.
* AMAZING #399. -- Danny

HOO-BOY!
I LOVE WHEN THAT HAPPENS!!
TIMING IS EVERYTHING!
I WISH YOU BOYS WEREN'T WEARING THOSE SILLY MASKS!
THE LOOK ON YOUR FACES WOULD BE *PRICELESS!*
JACK! GET THE CAMERA!
WHY?
WHY KEEP DOING THIS TO US?
"WHY" YOU ASK? SMOKE AND MIRRORS! SMOKE AND MIRRORS!
WHEN WILL THE TRUTH BE TOLD?

THE TRUTH, MY BOYS, IS...
...NEITHER OF YOU IS THE REAL ONE!
YOU REALLY ARE BOTH CLONES! A FAILED EXPERIMENT ON WHICH IT IS TIME TO PULL THE PLUG!
KEEP POUNDING AWAY, BOYS, BUT THIS PLACE IS GOING KABLOOEY IN ABOUT A MINUTE.
REALLY... I'M DOING YOU BOTH A FAVOR. WOULDN'T YOU RATHER GO CLEANLY THAN END UP LIKE POOR OLD GWEN?
Oh, AND BOYS, THE REAL PETER PARKER IS REALLY HERE SOME-WHERE.
WHY DON'T YOU SPEND YOUR LAST MINUTES LOOKING FOR HIM?
HEY, YOU NEVER KNOW, MAYBE YOU'LL GET A FINAL LOOK AT THE MAN OF WHOM YOU ARE BOTH JUST COPIES!

PUT YOUR BACK INTO IT! WE'VE GOT TO BE ABLE TO GET THROUGH!
WHAT? YOU DON'T THINK I'M TRYING HARD ENOUGH?
TRY RIPPING DOWN THE WALL AROUND THE MIRROR.
HER TOO?
IS THIS WHAT I'VE GOT TO LOOK FORWARD TO?
NO WAY!
YO! YOU'LL NEVER BREAK THROUGH IN TIME! THE DOOR!
IF YOU BOTH TRY YOU CAN OPEN THE DOOR!
GET OUT OF HERE! LIVE! AND IF YOU TWO HOT-SHOT SCIENTISTS HAPPEN TO FIGURE OUT A SOLUTION TO THIS DEGENERATION THING...
...DON'T FORGET WHO HELPED YOU TODAY!
LET'S DO IT!
DON'T HAVE TO TELL ME TWICE.